THE
ICE HOCKEY
ANNUAL

2004-05

THE
ICE HOCKEY
ANNUAL

EDITED AND COMPILED BY STEWART ROBERTS

First published in Great Britain by
Stewart Roberts
The Old Town Hall
142 Albion Street
Southwick
Brighton BN42 4AX

Cover Design by **Channel Graphic Communication**

British Library Cataloguing-in-Publication Data.
A catalogue record for this book is available from the British Library.

The Ice Hockey Annual 2004-05

ISBN 0-9536410-5-8

The Ice Hockey Annual's official website is at www.graphyle.com/IHA.
Past editions of *The Ice Hockey Annual* are archived in the Hockey Hall of Fame, London Life Resource Centre, Toronto, Canada.

Printed in Great Britain by **L & S Printing Co Ltd**
Hazelwood Close, Hazelwood Trading Estate, Worthing, West Sussex BN14 8NP

CONTENTS

COVER - Belfast Giants and Great Britain defenceman, **LEIGH JAMIESON**, was also a member of the GB under-20 team that won their group of the World Junior Championship for the first time. The first winner of the **Vic Batchelder** Memorial Award as the Best Young British Player, he was voted the Best British Defenceman by the Writers' Association.

For more on **TONY HAND MBE**, see *Players in the News.*

Photo of Leigh Jamieson: Diane Davey

ACKNOWLEDGEMENTS

Welcome to the 29th edition of *The Ice Hockey Annual*. How old is that? Well, it's about a third as old as the National Hockey League, the world's longest running league. Closer to home, we started this project ten years before our cover star, **Leigh Jamieson**, was born.

A book of this nature needs a large number of people to keep it going so this is the place where we take time out to thank every single one of you publicly. Ah, if only that were possible. This book is big but not that big.

Instead, we'll ask most of you to accept a blanket 'ta, ever so' and use this space to praise those who have contributed above and beyond.

The UK's leading clubs play in three separate leagues (don't get us started) but fortunately, all three have competent statisticians because stats are the life-blood of this book.

We'll start by thanking the Elite League's **Antony Hopker** and our own **Gordon Wade** for keeping tabs on the new league's scoring and other numerological minutiae. Gordon, who's been with the *Annual* almost since our first edition, also compiles GB's World Championship stats. for us.

Craig Simpson sent us his figures for the British National League. Craig also compiles the weekly stats that go on the league's website. **Sue Tomalin** is our lady of the English Leagues though, sad to say, she gave up at the end of the season. Thanks for all you've done over many years, Sue.

Sue will be hard to replace but we can't think of a better person to try than **Malcolm Preen**. 'Sonic', as he's known, looks after the most comprehensive British hockey website at http://homepage.ntlworld.com/malcolm.preen/brit ish.html. He will be handling all the English IHA stats. This year he supplied the *Annual* with details of the Scottish and women's leagues.

Talking of websites, we make no excuses for using **www.iihf.com** for most of our world and European information. All the World Championship stats can be found there, seniors, juniors, men and women.

While never big on photos, the *Annual* hopes readers will agree that ours have improved each year. Some of this is down to improved technology, especially at our printers, but it still takes a sharp eye to snap a decent photo of a fast-moving sport like ice hockey.

So we're very grateful to our photographers, from the left: **Tony Boot**, **Roger Cook**, **Dave Page**, **Chris Valentine**, and one of our favourite ladies, **Diane Davey**.

Helping us to keep the *Annual* going all these years are our advertisers. Where would we be without them? When you need the services these organisations supply, please remember these people support your favourite hockey publication.

We're delighted to have **Bauer-Nike** back on board this year as they've been supporters of the *Annual* since the early days. The famous brand is now being distributed in this country by **Wheels Skates** of Stockport.

Another of our staunch supporters is **Airport and Road Equipment** who are the sole importers of the famous **Zamboni** resurfacing machine. Ice hockey would be much slower without this vital piece of equipment!

Igloo can supply many of your equipment needs. The man behind this recently established business is **Kevin Barker**, who also brings you *The Hockey News* from Canada.

NASN, the North American Sports Network, is the exciting new TV channel designed especially for us NHL nuts. Don't miss it. And *Powerplay* is the sport's weekly mag. Buy it!

We're pleased to welcome a couple of new companies to our pages. The *Anglo-Czech Hockey School* provides a unique way of teaching youngsters the finer points of the European game and *Reid's Trophies* will supply all your trophy needs.

Back with us are *Specsavers*, the famous national chain of opticians who help Cardiff Devils and the GB national team, and *Crazy Kennys*, the growing online mail order business for hockey equipment.

Ian Green's *Armchair Sports* are the UK's hockey card specialist and a visit to *Ice N Easy*'s skate shop is a must the next time you're in iceSheffield.

D&P Trophies are the official trophy suppliers to the English IHA and *Trans Atlantic Sports* can supply you with a variety of hockey goodies via the internet.

Our final vote of thanks goes to *L & S Printing* of Worthing, who've put our rough jottings into an attractive package.

SR

EDITORIAL

The view from another planet

I was talking to a Martian the other day about our sport. Well, they've got ice up there, haven't they? Our conversation went something like this.

M: I didn't know you played ice hockey in your part of Earth.

SR: Not another one. All Earthmen say that, too. Yes, we do. In fact we have more rinks and modern arenas than most of those countries south and east of us. We call them the European Union now.

M: You must have a lot of good players then.

SR: Actually, we prefer to spend our money on importing them from the EU and that god-forsaken bit of frozen Earth across the big pond: Canada.

M: So you must be a rich hockey nation.

SR: Most of our club owners are, as we say, comfortable.

M: Where do you rank in the world?

SR: 25th.

M: Wow! I didn't know that many Earth nations played ice hockey. So what are you doing about improving your status.

SR: Not a lot. Our governing body hasn't any money and our big clubs aren't much interested in developing our own players. But we do have a top European coach who's working for nothing.

M: I see. But surely your national league is strong if you're choosing players from two continents.

SR: Er, we don't have a national league. Our comfortable owners aren't too comfortable with that idea, so we have two leagues.

M: I think I'm losing you now.

SR: We called in the organisation that runs world ice hockey, the International Ice Hockey Federation, to see if they could help.

M: Sounds like you need them.

SR: Thanks. Anyway, it was beyond them. They first gave the problem to a fellow you might know up there, **Frederick Meredith**? He was in charge of our last governing body when it went bust. He let the clubs who owed money carry on and set up a new league which then failed to pay its fees until halfway through the season.

After that he handed over to a colleague who persuaded the big clubs to kick their import habit - well, no, he didn't actually. He let them ice 11, one less than last year, but still the most in the EU apart from Germany who get much bigger crowds than we do.

He also devised some meaningless competition, which no one could agree what to call and where only half the teams played each other.

M: And one national league?

SR: Not a chance. A three-year plan was the best he could manage. Hard to get wins and losses out of that, isn't it?

M: Sounds like these people come from my planet.

SR: Funny, I thought that, too.

Some blue line thinking

We've used up quite a bit of space in the Annual trying to explain to you, dear reader, the rules and regs about imports and wage caps which seem to grow more complicated every year.

These days, apparently, team sports like ours even have to worry about such obscure immigration laws as the Working Holiday Makers Scheme.

I reckon it's time for some blue line thinking, sorry, blue sky thinking, as the fashionable businessmen call it.

Let's be bold and do away with import restrictions and wage caps.

Think about it. Wage caps are almost impossible to police effectively. The leagues now rely heavily on what they call the 'squealer' rule whereby one player sneaks on another if he hears that player might be getting too much money. Great for team morale that.

Teams' incomes vary only according to the size of their crowds and their success in finding sponsors. Imports are only one of the expenses that they have to take into account when working out their budgets.

Having more money does not necessarily mean you make better decisions over players.

My argument is that even with the import and wage cap rules we already have, Sheffield Steelers still win something every year and Nottingham Panthers rarely do!

I say let the clubs who make a success of their budgets and are skilful at picking and coaching players see that fairly reflected on the ice.

This might also be the quickest way to find out teams' real strengths and move more quickly towards one league - with promotion and relegation.

Enjoy your hockey and tell your friends.

Stewart Roberts
August 2004

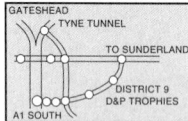

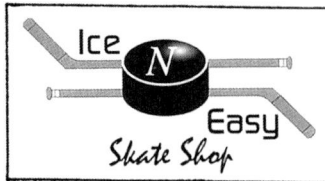

HONOURS AND AWARDS

HONOURS ROLL-CALL 2003-04

ELITE LEAGUE
Playoff Championship
SHEFFIELD STEELERS
Elite League
SHEFFIELD STEELERS
The Challenge Cup
NOTTINGHAM PANTHERS

***FINDUS* BRITISH NATIONAL LEAGUE**
Playoff Championship
GUILDFORD FLAMES
Findus **British National League**
FIFE FLYERS
Findus **Cup**
NEWCASTLE VIPERS

ENGLISH LEAGUES
Premier League Playoff Championship
MILTON KEYNES LIGHTNING
Premier League
MILTON KEYNES LIGHTNING
Premier Cup
PETERBOROUGH PHANTOMS
National League Playoff Championship
SHEFFIELD SCIMITARS
National League North
FLINTSHIRE FREEZE
National League South
INVICTA DYNAMO

SCOTTISH NATIONAL LEAGUE
CAMPERDOWN (Dundee) STARS
Caledonian Cup
FIFE FLYERS

WOMEN'S LEAGUE
SUNDERLAND SCORPIONS

Top League Points Scorers
Elite League
MARK DUTIAUME, Sheffield
British National League
TONY HAND, Edinburgh
English Premier League
KYLE AMYOTTE, Chelmsford

Best Goaltending Percentages
Elite League
ROB DOPSON, Sheffield
British National League
STEVE BRIERE, Fife
English Premier League
STEPHEN WALL, Peterborough

JASON RUFF

BRITISH ICE HOCKEY WRITERS' ASSOCIATION AWARDS

ALL-STAR TEAMS

ELITE LEAGUE
First Team

Goal	CURTIS CRUICKSHANK, Bas'stoke
Defence	DION DARLING, Sheffield
	KEVIN BOLIBRUCK, Sheffield
Forwards	JASON RUFF, Belfast
	JOHN CRAIGHEAD, Nottingham
	MARK DUTIAUME, Sheffield

Second Team

Goal	JAYME PLATT, Manchester
Defence	JEFF BURGOYNE, Cardiff
	STEVE O'BRIEN, Coventry
Forwards	STEVE GALLACE, Coventry
	MARK CADOTTE, Nottingham
	ERIK ANDERSON, Sheffield

BRITISH NATIONAL LEAGUE

Goal	STEVE BRIERE, Fife
Defence	PAUL DIXON, Guildford
	GREG KUZNIK, Fife
Forwards	DAN GONEAU, Fife
	TONY HAND, Edinburgh
	ADRIAN SAUL, Edinburgh

OTHER AWARDS

Best British Defenceman (Alan Weeks Trophy)
LEIGH JAMIESON, Belfast
Best British Netminder (BIHWA Trophy)
STEVIE LYLE, Cardiff
Best British Forward (BIHWA Trophy)
ASHLEY TAIT, Coventry
Best Young British Player (Vic Batchelder Memorial Award/*Bauer-Nike*)
LEIGH JAMIESON, Belfast
Top British Scorer (*Ice Hockey Annual* Trophy)
Not awarded

CURTIS CRUICKSHANK

POWERPLAY/EASTSIDE HOCKEY MANAGER PLAYERS OF THE MONTH

September
Elite League   LEIGH JAMIESON, Belfast
Brit Nat Lge   NATHAN REMPEL Br'nell
English Prem. Lge   JESSE HAMILL, P'boro
October
Elite League   PAUL SAMPLE, Belfast
Brit Nat Lge   TONY HAND, Edinburgh
English Prem. Lge   NICK POOLE, M Keynes
November
Elite League   C CRUICKSHANK Bas'stoke
Brit Nat Lge   STEVIE LYLE, Guildford
English Prem. Lge   ALLEN SUTTON, MK
December
Elite League   JODY LEHMAN, Coventry
Brit Nat Lge   TOMMI SATOSAARI,
                      Newcastle
English Prem. Lge   GARY CLARKE, M Keynes
January
Elite League   EVAN LINDSAY, London
Brit Nat Lge   DAN GONEAU, Fife
English Prem. Lge   SHANE MOORE, Swindon
February
Elite League   ASHLEY TAIT, Coventry
Brit Nat Lge   PAUL FERONE, Newcastle
English Prem. Lge   ANDY MOFFAT, Ch'ford
March
Elite League   KIM AHLROOS, Nott'ham
Brit Nat Lge   MILOS MELICHERIK, Guildford
English Prem. Lge   MATT COTE, Wightlink

BRITISH ICE HOCKEY WRITERS' ASSOCIATION AWARDS, contd.

PLAYER OF THE YEAR

Elite League   JASON RUFF, Belfast
Brit Nat League   TONY HAND, Edinburgh

JASON RUFF, the former NHL left-winger from British Columbia led the Elite League's scorers for much of the latter part of the season and was consistently among the top three. The Giants' captain had spent the previous five seasons in Europe, alternating between the German DEL and Belfast for whom he first played in season 2001-02.
Runner-up: **Curtis Cruickshank**, Basingstoke.

TONY HAND, who was awarded an MBE in the New Year's Honours List, was the heart and soul of the Capitals. To be specific, he was the player-coach and best forward on the team that he hand-picked jointly with his cousin and team manager, **Scott Neil**.
Tony's unsurpassed playmaking skills (he led the league in assists with 63 in 36 games, over twice as many as the runner-up) helped the low-budget club to a third place finish - their best ever - and playoff qualification.

COACH OF THE YEAR

Elite League   MIKE BLAISDELL, Sheffield
Brit Nat League   MARK MORRISON, Fife

MIKE BLAISDELL retained his Coach of the Year title as his superior recruiting and man management skills took his Steelers to the Elite League and Playoff Championship double.
To achieve this feat, 'Blaiser' had to build a new team as there were only three returnees from the Superleague double winners. He also gave ice-time to a handful of local players.
This is the Canadian's fourth Coach of the Year honour, and his third in four years. The Playoff trophy was his 13th in 11 years of coaching.
Runner-up: **Paul Thompson**, Coventry

After Flyers finished a disappointing seventh last season, **MARK MORRISON** was determined to build a strong side and Flyers quickly put distance between themselves and the rest of the league. Their first place finish was their second BNL triumph and the eighth major title of the coach's 11-year reign in Kirkcaldy. This is his third Coach of the Year title.

ALL-STARS

Clockwise from top left: Netminder **JAYME PLATT**, Manchester Phoenix; forward **JOHN CRAIGHEAD** Nottingham Panthers; defenceman **PAUL DIXON**, Guildford Flames; forward **MARK DUTIAUME**, Sheffield Steelers.

photos: Diane Davey, Dave Page, Chris Valentine.

QUOTES OF THE YEAR

MBE but no GB

"As much as I like playing for the national team, you can't keep coming back. My view is that they would be better sticking to the younger guys. I could go there [the World Championships] and do a job but I don't think I would make a big difference in the end." *Tony Hand MBE, Britain's finest home-grown player.*

Steelers for sale, maybe

"I will make it a condition of any sale that the Steelers remain in the Elite League." *Norton Lea, owner of Sheffield Steelers, laying down his main condition for selling the club.*

Help!

"The management team are very open about their limited experience at putting together a top level ice hockey product. Nonetheless, they all love the sport and are giving it a go. If you know anything about the sport and can contribute to this Herculean effort then it would be greatly appreciated if you'd come forward and give us a hand. There is still an awful lot of work to be done before Friday." *Rick Strang, spokesman for London Racers - apparently a professional team - three days before Racers were to host the league's first ever game.*

Disaster? What disaster?

"We've been playing well enough to be right in the thick of it; there are poorer teams in the league than us. Our bad luck will become folklore." *Roger Black, owner of the London Racers, after his team had extended their winless streak to 35 games.*

Phoenix arise....

"I'd have loved it to have been 10,000, five thousand would have been brilliant, but I'm more than happy with the 3,600 who turned out." *Neil Morris, owner of the Manchester Phoenix, on their opening game.*

...but only briefly

'The Arena has undergone an explosion in concert revenue, the recent Madonna concert sold 17,000 tickets in a day, at a cost of up to £150 per ticket. Therefore, understandably, the Arena is concentrating on that revenue and the Phoenix are lower in the pecking order.' *From the official transcript of the meeting of Phoenix fans on 6 July 2004, announcing that the team could no longer afford to play at the MEN Arena.*

Headlines of the Year

'Strikeforce is Saul in Hand, says Kaye'. *Over a story in the* Edinburgh Evening News *about Capitals' import* **Steve Kaye's** *scoring partnership with his countryman* **Adrian Saul** *and player-coach* **Tony Hand**.

The Scottish papers went a bit daft over Fife Flyers' forward **Dan Goneau**.

'Flyers Gon with the wins'. *From the* Scottish Daily Record *when he scored five goals in two weekend games.*

'He's just two Dan good'. *Over the* Scottish Sun's *piece about his two goals in the first game.*

'Critics told Dan he was Goneau'. *The* Scottish Sun *again, recalling his short spell with Bracknell Bees.*

This headline in Glasgow's Daily Record *is almost as painful as the operation it was describing*:
'New dad Paddy so Lochi tot Ava is a wee fighter' *Give yourself a wee dram if you guessed that this is about* **Patric Lochi's** *wife giving birth by Caesarean section to a 2lb 14oz baby girl.*

You should get out more, Stewy

"I didn't know what to expect from **Leigh** [**Jamieson**]. He worked very hard ... and showed great potential." *Rob Stewart, Belfast Giants' coach, on his new British signing. [Ed's note - defenceman Jamieson won The Ice Hockey Annual Trophy as MVP of the prestigious Hull junior tournament in May 2000 when he was 14.]*

Caution, mature player

"There is a rule in hockey that states that any player over the age of 35 shall not be hit or physically checked by an opposing player. Are you watching the game, [Nigel] Boniface? How about you, [Simon] Kirkham?" *Steve Moria, Basingstoke Bison's player-coach and leading goal scorer, writing tongue-in-cheek in the club programme. As everyone knows, 'Mo' has just turned 35.*

We couldn't possibly comment

'The best puck in town'. *London Racers' advertising slogan.*

"I doubt if I can have children. After all the box only gives you so much protection." *Jody Lehman, Coventry Blaze's goalie in an interview in* Loaded *magazine.*

One league?

Comments from the Elite League's movers and shakers on the biggest dilemma facing the sport:
"We need to see if having one league is workable. I'm not in this as a hockey fan - I'm a businessman so this one league needs to work financially. It's not simple." *Eamon Convery, the league's chairman.*

"I'm not in favour of one league because that would put half a dozen teams out of business. They couldn't compete with the likes of Sheffield, Nottingham or Belfast." *Mike Cowley, director of Coventry Blaze.*

"There are still question marks in commercial terms of how big the market is for professional ice hockey in the UK..." *Albert Maasland, owner of Belfast Giants, after the top two leagues announced their new working relationship in February 2004.*

Coach-speak for 'help!'

"Right now the team is on a bit of a downer but I believe it is stronger now than it was at the start of the season when we went on our unbeaten run." *Mike Ellis, player-coach of Bracknell Bees, on releasing GB forward, Darren Hurley.*

Real good hockey

"The hockey is real good, somewhere between the East Coast and American Hockey League. The league is more physical than most leagues in Europe and you get paid better than the East Coast League." *Steve Gallace, Coventry Blaze's Canadian forward.*

A thousand? Me?

"I thought it was a slight over-reaction to someone scoring a hat trick." *Doug McEwen, as his teammates poured on to the ice when the 40-year-old completed his hat-trick and scored his 1,000th goal in Britain. [More in Peterborough Phantoms' section - ed.]*

Done travelling

"It's a 70-mile round trip from my house to the Guildford rink and I was doing that five times a week. Then we played in Scotland for what seemed like every second game. I worked out I was doing about 1,500 miles a week. It was a huge strain on my family." *Tony Redmond, explaining his summer 2004 move from the BNL's Bracknell Bees to Basingstoke Bison in the Elite League.*

Absentee coach

"Mike [Blaisdell] will oversee the signing of a new head coach and then jointly work with that individual in signing the new Steelers' team for next season." *Norton Lea, Steelers' owner, confirming the continuing involvement of their coach despite his move to Saskatchewan.*

We're going to miss him

Mike Blaisdell, Sheffield Steelers' Hall of Fame coach, returned to Canada in the summer of 2004. Some of his comments from 2003-04:
"He picked on the smallest British kid on the ice. [Manchester's George] Awada is the biggest guy on the ice and he tried to run [Ryan] Lake's head into the glass. He's going to pay for that all year, I guarantee. I'll fine anybody who turns away from him. If players don't hit him every time, they'll get fined." *When an opponent went unpenalised after cutting one of his players during the third 'Roses' game of the season.*

"...teams like Cardiff give their guys good money from sponsors. I'm not saying they are breaking the wage cap but if a sponsor cuts a guy a cheque for £5,000 it helps!" *Especially cheeky one from the coach of a team that used to make a habit of overlooking wage caps.*

"It would be great for them [Ryan Lake and Paul Sample], our club and the sport if they were to develop and grow at Steelers into forceful, international-calibre forwards.
"The future of the Elite league is in the hands of home-grown players and these two are a great example for others to follow." *Belatedly making up for his notorious preference for Canadians.*

"Remember 1954" - Simms

"At the end of the day the only figures that matter when you are talking about Nottingham are 1954 - that's the last time they won the title. Most of their fans aren't old enough to remember that. And the reason is that Nottingham don't know how to breed winners....

"My advice for all the Steelers' fans who come to our home game with Nottingham on 27 December is to bring a banner, a poster, or a piece of paper with 1954 plastered on it. That should get the point across to Nottingham Panthers more than any other."
Dave Simms, Sheffield Steelers' director, fuelling the fire on the eve of the Boxing Day clash between the great rivals. We don't know how many fans carried out Simmsy's instructions but as regular readers of the Annual will know, Panthers last won the old British National League in 1955-56 and were [Heineken] British Champions in 1989.

With grateful acknowledgements to *Powerplay, the Daily Telegraph, Belfast Evening Telegraph, Belfast Sunday Life, Coventry Evening Telegraph, Manchester Evening News, Nottingham Evening Post, The Star (Sheffield), Scottish Sun, Reading Evening Post, London (Ontario) Free Press, and various websites and match programmes.*

PLAYERS IN THE NEWS

Tony Hand MBE

> MBE - **Anthony Hand**, coach and player, Edinburgh Capitals ice hockey team, for services to ice hockey - *the official announcement in the New Year newspapers.*

Yes, it was another memorable year for our finest home-grown player. Tony received the first ever 'gong' for a British ice hockey player in the 2004 New Year's Honours List.

Then, after a season when he was reunited with his home town team, Edinburgh Capitals, helping them to their highest finish in the British National League, he surprised his fans by leaving his native Scotland and signing as player-coach of the Belfast Giants.

Tony received his medal from Her Majesty the Queen on 29 June. (See cover photo). Wearing his Scottish tartan and formal highland regalia, he was one of the stars at a glittering ceremony at the Palace of Holyroodhouse in Edinburgh.

He said afterwards: "This is a great honour for me personally but it is also wonderful to have ice hockey highlighted in such a prominent way. I chatted briefly with Her Majesty and she congratulated me on my achievements and wished me success as coach of Belfast Giants."

The unique honour came in the middle of a special hockey season for the 36-year-old who was invited to play and co-coach the Capitals by his cousin **Scott Neil**, the team's general manager.

For the umpteenth time his line - with Canadians **Adrian Saul** and **Steven Kaye** - was the league's most prolific, finishing 1-2-3 in scoring with Tony as number one. His 63 assists were almost double his nearest rival's. Capitals' small home crowd and consequent strict budget stopped them winning silverware but they reached the playoffs, a rarity in recent times.

Perhaps it was his testimonial game at Murrayfield on 12 April - watched by a full house of nearly 3,000 - that lulled some of us into thinking the man was now going to take it easy and settle down in his beloved Scotland. But we greatly under-estimated his love of the game and his desire to coach when he's no longer able to play (like when he's 50, right?).

"I'm ambitious and I want to coach at the highest level," he told the Belfast press. "This is a major club playing in a top league. The opportunities offered to develop my coaching credentials are significant."

This will be his fourth season as a coach and his first in the Elite League. It will probably be his most challenging. Many Giants' fans stayed away last term after the club came close to bankruptcy in 2003 and he has been charged with filling up the 7,000 seats again.

He was unfazed by the size of his task. "I will be taking a wide, sweeping look at the talent available and I'm confident I can bring together a team that will entertain and delight the crowds, and bring some silverware back to the city."

In their spendthrift days, Giants won the Superleague and the playoffs, but Tony has a much more realistic budget to work with; Giants made a £30,000 loss in 2003-04.

As the *Annual* went to press, he had persuaded almost half (eight) of the Giants to return and a Canadian bruiser called **Mel** (**The Mangler**) **Angelstad** looked set to replace retired favourite, **Paxton Schulte**.

It should be another memorable year for, as one wag put it, our Miraculously Born 'Ere hero.

• Hand's appointment at the Odyssey was spoiled by the club's clumsy handling of his predecessor's dismissal. **Rob Stewart** was told he was out only 90 minutes before the press conference to announce his replacement.

■ Freelance writer, **Mike Appleton**, is writing a biography of Tony for publication late next year.

BritWatch
BEN O'CONNOR

The 15-year-old son of former Durham Wasp and Sheffield Steeler, **Mike O'Connor**, was picked by Canadian junior team, Windsor Spitfires, in the Ontario Hockey League priority draft on 1 May 2004.

Ben, a strapping 6ft defenceman like his father, went in the 14th round, 267th overall. He had been playing Midget AAA in London, Ontario.

At Christmas, the youngster played four games in New York for the England under-16s. Icing as a forward, he scored six goals.

COLIN SHIELDS

Glasgow-born **Colin Shields** was the top scorer in his third season with the University of Maine Black Bears and later attended Los Angeles Kings' NHL training camp.

Shields tallied 44 points (18 goals) in 44 games for Black Bears who were runners-up in Hockey East and went on to reach the final of the NCAA Frozen Four. He was named to the second All-Star team and was twice selected as Hockey East's player of the week.

The 24-year-old forward first went to North America at the age of 14 and in 2000 he became the second British born and trained player (after **Tony Hand**) to be drafted by the NHL when he was taken by Philadelphia Flyers.

THREE GENERATIONS OF NEILS

Nottingham Panthers made an additional signing this week, with outstanding 14-year-old prospect **James Neil** - son of the arena's former general manager **Vernon Neil** - coming in for special development from the club.

Neil might have an advantage over his young team-mates when it comes to dealing with 'stardom'. As well as his father playing for the old second string Trojans in the 1980s, his paternal grandfather, the late **Lawson Neil**, starred for Panthers in the 1960s.

And his maternal grandfather, **Billy Cobb**, scored the first Forest goal in European competition when he netted against Valencia in the Inter-City Fairs Cup in 1961.

Nottingham Evening Post, 21 May 2004

Flyers decided not to offer him a contract - partly due to the uncertainty in the league over the impending expiry of the Collective Bargaining Agreement with the players - so he snapped up Kings' invitation to attend their camp in July 2004. There he played alongside teenage prospect **Sydney Crosby** who is predicted to be the next **Wayne Gretzky**.

Shields, who flew back to Norway for his fourth World Championship with GB in April, received high praise from his coach at the Black Bears, **Tim Whitehead**. "He's playing real well at both ends of the ice," said the coach. "He's elevated his game physically and defensively, and he's also a natural scorer.

"He's now on the penalty kill and, of course, he's on the powerplay. He needs to continue to focus on his defensive game and he'll need that even more at the next level, but he's playing hard and producing and is a player we can use in all situations."

At the time of writing, Shields had not signed for a team in 2004-05 but was hoping to join a American Hockey League side.

▪ Viewers to the digital TV channel, North American Sports Network (NASN), were able to watch Colin in the NCAA Frozen Four final which was shown live in the UK.

JOE WATKINS

GB international netminder, **Joe Watkins**, spent the 2003-04 season in the USA with Bakersfield Condors of the East Coast Hockey League.

Watkins, 24, whose last UK team was Bracknell Bees, shared Condors' goaltending duties with **Peter Hirsch**, the Danish national team keeper. When the pair last met they were on opposite sides in the 2002 World Championships.

The Durham native bumped into some other familiar faces as former Superleague players **Johan Astrom**, **Kevin Reihl** and **Jimmy Drolet** were among his team-mates.

Condors finished fifth in their seven-team division and Watkins appeared in 26 games, winning seven and recording a save percentage of 88.1. But who cares about the hockey? Despite the league's name, Bakersfield is in sunny California.

▪ By a strange coincidence, Bracknell's goalie in 2003-04, **Scott Hay**, was an ex-Condor.

Farewell

Several leading players bid farewell to UK ice hockey in the summer of 2004.

RICK BREBANT

Rick Brebant, the British-Canadian forward who scored over 1,000 goals in this country, announced his retirement from the sport on his 40th birthday in February 2004.

The 5ft 9in dynamo won everything there is to win in the UK. During his 17 seasons he played over 800 games on eight different teams, winning 20 official competitions. In recognition of his outstanding achievements, he was inducted into the British Hall of Fame in 2004.

Actually, this was not the first time the pugnacious attacker had tried to quit playing the game he loved and played so well. In the mid-Nineties with Newcastle, Rick intended to stick to coaching but couldn't resist the temptation to lace 'em up. He turned out in 45 games for the Cobras.

In last year's *Annual*, we see that he had turned in his stick again after three seasons with Sheffield Steelers. But he had to have another go at coaching, this time with the new Manchester Phoenix. He put himself back in the fray for 36 games, ended fourth in the club's scoring and helped them into the Elite League playoffs.

Now the Elliot Lake, Ontario native has promised he will settle down back home in Canada and teach youngsters.

For more on Rick, see *Hall of Fame* section elsewhere in this *Annual*, and last year's edition.

FAREWELL

Clockwise from above left: **STEVE CHARTRAND** bids 'adieu' to Coventry Blaze; Hull Stingray **STEPHEN JOHNSON** takes his leave after 23 years; departing Belfast Giants' 'entertainer' **PAXTON SCHULTE**; 'enforcer' **MIKE WARE** waving goodbye to the Cardiff Devils fans.

Photos: Diane Davey, Arthur Foster, Dave Page, Coventry Evening Telegraph.

STEVE CHARTRAND

Another high scoring Canadian decided to hang up his skates, this time after 13 seasons.

Coventry Blaze forward **Steve Chartrand** was eight times leading marksman on his team, seven with Solihull and Coventry and once with Blackburn Hawks. In 612 games, he scored 1,898 points, including 931 goals. He had just 380 penalty minutes.

In season 2002-03 the 35-year-old centreman skippered the Blaze as they lifted the league and playoff titles in the British National League.

The French-Canadian first played in the Midlands for Solihull Barons in 1990-91. Apart from a year in Blackburn in the mid-Nineties (and five games for his first British side, Whitley Warriors), he played for the same club. He saw them change their name to Blaze in 1996 and move to Coventry in 2000.

In honour of his loyalty and his achievements, his number 12 shirt was raised to the rafters of the Coventry Skydome at the end of the season and he was to have a testimonial game at the start of 2004-05.

Last year, Blaze finished higher than ever before, fourth in the Elite League. "This has been my only full season in the top league in the country and I think it's time to call it a day and go out at the top," said 'Frenchie'. "I've been giving 100 per cent, but in this league sometimes it isn't enough."

His coach **Paul Thompson**, said: "Steve has led us through the dark times and stayed with us to savour the good times. I want to thank him for being my captain and go-to guy for many years."

STEPHEN JOHNSON

British forward **Stephen (Quacks) Johnson** ended his remarkable 23-year playing career by breaking the 1,000-game barrier.

When knee ligament damage forced the 37-year-old to hang up his skates in January 2004, he had racked up 1,013 games in official competitions. His last team, Hull Stingrays, honoured their captain by having his number 10 shirt retired.

The former Great Britain international scored 611 goals and 989 assists for a nice round 1,600 points since breaking into senior hockey, aged 15, with his home town team Durham Wasps. He spent just over a minute a game in the penalty box, with 1,183 minutes.

He was capped 23 times for GB in the Nineties, scoring ten goals and 22 points.

Stephen is the son of **Peter (Jonker) Johnson** and the brother of **Shaun** and **Anthony**, one of two famous hockey families (the others are the Coopers, **Stephen**, **Ian** and their father, **Brian**) who helped to make Wasps one of the most successful teams of the Eighties.

Shaun, the youngest of the three Johnson boys, is the only one still playing, at Newcastle Vipers.

Stephen first came to Hull in 1996 after the Wasps had been bought by **Sir John Hall** of the Newcastle Sporting Club.

He told the *Annual*: "I've recently started my own business which doesn't leave me a lot of time for playing and practising. What with that and the injuries I've picked up over the years, I just thought it was time to call it a day." When we queried the origin of his nickname, he just laughed and said: "You'd better ask my dad."

Joint Stingrays' owner, **Sue Pack**, paid tribute to him, saying: "We have not known 'Quacks' long but we hold him in the highest esteem. We were delighted with the job he did for us last year and his injury hurt us as he was our captain and our most senior British player. We always found him very professional and a really good guy."

PAXTON SCHULTE

Belfast Giants' 6ft 2in winger, who works on a farm in his home town of Edmonton, Alberta during the off-season, was not employed for his delicate touch around opposition nets.

In 328 games in his six seasons here, **Paxton Schulte** spent 22 hours in the sin-bin, 1,351 minutes. With one of the shortest fuses in the game, he justly earned the reputation for being one of its most feared practitioners.

"I like to think I'm respected and if being respected means I'm feared then so be it. I'm there to look after my team-mates when things get out of hand and I'm quite happy doing that. But when I drop the gloves, I drop them."

Despite his aggressive nature, the man could score. He was among his clubs' top six points scorers in five of his six seasons, the first two of which he spent with Bracknell Bees.

He won three Superleague trophies, including the playoffs with Giants, and in season 2001-02, he bagged ten powerplay goals, two hat-tricks and five game-winning goals.

Last season was difficult for Schulte as the Elite League attempted to cut down on the rougher aspects of the game. He was the league's biggest penalty taker with 352 minutes, around double his usual tally, and he was involved in a couple of particularly nasty incidents.

It came as a shock to the Giants' fans when a few days before the end of the season he announced his intention to retire. He told the *Belfast Telegraph* he had become increasingly frustrated and felt it was time to go "before I do something stupid".

It was not a popular decision. He was well liked at the Odyssey where he was one of the original Giants in 2000. He was a big attraction, not just for the mayhem he caused on the ice but for his warmth off it. He never refused an autograph request and made numerous visits to local schools and hospitals.

The feeling in the city was that Mr Belfast Giants jumped before he was pushed.

MIKE WARE

The shaven-headed Canadian played only five games in the NHL but it was long enough to earn him the monicker, Iron Mike. The tag stuck when **Mike Ware** came to Britain in 1992.

The 6ft 5in giant from North York, Ontario mixed it with the biggest bruisers in the Superleague and Elite League. In 347 games with Cardiff Devils, London Knights and Sheffield Steelers, he chalked up 1,093 penalty minutes but only 55 goals.

When he left Steelers, they signed another former NHL hard man, **Dennis Vial**, and he challenged Ware to a fight when he returned to Sheffield Arena with the Devils. Afterwards, Ware skated to the penalty box while Vial had to be dragged off the ice by the stewards.

'Goon!', you cry, but not loudly enough for him to hear, of course.

Anyway, he didn't win all his fights. In his spell with the Oilers, he tangled with the NHL's most famous enforcer, **Marty McSorley**, then with **Wayne Gretzky**'s LA Kings. "I'd like to call it a draw, but I'd be lying," said Ware.

In fact, it was Marty's brother, **Chris McSorley**, who brought the right-winger down from Edinburgh to play for Superleague's London Knights. This was in 1999-2000, McSorley's first season, when the *Annual* described the London Arena as 'Slap Shot-on-Thames'.

We'd almost forgotten that Mike played four seasons in the old British League, three of them as **Tony Hand**'s 'minder' in the Scottish capital before he joined Devils in the league's last campaign.

He played 201 games in the BL, where he was able to concentrate more on scoring with 153 goals and 332 points. But he still found time, 1,034 minutes to be precise, to visit his old haunt opposite the team benches.

But - and this is the final proof that the 37-year-old was a brute on the ice - in his private life Mike is 'modest, quiet and gentle, and doesn't like reliving his more grisly moments', according to an affectionate farewell tribute in the *South Wales Echo*.

"I'd love to play forever but that's just not possible. I have a back problem and I'm a family man so I have to think about the future," he said.

British rinks will be less fun for spectators now that Iron Mike Ware has decided to return home to Canada and join a hockey school as a full-time coach. We hate to think what he'll teach the little blighters.

Dave Whistle

ISERLOHN ROOSTERS FIRE COACH AFTER THIRD STRAIGHT LOSS

Frank Johne, Munich, Germany, 5 Oct. 2003
'After suffering their third straight defeat in Friday's 5-2 loss to the Hamburg Freezers, the slumping Iserlohn Roosters decided to axe head coach **Dave Whistle** on Saturday morning.

'Whistle's DEL rookie season lasted only nine games in which he led the Roosters to three wins, one regulation tie and five losses.

'"We have been monitoring games and practices closely for a long time," the Roosters stated in a press release. "Despite continuous communication and extraordinary assistance on our part, Dave Whistle was not able to realise our ideas. The team's primary goal is avoiding relegation. At the moment, we have the impression that this goal is in danger. That's why we felt forced to make this move."

'The Ontario native was brought in this off-season after fan favorite **Greg Poss** decided to take the head coaching reins at the Nürnberg Ice Tigers after eight years in Iserlohn.

'At only 37 years of age, Whistle has already won three championship rings as a head coach in the British Superleague, two with the Belfast Giants and one with the Bracknell Bees.'
- *www.prohockey.de*

■ Season 2003-04 was an eventful one for 'Whis'. When he returned to this country on 10 December to sign as coach of Cardiff Devils, he found his sponsor was to be KF Concepts. This is the, shall we say, enterprising firm whose directors were later arrested for fraud. See *Review of the Year* for more.

■ One of Roosters' players, **Ian McIntyre**, decided to return to Canada shortly after his coach was sacked and was threatened with legal action by the German club. McIntyre, who played for Devils and London Knights in the Superleague, signed for London Racers in August 2004. More on this in *International Round-Up* elsewhere in the *Annual*.

Rick Plant

Rick Plant, Guildford Flames' all-time leading British scorer, was suspended for 18 months by Ice Hockey UK after testing positive for a banned stimulant during a routine random drug test after a BNL game on 6 December 2003.

He is ineligible to play or to have any involvement in ice hockey until 31 August 2005.

Accepting the decision, Flames said: 'There is not a bad thing we can say about this classy young man. This is a very difficult situation and we are assisting him in dealing with these unfortunate circumstances."

THE GREAT ICE WAR

IIHF occupies UK

The disastrous experiment with fully professional ice hockey, known as Superleague, ended in 2003 with the league in liquidation and the sport's organisation in disarray, *writes the editor*.

As we reported in last year's *Annual*, the big arena clubs - Nottingham, Sheffield and Belfast - then got together with five other teams and formed a new league - the Elite League - against the wishes of the national governing body. Ice Hockey UK wanted the remaining Superleague clubs to settle the league's bills and join the British National League in one national league.

The argy-bargy lasted all summer with IHUK, under the chairmanship of Scot **Stuart Robertson**, refusing to recognise the new league but unable to exert their authority.

IHUK's weakness was partly due to their financial position which had worsened, ironically enough, because Superleague were in arrears with the payment of their fees. There were also divisions within Ice Hockey UK itself and a simmering row with their sometime rival, the English Ice Hockey Association.

CRISIS BEFORE SEASON OPENS

The fees, which were also payable by the British National League, entitled the leagues to do deals direct with TV companies and sponsors.

The crisis came to a head just days before the opening of the 2003-04 season. In a move unprecedented in the UK, the world governing body, the International Ice Hockey Federation, stepped in to try and bring some order.

A letter dated 27 August 2003 from the IIHF's general secretary, **Jan-Ake Edvinsson**, to Mr Robertson confirmed that 'the IIHF Council has decided that the administration of Ice Hockey UK will now be under the temporary supervision of the IIHF in exercising its supervisory role regarding the temporary affiliation of the Elite League to IHUK.'

The letter went on: 'The IIHF will administer the ITCs [International Transfer Cards needed by players moving from one country to another] to and from the Elite League clubs and other international matters with immediate effect.'

To say this was a controversial move would be an understatement. It was an embarrassment to Mr Robertson and his allies in Ice Hockey UK, who believed they had acted responsibly in refusing to recognise the new Elite League.

It annoyed many people when the world body asked their Council member, **Frederick Meredith**, to conduct a fact-finding mission. Mr Meredith was the last president of the British Ice Hockey Association, the forerunners of IHUK. He had presided over the virtual bankruptcy of the BIHA, forcing its own collapse in 1998 after 85 years.

And most BNL clubs were incensed when Mr Meredith recommended that the Elite League should be recognised without any strings so that the new season could start, pending further meetings of the clubs and the IIHF.

"ELITE HAVE DAMAGED OUR BUSINESS"

Martin Weddell, the general manager of Bracknell Bees, told the *Annual*: "We're furious with the IIHF. Their failure to punish the Elite League has strengthened [the league's] cause and increased their egos. [The Elite League] have damaged our business by six figures". The damage was caused by the summer-long wrangling which resulted in a severe drop in season ticket revenues at many rinks.

When the season started on 12 September 2003, the new league were still trying to put their organisation in place and several Basingstoke and London players were without ITCs.

Respected administrator, **Brian Storey**, who had worked for Superleague for six years, had been unable to agree terms with the new league who handed the job to **Andy French**, Superleague's officials' manager and a former GB team manager.

NEW LEAGUE OFFICIALS

Andy was given the title of Hockey Operations Manager and worked from his home near Cardiff as the league decided against the expense of a separate office.

The Elite League did not agree terms, either, with **Gordon Wade**, the sport's longest serving statistician. The stats were handled instead by freelance reporter, **Antony Hopker**, who is based in Coventry.

Meanwhile, Ice Hockey UK got busy drawing up new rules and regulations to clarify the way the sport is run. At the IIHF's insistence, these had to be approved by the Federation at their semi-annual congress in October.

Come 30 September and the Elite League had missed two payment deadlines. Among the league's demands were understood to be a two-year deal. IHUK threatened to withdraw the officials for that weekend's games.

THE ELITE LEAGUE'S BOARD OF DIRECTORS

Pictured at the Playoff finals in Nottingham, April 2004. *Left to right:* **Mark Johnson** (Basingstoke Bison), **Albert Maasland** (Belfast Giants), **Bob Phillips** (Cardiff Devils), **Mike Cowley** (Coventry Blaze), **Andy French** (league administrator), **Eamon Convery** (league chairman), **Roger Black** (London Racers), **Harry Howton** (Milton Keynes Lightning), **Neil Morris** (Manchester Phoenix), **Neil Black** (Nottingham Panthers), **Norton Lea** (Sheffield Steelers).

INTERNATIONAL ICE HOCKEY FEDERATION

Zurich, Switzerland, February 19 2004

IIHF and British officials review panel findings in order to improve ice hockey in Great Britain

Representatives of professional ice hockey clubs from the British National League and the Elite Ice Hockey League, and representatives from Ice Hockey UK and the International Ice Hockey Federation met on Wednesday, February 18, near the East Midlands Airport in Great Britain to review, analyse and discuss the findings of the six-member Review Panel on the future development and growth of professional ice hockey in Great Britain.

The IIHF was represented by its Director of Sports, Mr. **Dave Fitzpatrick**.

This initiative began last November in Bracknell when the same representatives attended a general meeting to discuss the way forward for professional ice hockey in Great Britain. A six-member Review Panel, representative of the attendees was created during this meeting to review the current operations of both the FBNL and EIHL and prepare proposals for the future growth of professional ice hockey in the United Kingdom.

Today the participants openly and thoroughly discussed the various options and proposals put forward by the six-member panel.

Following the review all participants expressed their commitment to developing the game in a professional and structured manner, committing to work towards improving the World Ranking of Great Britain ice hockey and the development of British players.

During the meeting today the clubs and league participants, assigned with the responsibility and respective authority to decide such issues, made the following proposals. All attendees accepted these proposals as a starting point to develop the professional game in Great Britain:

Recommend that more factual information was required to base large restructuring decisions at this time.

Recommend that the FBNL and the EIHL operate in 2004-05 as independent leagues, operating their competitions with their member teams.

Recommend that all FBNL and EIHL teams and leagues learn from the experiences of joint competition between the teams of both leagues.

Recommend that the decisions to guide the development of the professional sport be based on known and actual facts and data.

Recommend operating a three-year plan, making calculated steps and decisions based on facts in the ongoing initiative to integrate professional clubs into a strong national league.

Recommend that a national cup competition involving all FBNL and all EIHL clubs be organised and operated in year one and, depending upon the experiences, operate again in year two.

Points from all games in the national cup competition will be counted in individual league standings within both the FBNL and EIHL leagues.

The national cup competition game schedule will be developed for securing dates and facilities in the near future

Recommend that the national cup competition game schedule duration and timing be developed in a manner that supports the independent game schedule of both leagues.

Recommend that principles be structured to address parity of competition. The following proposals were adopted to achieve this goal:

all FBNL teams and EIHL teams use a maximum salary cap of £6,900.

all FBNL teams and EIHL teams operate a minimum team size of 16 players (including two players under 20 years of age) plus two goalkeepers.

all FBNL teams and EIHL teams to limit the number of imports to 11 in 2004-05 season and reduce to 10 in 2005-06 season.

all FBNL teams and EIHL teams clubs, in their commitment to developing the talent base, accept the obligation and will attempt to limit the maximum number of imports to 10 in the 2004-05 season.

that bench size be set with a maximum of 22 players and goalkeepers.

The members expressed their commitment to the future and agreed that a cautious and careful approach to the future development of the sport was an essential ingredient for success. The IIHF was also requested to assist the realisation of this project with the support of their Marketing Committee's expertise for the sponsorship and television aspects.

Peace in our time?

The escalating row persuaded the IIHF to bring forward by three weeks their first full meeting with representatives of the sport here. The Federation's Director of Sport, **Dave Fitzpatrick**, chaired a two-day meeting in Glasgow with IHUK and the 15 top clubs on 6 and 7 October.

Though Mr Fitzpatrick did his best - one club praised him as "diplomatic" - the meeting was not a great success. The Elite League questioned the need for IHUK's existence, and admitted they had ignored an IIHF ruling and allowed London Racers to play on the opening weekend, even though 11 of their players did not hold a valid transfer card.

(The matter was referred to the IIHF's disciplinary committee and the club was later understood to have been fined £2,000, a slap on the wrist as the amount laid down in the rules is around £25,000. Neither the IIHF nor IHUK was prepared to disclose the punishment to the *Annual*. We understand that IHUK are now more strict with clubs over the ITC rules procedure.)

> In October 2004, the Elite League clubs failed to pay Ice Hockey UK £27,000 in outstanding fees.

The Elite clubs did eventually sign a contract agreeing to play to IIHF/IHUK rules but they still failed to pay their outstanding fees which were now understood to total £27,000.

On 12 November, the sides met again, this time in Bracknell, though Nottingham's **Neil Black** ('unwell') and Sheffield's **Norton Lea** (unknown) were conspicuous by their absence.

The meeting, again chaired by Mr Fitzpatrick, set up a working party to look into 'the available options for the future of British professional ice hockey'. The working party consisted of -
Elite - **Eamon Convery** (chairman), **Albert Maasland** (Belfast) and **Mike Cowley** (Coventry)
BNL - **Martin Weddell** (Bracknell), **Tom Muir** (Fife) and **Darryl Illingworth** (Newcastle).

All clubs were sent a questionnaire asking for their views.

WORKING PARTY "CAN'T AGREE"

The working party was met with scepticism by some clubs. "They can't even agree on the basics," complained Weddell. "They [the EL] agree something then go off and say that they can't get all their members to agree to it. They're only interested in entertainment. They don't want rules, only vague agreements."

It was not until 17 February 2004 that the Elite League finally paid their outstanding dues to IHUK.

The reason for this sudden change of heart did not take long to become clear. All the clubs and IHUK met the IIHF again the next day to hear the results of the working party's deliberations, and make a final decision on the structure of the sport.

After a five-hour meeting at East Midlands airport, the Federation published 'a three-year plan' for the running of the 'professional leagues'. [See the IIHF's letter on the previous page].

> "[The Elite League] are only interested in entertainment. They don't want rules, only vague agreements." *Martin Weddell, Bracknell Bees.*

Sadly, these did not include the creation of the fans' favourite, a single national league - at least not straight away. Instead, there was a messy - some might say classically British - compromise of a 'crossover' league, featuring the first games between the two leagues for nine years. But as teams in the same leagues were not to meet each other in this competition, it was purely a political league, a getting-to-know-you exercise.

IMPORTS REDUCED TO 11

The Elite agreed to reduce their imports but only by one to 11 per team, and ten in 2005-06. The BNL's limit is already seven or eight, 50 per cent of the team.

The IIHF also politely suggested that rather than blame each other for the state of the game, the clubs should monitor their costs carefully so that any further restructuring of the sport was based on hard financial facts.

Warming to their task of sorting out our sport, the world body even offered the expertise of their marketing committee.

After holding their own meetings to ratify the Federation's proposals, both leagues publicly welcomed them. Eamon Convery, the chairman of the Elite League, said: "The proposals for a sensible and gradual coming together of the two bodies are welcomed by all and I am sure that the on-ice competition ... will generate a lot of interest and help forge even better working relationships."

The BNL's general manager, **Gary Stefan**, was a little more cautious: "This has been a great step in the right direction but there are many more steps to come."

Not everyone was happy, though. One BNL club rep said: "Most of the items were agreed on the Elite League's terms."

■ After the Elite League paid their fees, Eamon Convery and Coventry Blaze director, **Mike Cowley**, joined the Board of Ice Hockey UK.
■ For more on Ice Hockey UK's finances, see *Review of the Year*.

REVIEW OF THE YEAR

ICE HOCKEY UK
GB's five-ring circus

Great Britain's ice hockey team will not be playing in the 2006 Winter Olympic Games in Turin, Italy.

Despite many promises to the contrary by Ice Hockey UK through the national team coach, **Chris McSorley**, when it came to the crunch the governing body realised that they simply couldn't afford the costs of trying to qualify.

At the IIHF's annual congress in Prague in May 2004, Britain were the only country of the 21 needing to qualify to decide against entering the Olympic Qualifying Tournament.

The decision was taken by IHUK chairman **Stuart Robertson** and his deputy **Neville Moralee**, the only IHUK representatives to attend the meeting. In a statement afterwards, the governing body said:

'Ice Hockey UK was forced, very reluctantly and after consultation with head coach Chris McSorley, members of the board of directors and **Frederick Meredith** (who is an International Ice Hockey Federation council member), to withdraw the team as we had no funding for this event.

'It has been estimated that we would need in the region of £15,000 to £30,000 to compete in these qualifying rounds.'

McSorley said: "Although disappointed, I believe that it is extremely important to channel all available funds to the development of the under-20s programme. Although all of us would have enjoyed the competition we must remain realistic in our goal of development.

"To quash any rumours, my commitment to the Great Britain programme is as strong now as it has ever been."

Had Britain gone ahead, they would have had to battle through two rounds of qualifying, in November 2004 and February 2005, before reaching the final 12. As the world's eight leading nations, plus hosts Italy, had byes into the final round, this left only three spots open for the 21 qualifying nations.

The chances of GB being one of those three - they are currently ranked 25th in the world - was considered too slim to justify the expense. Moreover, holding the two qualifying rounds in the same season (last time they were spread over two years in 2000 and 2001) would have increased IHUK's cash-flow problem.

Frankly, we find IHUK's decision hard to disagree with. Moreover, we see no chance of

the situation improving until our leading clubs have been persuaded to see the benefits in investing time and money in our national side.

But IHUK left themselves open to criticism over the way the decision was taken and explained to the sport. Mr Moralee told the GB Supporters Club AGM in August 2004 that they only realised it was possible to withdraw from the qualifiers when they were in the IIHF meeting, and that left them no time to consult anyone, apart presumably from Messrs McSorley and Meredith.

This seems odd as it means that they went into the meeting with the intention of competing, even though they knew that the games were going to combine high risk with high cost.

The Supporters Club, who have been the national team's biggest backers for a number of years, were furious that they were not consulted over GB's unexpected withdrawal.

When they did find out, they immediately offered financial assistance of £10,000, with donations from *Powerplay* magazine and *Specsavers*. This was accepted but it was too late for the IIHF to change the complicated qualifying schedule.

Your editor must declare an interest here as a member of the GBSC. That said, we can understand the governing body's reluctance to rely on the fans for money as the supporters would then rightly feel that they could influence decisions about the running of the team. That would not make for a happy time for anyone.

But the fact that our governing body can't raise even a modest five-figure sum for the most important event in the sporting calendar should give everyone in British ice hockey pause for a lot of thought.

Ice Hockey UK posts heavy loss

The reason for Ice Hockey UK's Olympic decision became abundantly clear after an inspection of their accounts which revealed a loss of almost £100,000 for the year ended 30 June 2003. What's more, the governing body needed a loan from the IIHF to keep them afloat.

IHUK receives income from only a few sources. The top two leagues, the IIHF, regional bodies like the English IHA (which includes the English Premier League), youth training fees and the sale of rule books. That's about it. In all, this amounted to £277,107 for the year 2002-03.

The outgoings were to cover the costs of the national teams (that's all ages and both sexes), fees to the IIHF for the transfer cards needed by players from overseas (costing around £450 a card, depending on the exchange rate), expenses of youth training and the costs of the rule books. That lot totted up to £237,287.

That left a profit of around £40,000. But then there were £140,000 of administration costs and expenses. The major items were £30,000 to the staff at IHUK's Nottingham headquarters, and £20,000 to **Darryl Easson**, their (former) junior technical director (we're using round figures).

But these amounts were dwarfed by 'bad debts' amounting to £60,000. Of these £22,000 were unpaid fees by Superleague and the rest related to their bankrupt predecessors, the British Ice Hockey Association.

The bottom line was a loss of £98,181.

There is some good news, though. Subject to scrutiny of the accounts by the Board at their September meeting, IHUK should make a small profit (before tax) for the year ended 30 June 2004. This was achieved mostly by cutting back on the funds made available to the national teams including, of course, not sending a senior men's team to the Olympics.

UK RECEIVES LOAN FROM IIHF

The governing body received an interest-free loan of 90,000 Swiss francs (£42,000) from the International Federation in 2004. This is repayable over three years and should ensure that the governing body remains in the black for the foreseeable future.

■ **Neville Moralee**, a retired schoolmaster who is the finance director of the English IHA, replaced **Stuart Robertson** as chairman of Ice Hockey UK on 1 July 2004. Mr Robertson took on the role of general manager of the Fife Ice Arena in early 2004.

The full list of the 11-strong Board of Directors of Ice Hockey UK is at the back of the *Annual* under *Governing Bodies*. Each of the six bodies represented on IHUK has one vote on the Board.
☒ Ice Hockey UK released **Simon Kirkham** after only 21 months as their referee-in-chief. In a brief statement to the *Annual* on 4 August 2004, the governing body said that the duties he undertook were largely duplicated by the chief referees of their 'partner organisations' - primarily the Elite League, the BNL and the English IHA - and that his position had thus become superfluous.

Simon's primary duties were acting as liaison between the leagues and working with the IIHF in licensing the UK's referees and linesmen.

We understand that the Board's financial position contributed to their decision.

ELITE LEAGUE
Steelers win double, lose coach

Sheffield Steelers won the league and playoff double in the first season of the Elite League, but their coach, **Mike Blaisdell**, returned to Canada after the season and the club was put up for sale as their crowds fell by nearly a fifth.

With the country's leading teams playing in separate leagues, the new Elite League was based around their three arena clubs - Belfast Giants, Nottingham Panthers and Sheffield - who subsidised several of the other five.

The Elite's biggest money-spinner, as it was in the Superleague, was the derby games between the Panthers and the Steelers. The teams met 11 times in all, attracting 66,533 fans, meaning that more than one in ten of the crowds at Elite League games were fans of either the Panthers or the Steelers.

STEELERS FOR SALE

While the league congratulated itself on getting through the season against the predictions of their many critics, they delayed until February before paying their fees to the governing body. Their refusal to pay up before the season started led to a long wrangle with Ice Hockey UK who only agreed to recognise the league at the insistence of the world governing body, the International Ice Hockey Federation.

Despite Steelers' success on the ice, owner **Norton Lea** told the fans in November that he might sell the club. He was reported to have had negotiations with local businessman, **Robin Edwardes**, and **Chris McSorley**, the coach of the GB national team, but neither ended in the purchase of the 13-year-old team

Blaisdell, who was voted into the British Hall of Fame after winning a record 13 titles in the UK,. returned home to Canada but agreed to act as the club's director of player personnel.

The newly formed London Racers were on their third coach, second home rink and 41st game before they recorded their first win - in front of an official crowd of just 598.

The league's best non-arena side was Coventry Blaze. Under **Paul Thompson**, the only British coach among the eight clubs (until the late appointment of Scot **Paul Heavey** by Manchester), the former British National League side finished third and competed in the playoffs.

In July 2004, Manchester Phoenix announced that they were suspending operations for 12 months as they were unable to afford the rent of the cavernous MEN Arena. But they expected to be back in action in a temporary rink in 2005.

Rise and fall of Phoenix

The brave attempt by local businessman, **Neil Morris**, to revive professional ice hockey in Manchester's MEN Arena, ended on 8 July 2004, barely a year after he had formed the team, Manchester Phoenix.

GIANTS' FLEXIBLE FRIEND

"There was a time when it was 50-50 if there would even be a team.

"I gave my confidence to the owners, even down to using my own credit card to book flights for guys to come over here, though I knew what happened the year before when one guy bought equipment on his credit card and ended up losing £4,000 because he never got it back.

"I used my credit card most of the year because the club couldn't get a credit card and a lot of people won't take cheques from the club any more.

"I got my money back but if I hadn't used my card then I don't know how things would have got paid."

Rob Stewart, *Belfast Giants' coach, explaining how he kept the club alive in the summer of 2003 after it came close to financial collapse.*

The decision to put the club 'into mothballs' for one season was taken the day after a meeting of local fans came out against the idea of the team carrying on and playing their 'home' games at Deeside or iceSheffield.

Phoenix played 27 Elite League games and one playoff contest at the vast 17,250-seat MEN Arena but attracted only 2,068 fans a game. Crowds dipped as low as a thousand on more than one occasion. They were the second team to play at the MEN after the Storm collapsed with heavy debts early in the 2002-03 season.

As early as October, Mr Morris admitted he had taken out a loan to keep the Phoenix going. He said the rent of the MEN amounted to almost half the club's total budget. At other Elite clubs, rent was only 15 per cent of their costs.

It was all a far cry from the day in February 1997 when, with the house liberally papered by Ogden Entertainments (the arena operators at the time), the Storm played to a European record crowd of 17,245. Under general manager **Dave Biggar** (now in the USA with the Madison Square Garden Corporation), Ogdens organised a superb evening that was unequalled anywhere in the UK, and probably in Europe.

This was impossible to repeat on the Phoenix's limited budget.

Mr Morris, who agreed to remain on the board of the Elite League, was unbowed by his difficult 12 months. He declared that the Phoenix would have a new home in the Greater Manchester area in time for season 2005-06. (For more on this, see *New Rinks News*.)

The loss of the Manchester side only two months before the new season opened, left the Elite League with only seven teams. Coach Paul Heavey, who had joined the club in February in time to push them into the final playoff spot, moved to Scottish League club, Paisley Pirates.

Black season for Racers

Another page in the colourful history of London ice hockey was turned with the formation of London Racers in the summer of 2003.

Opinion was divided over **Roger Black**'s idea of putting a fully professional team into the unheated Alexandra Palace rink which had seating for around 750. Mr Black thought it was a brave move, everyone else thought he was barmy, especially after he had so many disagreements with management that he left himself only a few weeks to put a team together.

But somehow, against all the odds, Roger's Racers not only hit the ice on time (if not entirely legally - see later) but also survived the entire season. Not that they exactly lived happily ever after as they got through two rinks, three coaches, three general managers, 32 players, a long dispute with the IIHF and only four wins.

The team was created because the new Elite League were keen for recognition in the nation's capital city, something which London Knights had

---

RACERS BIGGER THAN KNIGHTS - OWNER

"The Knights played at the Docklands Arena which lacked atmosphere because it was never full. But we hope to attract between 2,000 and 4,000 to Alexandra Palace and they will be right up close to the action so the noise will be tremendous." **Roger Black**, *Racers' owner, in the London Metro newspaper on the eve of their opening game.*

---

brought to the Superleague. But long before the end of the season, other Elite clubs were saying privately that the league would have been better off without a team that lost 51 games.

In any case, it is doubtful that few except the most rabid ice hockey fans ever knew of their existence. Racers' average crowd was barely 500.

Mr Black, a cousin of Nottingham Panthers' owner, **Neil Black**, had been running an amateur side, Haringey Racers, in the English Premier League from Alexandra Palace in north London.

His new team's logo first appeared on the rink boards at the final Superleague playoff finals in his cousin's home arena in April 2003, but four months went by before he hammered out an agreement with the Ally Pally management.

THE WINNERS

Left: 16-year-old forward **SHAUN THOMPSON** of Slough, is presented with *The Ice Hockey Annual* Trophy as the Most Valuable Player of the English Junior Inter-Conference Championship at Hull by organiser **Geoff Hemmerman**; Sheffield Steelers' All-Star defenceman **KEVIN BOLIBRUCK** receives his championship medal from sponsor **Kevin Foster**.

Photos: Arthur Foster, Diane Davey

Not only did the club have barely four weeks to prepare for the new season, but their first choice as coach resigned without, as far as we know, ever setting foot inside the rink.

This was Canadian politician, **Gary Carr**, who memorably - and only partly inaccurately - described his new place of work as 'an historic Victorian recreation centre near Piccadilly Circus'. No official reason was given for his decision but we doubt that he's kicking himself.

A Swede, **Peter Ekroth**, took his place but struggled with a team he hadn't picked.

If the coaching was shot to pieces, their admin was shattered, too, as Racers took to the ice for their opening two games against Sheffield (home) and Manchester (away) with no fewer than 11 ineligible players. [For more on this, see *The Great Ice War.*]

Behind the scenes, relations between rink and club were fraught. Several thousands pounds' worth of work was urgently needed to bring the rink up to an acceptable standard for pro hockey. The small community rink, housed in part of the 125-year-old building, had not been designed with this in mind.

By October, these differences had reached breaking point and Racers took their equipment up the road to the Lee Valley Ice Centre in Hackney. The team had played just nine games at Ally Pally and Black admitted that the crowds had dwindled from 900 on opening night to as few as 50.

Canadian politician **Gary Carr**, the coach-who-never-was of the London Racers, was elected Liberal MP for the Ontario riding of Halton in 2004. Carr was a junior player with Toronto Marlboros when they won the Memorial Cup in 1975.

The fans' biggest complaint, apart from the cold and the restricted viewing, was holding games on a Friday night which forced them to battle through the London traffic chaos.

Though the club claimed the facilities were 'improved' at Lee Valley, where the capacity is listed as 1,000, there are no seats with a clear view of the ice. Despite this, the crowds seemed little affected by the change of venue, staying - officially, anyway - around the 500-mark.

With an horrific losing record of 51 defeats in 56 games, Racers attracted only a cult following, many of them probably bewhiskered fans of the much-missed (amateur) Lee Valley Lions of the Eighties. Their first win didn't come until their 41st game, on 30 January when they whitewashed Cardiff Devils 3-0 at home.

Unfortunately, when the club left Ally Pally it destroyed the Haringey Racers who had been acting as the London's team's farm side. Both teams were controlled by Roger Black and the unhappy rink management insisted that they came as 'one package'.

Goalie scores

Coventry Blaze netminder **Jody Lehman** joined a select band of ice hockey keepers when he scored a goal on 20 December 2003. Reporter **Antony Hopker** filed this story for the local paper, the *Coventry Evening Telegraph*:

'[Lehman] fired the fourth goal in Coventry's 4-2 Elite League win over Basingstoke Bison. Bison had pulled their netminder, **Curtis Cruickshank**, for the extra skater as they tried to force a draw. Lehman collected the puck as Basingstoke dumped it towards the Coventry net. Firing a shot over the heads of all the players, it bounced and continued into the Bison net.

LIFE AMONG THE ELITE

Cardiff Devils sensibly took to the air for their first Elite League game in Belfast. But to save the hefty excess baggage bill, their hockey kit went by road along with equipment man, **Tony Day**, and rink manager **Chris Hartrey**.

"I had visions of a comfortable flight, maybe a game of golf in the afternoon and then a beer or two after the game," Day told *Powerplay*.

Instead, they spent almost two days travelling, driving through Wales, England and Scotland, catching the ferry to Ireland - then back the same way.

■ Coventry Blaze and Basingstoke Bison also flew to Northern Ireland, each chartering a small plane for the journey.

'Lehman, 28, from North Battleford, Saskatchewan, said he had wanted to become one of the few goalies to score in a game since he was 14. "I've been trying that for a long, long time and it feels so good to achieve it," he said.

'"I got the puck when the forward hit it into the zone. I shot and I thought it was going to cut more and miss the net and maybe hit the post, but it held its line."

'The former netminder with the ECHL's South Carolina Stingrays added with a grin: "I've finally got the monkey off my back. Maybe I can relax a bit now and I won't be so tense when I go for number two."'

The paper later reported that Blaze fan **Timothy Robins** of Birmingham scooped £5,000 after he laid £100 at 50-1 against Lehman scoring in 2003-04.

Bookies William Hill said Mr Robins had made the same bet last season but was unsuccessful. Their spokesman, **Graham Sharpe**, said: "We

WITH THE GREATEST OF EASE

Coventry Blaze netminder **JODY LEHMAN** leaves the ice to attend to urgent business; team-mate **Russ Cowley** looks on.

Photo: Dave Page

hadn't been too worried about having to pay out – but from now on we'll be putting this type of bet on ice."

▪ Goals scored by netminders are naturally a rarity but Lehman's feat of scoring into an empty net is not unprecedented.

More unusual is for a goalie to score into an attended net, though in the only recorded case in the UK the puck received some help in its direction. Peterborough's **Tony Melia** was credited with a goal against Bracknell Bees' keeper **Dave Langford** in a British League game at Peterborough on 14 January 1996.

Melia's clearance struck Bees' defender **Chris Brant** and deflected into the net. Melia, a British-Canadian, received the credit as the last attacking player to touch the puck.

Nevertheless, the Hockey Hall of Fame in Toronto liked the feat so much that they arranged for Melia's jersey to be hung in the Hall. Canadian experts could trace only three previous occasions when this had happened.

▪ *A goal and a shutout* Cape Fear FireAntz goalie **Kevin Fines** scored a goal and kept a clean sheet in a game in the USA's South East League last season.

The 23-year-old rookie from Sarnia, Ontario shot the puck into the open net with 20 seconds left to give FireAntz (coached by former Slough Jet **Scott Rex**) a 3-0 shutout victory over Winston-Salem. He had 24 saves for his goose egg.

Scott Young

Defenceman **Scott Young**, the captain and driving force behind the Dundee Stars, disgraced himself and the sport after striking two officials in a British National League game.

The league banned the former GB international for two years for punching referee **Paul Staniforth** and linesman **Marco Coenen** in a game at Hull on 9 November 2003.

Young, 38, who was Hull's captain in 2002-03, lost his temper after being handed a five-minute major and a game misconduct for slashing late in the third period. Explaining the ban, **Gary Stefan**, the BNL's general manager, said: "There is no place in the sport for this sort of action."

According to the report in the *Hull Daily Mail*, Young appeared to throw a volley of punches at Staniforth, moments after pushing Coenen to the ice. The incident occurred as Young was being ejected for hitting Stingrays' Ukrainian star **Slava Timchenko** with his stick.

Obviously incensed by the player's action, Coenen - in breach of the officials' normal code of slience - spoke out. "I can't believe it happened," he told the paper. "I've worked over a thousand games in more than 10 years as an official and I've never seen anything like this before. As soon as I told Young in the penalty box he had to leave the ice he completely lost it.

"Before I even realised what was going on he punched me on my chin, trying to get by me and when I got up from the ice he had punched the referee as well."

Unusually for a banned player, Young also went public, admitting that he punched Staniforth. In an interview with the Scottish *Sun* headlined 'It was about time somebody thumped a ref', Young described his reaction to the ban in terms that should ensure he never returns to play in this country.

"I don't know if I'm sorry for what I did...He was trying to get Hull to win...The refereeing is a disgrace and has been every year since I came over...".

Young, a colourful character who was a fan favourite wherever he played, first came to Britain in 1993 with Teesside Bombers. Their top scorer, he also accumulated 207 penalty minutes in 36 British League games.

500% ROADSHOW ENDS WITH ARREST

The man behind a multi-million pound investment scheme that offered returns of 500% or more has been arrested after a seven-month investigation by the Serious Fraud Office and Kent police.

Kevin Foster, a 46-year-old former insurance salesman from Doddington, Kent, was arrested last Tuesday. A spokeswoman for the Serious Fraud Office said: 'He has been arrested on suspicion of conspiracy to defraud, and theft.' It is understood that Foster went voluntarily to Sittingbourne police station, accompanied by his solicitor.

Foster's *KF Concept* organisation, which operates gambling syndicates and puts money into network marketing businesses, attracted thousands of investors after holding roadshows around the country.

It gained publicity by supporting local charities and sponsoring sports teams including the **Cardiff Devils** ice hockey squad and Llanelli football club. But in February, the Financial Services Authority raided Foster's £2 million luxury farmhouse, where he keeps a collection of llamas, peacocks and koi carp.

FSA lawyers won High Court orders banning Foster, his wife Elaine, and another KF Concept boss, **Kevin McNab** of Llanelli, from operating any unauthorised investment schemes.

Their assets and bank accounts were frozen. After studying evidence seized in the raid, FSA officials called in the Serious Fraud Office. Foster will be fighting the FSA in a civil court case set down for next month.

Tony Hetherington, Mail on Sunday
22 August 2004
Editor's note - KF Concept also sponsored the Elite League's Playoff finals in Nottingham. We understand all sponsorship monies were paid in advance - in cash!

In case we hadn't got the message, he took time out to slag off the whole sport in the Scottish *Sun*. "That ban is nothing," he said. "It just means I can't play in Britain any more. That doesn't matter because hockey is going nowhere in this country."

After such a furore, you'd think that Stars would be glad to see the back of the man. Not according to club director, **Charlie Ward**. "It is extremely sad for both the club and the fans that such a charismatic and talented player should have left the club on such a sorry note", he said in a press statement. "We would like to thank Scott, who enjoyed playing his hockey in Dundee, for his contribution to our success over the past two seasons and wish him the very best for the future."

Still, he did add an apology to Mr Staniforth and thank the league for 'their full and thorough investigation'.

Young was capped 16 times for GB between 1999 and 2002 and enjoyed Grand Slam wins with both Superleague's Ayr Scottish Eagles and the Stars. He was rated as one of the best defencemen in the country.

Hull's coach **Rick Strachan**, a former GB team-mate, said the incident was a sad way for the defender to end his time in this country. "Scott's had a great career here, but I think he's going out the wrong way. He will be remembered for all the wrong reasons."

Though the ban made Young ineligible to play in any league under the International Ice Hockey Federation's jurisdiction (the affair was also reported in the Canadian media), that didn't prevent him signing for a North American team. The professional leagues across the Atlantic are not members of the world governing body.

On 20 December, the Cape Fear FireAntz of the South East (USA) Hockey League announced that they had signed Young. The FireAntz are owned by one-time Medway Bears' star, **Kevin MacNaught** and coached by **Scott Rex**, who played and coached in Britain for several years, most notably with London Knights and Slough Jets.

Blaze, Devils in record brawl

The final Elite League game of the season at the Coventry Skydome between the Blaze and the Cardiff Devils erupted in chaos when the two benches collided in a massive brawl.

Referee **Andy Carson** was at the centre of the row during the game in which he assessed a total of 217 penalty minutes - a league record - and ejected seven players. After several fights broke out with 20 seconds left in regulation, the teams were ordered to the dressing room for a 15-minute cooling-off period.

The 14 March game had been unremarkable going into the final period, with Cardiff leading 2-1. **Mike Ware** had put the Devils in front, **Ashley Tait** equalised and **Ivan Matulik** restored the lead.

At 47.52, Matulik reacted furiously when Carson declined to call a penalty after the Slovakian was caught by Tait's stick. Tait apologised immediately, but despite Matulik's bloodied face Carson ejected him for 'abuse of official' while Ware, who remonstrated with Tait, was given a match penalty.

When the game resumed, **Michael Tasker** equalised at 52.47, **Graham Schlender** gave Blaze the lead at 58.05 only for **Dennis Maxwell** to tie it up again, 3-3, at 58.49.

Then mayhem broke out as Maxwell challenged the Blaze bench, sparking a huge brawl. The Devils' hard man had two fights, one with Schlender, the second at 59.41 with **Gareth Owen**. Maxwell, **Ed Patterson** and **Jeff Brown** for the Devils, and Schlender, **Tom Watkins** and **Frank Evans** for Coventry were all ejected.

When the game restarted a second time, Blaze spent nearly all of overtime on the powerplay. There were just three seconds left in the five-minute extra session when **Hilton Ruggles** scored the winner.

After reviewing the videotape, the league's disciplinary committee suspended Brown for two games, Maxwell for one game and Coventry's coach **Paul Thompson** for one game. This trio were out of the line-ups when the teams met again only four days later in Cardiff for the league playoffs.

Ware's match penalty was reduced to a game misconduct.

Devils' coach, **Dave Whistle**, struck a late blow by publicly blaming the ref. "I truly believe the referee has something against Ivan [Matulik] on a personal basis," he fumed to the *South Wales Echo*. "If the ref had called that initial high stick I truly believe none of this would have happened."

No fights please, we're Elite

The Elite League became the first league in the UK, to our knowledge, to apply strict IIHF rules for fighting and roughing in season 2003-04.

In their magazine *Slapshot*, the league made it clear that any player who dropped his gloves for a fight would be assessed a double minor and a 10-minute misconduct, though the latter would be at the ref's discretion.

A repeat bout between the same opponents 'would be likely' to lead to a major plus game misconduct. This penalty could also be applied to a first bout if the ref considered it appropriate.

Fighting - the IIHF rather quaintly calls it fisticuffs - calls for an automatic match penalty. But Manchester's coach, **Rick Brebant**, disagreed with the new rule and suggested the NHL's five-minute fighting major would be more appropriate. And if a player fights twice in a game, he argued, he should get thrown out.

Brebant wrote on the club's website: "It's simple. The players and coaches know exactly what is on the line in terms of punishment and the fans don't get outraged at the officials.

"The double minor and misconduct means a player misses 14 minutes of play - almost a quarter of the game - for one incident. We haven't got the depth of roster to accommodate that kind of punishment.

"Don't get me wrong. I'm not encouraging more fighting, but let's be honest. The fans enjoy a good dust-up now and again, it helps sell tickets. And the five-minute major keeps the game honest as generally only the heavyweights go at it. It makes for a cleaner, faster and more entertaining game."

Two-way contracts

The Elite League made a controversial move in their first season to try and bridge the gap between the professional game and the lower reaches of senior hockey for promising young native players.

The eight clubs were mindful of the over-reliance on imports which had contributed to the downfall of Superleague, and they made a lot of noise about icing at least 50 home-grown players.

To help them reach this target and to keep within their stricter wage cap, they said they had reached an agreement with the English IHA. This allowed the Elite to 'borrow' under-25-year-old British-trained players from the English Premier League to help them develop, while allowing the player to continue competing on the lower team.

This was known as a two-way contract. But things didn't quite turn out that way. For a start, some of the contracts involved dual nationals who have been around for some years.

DEVELOPING DOUGIE

The most notable was Peterborough Phantoms' veteran forward, **Doug McEwen**, a former GB international, who played five games with his old club, Cardiff Devils. It must have been a strange sensation for Dougie, skating round the Wales National Ice Rink and gazing up at his number 7 shirt which was retired some time ago.

Then there was **Nicky Chinn**, British certainly, Welsh even, but hardly an up-and-coming youngster any more. He was 31 last season. He played 13 games in the Elite for Nottingham (11) and Basingstoke (2) and 17 in the English Premier with Slough. But he spent most of the season in the BNL with Bracknell (40 games). More like a three-way contract, eh, Chinny?

A more sensible use of the scheme was made by English defenceman, **Leigh Jamieson**, who was voted the Elite League's best young player during his time with Belfast Giants. Leigh, 18, who made his World Championship debut in 2004, also played seven English Premier games with his home town team, Milton Keynes.

Incidentally, Leigh almost went to Canada to join a team in the Western Hockey League, one of the world's top junior leagues. His Giants' team-mate, **Paxton Schulte**, said in January: "He's the right age, good size, big for someone so young. It would be interesting to see how far he could go in the WHL. If he was drafted [by the NHL], that would be awesome. But he needs to go this year, otherwise he'll miss out."

We understand **Rob Stewart**, Leigh's coach at Belfast, was not impressed with the idea.

James Pease, 22, who failed to keep his place with Coventry Blaze, was released on a two-way contract to the Lightning. The 22-year-old defenceman played only seven Elite League games with the Blaze but they described him as "benefiting from the regular ice time and a vastly improved player". He remained as coach of Coventry's under-12s.

Blaze also let forward **Gareth Owen** go on a two-way contract with Solihull Kings as he had spent much of the season at Coventry as a spectator. His coach at Coventry, **Paul Thompson**, said: "He's not one of the young players who can benefit from being on the bench in games and he wants to get out there."

Defender **James Morgan**, who began the season with Nottingham Panthers of the Elite League, surprised fans by suddenly announcing in early December that he was retiring from the sport to work for his family business in Peterborough. The surprise turned to annoyance when he later joined the Peterborough Phantoms of the English Premier League.

Still only 21, our Jim has already earned a reputation for being a bit of a wanderer. He's previously played in Canada as well as for Peterborough, Milton Keynes and Guildford in the BNL and Bracknell in the Superleague.

PLANET ICE'S REVOLVING DOORS

Many of these moves caused ripples around the English Premier League. One EPL club owner called them "a farce" and wanted them outlawed. Maybe this was because the traffic seemed to flow mostly between clubs in the Planet Ice sphere of influence - Milton Keynes and Peterborough in the EPL and the Elite's Basingstoke.

These teams had the biggest turnover of players, icing 32 who competed for other sides during the season (mainly for each other), an average of more than ten per club.

■ **Tony Hand**, the player-coach of the BNL's Edinburgh Capitals, was one of those approached by the Elite League to sign a two-way contract, according to a report in the Scottish *Sun*. Britain's best home-grown skater was quick to turn down the offers from Coventry Blaze and Sheffield Steelers.

"My job right now is to try and help Edinburgh win and I would be concerned about getting injured [playing for another team]," he told the paper in December 2003. He went on to rubbish the whole scheme.

"I think it is wrong that teams are allowed to do it. You have a situation where you have two leagues and I'd like to see them combine. I don't think passing players over - left, right and centre - is the way forward."

■ *BNL and EPL clubs form alliance* Two BNL clubs agreed two-way contracts with EPL sides. Hull Stingrays agreed to release Brit **Karl Hopper** and their top scorer **Slava Koulikov** to Chelmsford Chieftains at the end of the league season as Stingrays had not qualified for the playoffs. Defenceman Hopper, who made his GB debut in 2003, spent season 2000-01 with Chieftains.

A joint press release in October 2003 from the BNL's Guildford Flames and the EPL's Slough Jets confirmed that the two clubs had formed an alliance 'to help promote the development of young British talent in Berkshire and Surrey'.

Slough also formed a 'mutually beneficial partnership with the Elite's London Racers in June 2004. In a statement, the clubs said they would 'work closely together in many areas, including player recruitment and retention, training and young player development, public relations, marketing and ticket sales'.

■ *Two-way contract for manager* Edinburgh Capital's general manager, **Scott Neil**, was appointed in October 2003 to the same post with Sheffield Steelers - at the same time!

Neil, a former GB international forward who has played for both clubs, worked Tuesdays, Wednesdays and Thursdays for Steelers and the rest of the week back with his home-town side.

In his manager's role at Capitals, he was the first to sign Slovakian and other east European players in any numbers, a move that was so successful that several other clubs followed suit last season.

Canadians help to sell clubs

The Elite League took a novel approach to marketing its teams in season 2003-04, employing six Canadians on work experience after graduating from university.

Five clubs - Basingstoke, Belfast (2), Cardiff, London and Manchester - took up the league's offer of help, though Bison were the only team who thought it appropriate to inform the ice hockey press (bit more work experience needed there then).

Bison told us (to be honest we stumbled across the information on their website) that their 'dynamic team' was made up of **Lydia Howton, Julia Freeman, Phil Roy** and **Chris Slater.**

Lydia, said the announcement, has an extensive background in promotions and game day operations which will prove to be an asset to the team. Julia previously worked in the event co-ordination and fund raising departments at the Ottawa Senators Hockey Club of the National Hockey League.

New forward Roy was the team captain and defenceman Slater (who left the team halfway through the season without any information being sent to the press) joined Bison from Superleague's London Knights.

The new marketing team, the notice went on, is responsible for tackling the advertising, promotions and sponsorship within the club. The team is challenged with getting 'bums in the seats' to the Bison Ice Hockey Club.

So much for the hype. One of the 'dynamic team' told the *Annual* at the end of November: "I've not made much progress at all. Most of the local businesses are not interested in ice hockey as previous club owners have messed them about. And, anyway, we don't have enough staff here to handle any sponsorship deals if I got them."

BRITISH NATIONAL LEAGUE
Lose sponsor and star player

The *Findus* British National League did not have far to look for their troubles. At the end of season 2003-04, the frozen food company allowed their £500,000, three-year sponsorship of the league to lapse.

A further blow came when Edinburgh Capitals' player-coach, **Tony Hand**, the jewel in the league's crown, moved to the Elite League to take a similar role with Belfast Giants.

We understand that *Findus* pulled out mainly because they are running down their operations in the UK. No replacement backer had been found as we went to press in August 2004.

This left the league with no choice but to make stringent cutbacks. Contracts with their general manager **Gary Stefan**, and their marketing company, String Online, run by **Lesley Wickham**, were not renewed. Secretary **Stan Wiltshire**, who had left at the start of the season, was not replaced.

Bob Bramah, a former chief referee with Ice Hockey UK and the BNL's director of officiating (among many other hockey roles over the years) took over the league's admin. as their technical director, and Edinburgh's **Keith Butland** became their new webmaster.

'England' v 'Scotland'

The prize for the most bizarre games played during the season in any of the senior leagues must go to the FBNL's 'All-Star' games.

These were billed as England versus Scotland and many of us old hands became misty-eyed at the thought of being able to watch real Englishmen play real Scotsmen just like they did up until the early Eighties.

After all, the league likes to promote itself as a loyal supporter of home-grown talent with 50 per cent of its rosters being born and bred here.

We soon dried our eyes. The league actually meant English clubs playing against teams from north of the border. And at the last minute the players were changed from the advertised line-ups with no reasons given. Among those pulling out were the two of the league's finest native talents - **Tony Hand** and **David Longstaff**.

Eventually, ten Englishmen played for 'England' - **Danny Meyers, Greg Owen** (Bracknell), **Paul Dixon, Neil Liddiard** (Guildford), **Mark Florence, Kevin Phillips** (Hull), **Scott Moody, Stuart Potts, Richie Thornton** and **Jonathan Weaver** (Newcastle) - and the same number of Scots turned out for their home country - **Paul Berrington, Paddy Ward, Gary Wishart** (Dundee), **Laurie Dunbar, Steven Lynch, Iain Robertson, Craig Wilson** (Edinburgh), **Kyle Horne** and **Adam Walker** (Fife).

But that was mostly in Kirkcaldy. The first game in Bracknell on 10 February was a farce with only Dunbar, Horne, Walker and Ward travelling south. Unbelievably, seven English players from Slough Jets - who are not even in the league - played for 'Scotland'.

The four Scots apparently spent 20 hours on the road to and from Bracknell, getting home at dawn, while the English took a plane to Edinburgh for the second game. Dundee's **Charlie Ward** was furious that the league allowed them and accused them of treating the Scots as "second-class citizens".

Gary Stefan defended the BNL. "If the clubs wish to pay for their players to fly and stay overnight, that is entirely up to them."

Stefan claimed he had tried to persuade the clubs to stage a full England-Scotland international and put the best face he could on the games' chaotic organisation.

"We were very encouraged with the level of play," he said. "It was disappointing, of course, that injury and illness kept many of the Scottish players away [from Bracknell]. But it did give some of Slough's young players, like **Matt Towalski**, one of GB's under-20 gold medalists, a chance to showcase their talents."

For the record, 'Scotland', coached by Fife's **Mark Morrison**, outplayed **Stan Marple**'s 'England', 6-3 in Bracknell and 5-2 seven days later in Kirkcaldy. Both coaches are Canadian, of course. With the games being played in mid-week as friendlies with little body contact, crowds were poor at around 800 a game.

WHAT'S IN A NAME?

The New Year announcement that Newcastle's arena would be dubbed the *Metro Radio* Arena brought out some wry comments from Vipers' fans, who are obviously unimpressed by the building, whatever its name.

- How about the 'Right the game is over, chuck everyone out the nearest fire exit Arena'.
- the '£1.60 for a couple of chips and dip Arena'.
- the Green Shed.
- the 'Where on Earth is the Arena'.
- the 'When will it be finished Arena'.
- the 'More boring than Hull Arena'.

Thanks, guys. We get the picture.

IMPORTS

New law encourages foreign players

As if sport doesn't have enough legislation to contend with, in August 2003 the government made changes to the UK immigration rules under the Working Holiday Makers Scheme (WHMS).

The changes enable people from Commonwealth countries, aged between 18 and 30, to come and work here as professionals for up to two years, without needing to apply for a work permit.

As we need hardly point out, Canada is a Commonwealth country.

As so often happens, the changes were not intended to affect sport. In this case, they were designed to help ease the jobs crisis in the catering and other industries. In practice, though, they affect several sports, especially ice hockey, cricket and rugby.

Prior to the changes to the WHMS, anyone entering the UK under the scheme was prohibited from taking any job in a professional sport, paid or unpaid, if they played in front of a paying audience.

The government was duly bombarded with complaints from various sporting bodies. Ice Hockey UK, the Elite League and the Ice Hockey Players Association (GB), the players' union, argued that the changes would have a detrimental effect on the development of our domestic talent: clubs could employ Canadians without any connection to this country and without needing to keep to the strict criteria laid down for work permit players (see *League Organisation* section elsewhere in the *Annual*.)

Less than a year after the changes were introduced, the Dept of Culture, Media and Sport bowed to the pressure and asked sporting bodies to make official written representations.

The Central Council for Physical Recreation (CCPR), the umbrella body for national sports organisations, responded in August 2004, urging 'a return of the exemption for sports and entertainment that previously existed in the scheme...'

Until the matter is resolved, clubs are free to bring over Canadians (aged 18-30) from lower leagues than the East Coast Hockey League, which is still the baseline league for imports needing work permits.

MATCH OFFICIALS

Moray Hanson

Jenny Wiede of the International Ice Hockey Federation kindly supplied the *Annual* with this report on one of world ice hockey's fastest rising referees, our own **Moray Hanson**.

In May 2004, Scot **Moray Hanson** became the first person to play and referee in a World Championship.

Exactly ten years after guarding Britain's goal at the Pool A championships in Bolzano, Italy, the Edinburgh chef was selected to officiate in four games at the championships in Prague, the capital of the Czech Republic.

Hanson, now 39, played with Murrayfield Racers and was consistently one of the top three goaltenders in the *Heineken* League. He played in the 1989 and 1991 World Championships before being voted GB's top player in his last appearance with the squad in 1994.

Two years later, he decided to go from being the man behind the mask to the man in the stripes. The change came after the British League decided to restructure in 1996, and he thought it was a natural time to put the pads to rest and give officiating a chance.

"It was never my plan to become an referee," he said. "But it seemed like a good way at the time to stay involved with the game."

He earned his stripes in the old Premier Division where he spent three years as a linesman after working youth games around Scotland and England.

Next, he decided to try out as a referee and he once again he moved quickly up the ranks. Most referees take several years before they are invited to officiate at the international level, but after only one season he was approached by Ice Hockey UK to be one of their international ➤

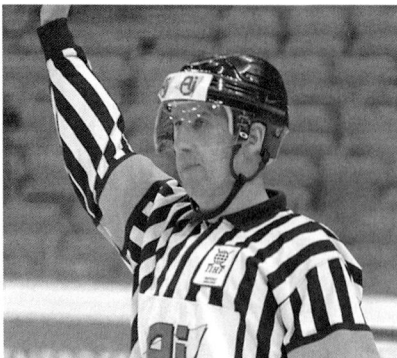

MORAY HANSON

representatives. "I was pretty stunned when I got the phone call," he said. "I knew that they had a ranking system and that only the top three or so got such a call."

Once referees are 'in the system,' they start in the lower division World Championship events and work their way up, depending on evaluations from the supervisors. In Hanson's case, that meant officiating the Division II World Championships in Madrid and Yugoslavia, and then the Division I Championships in Hungary last year.

This year he got another phone call that stunned him. "When they told me that I had been assigned to work the World Championships here in Czech, I was amazed," he said. "It was my goal as both a player and an official to be at the highest level possible, and here I am near the top."

A clue to his remarkable rise came in his reply to his local paper as to how he would handle the big stars of the international game. "I'll treat them the same way I do the juniors at Murrayfield," he said.

The feat of being invited to the 2004 tournament is rare not only because Hanson is a former goaltender, but also because he hails from a nation that has not played at the top World Championship level in ten years.

He says there are several misconceptions that people have about the officials on the ice. "We're just normal people who love the game," he explains. "We don't have favourites, we're here to do a job. We have bosses that watch us just like everyone else."

Still, he admits there is no such thing as a perfect game. "If you ask any referee, or even any coach, I think they would tell you that there are mistakes in every game. But obviously if you want to keep moving up, you have to minimise those mistakes."

If Hanson practices what he preaches, he hopes that the next stunning phone call will come in 2006, just a few months before the world goes to the Winter Olympics in Turin.

■ Two other British-based officials worked as linesmen in Prague. Canadian **Matt Folka** was assigned four contests and Dutchman **Marco Coenen** skated in six. In his fifth game on May Day, Coenen was unlucky to be injured by a flying stick with five minutes left. He required six stitches and had to attend hospital for dental treatment.

TELEVISION
Another good year for NHL fans

For NHL fans, this was a memorable year. Not only was it the first full season of four or five games a week via the *North American Sports Network (NASN)*, but there was also one a week on *Channel Five* for a sixth season.

For fans of British ice hockey, however, the year was completely unmemorable as only the highlights of the Elite League's playoff finals appeared on our national TV screens. And they were on pay-TV.

The action from the Elite League playoffs amounted to about half of the one-hour highlights programme on *Sky Sports 3*, shown a few days after the games in Nottingham.

It was good to see, literally, our old friends **Paul Ferguson** and **Richard Boprey** who appeared in front of the cameras to present the programme as well as behind the mikes for the commentary on the final between Steelers and Panthers. This was their first appearance together on *Sky*.

Produced by TSN Productions, the show also gave us a few minutes of each of the semi-finals, with voice-over from **Daniel Routledge**, and interviews with the coaches **Mike Blaisdell** and **Paul Adey**, plus a couple of players.

This was a good effort from all concerned and made us wonder why the league and the TV channel couldn't have done something similar on a weekly basis throughout the season. Maybe it had something to do with the league leaving it until halfway through the season before sorting out their differences with the governing body.

☑ Our spies tell us that *ITV Yorkshire* showed Steelers' goals and an interview with Blaisdell, and *BBC Yorkshire*'s *Look North* showed the on-ice celebrations at the NIC.

During September 2003, *ITV* screened a late night sports show, hosted by **John Fashanu**, called *Losing It*. This was a light-hearted look at how sportsmen 'lose it' in the heat of battle on the playing field.

Ice hockey was featured in the shows on 12 and 26 September with fights and other unsavoury moments from various Superleague games being shown. Cheap thrills, exploitation, gratuitous violence? Yup, you've got the picture.

At least the knowledgeable **Gary Moran** (Nottingham Panthers) and **Dave Simms** (Sheffield Steelers) fronted the programme and provided intelligent analyses of what drives hockey players to behave like this.

OH NO! NOT THEM AGAIN

"We have put this project together as the British National League is not pulling in the crowds [for Dundee Stars] and the Scottish National League [Dundee Tigers] is going nowhere." *Joe Guilcher, manager of Dundee Tigers, on his ambitious plans to enter the team in the Elite League in 2004-05. Dundee Evening Telegraph, 9 March 2004*

Ed's note: Joe is the brother-in-law of **Tom Stewart**.

'Dundee Tigers have named the two coaches who will lead them next year if they are successful in their Elite League application.

'The coaches' agents gave Tigers permission to release their names and they are **Dan Bouchard**, who has played for Boston Bruins, Calgary Flames and Quebec Nordiques in the NHL and coached Swiss side Fribourg Gotteron, and **Jean Pronovost**, who has played for Pittsburgh Penguins and Washington Capitals in the NHL'

Dundee Evening Telegraph, 10 March 2004

Our objection to this sort of prog. is that soccer and other sports get plenty of air-time to show their good sides so they can afford to brush off the occasional brickbats. But here poor old ice hockey was getting it in the neck again without much coverage of their games for balance.

The sport has only itself to blame. We understand that Black Diamond Productions, the video production company used by Superleague, sold the game videos to *Granada Sport* to help in the making of the programme.

What happened to the highlights of the March 2003 BNL finals which the league promised us would be shown on ITV1 'later in the year'? Er, which teams were in the final? Coventry Blaze and Cardiff Devils. And which league were they in for 2003-04? Right.

No, we mustn't jump to conclusions. In October 2003, the BNL finally gave their official answer. Actually, it was posted by one of the league's marketing people in an internet chatroom, as you do.

'The filming [of the finals] was carried out as part of an on-going documentary collation of ice hockey in general. The fact that the teams are [now] in a different league makes no odds. It was to promote the sport as a whole. It was never recorded as a promo.

'Unfortunately, all the c**p that has [gone on] and is still going on has tainted the appeal of the sport to those controlling what goes on our screens, but the project is still very much alive, despite speculation and guesswork.'

We're relieved to report that this gentleman is no longer involved with the league.

ENGLISH NATIONAL LEAGUE
Eat 'em raw! Redskins are back

Ice hockey returned to the Streatham High Road rink on 21 September 2003, almost 30 years to the day since the previous team made its debut on 29 September 1973.

The game - a 5-2 loss to Oxford City Stars - was the first time senior hockey had been played in the rink since season 1993-94. It attracted a crowd of 400, modest by the standards of Streatham's glory days, but the Redskins now play in the English National League South, the lowest level of the sport.

The team was coached by **Adam Goldstone** who provided a link with the first Redskins who were managed by his father **Alec Goldstone**.

Manager **Steve James** played for the club in that era, and the team was captained by **Joe Johnston**, who told his local paper before Redskins' first game:

"I was just a junior when the last team was active. It was such a shame when the club closed. Many of our fans went to support London Knights in Docklands to keep their interest in the sport. But with them gone now, it gives us a chance to re-establish ourselves and the sport in London. I am very proud to be captain."

Ice hockey was first played in the venerable south London building as long ago as 1931, making Streatham the country's oldest ice hockey club still in existence. But Streatham teams have had a chequered career in those 73 years, reflecting the ups and downs of the sport nationally.

The first side won four league championships and three Autumn Cups between 1931 and 1960. Two of the league titles and two of the cups came in the professional, all-Canadian English National League which was the strongest in the country until the advent of Superleague.

The first Redskins - the nickname was adopted in 1976 - were British Championship finalists in 1982 and reached the British Championship semis at Wembley in 1985 during the *Heineken* League era.

The rink was sold to a property developer in 1990 and Redskins did not play the following season while the building was refurbished. When they returned the next year, they found almost all the seats had been removed: the team lasted only two more seasons.

Plans are currently in hand to demolish the historic rink, which is run by Starburst, the operators of the Gillingham Ice Bowl. A new rink is included in a complete rebuilding of that part of the High Road by developers *Tesco.* The scheme allows for the existing rink to remain open until the new one, to be erected on the site of the old Streatham bus garage, is ready.

Ayr Centrum - can it survive?

The fans of Superleague's (Ayr) Scottish Eagles, which collapsed with heavy debts in November 2002, are now fighting to save the club's home rink, the Centrum at Prestwick Toll.

The star-crossed 2,745-seat arena, which only opened in 1996, closed in April 2003 and is now the subject of heated debates in Ayr.

The latest scheme - to turn Centrum into a curling centre of excellence - was quashed in August 2004 when it failed to receive backing from the Lottery.

One of the most modern arenas in Scotland, fondly remembered by all fans who went there, Centrum is still owned by construction group, Barr Holdings. Barr have undergone major changes since running up losses of £8.5 million in their last financial year, mostly due to their ill-advised diversification into leisure.

The group's managing director, **Bill Barr**, who owned the Eagles and Ayr Utd football club, retired in May 2003. He was criticised in the group's annual report for "straining the balance sheet" by running up losses on both clubs.

The new owners concluded in January 2004 that there was no future for skating in the area. "Companies such as ours should not run centres like this," said director **Tony Rush**.

Frustratingly for the Eagles' fans, however, Barr Holdings seem in no rush to rid themselves of the arena. BH have negotiated a dispensation from SportScotland giving them until January 2005 to repay the £500,000 they received in 1996 to complete the rink, and removing the requirement for them to operate it. But the company have given little encouragement to potential new owners who have shown interest in retaining the ice pad.

An 'England-based ice rink operating company' were reportedly interested in acquiring Centrum but were unable to persuade Barr to give them an asking price.

Friends of Eagles Hockey are keeping the pressure on Barr, SportScotland and South Ayrshire Council to find a solution which includes an ice based future for the arena.

For the latest news of the fans' fight, go to www.friendsofeagleshockey.co.uk.
■ There are still no plans to reinstate ice hockey in Scotland's other state-of-the-art ice arena at Braehead on the outskirts of Glasgow. Eagles played five games there at the start of the 2002-03 season.

Ayr's 75th birthday book

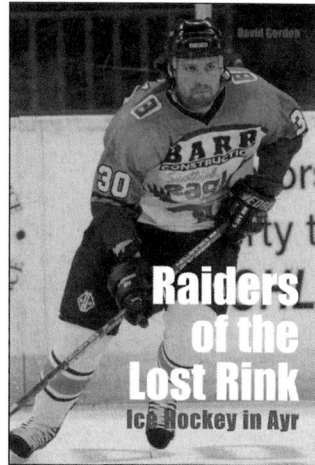

Raiders of the Lost Rink
Ice Hockey in Ayr

Followers of Ayr ice hockey can pass the time while the battle rages over Centrum by reading a new book on the history of the sport in their seaside town.

Local man **David Gordon**, a member of the British Ice Hockey Writers Association, has written *Raiders of the Lost Rink*, which is due to be published in late 2004 by Tempus Publishing, price £17.99.

It promises to be an absorbing and detailed account, containing many rare photographs and extensive interviews with the likes of **Stan Christie, Paul Bedard, Alastair Reid** and **Dino Bauba** among others, chronicling the triumphs and tribulations of ice hockey in Ayr.

Starting in 1929 when the sport was an exclusive pastime of the wealthy, Ayr's ice hockey history parallels the history of the game throughout the UK in the past three-quarters of a century and is an essential read for anyone with an interest in the sport.

Ice hockey historian David, who lives in Alloway and is a personnel manager with East Ayrshire Council, has been involved with the sport as supporter, player and writer since seeing his first match at Beresford Terrace as a small boy back in 1969.

His family involvement goes back further. His dad, **Tom Gordon**, was the former Ayr Raiders' correspondent of *Ice Hockey World* in the early 1950s. His uncle, **Ian Gordon**, covered the Ayr Balmorals and Ayr Rangers of the early 1960s, when sports editor of the *Ayrshire Post*.

David completed the research and writing of his book almost a year ago: "It was unintentional that the publishers have held off production until 2004," he said, "but it is a pleasant coincidence that it will be coming out on the 75th anniversary of an Ayr team's first ever match, and the 65th anniversary of the opening of their first purpose-built rink at Beresford Terrace."

Further details are available from www.tempus-publishing.com (tel 01453-883300). The book is also available from www.amazon.co.uk.

Powerplay

Steve Clarke took over as editor of the weekly magazine for the first issue of 2004. Former editor **Simon Potter** stayed on as statistician.

Steve, the owner of the magazine's printers, Keyprint of Peterborough, bought the 12-year-old weekly from Simon in January 2002.

Cumming and Ashcroft star in 84th Varsity Match

Cambridge University gained revenge for their overtime defeat in 2003 with a 5-1 trouncing of their arch rivals, Oxford University, in the 84th Varsity Match at Oxford on 7 March 2004.

As is traditional in the longest running battle in European hockey - dating back to 1900 - the game was played with an edge throughout, entertaining a crowd of almost a thousand.

Matt Cumming (Sidney Sussex) and captain **Andrew Ashcroft** (Wolfson) each scored twice for the Light Blues and it was the last minute of time before **Jamie Smith** (St Peter's) broke American **Brian Barrett**'s (Jesus) shutout bid.

Cumming, a budding lawyer from Toronto, won the man of the match award. The most experienced player on the ice, he played at Yale University before turning pro in Germany for a few years.

Ashcroft, who is studying engineering, took the Cawthra Cup as Cambridge's player of the game while Oxford's best player was **Sam Salisbury** (Wolfson) who was awarded the prestigious new Pearson Cup. This was the last Varsity Match for Ashcroft, a native of Sudbury, Ontario, who has scored in each of Cambridge's three victories in the last four years, for a total of eight goals.

Oxford, the perennial winners with 55 since the turn of the century, have won the Patton Cup only twice in the last seven outings. Cambridge's win took their all-time tally to 27. Two matches have been drawn.

The architect of the Light Blues' victory - as he has been of all their recent successes - is **Prof Bill Harris**. **Michael (Moose) Talbot** guided their opponents and the *Annual* is grateful to him for overcoming his dark despair to provide us with the harrowing details of his team's defeat.

■ The Pearson Cup was donated to Oxford University by the Canadian Ambassador, **Geoff Pearson**, in memory of his father, the **Rt. Hon Lester B Pearson**, a former Dark Blue who became Prime Minister of Canada. Lester Pearson was a big hockey fan whose name is also on the NHL's Players' Player trophy.

■ A player is eligible for the Varsity Match provided he is registered for a degree at one of the universities. Neither university has athletic scholarships.

■ In the Women's Varsity Match, Oxford beat Cambridge 11-4 - as they have in all eight matches we have recorded.

Overseas visitors

AIK STOCKHOLM, Sweden One of the best club sides in Europe, who share Stockholm's Globe Arena with Djurgarden, played three games in three days against two Elite League teams in September 2003.

5 Sept **Cardiff Devils-AIK 3-2.**

Devils' goal scorers: Ivan Matulik 2, Merv Priest.

English netminder **Joe Watkins** guested for Devils but faced only 18 shots as AIK took it easy in this pre-season friendly.

Devils poured 52 shots on AIK's net and their coach **Glen Mulvenna** said: "We played with guts and determination. We've been on the ice three times but AIK have been training for two months."

6 Sept **Nottingham Panthers-AIK 1-4**

7 Sept **Coventry Blaze-AIK 1-3**

Blaze goal scorer: Ashley Tait.

SC BIETIGHEIM-BISSINGEN, Germany

6 Sept **Sheffield Steelers-Bietigheim 3-6**

Steelers' goal scorers: Steve Ellis, Dion Darling, A N Other.

The Steelers from the German Bundesliga (one below the DEL) beat their English counterparts comfortably, but Sheffield's coach **Mike Blaisdell** said: "If we played them again in a month, the score would be a whole lot different. We had to play five imports down and we iced nine British lads. We've been on the ice four times and they've been together for a month so I was really pleased. "

'Miracle' on film

The second major movie about the USA's gold medal triumph in the 1980 Olympics, entitled 'Miracle', was released in the New Year, starring **Kurt Russell** as the USA's coach, **Herb Brooks**.

Brooks worked closely with Russell on the making of the film but, sadly, he was unable to see the finished product as he was killed in a driving accident before the film came out. (See our *North American Leagues* section for more on Brooks).

Former Cardiff Devil enforcer, **Mike McWilliam**, appeared in the movie as a Russian hockey player.

The 1980s film commemorating the event - *Miracle on Ice* - featured **Keenan Wynn** as Brooks.

• The word 'miracle' was used to describe the USA win because the team comprised mostly players from USA colleges, rather than the NHL, against the Soviet Union's mighty Red Machine.

The Americans' gold medal was the most unexpected since GB won the 1936 Olympics but, sadly, we've yet to hear of anyone wanting to make a film of that.

ATTENDANCES

OVERALL PICTURE	2003-04 TOTAL	ATTENDANCE GAMES	AVERAGE	2002-03 AVERAGE	*AVE. DIFF. ON 2002-03
ELITE LEAGUE					
League	513,205	224	2,291	3,627	down 37%
Challenge Cup	24,613	6	4,102	3,702	diff. teams
Playoffs	34,640	12	2,887	3,373	down 14%
Playoff Finals	19,886	3	6,629	6,285	up 5%
TOTALS	**592,344**	**245**	**2,418**	**3,565**	**down 32%**
FINDUS **BRITISH NATIONAL LEAGUE**					
League	135,764	126	1,077	1,316	down 18%
Playoffs	40,006	30	1,334	1,483	down 10%
Findus Cup	62,332	42	1,484	1,467	no diff.
TOTALS	**238,102**	**198**	**1,203**	**1,362**	**down 12%**
ENGLISH NATIONAL LEAGUE					
Premier Division	79,894	144	555	496	up 12%
Playoffs	20,303	30	677	615	up 10%
TOTALS	**100,197**	**174**	**576**	**509**	**up 13%**
GRAND TOTALS	**930,643**	**617**	**1,508**	**1,606**	**down 6%**

* Elite League's crowds are compared with Superleague's.

THE TOP LEAGUE CROWD-PULLERS			2003-04 LEAGUE	ATTENDANCE Total	Average+	2002-03 Average	Notes/ Changes
1	(2)	Sheffield Steelers	Elite	109,494	3,911	4,766	down 18%
2	(3)	Nottingham Panthers	Elite	108,157	3,863	4,654	down 17%
3	(1)	Belfast Giants	Elite	93,803	3,350	5,277	down 37%
4	(5)	Coventry Blaze	Elite	60,625	2,165	2,043	up 6%
5	(-)	Manchester Phoenix	Elite	57,895	2,068	#	#
6	(9)	Cardiff Devils	Elite	45,200	1,614	1,481	up 9%
7	(8)	Guildford Flames	BNL	26,587	1,477	1,624	down 9%
8	(7)	Fife Flyers	BNL	26,108	1,446	1,644	down 12%
9	(6)	Newcastle Vipers	BNL	24.947	1,386	1,882	down 26%
10	(11)	Bracknell Bees	BNL	19,498	1,130	1,381	down 18%
11	(10)	Dundee Stars	BNL	19,406	1,066	1,468	down 27%
12	(13)	Milton Keynes Kings	EPL	19,309	1,073	1,092	no diff.

List includes teams that averaged at least 1,000 fans to league games (excluding playoffs).
Last season's position in brackets.
+ Home games - Elite League teams each played 28; British National League (BNL) teams and English Premier League (EPL) side, Milton Keynes, each played 18.
 # The last recorded average crowd over a full season in Manchester was 4,085 for Storm in 2001-02. Figures are based on the leagues' own media information releases where available.

NOTES

⊠ The Elite League's average of 2,418 fans per game is the same as in the old Premier Division of the British League in 1995-96 when the average was 2,454.
⊠ the Grand Total of 930,643 is the lowest attendance recorded by *The Ice Hockey Annual* since 1990-91. The total average crowd of 1,508 is the lowest since 1991-92 when it was 1,466.

NEW RINKS NEWS

Most of the plans we've read about in 2004 are for large, multi-purpose arenas with ice. After the rash of such buildings in the north and Midlands (Manchester, Newcastle, Nottingham and Sheffield), the latest plans are in the south and west - Brighton, Bristol, Cardiff, Croydon and Southampton.

The difficulty with such ambitious schemes is persuading private investors to finance them. All the existing arenas - apart from Newcastle - were financed through the public purse.

In any case, these venues are a mixed blessing for ice hockey these days. In truth, they were needed several years ago when the professional Superleague was trying to gain a foothold in the imagination of the sporting public.

The lesson of Superleague is that ice hockey is most at home in 3,000-seaters, something like Coventry. Of the rinks on the drawing boards, only Manchester's Sportscity is close to this size.

Some details of the current plans -

We're starting with **BRIGHTON** because it's first alphabetically and not just because your editor is closely involved in the Brighton International Arena Consortium which was selected in October 2003 to build a £50 million twin-rink and leisure complex next to Brighton Marina.

As mentioned in last year's *Annual*, the design is based on that for Nottingham's National Ice Centre. The consortium was negotiating with several investors and hoped to submit a planning application before the end of 2004. The arena would be home for a revived Brighton Tigers who last played in the town in season 1964-65.

We also listed a twin-pad, 7,000-seater at **BRISTOL** in our last edition and this, too, has made progress. The local authority was due to decide on 1 September 2004 between two bidders: the Brighton International Arena Consortium and the SMG Orion Consortium, SMG being the operators of the Belfast, Manchester and Newcastle arenas.

A start on building the roads and the rest of the infrastructure for the £700 million **CARDIFF BAY** Sports Village was scheduled for the end of 2004. Work began on preparing the site in December 2003 and the long awaited scheme is expected to be completed in seven/ten years. No date has yet been set for building the sports and leisure facilities which will include a 10,000-seat arena to house Cardiff Devils and a 'full size leisure ice pad'.

CROYDON

The mixed use development next to East Croydon station, for which planning permission was granted in December 2003, includes a 12,500-seat multi-purpose arena.

SOUTHAMPTON

Plans for a 7,000-seat multi-purpose arena on the West Quay site have stalled since the local authority granted permission in October 2002 to the Bravo Consortium to submit a planning application. It seems that the consortium, who include Clear Channel, one of the world's leading entertainment providers, have had trouble raising the necessary finance.

GREATER MANCHESTER

Altrincham

Sterling St James were selected by Trafford Council in June 2004 to submit a planning application for an ice rink - to replace the old one which closed in April 2003 - plus an hotel, shops and housing in the town centre. But then the newly elected Tory administration decided to re-open the tendering process as it did not agree that Sterling St James had the best scheme.

The Annual believes that Planet Ice is interested in running the new rink.

Sportscity/Eastlands

A £260 million gambling complex next to the City of Manchester stadium in Beswick could be the new home of Manchester Phoenix.

The bid to build the complex was won in July 2004 by a consortium including major casino operators, Kerzner International.

The financing of the scheme, which includes a 4,000-seat arena with ice, depends on the relaxation of the gambling laws which are currently being considered by the government.

If Manchester is granted a gambling license under the new law, it will give the green light to Phoenix. As the new rink is not expected to open until 2008, the club hope to receive permission to build a temporary 3,000-seat rink - constructed of laminated timber of Finnish design - in time for season 2005-06.

The club feels this would help to prove that ice sports can be successful in this size of building after the collapse of the Storm in the huge and expensive MEN Arena, and the closure of the small and old Altrincham rink.

Major Teams 2003~04

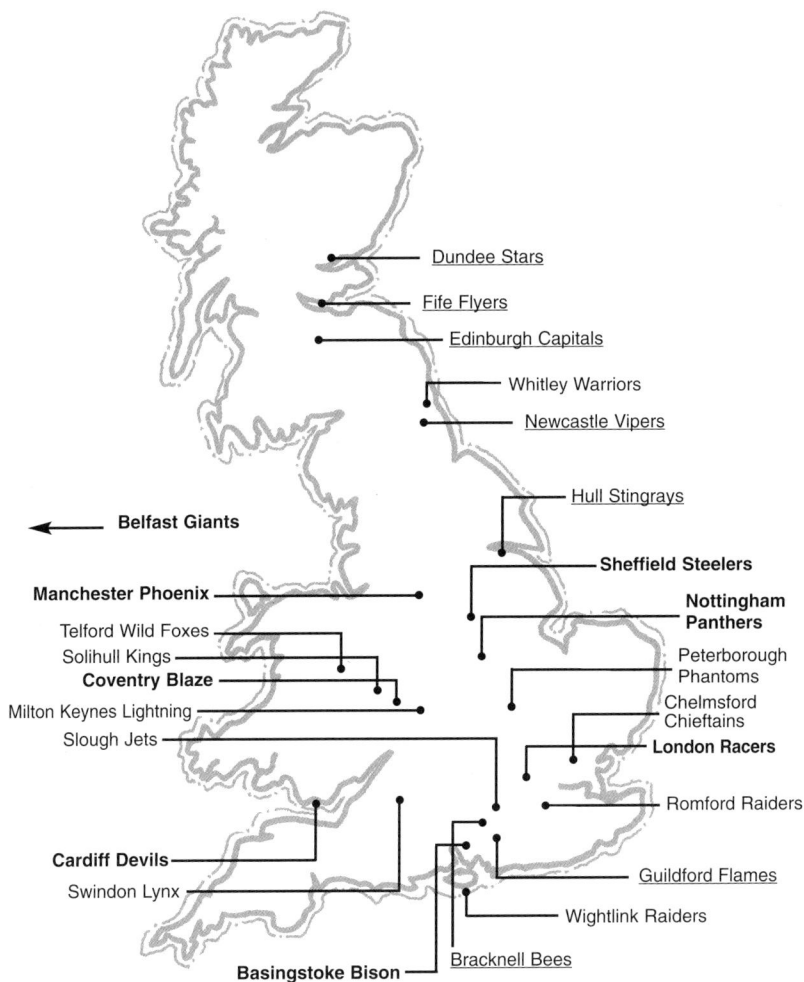

Dundee Stars

Fife Flyers

Edinburgh Capitals

Whitley Warriors

Newcastle Vipers

Hull Stingrays

Belfast Giants ←

Sheffield Steelers

Manchester Phoenix

Nottingham Panthers

Telford Wild Foxes

Solihull Kings

Coventry Blaze

Peterborough Phantoms

Milton Keynes Lightning

Chelmsford Chieftains

Slough Jets

London Racers

Romford Raiders

Cardiff Devils

Swindon Lynx

Guildford Flames

Wightlink Raiders

Basingstoke Bison

Bracknell Bees

Elite League   British National League   English/Scottish Leagues

BASINGSTOKE BISON

PLAYER	ALL COMPETITIONS					ELITE LEAGUE				
Scorers	GP	G	A	Pts	Pim	GP	G	A	Pts	Pim
Joe Ciccarello (I)	54	27	36	63	75	54	27	36	63	75
Steve Moria	56	33	28	61	22	56	33	28	61	22
Blake Sorensen (I)	56	16	23	39	80	56	16	23	39	80
Phil Roy (I)	49	14	17	31	44	49	14	17	31	44
Martin Filip (I)	54	16	14	30	34	54	16	14	30	34
Matt Reid (I)	26	10	15	25	30	26	10	15	25	30
Doug Schueller (I)	30	3	17	20	24	30	3	17	20	24
Kim Vahanen (I)	56	1	11	12	74	56	1	11	12	74
Darren Hurley 7	28	6	5	11	59	28	6	5	11	59
Markus Takala (I)	22	2	9	11	14	22	2	9	11	14
Dave Geris (I)	56	4	6	10	151	56	4	6	10	151
Richard Hargreaves	55	3	6	9	77	55	3	6	9	77
Christian Widauer (I)	56	3	6	9	75	56	3	6	9	75
Chris Slater (I)	18	2	7	9	75	18	2	7	9	75
Jesse Hammill 5	7	1	2	3	20	7	1	2	3	20
Michael Wales 2	12	1	2	3	42	12	1	2	3	42
Jaromir Kverka (I)	15	1	2	3	10	15	1	2	3	10
Norman Pinnington 4	13	0	3	3	24	13	0	3	3	24
Curtis Cruickshank (N) (I)	54	0	3	3	26	54	0	3	3	26
Nicky Chinn 1	2	1	1	2	6	2	1	1	2	6
Luc Chabot	2	0	2	2	0	2	0	2	2	0
Mark McCoy 3	11	0	2	2	2	11	0	2	2	2
James Hutchinson	44	0	2	2	18	44	0	2	2	18
Gary Clarke 2	1	1	0	1	0	1	1	0	1	0
Shaun Thompson	39	1	0	1	2	39	1	0	1	2
Nicky Watt	47	0	0	0	24	47	0	0	0	24
Bench Penalties					16					16
TEAM TOTALS	56	146	219	365	1024	56	146	219	365	1024
Netminders	GPI	Min	SOG	GA	Sv%	GPI	Min	SOG	GA	Sv%
Curtis Cruickshank	54	3103	2099	163	92.2	54	3103	2099	163	92.2
Dean Skinns	13	293	178	24	86.5	13	293	178	24	86.5
Empty Net Goals			8	8				8	8	
TEAM TOTALS	56	3396	2285	195	91.5	56	3396	2285	195	91.5

Also appeared: Adam Carr (2), Bari McKenzie (2), Chris McEwan (2), Jamie Randall (6)

Also played for: 1 Nottingham Panthers, Bracknell Bees, Slough Jets; 2 Milton Keynes Lightning; 3 Sheffield Steelers; 4 London Racers; 5 Peterborough Phantoms; 6 Romford Raiders; 7 Bracknell Bees.

Shutouts: Cruickshank - league: 11 Oct v Manchester Phoenix (36 saves), 5 Dec at Manchester Phoenix (45).

All Competitions = league and Challenge Cup

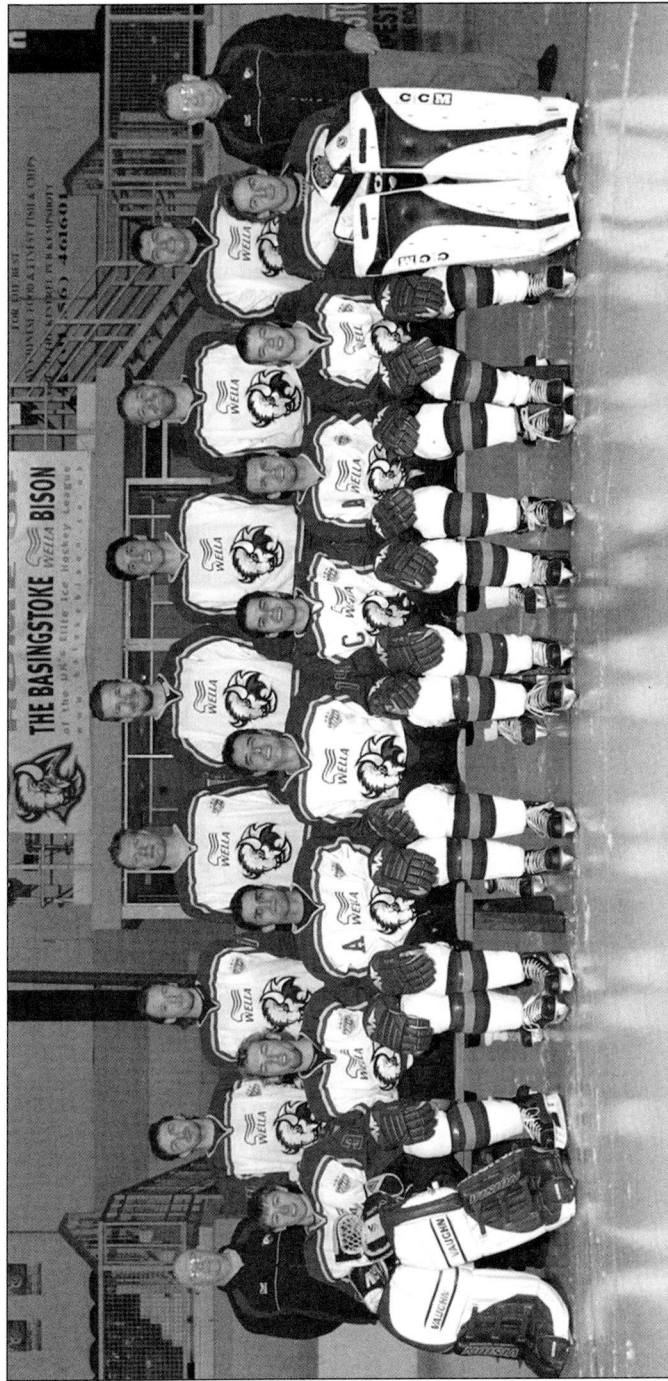

BASINGSTOKE BISON *left to right, back row:* Tony Skinns (bench crew), Martin Filip, Christian Widauer, Kim Vahanen, Dave Geris, Darren Hurley, Doug Schueller, Jaromir Kverka, Alan Parrott (bench crew); *front row:* Dean Skinns, Richard Hargreaves, Joe Ciccarello, Steve Moria, Phil Roy, Blake Sorenson, Shaun Thompson, Curtis Cruickshank.

Photo: David Taylor

Curtis keeps Bison in battle

GRAHAM MERRY

It was all change for the Basingstoke Bison as a new team entered the new Elite League, wearing a new green strip and a new logo.

All that stayed the same were sponsor *Wella*, player-coach **Steve Moria** and back-up netminder **Dean Skinns**.

As well as the expected Canadians and Americans, Moria signed the team's first Austrian, **Christian Widauer**, and their first Czech, **Martin Filip**. With a couple of Finns and a few Brits, the changing room had a genuinely cosmopolitan atmosphere.

Bison also iced five players on two-way contracts with English Premier League clubs, Peterborough and Milton Keynes.

The season opened badly with most of the new players forced to sit out the first weekend due to problems with their International Transfer Cards. But this didn't affect Canadian goalie, **Curtis Cruickshank**, who cheered the fans with a superb performance at the National Ice Centre, limiting Nottingham Panthers to a 2-1 win.

This was to be the first of many outstanding displays by the former North American minor leaguer who was voted onto the All-Star team at the end of the season.

But it was a different story the following night in Belfast when the Giants took the tired Herd apart, 10-4. One of the goals came from temporary signing **Nicky Chinn**, while bench coach, **Luc Chabot**, who had also been pressed into action, collected two assists.

A week later, a home victory over Coventry gave the fans hope and the wooden spoon was soon forgotten. As the season progressed Bison climbed as high as fifth. Their best spell came in November with a brilliant 7-2 revenge win over the Giants in Hampshire, followed by home and away wins over the Panthers in four days.

In other high spots, 19-year-old Skinns back-stopped his side to victory, and 16-year-old **Shaun Thompson** became the youngest player to score in the top flight of the British game for over a decade. [Editor's note - Shaun later won *The Ice Hockey Annual* trophy as the MVP of the major junior tournament in Hull.]

Two things spoiled Bison's season. Though they played some great hockey on the road, taking points from everywhere except Sheffield, their home form let them down. And their offence fired on only one line with Moria and **Joe Ciccarello** being the main marksmen.

But it was only on the final weekend that they eventually conceded defeat, narrowly missing out on the sixth and last playoff spot.

PLAYER AWARDS

Players' Player (Mark Scotchmer award)
                                    Curtis Cruickshank
Most Valuable Player   **Curtis Cruickshank**
Coach's Player   **Dean Skinns**
Captain's Player   **Blake Sorensen**
Best British Player   **Richard Hargreaves**

LEADING PLAYERS

Joe Ciccarello *born 8 March 1972*

The Italian-Canadian forward was the club's top points scorer after making the short journey down the M4 from Bracknell. A fast skater who gave his all for the team and netted the team's only hat-trick of the season.

Curtis Cruickshank *born 21 March 1979*

The Ottawan was rated as one of the finest netminders in the club's history. He won several games for Bison and was voted man of the match in seven of the eight league venues. Popular with the fans, he was a great ambassador for the club.

Phil Roy *born 16 January 1977*

The Herd's French-Canadian captain led by example. In one game he was helped off the ice after being hit by the puck only to return for his next shift. A solid blueliner, he also got his fair share of goals and was an important part of the powerplay.

FACT FILE 2003-04

Elite League: Seventh
Playoffs: Did not qualify
Challenge Cup: Sixth

HISTORY

Founded 1988 as Beavers. Name changed to Bison in May 1995.

Leagues Elite League 2003-04; British National League 1998-2003; Superleague 1996-98; British League, Premier Div 1993-96; British League, Div One 1990-93; English League 1988-90.

Honours: British League, Div One & playoffs 1992-93; English League (promotion) playoffs 1989-90. *Benson and Hedges* Plate 1999-2000 & 2000-01.

BELFAST GIANTS

PLAYER	ALL COMPETITIONS					ELITE LEAGUE					PLAYOFFS				
Scorers	GP	G	A	Pts	Pim	GP	G	A	Pts	Pim	GP	G	A	Pts	Pim
Jason Ruff (I)	58	38	55	93	140	52	35	50	85	134	4	1	3	4	4
Curt Bowen (I)	53	28	43	71	98	47	27	39	66	86	4	0	2	2	10
Brad Kenny (I)	62	33	36	69	38	56	32	36	68	36	4	1	0	1	2
Colin Ward (I)	51	28	32	60	52	47	27	31	58	50	4	1	1	2	2
Paxton Schulte (I)	60	21	35	56	424	54	21	31	52	352	4	0	2	2	66
Todd Kelman (I)	62	16	37	53	48	56	14	36	50	46	4	1	0	1	2
Paul Sample	62	18	22	40	72	56	16	22	38	66	4	1	0	1	4
Shane Johnson	61	9	22	31	110	55	9	21	30	94	4	0	0	0	16
Sean Berens (I)	17	10	16	26	12	17	10	16	26	12					
Jason Bowen (I)	54	8	15	23	176	48	8	14	22	166	4	0	0	0	4
Leigh Jamieson 1	58	6	10	16	84	52	6	10	16	80	4	0	0	0	4
Rob Stewart (I)	43	2	13	15	49	37	2	13	15	49	4	0	0	0	0
Mark Finney	26	3	7	10	35	20	3	6	9	33	4	0	1	1	2
Mark Morrison	61	4	3	7	28	55	4	3	7	28	4	0	0	0	0
Graeme Walton	49	0	4	4	28	43	0	4	4	28	4	0	0	0	0
Gareth Martin	56	3	0	3	6	53	3	0	3	6	1	0	0	0	0
Colin Ryder (N) (I)	62	0	3	3	12	56	0	3	3	12	4	0	0	0	0
Grant Taylor	12	1	0	1	2	10	1	0	1	2	2	0	0	0	0
Bench Penalties					12					10					2
TEAM TOTALS	62	228	353	581	1426	56	218	335	553	1290	4	5	9	14	118

Netminders	GPI	Min	SOG	GA	Sv%	GPI	Min	SOG	GA	Sv%	GPI	Min	SOG	GA	Sv%
Colin Ryder (I)	62	3707	1847	195	89.4	56	3342	1698	175	89.7	4	245	93	9	90.3
Chris McGimpsey	5	57	33	6	81.8	5	57	33	6	81.8					
Empty Net Goals			6	6				4	4				2	2	
TEAM TOTALS	62	3764	1886	207	89.0	56	3399	1735	185	89.3	4	245	95	11	88.4

Also appeared: Adam Brittle (2), Tom Carlon (2).

Also played for: 1 Milton Keynes Lightning; 2 Telford Wild Foxes.

Shutouts: Ryder - league: 17 Oct at Manchester Phoenix (22 saves),
28 Dec v London Racers (22).

All Competitions = league, playoffs and Challenge Cup

Giant nothing

STUART McKINLEY

A season that "promised a lot but delivered nothing", is how coach **Rob Stewart** summed up Giants' campaign. Ultimately, it was the fact that nothing was delivered in terms of silverware that cost him his job just a few weeks after the season finished.

Stewart had been promoted from assistant coach to take over from the Germany-bound **Dave Whistle**. It was something of a poisoned chalice as financial problems hit the club and he was fortunate to be able to put a team on the ice for the opening fixture at home to Coventry. Only an agreement from creditors to accept part payment of their huge debts saved Giants, just three seasons after their formation.

Jason Ruff, who played a major part in Giants' Superleague triumph of 2001-02, was brought back in the big coup of the summer. As the new Elite League placed a large emphasis on home-grown players, Stewart signed four Irishmen - goaltender **Chris McGimpsey**, forwards **Gareth Martin** and **Mark Morrison**, and, later, defenceman **Graeme Walton**. They were the first locals to play for the side.

Opening night was one to forget, though, as the British National League champions left Belfast with a 5-2 win behind them. That was followed, however, by an eight-game unbeaten run as Giants hit the top of the Elite League table. Indeed Blaze were the only team to beat the Giants during a run of 15 wins in their opening 18 games.

Sean Berens also returned to Belfast. He was a linemate of Ruff's in the Superleague and once again lit up the Odyssey - until a Swiss club snapped him up just days before a release clause in his contract was due to expire. He was never really replaced and it was when injuries hit that his loss was most keenly felt.

It was the players who mattered most who went down with injuries, too. **Jason Bowen**, **Colin Ward** and Ruff, all missed games.

The league finished with a whimper, but there was still hope of making an impact in the playoffs. In the end, though, just one point and five goals from their four games meant the season ended early for the Giants.

Paxton Schulte's continued run-ins with officials saw him thrown out of more games than anyone cares to remember, and a suspension or two did nobody any favours. But he was a big fan favourite and he and Ward, who both retired at the end of the season, will be greatly missed.

So will *Harp Lager*, who decided not to renew their sponsorship deal with the club.

LEADING PLAYERS

Todd Kelman born 5 January 1975

The Calgary native went from being one of the youngest members of the team to an experienced head almost in the blink of an eye. He led by example, playing the best hockey of his career.

Jason Ruff born 27 January 1970

Despite injury problems during his year in Germany, the left-winger had lost none of his skill and know-how. Rightly voted MVP by his team-mates and the Writers' Association.

Colin Ward born 5 September 1970

Gave his all in every game he played for the team as he made sure his last season was one to remember. Was badly missed during a month out with a broken foot. His number 11 shirt was hoisted to the rafters of the Odyssey after the last game.

BELFAST GIANTS *left to right*, *back row*: Jason (Taff) Ellery (equipment), Paul Sample, Shane Johnson, Graeme Walton, Todd Kelman, Jason Bowen, Leigh Jamieson, Brad Kenny, Mark Finney, Gareth Martin, Mark Morrison, John Elliott (manager); *front row*: Chris McGimpsey, Paxton Schulte, Curt Bowen, Jason Ruff, Rob Stewart, Colin Ward, Colin Ryder.

Photo: Michael Cooper.

BRACKNELL BEES

PLAYER	ALL COMPETITIONS					FINDUS BRITISH NATIONAL LEAGUE					PLAYOFFS				
Scorers	GP	G	A	Pts	Pim	GP	G	A	Pts	Pim	GP	G	A	Pts	Pim
Nathan Rempel (l)	64	46	37	83	80	35	27	21	48	28	14	10	8	18	8
Scott Allison (l)	63	26	47	73	223	35	20	27	47	114	13	3	11	14	79
Greg Owen	62	21	35	56	32	36	15	23	38	16	11	3	8	11	6
David Matsos (l)	55	23	27	50	32	28	11	16	27	12	14	6	5	11	10
Daryl Lavoie (l)	38	7	37	44	134	19	5	19	24	81	4	0	1	1	0
Mike Ellis	59	15	29	44	36	34	5	17	22	28	10	4	4	8	4
Nicky Chinn 2	40	5	31	36	115	26	3	26	29	50	14	2	5	7	65
J-P Soucy (l)	64	9	27	36	194	36	4	14	18	85	14	3	7	10	55
Danny Meyers	64	5	25	30	80	35	1	12	13	42	14	1	7	8	4
Mark Richardson	58	13	12	25	20	32	5	5	10	4	11	4	5	9	16
Corey Lyons	22	11	12	23	6	15	10	11	21	6	7	1	1	2	0
Ryan Aldridge	63	7	10	17	117	34	4	4	8	85	14	2	3	5	12
Darren Hurley 3	24	7	4	11	97	10	2	1	3	54					
Curtis Sheptak (l)	11	1	5	6	4	8	1	3	4	0					
Andrew Sande	13	3	1	4	6	2	0	0	0	2					
Chris Crombie (l) 1	14	2	2	4	10	2	1	0	1	4					
Ross McDougall	55	0	4	4	22	30	0	1	1	12	12	0	2	2	2
Adam Hyman	50	1	2	3	22	25	1	0	1	6	12	0	1	1	6
Danny Hughes	60	1	2	3	4	34	0	2	2	4	12	1	0	1	0
Tyrone Miller	23	1	1	2	18	12	1	0	1	10	11	0	1	1	8
Stephen Murphy (N)	27	0	1	1	0	8	0	1	1	0	7	0	0	0	0
Scott Hay (N) (l)	42	0	1	1	39	28	0	1	1	14	12	0	0	0	25
Bench Penalties					4										2
TEAM TOTALS	65	204	352	556	1295	36	116	204	320	659	14	40	69	109	302

Netminders	GP	Mins	SOG	GA	Sv%	GP	Mins	SOG	GA	Sv%	GP	Mins	SOG	GA	Sv%
Scott Hay (l)	43	2563	1391	116	91.7	28	1694	893	79	91.2	13	746	423	30	92.9
Stephen Murphy	21	1238	574	50	91.3	8	494	234	22	90.6	1	60	37	4	89.2
Tom Annetts	2	50	19	2	89.5	1	20	10	1	90.0					
David Wride	4	110	55	8	85.5	1	10	9	0	100	1	34	15	2	86.7
Empty Net Goals			2	2				1	1				1	1	
TEAM TOTALS	65	3961	2041	178	91.3	36	2218	1147	103	91.0	14	840	476	37	92.2

Also appeared: David Poulton, Luke Reynolds, Kent Nobes (4).

Also played for: 1 *Wightlink* Raiders; 2 Basingstoke Bison, Nottingham Panthers, Slough Jets; 3 Basingstoke Bison; 4 Peterborough Phantoms, *Wightlink* Raiders.

Shutouts: Murphy - cup: 21 Sept at Edinburgh Capitals (28 saves),
28 Sept v Fife Flyers (22);
Hay - league: 4 Jan at Hull Stingrays (17 saves), 18 Jan v Fife Flyers (26),
1 Feb v Newcastle Vipers (35), 14 Feb v Dundee Stars (37).

BRACKNELL BEES *left to right*, *back row*: Simon Lazarczuk (apprentice), Adam Hyman, Joe Reynolds, Danny Meyers, Andrew Sande, Chris Crombie, Luke Reynolds, Ross McDougall, Brian Miller (equipment); *middle row*: Tom Annetts, David Poulton, Mark Richardson, JP Soucy, Alex Barker (apprentice), Nathan Rempel, Greg Owen, David Wride; *front row*: Scott Allison, Mike Ellis, Darren Hurley, Stephen Murphy, David Matsos, Ryan Aldridge, Daryl Lavoie.

Photo: Bracknell and Wokingham Times.

Bee-ridesmaids

ALAN MANICOM

New player-boss **Mike Ellis** assembled virtually a completely new team for Bracknell Bees' first campaign in the *Findus* British National League.

An unbeaten eight-match start went a long way to resurrecting fans' interest after last season's abject surrender in the Superleague.

But although Bees finished the season with an against-all-odds appearance in the Playoff final, there were a lot of ups and downs as a rapidly changing side struggled for consistency while battling with injuries to key players.

When Bees failed to win a single game in October and suffered defeats in their opening two league games, Ellis proved he was not afraid to make tough decisions. He axed not only defenceman **Andrew Sande**, but also **Chris Crombie**, a personal friend he had brought with him from Basingstoke Bison in the summer.

Captain **Dave Matsos** was sidelined for several weeks with a knee injury and GB netminder **Stephen Murphy** was ruled out for the rest of the league campaign after aggravating a shoulder injury in a charity basketball match.

Import **Scott Hay** replaced him leading to the release of forward **Darren Hurley**, the only surviving member of last season's squad. His place was taken by **Nicky Chinn**, who joined permanently after being brought in for the second leg of their *Findus* Cup semi-final against his former club, Guildford Flames.

Any chance of a settled team was dashed when Canadian international **Curtis Sheptak** flew off to join La Chaux-De-Fonds in the lucrative Swiss A League. And only days later another defenceman, assistant coach **Daryl Lavoie**, took the full force of a slapshot and fractured a leg, forcing Ellis to switch from forward to defence.

Lavoie had barely returned from his broken leg when he was the victim of another stray puck which fractured his skull. **Corey Lyons**, the former London Knights and Guildford forward, missed playoff games with a back injury after Bees finished the regular season in fourth place.

Ellis missed games, too, with a bruised retina, as his side took third place in the playoff qualifying table, and top British forward **Greg Owen** ruptured knee ligaments while helping Bees to beat league winners, Fife, in the semis.

But a thrilling final with Guildford, in which neither team were more than a goal ahead on aggregate until the last few minutes of their three-hour derby showdown, proved one step too far for Bees' weary and depleted squad.

PLAYER AWARDS

Player of the Year	Scott Allison
Players' Player	J P Soucy
Coach's Award	Greg Owen
Best Forward	Scott Allison
Best Defenceman	J P Soucy
Most Improved Player (Paxton Ward Trophy)	
	Mark Richardson
Best British Player	Danny Meyers

LEADING PLAYERS

Scott Allison *born 22 April 1972*

The left-winger's fiery, aggressive style made him an instant favourite with fans who had grown tired in previous seasons of seeing their team being bullied out of games.

Scored some vital goals and was always instrumental in firing the team up when they needed to dig deep.

Greg Owen *born 19 June 1981*

In a league that relies heavily on home-grown talent, the centreman was the team's leading British scorer, finishing third overall. Weighed in with a hefty 21 goals in all competitions before being cruelly denied an appearance in the playoff final by a knee injury.

Nathan Rempel *born 7 February 1977*

The former Team Canada right-winger played in all but one of Bees' 65 cup, league and playoff games, netting 46 goals to finish as top scorer. A lethal finisher and tough competitor.

FACT FILE 2003-04

British National League:	Fourth
Playoffs:	Runners-up
***Findus* Cup:**	Runners-up

HISTORY

Founded: 1987.

Leagues: British National League 2003-04; Superleague 1996-2003; British League, Premier Div. 1991-95; British League, Div. One 1995-96, 1990-91; English League 1987-90.

Honours: Superleague 1999-2000, Promotion Playoffs 1991-92, English League 1989-90.

CARDIFF DEVILS

PLAYER	ALL COMPETITIONS					ELITE LEAGUE					PLAYOFFS				
Scorers	GP	G	A	Pts	Pim	GP	G	A	Pts	Pim	GP	G	A	Pts	Pim
Vezio Sacratini (I)	59	14	52	66	106	54	14	48	62	104	3	0	3	3	0
Dennis Maxwell (I)	57	25	24	49	245	51	23	22	45	231	4	1	2	3	2
Ivan Matulik	63	24	18	42	126	56	22	16	38	120	5	2	2	4	2
Jeff Burgoyne (I)	61	11	24	35	64	54	10	24	34	58	5	1	0	1	6
Russ Romaniuk (I)	49	15	18	33	73	42	13	17	30	34	5	1	1	2	10
Ed Patterson (I)	44	13	19	32	82	37	10	16	26	68	5	3	2	5	4
Jonathan Phillips 4	63	17	12	29	72	56	17	11	28	66	5	0	1	1	6
Mike Ware (I)	54	11	15	26	181	47	8	14	22	167	5	3	1	4	6
Jeff Brown (I)	61	6	20	26	118	56	6	19	25	110	3	0	0	0	4
Jeff Ulmer (I)	9	9	9	18	6	9	9	9	18	6					
Matt Myers	59	6	9	15	79	52	5	7	12	48	5	1	2	3	6
Jason Becker (I)	26	2	11	13	8	20	2	7	9	8	5	0	4	4	0
Merv Priest	17	5	4	9	14	17	5	4	9	14					
Frank Evans (I) 3	23	4	4	8	60	23	4	4	8	60					
Phil Hill	62	3	5	8	34	55	3	5	8	22	5	0	0	0	10
Jason Stone	63	2	6	8	36	56	2	6	8	34	5	0	0	0	0
Neil Francis	60	1	3	4	38	53	1	2	3	34	5	0	1	1	4
Jason Cugnet (N) (I)	30	0	3	3	2	23	0	2	2	0	5	0	1	1	2
James Manson	62	0	3	3	26	55	0	2	2	24	5	0	1	1	2
Doug McEwen 4	5	1	1	2	2	4	1	1	2	2	1	0	0	0	0
Eoin McInerney (I) (N)	30	0	1	1	18	30	0	1	1	18					
Bench Penalties					16					12					4
TEAM TOTALS	63	169	261	430	1406	56	155	237	392	1240	5	12	21	33	68

Netminders	GPI	Min	SOG	GA	Sv%	GPI	Min	SOG	GA	Sv%	GPI	Min	SOG	GA	Sv%
Jason Cugnet (I)	30	1820	822	72	91.2	23	1400	645	59	90.9	5	300	129	9	93.0
Eoin McInerney (I)	30	1818	937	88	90.6	30	1818	937	88	90.6					
Barry Hollyhead 5	3	180	71	8	88.7	3	180	71	8	88.7					
Empty Net Goals			9	9				8	8				1	1	
TEAM TOTALS	63	3818	1839	177	90.4	56	3398	1661	163	90.2	5	300	130	10	92.3

Also appeared: Gary Clarke (1), Darren Cotton (2), Phil Manny, David James.

Also played for: 1 Basingstoke Bison; 2 Cardiff Devils, Nottingham Panthers; 3 Coventry Blaze; 4 Peterborough Phantoms; 5 Milton Keynes Lightning.

Shutouts: Cugnet - league: 12 March at Manchester Phoenix (17 saves); playoffs: 25 March v Nottingham Panthers (15).

All Competitions = league, playoffs and Challenge Cup

Whistle blows hot

The new-look *Thomson* Cardiff Devils made a fine run in the Elite League playoffs but perhaps even more important after their chequered history, they claimed to have made a modest profit for the first time in 18 years.

Former fan favourite **Shannon (Shinedog) Hope** returned to the city and headed the club's commercial department. After the decision was finally made to switch from the British National League, he re-signed coach **Glenn Mulvenna**.

Mulvenna built his side around old heroes, **Vezio Sacratini** (back after a spell with London Knights), **Ivan Matulik**, **Mike Ware** and **Jeff Burgoyne**, and brought in feisty forward, **Dennis Maxwell**, also from the Knights.

Several Welshmen played key roles, including GB internationals **Matt Myers** and **Jonathan Phillips**, **Philip Hill**, **James Manson** and **Jason Stone**.

The results failed to come at the start and by early December the team were only one place off the bottom of the table.

Mulvenna was sacked amid controversy, with the coach first resigning after hearing of his possible replacement by former Belfast and Bracknell coach, **Dave Whistle**, and then agreeing to return after being given the dreaded vote of confidence and a new contract, reportedly with a 'no-sack' clause.

'Shinedog' briefly took the reins himself, saying: "We've been playing like a team without direction." With goalie **Eion McInerney** on the verge of quitting to become a fireman back in Canada, Hope announced that the new coach would be, er, Whistle.

The new man, who had enjoyed considerable success with the Giants and Bees, duly turned the side around. **Jason Cugnet** replaced McInerney and finished third in the netminding averages, reflecting the side's much improved defence as Devils qualified for the playoffs with a fifth place finish.

They got safely through their playoff group to reach the semi-finals at Nottingham and put up a determined battle against eventual champs, Sheffield Steelers, before being knocked out.

But the club's future remains cloudy. Their lease on the Wales National Ice Rink is due to expire at the end of season 2004-05 and it remains to be seen if the rink owners, Cardiff County Council, will keep their promise to fans that the team "will never be without a rink".

Work on the much-delayed Sports Village in Cardiff Bay was not due to begin until the end of 2004 and the arena, which is to be Devils' home, is not included in the first stage of the development. (*See New Rinks News* - ed.)

PLAYER AWARDS

Player of the Year	**Jeff Burgoyne**
Players' Player	**Jonathan Phillips**
Best British Player (Norman Watkins Memorial Award)	**Jonathan Phillips**
Travelling Supporters' Player	**Eoin McInerney**
Most Improved Player	**Matt Myers**

LEADING PLAYERS

Jeff Burgoyne *born 26 February 1977*

Voted a second team All-Star by the ice hockey writers, the former ECHL rearguard from Penticton, BC was a major asset in his second season with the club. But he admitted he felt like quitting when things turned sour in mid-season.

Matt Myers *born 6 November 1984*

Cardiff-born Myers has come up through the club's junior system. A skilful centreman who is growing in strength and toughness, he was a hit not only with Devils but also with GB. Travelled regularly from university in Nottingham.

Mike Ware *born 22 March 1967*

Nobody messed with the Devils while Iron Mike was around! The Canadian winger racked up 167 minutes in his league games alone and was always an intimidating presence. Retired after 20 years playing professionally on both sides of the Atlantic.

FACT FILE 2003-04

Elite League:	Fifth
Playoffs:	Semi-finalists
Challenge Cup:	Semi-finalists

HISTORY

Founded 1986.

Leagues Elite League 2003-04; British National League 2001-03; Superleague 1996-2001; British League, Premier Div. 1989-96; British League, Div. One 1987-89; British League, Div. Two 1986-87.

Honours Superleague Playoff Champions 1999; British League and Championship winners 1993-94, 1992-93, 1989-90; British League winners 1996-97; *Benson and Hedges Cup* winners 1992.

CARDIFF DEVILS *left to right*, *back row*: Jonathan Phillips, Neil Francis, Merv Priest, James Manson, Jeff Burgoyne, David James; *middle row*: Nathan Craze, Frank Evans, Phil Manny, Matt Myers, Phil Hill, Jeff Brown, Jason Stone, Mike Brabon; *front row*: Joe Watkins, Vezio Sacratini, Ivan Matulik, Mike Ware, Glenn Mulvenna (coach), Russ Romaniuk, Dennis Maxwell, Eoin McInerney.

Photo: Adrian Rapps

CHELMSFORD CHIEFTAINS

PLAYER	ALL COMPETITIONS					ENGLISH PREMIER LEAGUE					PLAYOFFS				
Scorers	GP	G	A	Pts	Pim	GP	G	A	Pts	Pim	GP	G	A	Pts	Pim
Kyle Amyotte (I)	48	73	62	135	150	31	56	46	102	112	6	4	4	8	28
Andrew Power (I)	40	40	64	104	226	30	36	46	82	120	4	1	2	3	102
Lee Cowmeadow	48	45	37	82	28	32	28	32	60	24	6	8	2	10	0
Andy Hannah	47	31	33	64	209	29	16	23	39	147	6	5	2	7	22
Richard Whiting	44	14	37	51	50	32	13	30	43	34	4	0	2	2	6
Scott McKenzie	30	13	15	28	12	14	8	9	17	6	5	0	2	2	4
Antti Makikyro (I)	48	7	21	28	50	30	4	12	16	38	6	1	3	4	2
Ross Jones	47	5	17	22	48	29	3	9	12	16	6	0	1	1	26
Jon Beckett 1	19	7	14	21	34	17	7	13	20	22					
Jake French	32	4	16	20	32	20	3	12	15	28	2	0	1	1	0
Slava Koulikov 2	10	6	12	18	2	1	2	0	2	0	6	3	9	12	0
Anthony Leone	44	8	6	14	22	26	6	5	11	20	6	2	0	2	0
Lee Brears	21	4	10	14	6	14	4	9	13	6	0	0	0	0	0
Dan Cabby	33	3	9	12	8	24	3	6	9	4	4	0	1	1	4
Russell Bishop	40	2	10	12	8	26	1	9	10	4	6	0	1	1	0
Richard Gunn	20	5	4	9	2	18	5	4	9	2					
Daniel Wright	39	2	7	9	6	22	2	5	7	6	6	0	2	2	0
Shaun Wallis	36	6	2	8	101	23	4	2	6	69	6	2	0	2	2
Andrew Clements	32	5	2	7	12	23	5	2	7	10	3	0	0	0	0
Craig Metcalfe	4	2	4	6	2	4	2	4	6	2					
Chris Wise	5	3	1	4	0	4	2	1	3	0					
Chad Reekie 3	23	2	2	4	12	8	1	1	2	2	6	1	1	2	2
Karl Hopper 2	10	0	4	4	32	1	0	0	0	0	6	0	3	3	26
Ricky Mills	1	0	3	3	0	1	0	3	3	0					
Glen Moorhouse	32	0	3	3	14	22	0	2	2	10	4	0	0	0	0
Andy Moffat (N)	43	0	2	2	6	28	0	2	2	2	3	0	0	0	0
Bench Penalties					14					14					0
TEAM TOTALS	50	287	397	684	1086	32	211	287	498	698	6	27	36	63	224

Netminders	GPI	Mins	SOG	GA	Sv%	GPI	Mins	SOG	GA	Sv%	GPI	Mins	SOG	GA	Sv%
Andy Moffat	40	2185	1328	154	88.4	25	1353	789	100	87.3	3	172	119	19	84.0
Alan Blythe	12	409	277	38	86.3	8	261	161	23	85.7	3	108	92	13	85.9
Ben Clements	11	405	223	37	83.4	8	305	159	25	84.3	2	80	57	10	82.5
Empty Net Goals		1		1			1		1						
TEAM TOTALS	50	3000	1828	230	87.4	32	1920	1109	149	86.6	6	360	268	42	84.3

Also played for: 1 Romford Raiders; 2 Hull Stingrays; 3 Fife Flyers

All Competitions = league, playoffs and Premier Cup

CHELMSFORD CHIEFTAINS *left to right, back row:* Dean Birrell (coach), Russell Bishop, Andy Hannah, Jake French, Shaun Wallis, Andrew Power, Jonathan Beckett, Lee Cowmeadow, Antti Makikyro, Glen Moorhouse, Gordon Crawford (physio), Ollie Oliver (owner); *front row:* Ben Clements, Danny Wright, Ross Jones, Kyle Amyotte, Andy Moffat, Richard Whiting, Anthony Leone, Richard Gunn, Alan Blyth.

One up

IVOR HOBSON

Chieftains climbed to fourth place in the English Premier League, one better than the previous season, but disappointed their fans with a poor post-season.

With **Erskine Douglas** returning to Romford, **Dean Birrell** replaced him as head coach. Among his key signings were **Lee Cowmeadow** from Cardiff who scored almost a goal a game, **Scott McKenzie** from Fife, Solihull's **Antii Makikyro** and the dependable Isle of Wight netminder **Andy Moffat** who replaced **Chris Douglas**.

Otherwise, Chieftains' line-up had a familiar look as they took to the ice for their season opener. Leading scorers **Kyle Amyotte** and new team captain **Andrew Power** returned alongside the growing band of local players. These included **Ross Jones** and **Richard Whiting** who was appearing in his tenth season with the Tribe.

Andy Hannah, who doubled as assistant coach, finished fourth in club scoring. But he also became Chieftains' all-time penalty leader with 1,082 minutes in 326 games.

Over the first couple of months, the team won only four of 13 games as they faced a tough schedule that included seven games against the eventual top three clubs, Their form suffered further as they were at full strength in only three of these contests as injuries piled up. As many as five regulars were out at any one time, not to mention suspensions.

Their fortunes changed when they became the first team to beat Milton Keynes with an impressive 6-4 victory in mid-October. Then they strengthened their blueline by signing their former captain, **Jake French**, from Invicta and Fife's junior GB defenceman, **Chad Reekie**.

After a bad New Year, they hit their stride and a nine-game unbeaten streak secured fourth place in the league and a spot in the semi-finals of the English Premier Cup. In late signings, Chieftains acquired **Craig Metcalfe** as cover for the injured Makikyro, plus Hull's leading scorer, **Slava Koulikov**, and **Karl Hopper**. So expectations were high when Amyotte scored hat-tricks in the final two league games.

In the opening playoff game at Milton Keynes, Chieftains held their nerve for 40 minutes trailing only 4-3. But then Power was thrown out (the first of three such dismissals in the post-season) and they slumped to a 7-3 defeat. They could only record a solitary victory over Telford to finish third in the group.

The cup semi-final was a close run affair but Peterborough ran out 7-4 winners on aggregate.

PLAYER AWARDS

Player of the Year	**Lee Cowmeadow**
Coach's Player	**Richard Whiting**
M&G Investments *Players' Player*	
	Lee Cowmeadow
Candol *Best Defenceman*	**Andy Moffat**
Best Forward	**Kyle Amyotte**

LEADING PLAYERS

Jake French *born 6 June 1975*

A selfless defenceman always willing to put himself between the puck and the goal at whatever cost. Rejoined the team after two seasons at Invicta. Broke the 200-game barrier with 235 games for the Tribe despite work commitments.

Chad Reekie *born 7 January 1986*

A third line defenceman on the Fife Flyers, Chad's confidence grew as his ice-time increased. Part of the medal-winning GB under-20 team, he also played in Scotland's under-19s against England at Nottingham.

Richard Whiting *born 16 March 1977*

A talented team player who can let his stick do the talking or, if needs must, his fists. Made his debut in 1994 and has laced up for the Tribe in 393 games. A local lad, he stands 10th in Chieftains' all-time points scorers with 248.

FACT FILE 2003-04

English Premier League:	Fourth
Playoffs:	Third in group
Premier Cup:	Semi-finalists

CLUB HISTORY

Founded: 1987.

Leagues: English Premier League 2002-04, 1998-2001; English (National) League 2001-02, 1996-98 and 1988-93; British League Div One 1993-96; British League, Div. Two 1987-88.

Honours: League winners, Playoff champions and *DataVision* Millennium Cup winners 1999-2000.

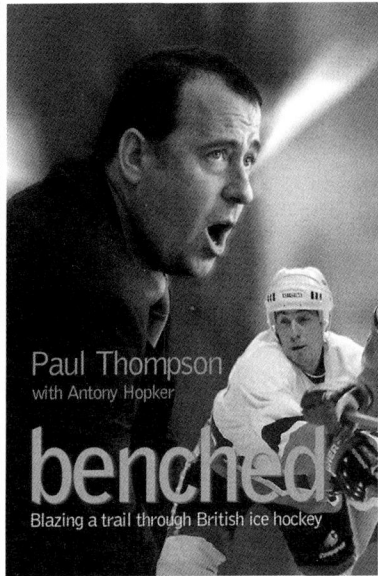

COVENTRY BLAZE

PLAYER	ALL COMPETITIONS					ELITE LEAGUE					PLAYOFFS				
Scorers	GP	G	A	Pts	Pim	GP	G	A	Pts	Pim	GP	G	A	Pts	Pim
Steve Gallace (I)	59	31	45	76	62	55	29	45	74	56	4	2	0	2	6
Ashley Tait	60	25	32	57	88	56	24	30	54	88	4	1	2	3	0
Steve O'Brien (I)	60	14	37	51	60	56	13	35	48	60	4	1	2	3	0
Joel Poirier (I)	60	24	24	48	50	56	23	23	46	42	4	1	1	2	8
Hilton Ruggles	60	23	24	47	72	56	22	23	45	66	4	1	1	2	6
Graham Schlender (I)	60	19	27	46	128	56	19	26	45	128	4	0	1	1	0
Michael Tasker	58	12	25	37	74	54	10	25	35	66	4	2	0	2	8
Steve Chartrand	56	15	17	32	32	52	15	15	30	30	4	0	2	2	2
Steve Carpenter	44	10	20	30	92	40	9	20	29	84	4	1	0	1	8
Shaun Johnson	41	8	15	23	10	37	8	13	21	10	4	0	2	2	0
Russell Cowley	46	3	8	11	14	42	3	6	9	14	4	0	2	2	0
Tom Watkins	55	2	7	9	72	51	2	5	7	70	4	0	2	2	2
Mathias Soderstrom (I)	58	1	8	9	46	54	0	7	7	44	4	1	1	2	2
Frank Evans 1	26	6	2	8	89	22	6	2	8	85	4	0	0	0	4
Lee Richardson	60	2	4	6	2	56	2	4	6	2	4	0	0	0	0
Jody Lehman (N) (I)	59	1	3	4	39	56	1	3	4	39	3	0	0	0	0
James Pease 2	7	0	1	1	22	7	0	1	1	22					
Gareth Owen 3	48	0	1	1	10	44	0	1	1	10	4	0	0	0	0
Adam Radmall	53	0	1	1	0	50	0	1	1	0	3	0	0	0	0
Bench Penalties					20					16					4
TEAM TOTALS	60	196	301	497	982	56	186	285	471	932	4	10	16	26	50

Netminders	GPI	Min	SOG	GA	Sv%	GPI	Min	SOG	GA	Sv%	GPI	Min	SOG	GA	Sv%
Jody Lehman (I)	59	3475	1742	162	90.7	56	3295	1661	149	91.0	3	180	81	13	84.0
Alan Levers	6	171	74	11	85.1	5	111	47	4	91.5	1	60	27	7	74.1
Empty Net Goals			3	3				3	3				0	0	
TEAM TOTALS	60	3646	1819	176	90.3	56	3406	1711	156	90.9	4	240	108	20	81.5

Also played for: 1 Cardiff Devils; 2 Milton Keynes Lightning; 3 Solihull Kings.

Shutouts: Lehman - league: 22 Nov at Cardiff Devils (25 saves),

5 Dec at London Racers (22), 7 Dec v Manchester Phoenix (20),

2 Jan at London Racers (24).

All Competitions = league, playoffs and Challenge Cup

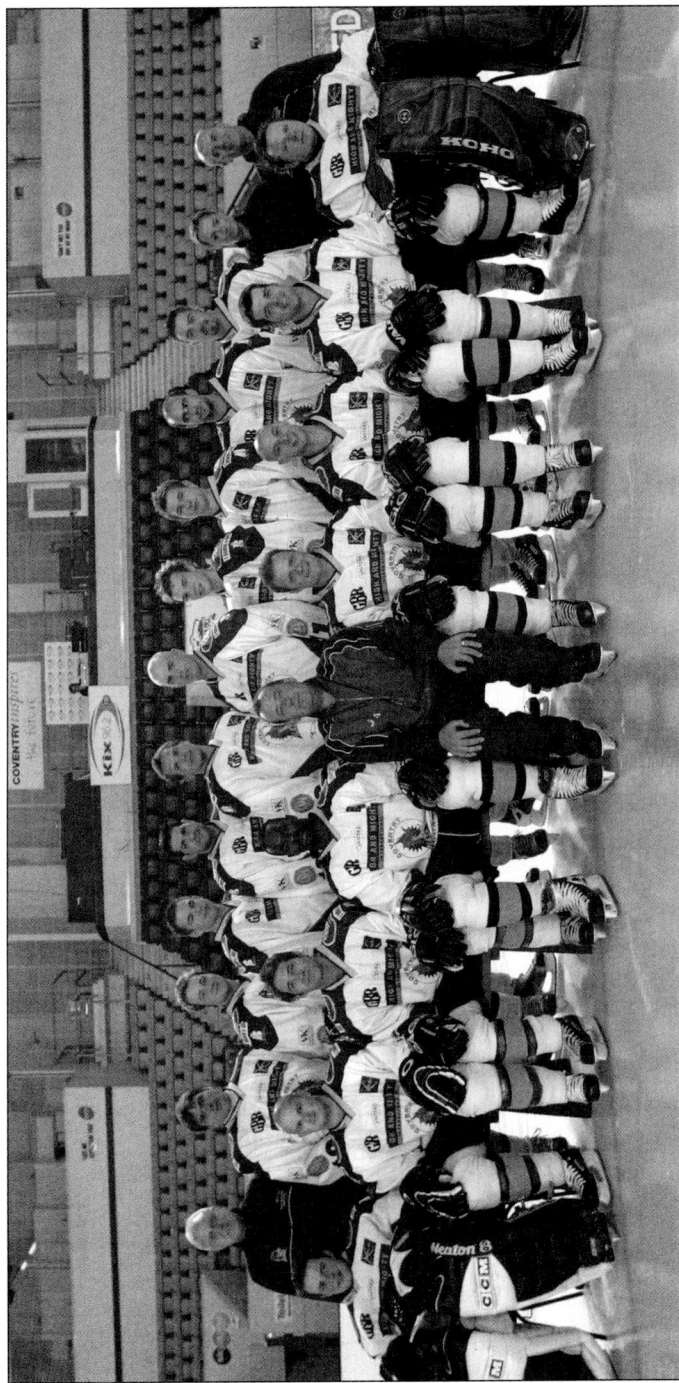

COVENTRY BLAZE *left to right*, *back row:* Steve Small (manager), Steve Chartrand, Adam Radmall, Steve O'Brien, Steve Gallace, Joel Poirier, Graham Schlender, Russ Cowley, Lee Richardson, Gareth Owen, Mathias Soderstrom, Sue Evans (physio), John Crook (equipment); *front row:* Alan Levers, Tom Watkins, Shaun Johnson, Hilton Ruggles, Paul Thompson (coach), Michael Tasker, Ashley Tait, Steve Carpenter, Jody Lehman.

Blaze amaze Elite

ANTONY HOPKER

An extraordinary year for Coventry Blaze ended with a feeling of disappointment as they failed to reach the Nottingham Playoff weekend. But looking back at the progress made in 12 months, there was plenty to cheer.

In the politicking of the summer, Blaze played a leading part in the formation of the new Elite League. The directors were adamant that the league would be a success, that it would help the club grow and that Coventry would be able to compete with the arena sides. And so it proved.

Blaze gave as good as they got from the opening day of the season. Flying to Belfast for the first time, they announced themselves with a convincing 5-2 win over the Giants.

The squad was largely the same as the one which had won the British National League the season before. In came **Steve O'Brien** and **Steve Gallace** from the North American ECHL, while **Graham Schlender** arrived from college in Canada to replace **Kurt Irvine**, who moved on after spending his entire career with the Blaze.

The season got off to a stuttering start. Coventry could indeed compete with the very best but perversely struggled against teams at the lower end of the table. The work rate was there but the individual quality was lacking.

Still, beating Sheffield 6-2 was a huge fillip; Blaze had a fantastic record against Nottingham; and they went the whole season undefeated against Belfast, beating them to third place.

Average crowds at the SkyDome rose above 2,300. But injuries proved a curse. **Steve Carpenter** was in and out all year, and **Shaun Johnson** and **Steve Chartrand** picked up knocks in a game against the Giants.

The forward shortage saw Gallace emerge as a leading scorer. His first game on the wing yielded a hat-trick and he went goal crazy for three months.

"I'm going to have words with his agent who passed him off as a defenceman," smiled coach **Paul Thompson** "If he'd been moved forward earlier he could be in the NHL by now!"

But Gallace's goals dried up and the team foundered in the run-in for the league. In January they missed a chance to overtake Sheffield at the top of the table.

Then they got off to a losing start to the playoffs when Thompson was banned for one game after a bench clearance in a meaningless final league contest against Cardiff Devils. Given the short nature of the competition, there wasn't enough time to regain momentum and Coventry finished winless in their group.

PLAYER AWARDS

Player of the Year	Steve O'Brien
Players' Player	Ashley Tait
Coach's Player	Joel Poirier
Best Forward	Joel Poirier
Best Defenceman	Steve O'Brien
Most Improved Player	Russ Cowley
Best British Player	Michael Tasker

LEADING PLAYERS

Steve O'Brien *born 26 July 1977*

Defender who sees the game with great clarity and was able to provide a defence-splitting pass. But his major contribution was his work rate: in some games he never seemed to leave the ice. He took his burden without complaining and chipped in with some vital points.

Joel Poirier *born 15 January 1975*

The team's most consistent player. When injuries hit, he converted from left-wing to centre and his unyielding effort won plaudits for a second successive season. His dedication provided much of the side's inspiration for the run-in when others lost their way.

Ashley Tait *born 9 August 1975*

The right-winger is perhaps the best British player around, scoring at a point-a-game pace in the league. His two-way game has also developed enormously in his two seasons under coach Thompson. Never stopped trying, even though he went through a lean period when the team struggled.

FACT FILE 2003-04

Elite League:	Third
Playoffs:	Third in group
Challenge Cup:	Fifth

HISTORY

Founded: 2000, after club moved from Solihull.

Leagues: Elite League 2003-04; British National League 2000-03.

DUNDEE STARS

PLAYER	ALL COMPETITIONS					FINDUS BRITISH NATIONAL LEAGUE					PLAYOFFS				
Scorers	GP	G	A	Pts	Pim	GP	G	A	Pts	Pim	GP	G	A	Pts	Pim
Dino Bauba (I)	57	24	47	71	182	35	18	30	48	122	10	3	4	7	26
Patric Lochi (I)	56	33	32	65	75	34	20	23	43	55	10	6	6	12	8
Jason Shmyr (I)	56	27	36	63	252	35	18	21	39	142	10	4	8	12	26
Derek DeCosty (I)	38	18	22	40	22	27	16	15	31	16	10	2	6	8	2
Paul Berrington	50	14	24	38	167	28	6	15	21	131	10	3	6	9	6
Gary Wishart	58	17	20	37	56	36	13	13	26	40	10	4	4	8	8
Dave Smith	50	10	11	21	24	28	7	9	16	8	10	2	1	3	6
John Downes	57	7	14	21	36	36	5	11	16	12	10	2	2	4	22
Johan Johansson (I)	58	3	18	21	22	36	2	16	18	14	10	0	1	1	2
Mark Thompson (I)	58	2	17	19	188	36	0	12	12	98	10	1	3	4	60
Paddy Ward	54	2	12	14	66	32	1	7	8	38	10	1	3	4	12
Scott Young	16	6	6	12	106	4	1	1	2	56					
Dominic Hopkins 2	41	2	8	10	26	32	1	7	8	22	9	1	1	2	4
John Dolan	42	4	5	9	2	31	4	2	6	2	9	0	3	3	0
Laurie Dunbar 1	8	0	2	2	0										
Andy Samuel	3	0	1	1	0	3	0	1	1	0					
Magnus Sjostrom (I)	5	0	1	1	6										
Craig Phillips	36	0	1	1	30	22	0	1	1	16	9	0	0	0	0
Dave Trofimenkoff (N) (I)	58	0	1	1	8	36	0	0	0	4	10	0	0	0	2
Chris Petrie	8	0	0	0	2	6	0	0	0	2					
Bench Penalties					8										4
TEAM TOTALS	58	169	278	447	1278	36	112	184	296	782	10	29	48	77	184

Netminders	GP	Mins	SOG	GA	Sv%	GP	Mins	SOG	GA	Sv%	GP	Mins	SOG	GA	Sv%
Dave Trofimenkoff (I)		3450	2002	204	89.8	36	2180	1293	135	89.6	10	570	313	32	89.8
Stewart Rugg		77	35	10	71.4	2	27	11	2	81.8	1	30	12	4	66.7
Empty Net Goals			5	5				3	3				1	1	
TEAM TOTALS	58	3527	2042	219	89.3	36	2207	1307	140	89.3	10	600	326	37	88.7

Also appeared: John Robertson

Also played for: 1 Edinburgh Capitals; 2 London Racers.

Shutouts: Trofimenkoff - league: 2 Nov v Newcastle Vipers (29 saves);
       cup: 10 Sept v Newcastle Vipers (37),
            14 Sept at Edinburgh Capitals (36).

All Competitions = league, playoffs and Findus Cup

Not so twinkly

ANDY HAMILTON

Stars' proud boast was that they were the only team to defeat the British National League champion side, Fife Flyers, home and away.

But in truth, victories over their local rivals were not enough to prevent the team who finished first two years ago and runners-up last time from having a disappointing season.

When player-coach **Tony Hand** departed for Edinburgh, his Canadian assistant **Roger Hunt** stepped up and pointed Stars in a different direction. A season of consolidation might be the kindest way of putting it.

Under the guidance of the Ward brothers, ice hockey has come a long way in Dundee, but falling crowds since their magnificent double-winning first season left Hunt without Hand's budget. Nevertheless, he put together a side capable of mixing with the best in a competitive league.

Surprisingly, it was their home form that let down the *Texol*-sponsored outfit. "I couldn't really put my finger on why that was the case," he admitted. "We played as hard every night as we have always done, but for some reason the Dundee Ice Arena was not the fortress for us that it has been in previous years, and that made it difficult for us to gain consistency."

YOUNG'S LEADERSHIP MISSED

Stars' cause was not helped by the loss of defensive lynch-pin **Scott Young** who was banned for the rest of the season after an altercation with a linesman at Hull in October. But the coach would not quite use that as a reason for their failure to land a trophy.

"It didn't help us, for sure," said Hunt, "but I felt we had enough talent in the side to overcome his loss. Maybe we lacked his leadership, because if there was one thing Scott brought to the team it was that never-say-die attitude. He was the heartbeat of the side and without him in the dressing room, maybe we didn't have that one player who could make a difference."

After failing to reach the latter stages of the *Findus* Cup, Dundee made a bright start to the league campaign. They were unbeaten in their opening ten games and were among the leading sides at Christmas.

But their performance fell away after that as influential players like **Paul Berrington** and **Derek DeCosty** missed large chunks of the season and the players were unable to pick up the pace in the playoffs when everyone was fit again.

PLAYER AWARDS

Player of the Year	**Johan Johansson**
Players' Player	**Dave Trofimenkoff**

LEADING PLAYERS

John Dolan

After beginning the season in the Scottish National League with Camperdown Stars, the young forward impressed Stars' coach in the Caledonian Cup games and established himself as a member of the squad. A player the Stars expect to be able to rely on in the future.

Paddy Ward *born 10 October 1984*

Signed from Edinburgh, the talented youngster, who played in Superleague with Ayr, became a fan favourite with quality performances that belied his years.

Gary Wishart *born 28 August 1981*

Still in his early 20s, he already has a great deal of experience. Became a reliable, mature player who finished as the team's leading British goal scorer.

FACT FILE 2003-04

British National League:	Sixth
Playoffs:	Sixth in qr-finals
Findus **Cup:**	Sixth
Caledonian Cup:	Fourth

HISTORY

Founded: 2001.

Leagues: *Findus* British National League 2001-04.

Honours: *Findus* British National League 2001-02; *Findus* Playoffs 2001-02; Caledonian Cup 2002.

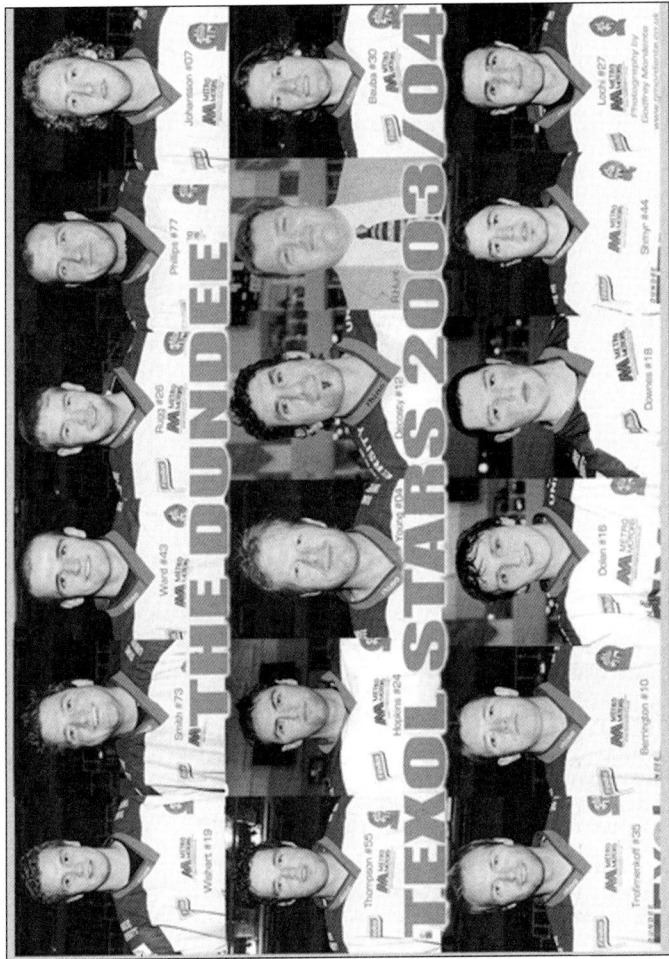

DUNDEE STARS *left to right, top row:* Gary Wishart, Dave Smith, Paddy Ward, Stewart Rugg, Craig Phillips, Johan Johansson; *middle row:* Mark Thompson, Dominic Hopkins, Scott Young, Derek DeCosty, Roger Hunt (coach), Dino Bauba; *front row:* Dave Trofimenkoff, Paul Berrington, John Dolan, John Downes, Jason Shmyr, Patric Lochi.

Photo: Godfrey Mordente

EDINBURGH CAPITALS

PLAYER	ALL COMPETITIONS					FINDUS BRITISH NATIONAL LEAGUE					PLAYOFFS				
Scorers	GP	G	A	Pts	Pim	GP	G	A	Pts	Pim	GP	G	A	Pts	Pim
Tony Hand	59	28	90	118	56	36	21	63	84	38	11	2	14	16	2
Adrian Saul (I)	56	42	39	81	44	35	31	32	63	22	11	9	2	11	4
Steven Kaye (I)	55	39	42	81	86	35	29	33	62	42	10	5	5	10	6
Martin Cingel (I)	57	33	34	67	76	33	18	25	43	38	12	9	5	14	32
Jan Krajicek (I)	53	17	35	52	44	29	12	26	38	28	12	2	6	8	8
Miroslav Droppa (I)	58	21	30	51	56	35	16	23	39	20	12	3	2	5	30
Mike Clarke (I)	60	7	22	29	42	36	5	12	17	16	12	0	6	6	6
Steven Lynch	60	6	16	22	28	36	2	10	12	20	12	2	3	5	6
Neil Hay	56	4	15	19	26	34	2	8	10	20	10	1	4	5	0
Laurie Dunbar 1	50	5	8	13	6	36	3	6	9	2	12	2	1	3	4
Iain Robertson	36	3	3	6	16	17	2	1	3	8	10	1	0	1	2
Craig Wilson	57	1	4	5	10	35	1	2	3	10	11	0	1	1	0
Lee Coyle	1	0	2	2	0						1	0	2	2	0
Ross Hay	46	1	1	2	0	28	1	1	2	0	10	0	0	0	0
Calum McBride	1	0	1	1	0						1	0	1	1	0
Daniel McIntyre	54	0	1	1	4	34	0	1	1	4	8	0	0	0	0
Ladislav Kudrna (N) (I)	60	0	1	1	8	36	0	1	1	6	12	0	0	0	2
David Beatson	55	0	0	0	46	34	0	0	0	26	11	0	0	0	6
Bench Penalties					12					12					
TEAM TOTALS	60	207	344	551	560	36	143	244	387	312	12	36	52	88	108
Netminders	GP	Mins	SOG	GA	Sv%	GP	Mins	SOG	GA	Sv%	GP	Mins	SOG	GA	Sv%
Blair Daly	2	6	6	0	100	1	2	2	0	100	1	4	4	0	100
Ryan Ford	2	40	24	1	95.8	2	40	24	1	95.8					
Ladislav Kudrna (I)	60	3592	1976	194	90.2	36	2156	1209	114	90.6	12	716	387	51	86.8
Empty Net Goals		6	6				2	2				1	1		
TEAM TOTALS	60	3638	2012	201	90.0	36	2198	1237	117	90.5	12	720	392	52	86.7

Also appeared: Alistair Flockhart (N), Calum Baker, Kevin Forshall, Steven Francey, Lewis Christie, Lewis Glasgon, Mark McRae, Sean Lamb.

Also played for: 1 Dundee Stars

Shutouts: Kudrna - league: 29 Nov at Hull Stingrays (23 saves),
7 Feb at Newcastle Vipers (23);
playoffs: 7 Mar v Guildford Flames (34).

All Competitions = league, playoffs and Findus Cup

EDINBURGH CAPITALS *left to right,* *back row:* Iain Robertson, Mike Clarke, Tony Hand, Daniel McIntyre; *middle row:* David Beatson snr, Ryan Ford, Ross Hay, Miroslav Droppa, Jan Krajicek, David Beatson, Craig Wilson, Les Gray; *front row:* Ladislav Kudrna, Steven Kaye, Martin Cingel, Keith Butland (club webmaster), Steven Lynch, Adrian Saul, Ali Flockhart.

Photo: Jan Orkisz.

Hand raises his Caps

ANDY HAMILTON

Edinburgh's general manager **Scott Neil** pulled off one of the summer's biggest signings when he persuaded **Tony Hand** to make an emotional return to his home town club.

The move paid off handsomely as the Murrayfield legend led from the front and coached the club to their best ever *Findus* British National League campaign.

The Caps already had a good import base with two Czechs, netminder **Ladislav Kudrna** and top defender **Jan Krajicek**, Slovakian forward **Martin Cingel**, and Canadians **Adrian Saul** and **Steven Kaye**. To these Neil added a good pair of defencemen in Canadian **Michael Clarke** and **Miroslav Droppa** from Liptovsky Mikulas in the Slovakian Extraleague.

After the new players got some Findus Cup games under their belts, they made a great start to the league campaign when a road trip to Bracknell and Guildford yielded maximum points.

Consistency was the key to Edinburgh's success throughout the league season and only twice did they lose two games in a row, while a run of six consecutive away victories at the turn of the year was pivotal in their eventual third place finish. With Hand in the side, they were always a threat in front of goal. His partnership with Saul and Kaye was one of the league's most potent attacking lines.

There was also some silverware for the club as they captured the now traditional Capital Cup over Christmas, defeating Newcastle in the semi-final and then Dundee in the short-format tournament.

They justified their high league finish with a Playoff Championship semi-final appearance which was achieved despite very mixed fortunes in the opening round. They lost only once at home (to in-form Bracknell) but picked up only one point on their travels (in Newcastle).

In the semis, they failed to repeat their league successes against the Flames and bowed out to the eventual champions.

"We maintained our improvement from the previous season," said Neil at the end of the campaign, "but we felt we could have done better at a crucial stage of the season.

"Maybe we don't have the budget of some of the sides that finished below us, but we got a good return for our investment from the players. A third place finish for a club like Edinburgh means we're on the right lines."

PLAYER AWARDS

Player Of The Year	**Tony Hand MBE**
Players' Player	**Miroslav Droppa**
Supporters' Player	**Miroslav Droppa**
Scottish Nat'l Lge Player	**Steven Francy**

LEADING PLAYERS

Miroslav Droppa *born 17 February 1977*
The Slovakian defender quickly settled into his new surroundings and had much to do with the success achieved by the Capitals. Formed an outstanding partnership with **Jan Krajicek**, which made the Edinburgh side difficult to beat.

Laurie Dunbar *born 22 September 1977*
Had an exceptional time with the Capitals after returning from an 18 months spell in Dundee and became an integral part of the second line in the latter part of the season.

Neil Hay *born 11 August 1981*
Profited from the experience of playing alongside Tony Hand on the first line and the confidence of the talented youngster grew as the campaign wore on. Edinburgh should benefit from his improvement for many seasons.

FACT FILE 2003-04

British National League:	Third
Playoffs:	Semi-finalists
***Findus* Cup:**	Seventh
Caledonia Cup:	Finalists

HISTORY

Founded: 1998. Previous teams in the Murrayfield rink were: *Murrayfield Royals* 1995-98 and 1952-66, *Edinburgh Racers* 1994-95; *Murrayfield Racers* 1966-94.

Leagues: *Capitals* - Findus British National Lge 1998-2004; *Royals* - British National Lge 1997-98, Northern Premier Lge 1996-97, British Lge, Div One 1995-96, British Lge 1954-55, Scottish National Lge 1952-54; *Racers* - British Lge, Premier Div 1982-95, Northern Lge 1966-82.

Past Honours: *Racers* - See *The Ice Hockey Annual 1998-99*.

FIFE FLYERS

PLAYER	ALL COMPETITIONS					FINDUS BRITISH NATIONAL LEAGUE					PLAYOFFS				
Scorers	GP	G	A	Pts	Pim	GP	G	A	Pts	Pim	GP	G	A	Pts	Pim
Karry Biette (I)	59	36	44	80	135	33	23	25	48	81	12	7	8	15	22
Dan Goneau (I)	47	32	47	79	68	33	22	37	59	42	2	1	0	1	2
Todd Dutiaume (I)	63	33	42	75	50	36	21	21	42	28	12	5	8	13	12
Paul Spadafora (I)	51	19	31	50	294	35	12	23	35	116	9	5	5	10	96
Mark Morrison (I)	61	20	27	47	62	34	13	19	32	30	12	5	3	8	10
Steven King	59	17	28	45	56	34	11	18	29	28	11	3	4	7	16
Greg Kuznik (I)	63	13	26	39	62	36	10	18	28	28	12	2	5	7	4
John Haig	63	12	25	37	80	36	8	13	21	62	12	2	6	8	2
Ian Fletcher (I)	57	8	27	35	36	30	3	19	22	20	12	2	4	6	0
Kyle Horne	63	3	16	19	20	36	2	12	14	16	12	0	3	3	0
Darryl Venters	63	7	10	17	16	36	4	8	12	10	12	1	2	3	4
Derek King	60	2	8	10	12	34	2	6	8	6	11	0	1	1	4
Andy Finlay	58	4	5	9	26	36	4	4	8	16	7	0	1	1	4
Adam Walker	52	1	4	5	0	31	0	4	4	0	8	1	0	1	0
Steve Briere (N) (I)	63	0	3	3	14	36	0	3	3	14	12	0	0	0	0
Euan Forsyth	48	0	2	2	2	29	0	2	2	2	7	0	0	0	0
Bench Penalties					4					2					0
TEAM TOTALS	63	207	345	552	937	36	135	232	367	501	12	34	50	84	176
Netminders	GP	Mins	SOG	GA	Sv%	GP	Mins	SOG	GA	Sv%	GP	Mins	SOG	GA	Sv%
Steve Briere (I)	63	3810	2026	170	91.6	36	2210	1170	96	91.8	12	720	383	27	93.0
Craig Arthur	1	30	18	4	77.8										
Empty Net Goals			1	1				1	1						
TEAM TOTALS	63	3840	2045	175	91.4	36	2210	1171	97	91.7	12	720	383	27	93.0

Also appeared: Lee Mitchell, Thomas Muir, Jamie Wilson, Mike Haston (N), Chad Reekie (1)

Also played for: 1 Chelmsford Chieftains.

Shutouts: Briere - cup: 12 Oct at Dundee Stars (33 saves);
league: 15 Nov v Edinburgh Capitals (26),
20 Dec v Newcastle Vipers (34);
playoffs: 6 Mar v Bracknell Bees (27), 13 March v Dundee Stars (30)

All Competitions = league, playoffs and Findus Cup

A Dan good season

MATTHEW ELDER Fife Free Press

The 2003-04 season marked a return to the top for Britain's oldest surviving club. Under the leadership of long-serving coach **Mark Morrison**, Flyers held off stiff competition to win the *Findus* British National League title on the second to last day of the season.

Around 200 supporters invaded Hull on 28 February for a nail-biting overtime victory that wrapped up their second title in four attempts.

Morrison, 40, in his eighth year as player-coach, admitted that the run-in had taken its toll. "Of all the championships I have won since I came to Fife this is the one that I'm glad is over because it just never seemed to end," he said. "But the players, many of whom were carrying injuries for a long time, persevered through it."

The season started with disappointment as a penalty shoot-out defeat to Newcastle Vipers robbed them of a place in the *Findus* Cup final. But they recovered to win their opening league match 4-1 at home to Stingrays and didn't look back. Within two months they had raced to a ten-point lead and there was talk of them winning the championship before Christmas.

With new front man, ex-New York Ranger **Dan Goneau**, firing on all cylinders and fellow Canadian **Greg Kuznik** emerging as one of the most consistent defencemen in the league, the side were unstoppable. They enjoyed an amazing run of 12 games without defeat, 11 of which were victories.

Guildford Flames were the Fifers' fiercest competition and they reduced the gap at the top of the table to just one point. But Flyers held their nerve to cross the finish line in first place.

"Our will to win was better than anyone else's and that's why we won it," explained Morrison. "We won the biggest trophy of the year – it's the one that shows you are the best team for the season."

Naturally, Morrison had hoped to add the playoff title to the league championship. Fife finished strongly in the quarter-finals but their semi-final draw against Bracknell Bees was not the one they would have chosen. With a number of players unable to travel due to work commitments, their away form against southern clubs had been shaky with only three wins all season.

But apart from a hiccup in the Cup, Flyers had always handled Bees at home, so it was a huge disappointment when Bracknell won 3-2 in Kirkcaldy. Another defeat in the return leg, though not as surprising, was just as depressing.

PLAYER AWARDS
Mirror of Merit   Dan Goneau

LEADING PLAYERS
Steve Briere *born 25 March 1977*
Every successful team needs a reliable netminder and Briere filled that role for Fife. Big saves in important matches helped his side to the league title, while a save percentage of 91.79 confirmed his position as the league's number one goalie.

Dan Goneau *born 16 January 1976*
Nobody in the league came close to matching the pace and skill of the Montreal-born centreman who played 53 games with New York Rangers, his coach's old team. Despite missing most of the playoffs through injury, he was runner-up in the club's scoring.

Greg Kuznik *born 12 June 1978*
An imposing figure in defence, his strength is his biggest asset. Some of the league's most feared snipers never got a sniff of the puck when he was around. His powerful shot contributed 13 goals.

FACT FILE 2003-04
British National League: Winners
Playoffs: Semi-finalists
***Findus* Cup**   Fourth
Caledonian Cup: Winners

HISTORY
Founded: 1938.
Leagues: (*Findus*) British National League (BNL) 1997-2004; Northern Premier League (NPL) 1996-97; British League 1982-96, 1954-55; Northern League (NL) 1966-82; Scottish National League (SNL) 1981-82, 1946-54, 1938-40.
Major Honours:
British Champions 1985.
Leagues: BNL 2003-04, 1999-2000; NPL 1997-98, 1996-97; British Lge, Div. One 1991-92; NL 1976-78; SNL 1951-52, 1939-40.
Playoffs: BNL 1999-2000, 1998-99.
Findus Challenge Cup: 2001-02; *Autumn Cup*: 1978, 1976, 1975; Scottish - 1950, 1948. *Scottish Cup*: 2001, 2000, 1999, 1998, 1995, 1994.

FIFE FLYERS *left to right, back row:* Fiona Cameron (physio), Allan Grubb (trainer), Mark Morrison (coach), Adam Walker, Euan Forsyth, Dan Goneau, Allan Anderson (bench coach); *middle row:* Lee Mitchell, Tom Muir jnr, Paul Spadafora, Daryl Venters, Greg Kuznik, Todd Dutiaume; *front row (kneeling):* Ian Fletcher, Derek King, Andy Finlay, Steven King, Karry Biette (asst coach), Craig Arthur, Kyle Horne; *in front:* Steve Briere, John Haig.

Photo: Fife Free Press

GUILDFORD FLAMES

PLAYER	ALL COMPETITIONS					FINDUS BRITISH NATIONAL LEAGUE					PLAYOFFS				
Scorers	GP	G	A	Pts	Pim	GP	G	A	Pts	Pim	GP	G	A	Pts	Pim
Milos Melicherik (I)	65	36	48	84	94	36	19	28	47	48	14	10	12	22	18
Ryan Vince (I)	65	41	38	79	66	36	22	18	40	26	14	7	12	19	18
Jozef Kohut (I)	63	35	30	65	130	35	20	18	38	86	13	11	9	20	12
Ratislav Palov (I)	56	25	33	58	18	36	16	20	36	12	5	2	2	4	0
Paul Dixon	61	10	40	50	16	35	7	20	27	8	12	2	8	10	2
Peter Konder (I)	49	12	34	46	74	32	9	22	31	66	14	3	10	13	6
Marian Smerciak (I)	63	12	28	40	66	36	4	20	24	30	14	3	6	9	20
Nick Cross	65	12	25	37	92	36	6	14	20	28	14	4	7	11	34
Rick Plant	51	11	22	33	20	36	9	14	23	12					
Neil Liddiard	65	3	22	25	130	36	3	14	17	80	14	0	5	5	22
Dominic Parlatore (I)	17	10	12	22	58	5	3	4	7	6					
Peter Michnac (I)	57	6	16	22	78	28	3	10	13	36	14	2	2	4	14
Mark Galazzi	62	12	8	20	38	33	5	5	10	16	14	3	3	6	14
Tony Redmond	38	3	17	20	12	15	1	6	7	0	14	1	6	7	6
Scott Levins (I)	21	11	5	16	56	10	7	4	11	28	11	4	1	5	28
Stan Marple	44	2	9	11	177	21	2	2	4	65	8	0	3	3	45
Frank Evans	4	0	1	1	4	4	0	1	1	4					
Stevie Lyle (N)	65	0	0	0	18	36	0	0	0	4	14	0	0	0	12
Rick Skene	5	0	0	0	2	4	0	0	0	2	1	0	0	0	0
Bench Penalties					10					2					0
TEAM TOTALS	65	241	388	629	1159	36	136	220	356	559	14	52	86	138	251
Netminders	GP	Mins	SOG	GA	Sv%	GP	Mins	SOG	GA	Sv%	GP	Mins	SOG	GA	Sv%
Stevie Lyle	65	3916	1777	157	91.2	36	2179	965	86	91.1	14	840	402	28	93.0
Joe Dollin	3	18	11	2	81.8	2	12	5	0	100					
Empty Net Goals			2	2				2	2						
TEAM TOTALS	65	3934	1790	161	91.0	36	2191	972	88	90.9	14	840	402	28	93.0

Also appeared: Simon Lavis (N), Mike Timms, Joe White (N), Chris Wiggins.

Shutouts: Lyle - league: 29 Nov v Bracknell Bees (27 saves),
20 Dec v Dundee Stars (19), 14 Jan at Newcastle Vipers (25),
11 Feb v Hull Stingrays (21);
playoffs: 6 March v Edinburgh Capitals (27)

All Competitions = league, playoffs and Findus *Cup*

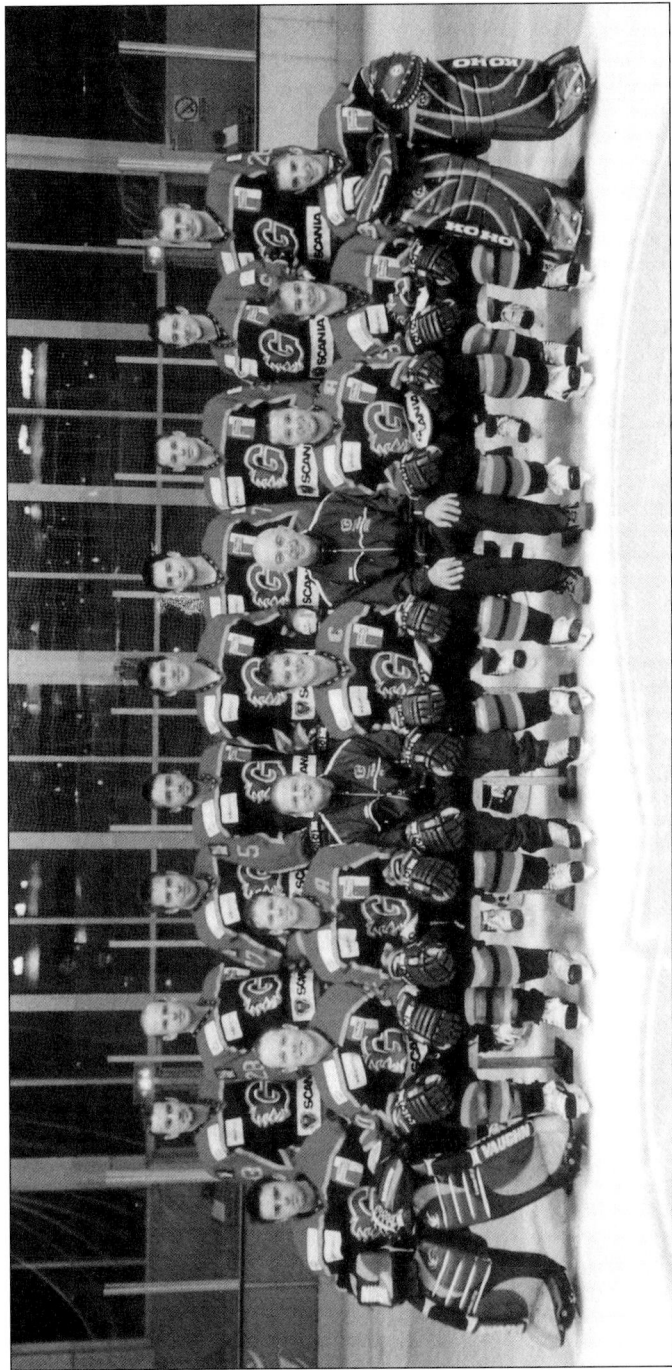

GUILDFORD FLAMES **left to right**, *back row*: Peter Konder, Jozef Kohut, Rick Plant, Marian Smerciak, Nick Cross, Mark Galazzi, Peter Michnac, Neil Liddiard, Rastislav Palov; *front row*: Stevie Lyle, Tony Redmond, Ryan Vince, Stan Marple (coach), Paul Dixon, Dave Wiggins (asst manager), Milos Melicherik, Michael Timms, Joe Dollin.

Saviours from the East

ROGER PECK

When coach **Stan Marple** said he would bring in imports from eastern Europe, few realised that the six Slovakians would help the Flames to their most successful *Findus* British National League season for three years.

Milos Melicherik, Rastislav Palov and **Jozef Kohut** were the forwards, with **Marian Smerciak** and young **Peter Michnac** on defence. Completing the Slovak crew later on was Edinburgh's leading scorer, **Peter Konder**.

Apart from **Paul Dixon, Tony Redmond** and **Rick Plant**, Marple made a clean sweep of his squad. In came Canadian forwards **Ryan Vince** from the ECHL's Dayton Bombers and **Domenic Parlatore** who was previously in Paisley and Hull.

Rounding out the club were three GB internationals: netminder **Stevie Lyle**, who had just taken Cardiff Devils to the playoff finals, defenceman **Neil Liddiard** and forward **Nick Cross** from Basingstoke Bison.

The season began on a high note as Flames finished on top of the *Findus* Cup table. In a dramatic semi-final weekend they fought off fierce local rivals, Bracknell Bees, to win on Cross's overtime goal. Their trip to the final in Newcastle, however, was an anti-climax as they went down 6-1 to the Vipers.

Worse still, the defeat fell in the middle of a four-game losing run in the league that eventually proved crucial in preventing the club from heading the league table.

In the New Year Marple added some size to his squad with 6ft, 4in, 235lb forward **Scott Levins** from Sheffield's Superleague side.

At last, on 11 January, Flames snapped their losing run and won 16 of their final 21 league games, making up 14 points on the league-leading Fife Flyers. The season ended a weekend too early with the Flames just one point behind the Scots.

The playoffs were the last chance for the bridesmaids to win some silverware. Their strong finish to the league carried over into March and they didn't disappoint, leading the playoff table after the first round.

They eased past **Tony Hand**'s Edinburgh side in their semi, and Bees stunned Flyers in the other, setting up the perfect local derby final. That's when the Slovaks really proved their worth. With the sides tied late in the second leg, Smerciak and Melicherik gave Flames a 9-7 aggregate victory and the coveted playoff trophy.

PLAYER AWARDS

Player of the Year	**Milos Melicherik**
Player's Player	**Ryan Vince**
Best British Player	**Paul Dixon**
Most Sportsmanlike Player	**Paul Dixon**
Top Points Scorer	**Milos Melicherik**

LEADING PLAYERS

Paul Dixon *born 4 August 1973*
Appointed assistant coach he combined these duties with his usual consistent defensive play. Was voted best British player by both his team-mates and the fans.

Milos Melicherik *born 7 October 1974*
The first season in the UK for this gifted playmaking centreman who had spent several seasons in the Slovakian Extraliga. A firm favourite with fans at the Spectrum, he finished as the team's leading points scorer.

Marian Smerciak *born 24 Dec 1972*
Another Slovak debutant and the most experienced. Combined his controlled defensive work with a dynamic shot, scoring several vital goals from the blue-line.

FACT FILE 2003-04
British National League:	Runners-up
Playoffs:	Champions
***Findus* Cup**	Finalists

HISTORY
Founded: 1992.
Leagues: (*Findus*) British National League (BNL) 1997-2004; Premier League (PL) 1996-97; British League, Div. One 1993-96; English League 1992-93.
Honours: BNL and Playoffs 2000-01, 1997-98; *ntl* Cup 2000-01; B&H Plate 1998-99.

HULL STINGRAYS

PLAYER	ALL COMPETITIONS					FINDUS BRITISH NATIONAL LEAGUE				
Scorers	GP	G	A	Pts	Pim	GP	G	A	Pts	Pim
Slava Koulikov 3	46	24	28	52	38	34	18	15	33	28
Andrei Nikolaev (I)	46	21	30	51	24	34	15	21	36	0
Evgeny Alipov (I)	46	14	24	38	52	36	8	18	26	42
Pavel Gomenyuk (I)	48	11	18	29	78	36	6	11	17	58
Slava Timchenko (I)	43	9	17	26	68	31	5	10	15	46
Brent Pope	45	5	18	23	186	33	4	15	19	122
Dru Burgess	17	5	8	13	10	17	5	8	13	10
Mike Bowman	46	5	7	12	8	36	3	7	10	8
Noel Burkitt (I) 1	27	5	6	11	24	15	1	4	5	8
Rick Strachan	20	2	6	8	6	20	2	6	8	6
Linus Schellin (I)	19	1	7	8	20	8	0	1	1	4
Stephen Johnson	26	2	5	7	20	15	0	2	2	12
Mark Florence	48	2	4	6	8	36	2	0	2	4
Kevin Phillips	44	0	4	4	26	32	0	3	3	24
Andy Munroe	48	2	1	3	16	36	2	0	2	10
Stuart Brittle 4	42	0	1	1	4	30	0	1	1	2
Karl Hopper 3	48	0	1	1	40	36	0	0	0	26
Anders Hogberg (N) 1	21	0	0	0	10	21	0	0	0	10
Bench Penalties					16					12
TEAM TOTALS	48	108	185	293	654	36	71	122	193	432
Netminders	GP	Mins	SOG	GA	Sv%	GP	Mins	SOG	GA	Sv%
Anders Hogberg 1	20	1231	677	63	90.7	20	1231	677	63	90.7
Pasi Raitanen 2	26	1528	770	92	88.1	14	844	387	57	85.3
Sam Roberts	5	175	88	22	75.0	4	139	74	18	75.7
Empty Net Goals			4	4				4	4	
TEAM TOTALS	48	2933	1539	181	88.2	36	2213	1142	142	87.6

Also appeared: Dave Phillips, Dave Pyatt, Tristian Rodgers (N), Luke Boothroyd, Nathan Hunt.

Also played for: 1 London Racers; 2 Newcastle Vipers, Sheffield Steelers; 3 Chelmsford Chieftains; 4 Telford Wild Foxes.

Shutouts: Raitanen - cup: 12 Oct at Edinburgh Capitals (46 saves); Hogberg - league: 28 Dec v Guildford Flames (40 saves)

All Competitions = league and Findus Cup

Troubles Packed up

CATHY WIGHAM

Hull Stingrays had nothing to brag about on the scale of sporting achievements in 2003-04. Finishing bottom by 20 points with just four wins and three draws from 36 league games hardly set the pulse racing.

To those outside hockey it would appear an embarrassing effort. To those inside it was more of a triumph for Milton Keynes-based owners **Mike and Sue Pack** and coach **Rick Strachan**.

The optimism stems not from the league table, but the fact that the club survived without the financial embarrassments and mid-season player exodus which dogged previous regimes.

Arriving in April 2003, the Packs promised stability with a capital 'S' and that the club would see the season out. Sceptics had seen it all before. But Christmas came and went . . . and Stingrays were still in business . . . with the novelty of signing, not axing, players over the festive period.

The seasonal highlights included victories over Guildford, a 6-1 thrashing of Dundee and a 4-1 challenge match win over Sheffield Steelers.

There were certainly other nights to forget, most usually at Guildford's Spectrum or in Edinburgh. But Stingrays were rarely embarrassed, competed in most games and provided plenty of highlights.

They also showed it wasn't necessary to spend a fortune to unearth talent, bringing in a Ukrainian contingent which included Olympic defenceman **Slava Timchenko**, world championship forwards **Andrei Nikolaev** and **Pavel Gomenyuk**, plus veteran **Evgeny Alipov**.

Despite the mid-season switch of ineffective forward **Noel Burkitt** for Canadian **Dru Burgess**, keeper **Pasi Raitanen** for **Anders Hogberg** and Swede **Linus Schellin** for Strachan, wins proved elusive.

In the end, Stingrays were always one or two players short of turning a just losing team into a winning one. The chronic problem was goal-scoring, with points particularly sparse from the British contingent. It didn't help having three imports on defence or having the ageing legs of Alipov (38) and Strachan (40) up front.

Nevertheless, Mike Pack - who holds a full-time job down in London - could look back and feel he's done what it said on the tin.

"We're tired a lot of the time," he said, "but if we didn't enjoy it we'd be total fruitcakes to keep it going. We achieved our number one objective and that was to finish the year without any financial disasters, no embarrassments for Hull or for ice hockey."

PLAYER AWARDS

Player of the Year	**Evgeny Alipov**
Best Defenceman	**Brent Pope**
Best Forward	**Andrei Nikolaev**
Most Improved Player	**Mike Bowman**
Spirit of the Game	**Stephen Johnson**

LEADING PLAYERS

Dru Burgess *born 7 December 1974*

The epitome of a hardworking, two-way hockey player, he arrived in January after a long-running passport wrangle and slotted seamlessly onto whatever line he played. Had an eye for goal and was a real motivating force on the bench.

Andrei Nikolaev *born 18 September 1972*

With an excellent shot, the Ukrainian finished as top goal scorer. He would have had even more but for a tendency to pass too much. Also an excellent penalty killer and probably the team's most consistent player.

Vyacheslav Timchenko *b. 16 Aug 1971*

The defenceman simply oozed class as befits a Pool A world championship and Olympic defenceman. He was easily the best blueliner, with silky stick skills, an unruffled temperament and an uncanny ability to irritate opponents.

FACT FILE 2003-04

British National League:	Seventh
Playoffs:	Did not qualify
Findus **Cup:**	Fifth in qr-finals

HISTORY

Founded: April 2003 by **Mike** and **Sue Pack**. The first club in Hull was *Humberside Seahawks* 1988-96 (known as Humberside Hawks 1993-96). Second club was *Kingston Hawks* 1996-99 (briefly Hull City Hawks 1998-99). Third club was *Hull Thunder* 1999-2003.

Leagues: *Stingrays* - British National League 2003-04; *Thunder* - British National League 1999-2003; *Kingston* - British National Lge 1997-99, Premier Lge 1996-97; *Humberside* - British Lge, Premier Div. 1991-96, British Lge, Div. One 1989-91, English Lge 1988-89.

Honours: *Humberside Hawks:* British League, Div. One 1990-91; English League 1988-89.

HULL STINGRAYS *left to right,* *back row:* Rick Strachan (coach), Noel Burkitt, Linus Schellin, Andrei Nikolaev, Slava Timchenko, Brent Pope, Karl Hopper, David Phillips, Andy Munroe, Kevin Phillips, Pavel Gomenyuk, Ken Jennison (equipment); *front row:* Pasi Raitanen, Stuart Brittle, Michael Bowman, Stephen Johnson, Slava Koulikov, Evgeny Alipov, Mark Florence, Sam Roberts.

Photo: Arthur Foster.

LONDON RACERS

PLAYER	ALL COMPETITIONS					ELITE LEAGUE				
Scorers	GP	G	A	Pts	Pim	GP	G	A	Pts	Pim
Mark Long (I)	55	13	15	28	76	55	13	15	28	76
Kalle Konsti (I)	48	19	8	27	4	48	19	8	27	4
Jani Touminen (I)	56	10	16	26	38	56	10	16	26	38
Erik Zachrisson (I)	56	8	10	18	46	56	8	10	18	46
Mark Scott (I)	31	6	11	17	36	31	6	11	17	36
Mojmir Musil (I)	31	8	8	16	12	31	8	8	16	12
Lukas Filip (I)	52	6	9	15	63	52	6	9	15	63
Brian McLaughlin (I)	56	2	13	15	44	56	2	13	15	44
Nick Burton	42	5	9	14	32	42	5	9	14	32
Warren Tait	52	5	8	13	36	52	5	8	13	36
Reine Rauhala (I)	20	3	9	12	10	20	3	9	12	10
Noel Burkitt (I)	16	4	6	10	20	16	4	6	10	20
Norman Pinnington 1	30	3	4	7	68	30	3	4	7	68
Jason Robinson (I) 2	33	3	4	7	94	33	3	4	7	94
Zoran Kozic 3	10	3	3	6	8	10	3	3	6	8
Markus Niemi (I)	19	2	3	5	52	19	2	3	5	52
Mike McKinnon (I)	52	1	4	5	97	52	1	4	5	97
Sean Murdoch (I)	8	2	1	3	2	8	2	1	3	2
Ville Kiiskinen (I)	11	1	2	3	6	11	1	2	3	6
Martin Sellgren (I)	12	1	1	2	24	12	1	1	2	24
Jani Touminen (I)	14	1	1	2	18	14	1	1	2	18
Timo Hurskainen (I)	9	0	1	1	4	9	0	1	1	4
Jouni Saarinen (I)	10	0	1	1	2	10	0	1	1	2
Dominic Hopkins 4	4	0	0	0	2	4	0	0	0	2
Niklas Ekman (I)	8	0	0	0	8	8	0	0	0	8
Anders Hogberg (N)(I) 6	17	0	0	0	8	17	0	0	0	8
Chris Bailey 5	31	0	0	0	71	31	0	0	0	71
Evan Lindsay (N) (I)	35	0	0	0	4	35	0	0	0	4
Bench Penalties					75					75
TEAM TOTALS	56	106	147	253	960	56	106	147	253	960
Netminders	GPI	Min	SOG	GA	Sv%	GPI	Min	SOG	GA	Sv%
Evan Lindsay (I)	35	1920	1264	136	89.2	35	1920	1264	136	89.2
Anders Hogberg (I) 6	17	995	591	73	87.6	17	995	591	73	87.6
Matt van de Velden	11	338	197	29	85.3	11	338	197	29	85.3
Markus Maier	2	120	61	10	83.6	2	120	61	10	83.6
Empty Net Goals			5	5				5	5	
TEAM TOTALS	56	3373	2118	253	88.1	56	3373	2118	253	88.1

Also appeared: Tom Wills (N) (3), James Day.

Also played for: 1 Basingstoke Bison; 2 Newcastle Vipers;
3 Slough Jets; 4 Dundee Stars; 5 Sheffield Steelers;
6 Hull Stingrays.

Shutouts: Lindsay - league: 30 Jan v Cardiff Devils (41 saves),
2 Mar v Basingstoke Bison (39).

All Competitions = league and Challenge Cup

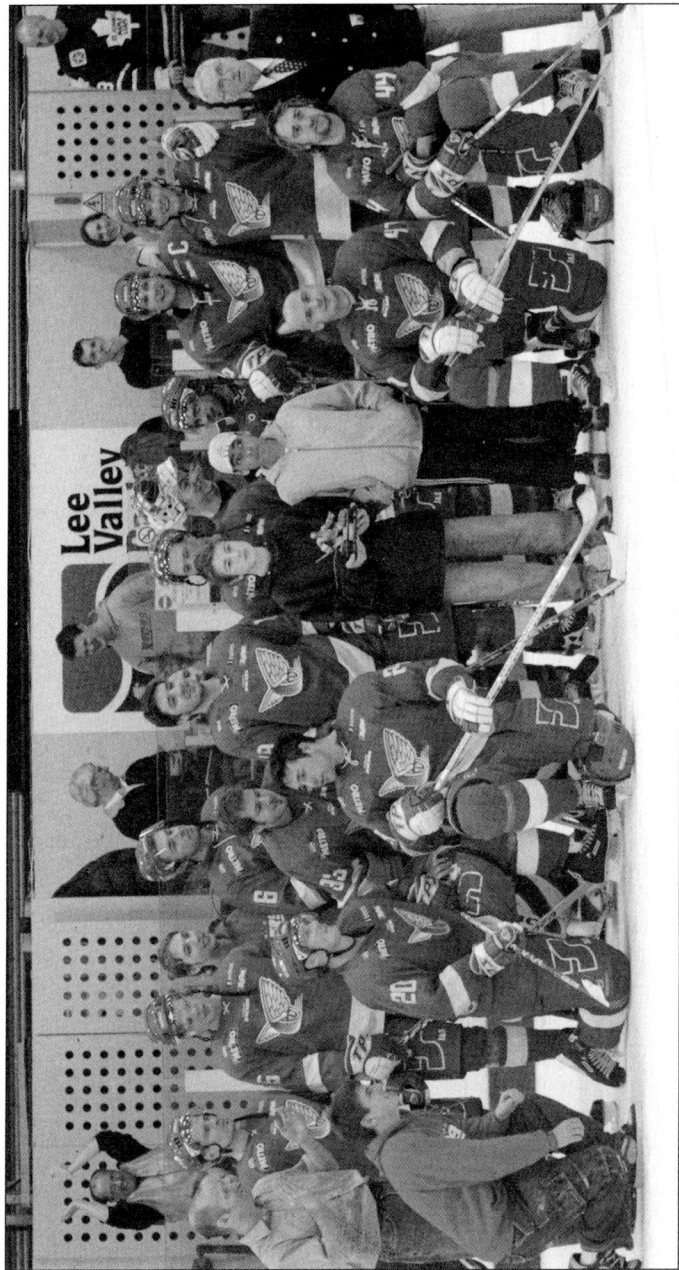

LONDON RACERS *left to right*, back row *(standing)*: Roger Black (chairman), Jani Touminen, Kalle Konsti, [equipment manager], Chris Bailey, Lukas Filip, Noel Burkitt *(behind Filip)*, Marc Long, Evan Lindsay, Warren Tait, Erik Zacrisson (captain), Mark Scott, Dave Richards Snr; front row *(players)*: Mike McKinnon, Matt van der Velden, Jason Robinson (coach), Mojmir Musil, Brian McLaughlin.

Photo: Diane Davey

Moving times

DAN WARD

Racers endured much, yet prevailed, in their inaugural season in the new Elite League.

The trauma of three coaches, three general managers, two rinks and a roster of 32 players - including three starting netminders - helped make the campaign truly unforgettable. But it was the never-say-die spirit of the players and management which made the similarly determined fans forever grateful that they kept top-flight hockey in the capital.

Racers evolved out of the English Premier League's Haringey Racers who iced at Alexandra Palace in north London. With the simultaneous demise of London Knights and the Superleague there was a very small window of opportunity to put together a team to keep the city represented at the top level.

Racers initially shared ice-time at Ally Pally with the Haringey side who acted as the farm team for the Elite outfit. At the end of October, however, they moved to Lee Valley Ice Centre in east London, which provided improved facilities. Unfortunately, the move couldn't accommodate the Haringey team who were forced to disband. Racers worked hard to find alternative contracts for their released players and in so doing built a strong relationship with the EPL's Slough Jets where a number of former Racers found a home.

London's Swedish coach, **Peter Ekroth**, who took charge just days before the season opener, had the unenviable task of asking a team he had not selected to play a system they had to learn on the job.

While the league was competitive in the early weeks, a gap began to grow between Racers and the rest as they reached game 14 before registering their first point, a 4-4 tie with the visiting Coventry Blaze.

The move to Lee Valley helped the team to settle but the fans were not flocking to see a side who, though winless, had a prodigious work-rate.

When defenceman **Jason Robinson** arrived from the BNL's Newcastle Vipers, the Canadian did not realise his new team had yet to win. Within weeks he had a further shock with the news that Ekroth was leaving, and he was asked to take charge. The 25-year-old seized the opportunity and the side became more competitive, although they still had to wait for that first elusive win.

By the close of the season Racers had three wins and 10 points, but a lot more pride than their league position suggested.

PLAYER AWARDS

Most Points:	Marc Long
Most Goals:	Kalle Konsti
Most Assists:	Jani Touminen

LEADING PLAYERS

Evan Lindsay born 15 May 1979

The talented, twice-drafted netminder would have had fonder memories of London if the team had employed more than one solid defensive line in front of him. Though the shot count he faced inevitably took its toll, he remained upbeat, professional and a fan favourite who will always be welcome in the UK.

Jason Robinson born 22 August 1978

The defender came to London with an experienced hockey mind and the size and willpower to make a difference. Though relatively young, he took over the coaching reins and was a success in the locker-room, on the ice and with the fans. Quiet and plain speaking, he let his play do the talking.

Warren Tait born 17 April 1981

Revelling in his ice-time, the forward made huge advances in his play. One of the team's most consistent performers and their best British player, he grabbed the opportunity to learn from the imported players alongside him.

Racers appeared on *CNN*'s World of Sport in early January. The programme is seen round the world and Racers received an e-mail from the *China Daily* newspaper who wanted to run an article on the team and British ice hockey. [No, we've no idea why, either.]
Powerplay

FACT FILE 2003-04
Elite League: Eighth
Playoffs: did not qualify
Challenge Cup: Eighth in qr-finals

HISTORY
Founded: 2003.
League: Elite League 2003-04.

MANCHESTER PHOENIX

PLAYER	ALL COMPETITIONS					ELITE LEAGUE					PLAYOFFS				
Scorers	GP	G	A	Pts	Pim	GP	G	A	Pts	Pim	GP	G	A	Pts	Pim
George Awada (I)	57	24	27	51	72	52	23	25	48	72	5	1	2	3	0
Mike Morin (I)	53	9	28	37	68	48	9	27	36	64	5	0	1	1	4
David Kozier (I)	55	17	11	28	60	50	16	11	27	56	5	1	0	1	4
Rick Brebant	36	2	26	28	64	33	2	25	27	60	3	0	1	1	4
Mark Bultje (I)	22	14	13	27	30	18	11	13	24	28	4	3	0	3	2
Darcy Anderson (I)	35	11	14	25	22	30	10	12	22	20	5	1	2	3	2
Miroslav Skovira (I)	26	12	11	23	27	26	12	11	23	27					
Mika Skytta (I)	43	9	13	22	22	38	9	12	21	16	5	0	1	1	6
Dwight Parrish (I)	60	7	15	22	66	55	7	12	19	60	5	0	3	3	6
Mike Lankshear (I)	49	7	14	21	40	44	7	14	21	38	5	0	0	0	2
Shin Larsson-Yahata (I)	25	4	15	19	10	25	4	15	19	10					
Petteri Lotila (I)	54	7	11	18	16	49	7	10	17	12	5	0	1	1	4
Chad Brandimore (I)	35	7	8	15	12	30	7	7	14	12	5	0	1	1	0
Jeff Sebastian (I)	15	2	8	10	8	15	2	8	10	8					
Eric Lind (I)	22	6	3	9	26	22	6	3	9	26					
Mark Lovell	59	3	4	7	30	54	3	4	7	28	5	0	0	0	2
Eric Greenhous	35	0	5	5	10	30	0	4	4	10	5	0	1	1	0
Mark Thomas	58	2	2	4	74	53	2	2	4	72	5	0	0	0	2
Jason Hewitt	61	2	2	4	52	56	1	2	3	52	5	1	0	1	0
Mikko Niemi	15	0	3	3	20	15	0	3	3	20					
Jayme Platt (N) (I)	60	0	2	2	24	55	0	2	2	24	5	0	0	0	0
Dwayne Newman 1	2	1	0	1	0	2	1	0	1	0					
Brian Worrall	21	1	0	1	0	21	1	0	1	0					
Nick Poole 1	2	0	1	1	4	2	0	1	1	4					
Russ Richardson	11	0	0	0	8	11	0	0	0	8					
Aaron Davies	38	0	0	0	6	33	0	0	0	6	5	0	0	0	0
Bench Penalties					28					24					4
TEAM TOTALS	61	147	236	383	799	56	140	223	363	757	5	7	13	20	42
Netminders	GPI	Min	SOG	GA	Sv%	GPI	Min	SOG	GA	Sv%	GPI	Min	SOG	GA	Sv%
Jayme Platt (I)	56	3251	1671	142	91.5	55	3242	1667	141	91.5	1	9	4	1	75.0
Dave Clancy	10	458	204	23	88.7	5	162	77	12	84.4	5	296	127	11	91.3
Empty Net Goals			2	2				2	2				0	0	
TEAM TOTALS	61	3709	1877	167	91.1	56	3404	1746	155	91.1	5	305	131	12	90.8

Also appeared: Alan Hough.

Also played for: 1 Milton Keynes Lightning.

Shutouts: Platt - league: 14 Sept v London Racers (24), 10 Oct v Sheffield Steelers (25), 15 Feb v Basingstoke Bison (29), 24 Feb at London Racers (32), 6 Mar at Coventry Blaze (37); playoffs: 21 Mar v Belfast Giants (31).

All Competitions = league, playoffs and Challenge Cup

Awada Phoenix

CHRIS BRIERLEY

Rick Brebant started the season as Manchester Phoenix's first coach and ended it by playing his last game in Britain. Arguably the country's greatest import, he worked night and day with club owner **Neil Morris** to get the team up and running following the shock demise of the Storm.

Working to the tightest of budgets he pulled together a team of tried and tested imports, unknown quantities and a bunch of local kids who had been playing roller hockey.

The first problem was getting disaffected fans - many of whom had been short-changed on their season ticket money the year before - back through the doors of the hugely expensive *MEN* Arena. By the end of the season Morris was claiming that fans new to hockey were replacing those who had left it.

The second problem was that several key players decided to leave early. Assistant coach **Jeff Sebastian** was tempted by a bigger pay cheque from a team in Italy, **Eric Lind** returned to his old club in the East Coast Hockey League, **Shin-Larsson Yahata** couldn't settle, and **Miroslav Skovira** decided to return to Slovenia.

The good news was that goaltender **Jayme Platt** turned out to be a franchise player while **George Awada** - appointed captain - gave 100 per cent in every game.

But the real success was in the development of local Brits **Mark Lovell**, **Mark Thomas**, **Jason Hewitt** and netminder **Dave Clancy**. They were given the ice time they needed and proved they have the potential to play at the highest level.

But Brebant's mixture lacked strength in depth and while Phoenix recorded wins against every club except Nottingham, the season was a battle to gain sixth place and make the playoffs.

Within weeks of the start the coach had donned his skates again but the pressure of doing two jobs was too much. In January he announced he would be quitting Britain and the game at the end of the season.

While retaining Brebant as a player, Phoenix appointed former Cardiff and Ayr boss **Paul Heavey** as head coach. His firm but cool-headed approach gave the team confidence and they clinched the final playoff spot.

The highlight of the season was beating Belfast home and away and drawing 1-1 with Sheffield in their 'home' game - at Steelers' training rink, iceSheffield - with Hewitt scoring the all-important goal.

Sadly, injuries put paid to their hopes in the playoff semi-final when they were wiped out by their bogey team, Panthers.

PLAYER AWARDS

Player of the Year	**Mike Lankshear**
Players' Player	**Jayme Platt**
Coach's Player	**Jayme Platt**
Best Forward	**George Awada**
Best Defenceman	**Dwight Parrish**
Rookie of the Year	**Mark Thomas**
Most Improved Player	**Mark Thomas**
Unsung Hero	**Carl Greenhous**

LEADING PLAYERS

George Awada *born 2 June 1975*
The big left winger was the team's leading scorer in goals and points and led from the front during a difficult season. His work ethic was second to none.

Mike Morin *born 20 July 1971*
He's been in Manchester for seven years but last season was probably his best. He played in every position bar netminder, played injured, and played his heart out in every game.

Jayme Platt *born 26 July 1978*
Without the inspirational American netminder, the team would never have qualified for the playoffs. In some games he kept the opposition at bay almost single-handedly. Statistics say he was not the league's best but the others didn't have to play behind the Phoenix' defence. Also a leader off the ice.

FACT FILE 2003-04
Elite League	Sixth
Playoffs	Semi-finalists
Challenge Cup:	Seventh

HISTORY
Founded: 2003 by local businessman **Neil Morris**. Previous club at the *MEN* Arena was the *Storm* who folded in October 2002.
Leagues: *Phoenix* Elite League 2003-04; *Storm* Superleague 1996-2002; British League, Div. One 1995-96.
Honours: *Storm* - *Benson and Hedges* Cup winners 1999-2000, Superleague champions 1998-99, British League Division One champions 1995-96.

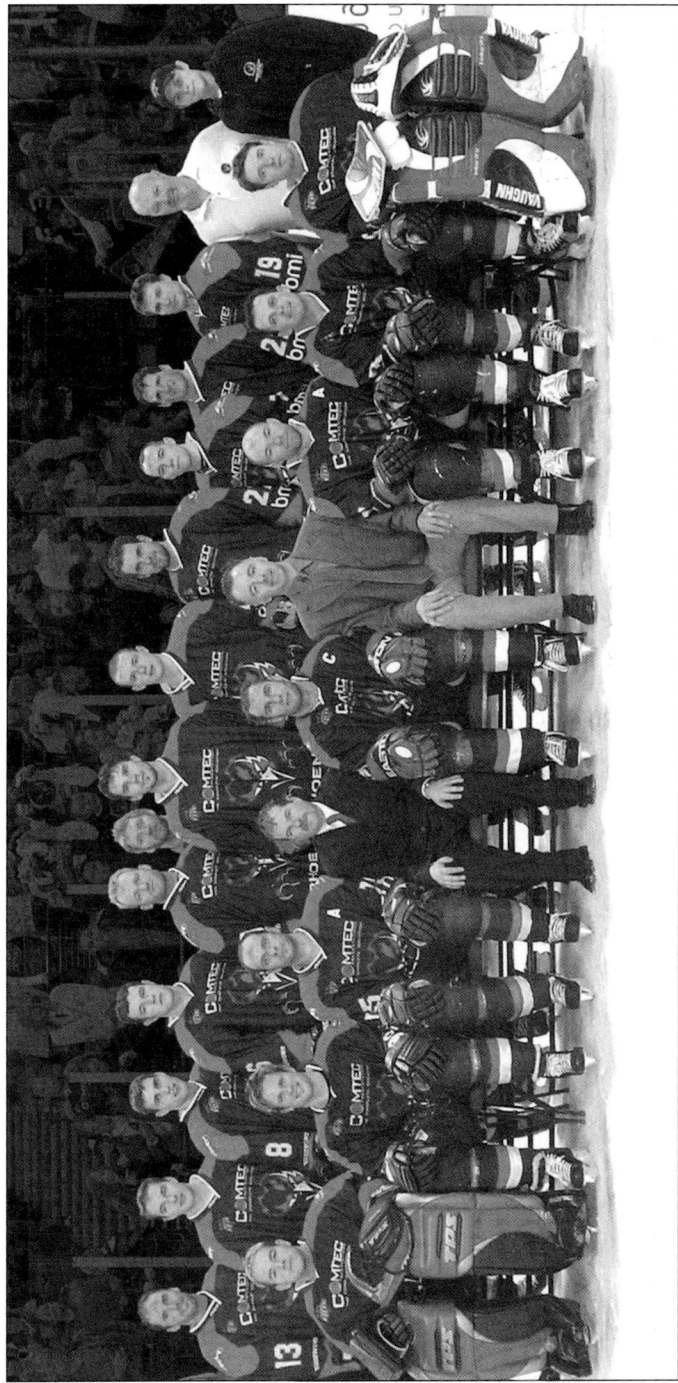

MANCHESTER PHOENIX *left to right,* *back row:* Chad Brandimore, David Kozier, Aaron Davies, Marc Lovell, Carl Greenhous, Andy Costigan (team manager), Mike Lankshear, Mark Thomas, Mika Skytta, Jason Hewitt, Darcy Anderson, Petteri Lotila, Paul Turner (equipment), Matt Turner (stick boy); *front row:* Dave Clancy, Mark Bultje, Mike Morin, Neil Morris (club owner), George Awada, Paul Heavey (coach), Dwight Parrish, Rick Brebant, Jayme Platt.

MILTON KEYNES LIGHTNING

PLAYER	ALL COMPETITIONS					ENGLISH PREMIER LEAGUE					PLAYOFFS				
Scorers	GP	G	A	Pts	Pim	GP	G	A	Pts	Pim	GP	G	A	Pts	Pim
Gary Clarke 2	52	83	52	135	46	32	55	32	87	18	10	13	10	23	16
Nick Poole 4	52	50	73	123	40	32	32	50	82	28	10	5	11	16	6
Mikko Skinnari (I)	52	34	57	91	12	32	23	38	61	4	10	5	9	14	4
Greg Randall	52	25	43	68	26	32	15	28	43	18	10	7	3	10	4
Kurt Irvine	44	9	39	48	318	30	9	28	37	227	8	0	7	7	71
Adam Carr 3	49	29	17	46	12	31	18	13	31	10	10	6	1	7	2
Michael Wales 3	40	15	24	39	169	25	9	18	27	123	9	3	2	5	26
Simon Howard	49	8	25	33	36	30	4	17	21	24	9	1	3	4	4
Dean Campbell	38	12	17	29	28	23	8	12	20	24	7	1	1	2	2
Dwayne Newman (I) 4	37	7	13	20	40	21	7	11	18	24	10	0	2	2	12
Barry McKenzie 3	44	12	6	18	32	27	6	3	9	20	10	5	1	6	4
Chris McEwan 3	48	3	14	17	18	29	3	11	14	18	10	0	2	2	0
Ross Bowers	26	9	7	16	10	14	2	6	8	2	7	1	0	1	6
Tom Griffiths	39	4	12	16	41	29	3	10	13	37	5	1	0	1	0
James Pease 5	48	4	11	15	90	31	4	9	13	62	9	0	1	1	12
Phil Wooderson	42	3	7	10	30	25	0	5	5	18	9	0	1	1	0
Geoffrey O'Hara	41	1	9	10	22	32	1	5	6	8	1	0	0	0	0
Adam Todd	2	2	1	3	0										
Tom Ledgard	2	1	2	3	0	1	1	1	2	0					
Leigh Jamieson 1	7	1	2	3	22	4	0	0	0	6	2	1	2	3	16
Tom Roles	3	0	3	3	0						1	0	0	0	0
Iain McGill	1	0	1	1	0						1	0	1	1	0
Allen Sutton (N)	52	0	1	1	4	32	0	1	1	2	10	0	0	0	0
Barry Hollyhead (N) 6	48	0	0	0	10	30	0	0	0	6	9	0	0	0	4
Bench Penalties					6					4					0
TEAM TOTALS	52	312	436	748	1012	32	200	298	498	683	10	49	57	106	189
Netminders	GPI	Mins	SOG	GA	Sv%	GPI	Mins	SOG	GA	Sv%	GPI	Mins	SOG	GA	Sv%
Allen Sutton	24	1377	482	39	91.9	15	900	306	25	91.8	3	180	70	3	95.7
Andrew Moore	1	28	12	1	91.7										
Barry Hollyhead 6	29	1714	710	67	90.6	17	1019	411	35	91.5	7	420	188	12	93.6
Empty Net Goals	1	1				1	1								
TEAM TOTALS	52	3120	1204	107	91.1	32	1920	717	60	91.6	10	600	258	15	94.2

Also appeared: Andrew Moore, Aram Todd, Carl Stevenson, David Coffey, Nick Mentiply.
Also played for: 1 Belfast Giants; 2 Basingstoke Bison, Cardiff Devils; 3 Basingstoke Bison; 4 Manchester Phoenix; 5 Coventry Blaze; 6 Cardiff Devils.
Shutouts: Sutton - league: 30 Aug v Solihull Kings (13 saves), 28 Sept at Solihull Kings (4), 12 Oct v Solihull Kings (14), 8 Nov at Slough Jets (24), 16 Nov v Swindon Lynx (12), 30 Nov v Slough Jets (22), Hollyhead - league: 2 Nov at Romford Raiders (18 saves).

All Competitions = league, playoffs and Premier Cup

MILTON KEYNES LIGHTNING *left to right, back row:* Geoff O'Hara, Tom Griffiths, Chris McEwen, Leigh Jamieson, James Pease, Ross Bowers, Bari McKenzie; *middle row:* Liam Nolan (physio), Adam Carr, Phil Wooderson, Michael Wales, Greg Randall, Dean Campbell, Kurt Irvine, Mikko Skinnari, Gary Clarke, Pete Nolan (physio), Andy Phillips (equipment manager); *front row:* Barry Hollyhead, Nick Poole, Harry Howton (chairman), Dwayne Newman, Vito Rausa (general manager), Simon Howard, Allen Sutton.

Poole's big fish

PAUL BROOKMAN

Lightning's inaugural campaign had been a success but the 2003-04 season was simply the best in the 14-year history of the sport in Milton Keynes.

They retained the English Premier League playoff trophy and went one better by cantering to the league title as well.

Coach **Nick Poole** made relatively few changes to the 2002-03 line-up and secured two-way deals with Elite League clubs for several players, including one with Belfast Giants for the city's own **Leigh Jamieson**. Giants liked him so much that he stayed and by the end of the season he was a GB senior international.

For Lightning it was evident by mid-October that league honours were almost certain as the side started with a 12-game winning streak. A solitary loss, 6-4 at Chelmsford, was followed by an even better 18-match winning run.

The league title was effectively clinched with two pre-Christmas wins over rivals, Peterborough Phantoms, and officially sealed on 17 January when Telford Wild Foxes were beaten 9-3 at Planet Ice.

But the early capture of the trophy proved detrimental to the team's motivation - they suffered three losses to Phantoms in February, including their only home defeat of the season.

One of Phantoms' losses was in the English Premier Cup – a result which cost Lightning top spot in their group and led to a dreaded semi-final trip to *Wightlink* Raiders. After having drawn 2-2 in the home leg, Lightning lost 9-6.

Poole's men were back at their best in the championship playoffs and they went through the group stages dropping just one point in a 1-1 draw back on the feared Isle of Wight.

The semi-finals pitched Lightning against Phantoms again. In the home leg Lightning were held to a 1-1 draw and it looked odds-on that Peterborough would go through. But a magnificent display, capped by a **Gary Clarke** empty-netter, gave the Buckinghamshire side a 4-2 win in the return.

Lightning went into the first leg of the final at Slough Jets hoping to keep the game tight with a solid defensive display, but they came away with a 7-0 victory thanks to a five-goal second period blitz. That made the second match at home before a crowd of 2,075 - the biggest for six years - somewhat academic. However, Jets were determined to restore their pride and battled hard until succumbing 5-2.

PLAYER AWARDS

Most Valuable Player	**Gary Clarke**
Players' Player	**Greg Randall**
Coach's Player	**Greg Randall**
Club Man of the Year	**Dean Campbell/Phil Wooderson**
Top Points Scorer	**Gary Clarke**
Best Defenceman	**Simon Howard**
Best Young British Player	**Michael Wales**
Most Improved Player:	**Ross Bowers**

LEADING PLAYERS

Simon Howard *born 21 September 1973*
London-born 'Howie' was Mr Reliable in defence which was the tightest in the league. He also contributed goals at vital times in important games.

Greg Randall *born 6 December 1978*
Almost a veteran on the team at the age of 25, he switched from forward to defence when captain **Dwayne Newman** suffered a long term injury, and turned out to be an excellent and natural D-man.

Mikko Skinnari *born 14 September 1975*
The popular Finnish forward was the backbone of the second line, often splitting defences with his great stickhandling skills. Finished third in the regular season points scorers behind Clarke and Poole, ending with more assists than goals.

FACT FILE 2003-04

English Premier League	Winners
Playoffs	Champions
Premier Cup	Semi-finalists

HISTORY

Founded: 2002. Original club founded 1990 as *Kings*. Rink closed 1996-98.

Leagues: *Lightning* English Premier League 2002-04; *Kings* Findus British National League 1999-2002; English League (Premier Div) 1998-99, 1990-91; British League, Premier Div 1994-96; British League, Div One 1991-94.

Honours: *Lightning* English Premier League (EPL) 2003-04; EPL Playoffs 2002-04; *Kings* English Cup 1998-99; British League, Div. One 1993-94.

NEWCASTLE VIPERS

PLAYER	ALL COMPETITIONS					FINDUS BRITISH NATIONAL LEAGUE					PLAYOFFS				
Scorers	GP	G	A	Pts	Pim	GP	G	A	Pts	Pim	GP	G	A	Pts	Pim
Jonathan Weaver	60	33	46	79	69	35	21	22	43	26	10	2	8	10	12
Matt Beveridge (I)	61	28	44	72	36	36	18	32	50	32	10	4	4	8	0
Paul Ferone (I)	54	23	37	60	202	30	13	21	34	96	10	3	5	8	6
Rob Wilson	59	19	38	57	96	36	10	26	36	44	10	3	4	7	34
Marc West (I)	24	11	31	42	28	11	4	12	16	14					
David Longstaff	29	15	21	36	28	19	12	15	27	20	9	2	6	8	6
Stephen Wallace	55	16	16	32	46	31	7	9	16	34	9	0	2	2	2
Rob Trumbley (I)	42	14	16	30	134	20	11	11	22	42	8	1	1	2	8
Stuart Potts	59	14	14	28	14	34	7	9	16	4	10	2	3	5	4
Simon Leach	54	4	23	27	106	30	2	14	16	62	10	0	0	0	22
Scott Campbell	31	3	9	12	58	20	0	7	7	34	10	2	2	4	20
Karl Culley	53	2	4	6	14	32	2	3	5	14	8	0	0	0	0
Scott Moody	60	1	5	6	34	35	0	1	1	18	10	0	0	0	8
Richie Thornton	61	3	2	5	18	36	1	1	2	12	10	2	0	2	0
Jason Robinson (I) 3	6	2	2	4	6	1	1	0	1	0					
Pasi Jarvinen (I)	7	1	3	4	4										
Tommi Satosaari (N) (I)	35	0	4	4	29	20	0	2	2	27					
Martin King	38	0	2	2	126	26	0	2	2	78	6	0	0	0	4
Andrew Thornton	26	0	2	2	2	18	0	1	1	2	7	0	1	1	0
Paul Graham	19	0	1	1	0	10	0	0	0	0	8	0	0	0	0
Kevin Bucas	56	0	0	0	10	32	0	0	0	0	9	0	0	0	2
Ian Defty	9	0	0	0	20	7	0	0	0	20					
Rory Dunn (N)	44	0	0	0	2	34	0	0	0	2	5	0	0	0	0
Pasi Raitanen (N) 1	25	0	0	0	2	15	0	0	0	2	10	0	0	0	0
Bench Penalties					24					10					4
TEAM TOTALS	61	189	320	509	1108	36	109	188	297	593	10	21	36	57	132
Netminders	GP	Mins	SOG	GA	Sv%	GP	Mins	SOG	GA	Sv%	GP	Mins	SOG	GA	Sv%
Tommi Satosaari (I)	35	2086	1220	110	91.0	20	1176	684	66	90.4					
Pasi Raitanen 1	25	1511	972	90	90.7	15	911	599	61	89.8	10	600	373	29	92.2
Stephen Wall 2	1	70	40	5	87.5	1	70	40	5	87.5					
Rory Dunn	1	27	11	2	81.8	1	27	11	2	81.8					
Empty Net Goals			3	3				1	1				2	2	
TEAM TOTALS	61	3694	2246	210	90.7	36	2184	1335	135	89.9	10	600	375	31	91.7

Also appeared: Michael Allinson, Bryan Dunn, Robert Wilson, Spencer Downey, Mark Lee (N).

Also played for: 1 Hull Stingrays, Sheffield Steelers; 2 Peterborough Phantoms; 3 London Racers.

Shutouts: Satosaari - cup: 11 Oct at Bracknell Bees (47 saves);

Raitanen - league: 25 Jan v Dundee Stars (26); playoffs: 7 Mar v Bracknell Bees (43), 17 Mar v Fife Flyers (34).

All Competitions = league, playoffs and Findus Cup

A cup and security

PETER ADAMS

In their second year, Vipers produced a six-goal blast to retain the *Findus* Cup, but perhaps the fledgling team's finest achievement was simply to survive.

An ugly incident in which skipper **Rob Trumbley** was attacked by a Guildford fan as he left The Spectrum ice in a September cup game set the tone for a testing season.

In November it emerged that Vipers were in financial trouble. The players' commitment was shown when the majority agreed to accept a pay cut to help stabilise the crisis. Inevitably though, there were dissenters.

A player who might have made a difference, blueliner **Jason Robinson**, quit. He had replaced the Finn, **Pasi Jarvinen**, but failed to settle on Tyneside.

On the ice, Vipers showed their fighting qualities by winning an epic *Findus* Cup semi-final second leg tussle in Kirkcaldy against Fife Flyers. Netminder **Tommi Satosaari** produced a display which had to be seen to be believed to keep Vipers in with a chance.

At the death, **Stephen Wallace** scored to send the tie into overtime. Satosaari saved 42 attempts in 70 minutes, and then four penalty shots as the Vipers won with one-on-one successes from **Matt Beveridge** and **Simon Leach**.

In December, owner **Darryl Illingworth** reassured fans about the future but the team lost a key player ahead of the cup final. 'WWF line' centre **Marc West** flew home, never to return despite saying otherwise.

Then moments before the final started, **David Longstaff** decided to risk his ankles which had been seriously damaged in a freak pre-season gym accident. It was as if Lobby's comeback had been scripted. In his first shift, the GB captain delivered a crunching check and at 9.36, he sensationally put Vipers ahead of the Flames.

With the trophy emphatically won, the club was in turmoil again when the stand-out Satosaari unexpectedly announced that he had accepted a big money offer to play in Slovenia.

Left in the lurch, Vipers were lucky that their 2002-03 shot stopper **Pasi Raitenen** was available: the Bear was outstanding at times.

Few games matched the excitement of the Flyers and Flames' cup ties, but for many the end of the season was a relief. Vipers would go where the Cobras, Riverkings and Jesters had not - into a third season.

PLAYER AWARDS

Player of the Year	Matt Beveridge
Players' Player	Jonathan Weaver
Best Forward	Jonathan Weaver
Best Defenceman	Rob Wilson
Most Improved Player	Stuart Potts
Most Valuable Asset	Rob Trumbley
Correspondents' Cup	Jonathan Weaver

LEADING PLAYERS

Matt Beveridge *born 18 March 1975*
The centreman showed why he was so highly rated by Invicta fans. He ended the season as the Vipers' top points scorer in league play and pushed Weaver hard for the honours.

Jonathan Weaver *born 20 January 1977*
The GB international played consistently at a high level in defence and attack, and at times produced plays that made fans yell "wow!" Thoroughly deserved his end of season accolades.

Rob Wilson *born 18 July 1968*
In his first season as player-coach, he showed great leadership qualities on and off the ice. His tremendous stamina and effortless skating again meant he regularly logged about 40 minutes' ice time every game.

FACT FILE 2003-04
British National League   Fifth
Playoffs   Fifth in qr-final grp
Findus **Cup**   Winners

CLUB HISTORY
Founded: Summer 2002 by speedway promoter **Darryl Illingworth** and former GB and Riverkings coach **Alex Dampier**.

Previous Clubs at the *Telewest* Arena were *Jesters*, *Riverkings*, *Cobras* and **Warriors**. No team 2001-02 after bankruptcy of *Jesters*.

Leagues: *Vipers* British National League 2002-04; *Jesters* Superleague 2000-01; *Riverkings* Superleague 1998-2000; *Cobras* Superleague 1996-98; *Warriors* British League, Premier Div 1995-96.

Honours: *Vipers Findus* Cup 2003 and 2002.

NEWCASTLE VIPERS *left to right, back row:* Stuart Potts, Ian Defty, Stephen Wallace, Karl Culley, Kevin Bucas, Martin King; *middle row:* Jason Robinson, Jonathan Weaver, Richie Thornton, Rob Wilson, Scott Moody, Matt Beveridge, David Longstaff, Marc West; *front row:* Tommi Satosaari, Paul Ferone, Rob Trumbley, Simon Leach, Rory Dunn.

Photo: David Glen-Walker/Touch The Sky Photography

NOTTINGHAM PANTHERS

PLAYER	ALL COMPETITIONS					ELITE LEAGUE					PLAYOFFS				
Scorers	GP	G	A	Pts	Pim	GP	G	A	Pts	Pim	GP	G	A	Pts	Pim
Mark Cadotte (I)	65	35	55	90	46	56	30	47	77	40	5	3	6	9	6
John Craighead (I)	63	45	32	77	228	54	39	30	69	182	6	5	1	6	8
Kim Ahlroos (I)	66	34	42	76	36	56	29	38	67	34	6	2	2	4	2
Lee Jinman (I)	36	25	41	66	46	26	20	27	47	38	6	2	10	12	4
Mikko Koivunoro (I)	57	13	46	59	119	47	12	40	52	101	6	1	2	3	16
Briane Thompson (I)	62	15	32	47	148	52	13	28	41	146	6	1	0	1	0
Joel Salonen (I)	61	16	30	46	32	51	15	24	39	28	6	0	4	4	0
David Struch (I)	66	13	33	46	24	56	11	30	41	18	6	1	2	3	4
David Clarke	52	17	21	38	55	44	14	16	30	49	4	2	2	4	4
Calle Carlsson (I)	65	7	31	38	56	55	7	30	37	50	6	0	1	1	2
Paul Moran	66	7	14	21	80	56	6	12	18	78	6	0	0	0	2
Robert Stancok (I)	60	3	16	19	102	50	2	14	16	86	6	0	1	1	2
Kristian Taubert (I)	59	5	11	16	63	49	4	10	14	63	6	1	0	1	0
Marc Levers	54	6	4	10	44	44	5	4	9	40	6	1	0	1	4
James Morgan 2	23	2	2	4	42	23	2	2	4	42					
Niklas Sundberg (N) (I)	64	0	3	3	8	54	0	3	3	8	6	0	0	0	0
Shaun Yardley 3	1	0	1	1	0	1	0	1	1	0					
Darren Cotton 2	2	0	1	1	0	2	0	1	1	0					
Lewis Buckman 3	10	0	1	1	14	8	0	1	1	14	2	0	0	0	0
Nicky Chinn 1	11	0	0	0	6	11	0	0	0	6					
Daniel Scott 4	29	0	0	0	2	23	0	0	0	2	6	0	0	0	0
Bench Penalties					12					8					2
TEAM TOTALS	66	243	416	659	1163	56	209	358	567	1033	6	19	31	50	56
Netminders	GPI	Min	SOG	GA	Sv%	GPI	Min	SOG	GA	Sv%	GPI	Min	SOG	GA	Sv%
Niklas Sundberg (I)	64	3761	1783	154	91.4	54	3160	1509	137	90.9	6	360	163	9	94.5
Geoff Woolhouse	9	240	111	16	85.6	9	240	111	16	85.6					
Empty Net Goals			5	5				5	5				0	0	
TEAM TOTALS	66	4001	1899	175	90.8	56	3400	1625	158	90.3	6	360	163	9	94.5

Also appeared: Paul Adey, Jason Buckman (3), Rhys McWilliams.

Also played for: 1 Basingstoke Bison, Bracknell Bees, Slough Jets; 2 Cardiff Devils, Peterborough Phantoms; 3 Peterborough Phantoms; 4 Solihull Kings.

Shutouts: Sundberg - league: 29 Oct v London Racers (19 saves), 4 Jan at Manchester Phoenix (20), 15 Feb at Coventry Blaze (33); playoffs: 20 Mar v Cardiff Devils (26).

All Competitions = league, playoffs and Challenge Cup

NOTTINGHAM PANTHERS *left to right*, *back row*: Scott (physio), Mikko Koivunoro, Robert Stancok, John Craighead, James Morgan, Kristian Taubert, Andy Worth (sponsor); *middle row*: Gary Moran (manager), Adam Goodrich (equipment), Mark Cadotte, Paul Moran, Marc Levers, David Struch, Kim Ahlroos, Joel Salonen, Paul Adey (coach); *front row*: Geoff Woolhouse, Calle Carlsson, Briane Thompson, David Clarke, Niklas Sundberg.

Photo: Dave Page

A trophy at last

MICK HOLLAND, Nottingham Evening Post

Celebrating their first trophy since 1998 with victory over their fiercest rivals at last gave the Panthers' faithful something to smile about.

But, realistically, it could - and should - have been more. In the end, it was that same Sheffield team they'd beaten on a memorable night at the *Hallam FM* Arena to secure the Challenge Cup who denied Panthers more glory.

Fans point to a poor Christmas period when they lost twice in successive nights to the Steelers as putting paid to Panthers' title hopes in the new Elite League. And there was no doubt that Sheffield's measly defence always had the edge against the flair of Panthers.

OK, so they beat Sheffield just twice in eight league games but, unlike their bitter enemies, Panthers didn't embark on a lengthy winless streak. They did, however, lose to teams they should have comfortably beaten, including setbacks against London and Basingstoke who inexplicably beat Panthers three times.

But make no mistake, this was a successful season for Panthers and it cannot be denied that **Paul Adey**'s outfit was the most attractive in the Elite League.

At a time of change when the pessimists were predicting poor hockey and unattractive play, Adey and the team's management must take credit for putting a virtually new team together.

The main returnees were **Briane Thompson**, who was installed as skipper, fellow defenceman **Kristian Taubert** and free-scoring winger **Mark Cadotte**. Also back were **Calle Carlsson, David Struch** and the much-travelled Finns **Kim Ahlroos** and **Mikko Koivunoro**.

New to this country were goaltender **Niklas Sundberg, Joel Salonen, Robert Stancok** and **John Craighead**, who was perhaps the biggest hit of the league. He arrived with a tough-guy image and finished with 39 league goals on top of his 228 penalty minutes.

Adey also gave Brits a chance with **David Clarke** at last fulfilling his immense potential and **Paul Moran** coming up with displays belying his tender years. There were nine guest players during the early weeks, chiefly from Peterborough and Solihull, but also including GB veteran **Nicky Chinn**.

Panthers were given a massive boost when former favourite **Lee Jinman** was released by his Swedish club and, with the departure of **James Morgan**, returned to spark his partnership with Cadotte.

Unfortunately, Sheffield had the final say . . . once again.

PLAYER AWARDS

Player of the Year	**Robert Stancok**
Players' Player	**Mark Cadotte**
Most Valuable Player	**Robert Stancok**
Most Consistent Player	**Kim Ahlroos**
GMB's Best Player	**David Clarke**
Best British Player	**Paul Moran**
Most Entertaining Player:	**Mark Cadotte**
Team Spirit (Gary Rippingale Memorial Award):	**Geoff Woolhouse**

LEADING PLAYERS

Mark Cadotte *born 11 March 1977*
The speedy winger is one of the smallest players on the circuit at 5ft 8in but he once more made a huge contribution, especially on the return of his old line-mate, **Lee Jinman**. Top-scored with 77 points (30 goals) to finish third in the league.

John Craighead *born 23 November 1971*
The instantly recognisable winger came to Panthers as a one-man replacement for last season's quartet of enforcers. But he showed great skills and an eye for goal, and led the league's goal scoring with 39. He also ensured that Panthers weren't a team to be messed with.

Robert Stancok *born 13 February 1976*
Another newcomer to Britain, the cultured 6ft 3in Slovakian defenceman was a classy addition to the blueline and enjoyed his first season away from his homeland. The fans appreciated his cool head and ability to play the puck smoothly out of defence.

FACT FILE 2003-04

Elite League	Runners-up
Playoffs	Finalists
Challenge Cup	Winners

HISTORY

Founded 1946. Re-formed 1980. Club suspended operations 1960-80. Purchased by Aladdin Sports Management in 1997. Moved to the National Ice Centre in August 2000.

Leagues Elite League 2003-04; Superleague 1996-2003; British Lge (BL) (Premier Div) 1982-96 and 1954-60; English Nat Lge (ENL) 1981-82 and 1946-54; Inter-City Lge 1980-82.

Honours: British Champions 1989; League - BL 1955-56, ENL 1953-54 and 1950-51; Challenge Cup 2003-04; Autumn Cup winners 1998, 1996 & 1994 *(B&H)*, 1991, 1986, 1955.

PETERBOROUGH PHANTOMS

PLAYER	ALL COMPETITIONS					ENGLISH PREMIER LEAGUE					PLAYOFFS				
Scorers	GP	G	A	Pts	Pim	GP	G	A	Pts	Pim	GP	G	A	Pts	Pim
Doug McEwen 3	51	50	55	105	87	32	31	37	68	73	8	7	7	14	4
Jon Cotton	52	40	47	87	100	32	28	25	53	76	8	3	9	12	12
Jesse Hammill 4	45	29	39	68	223	28	22	34	56	171	7	5	0	5	38
Jake Armstrong	51	19	47	66	118	31	11	29	40	84	8	3	6	9	16
Antti Kohvakka (I)	51	13	46	59	86	32	7	27	34	66	8	2	4	6	4
Shaun Yardley 5	49	27	27	54	101	30	20	15	35	73	8	1	5	6	22
Lewis Buckman 5	42	33	19	52	54	24	17	12	29	36	8	6	2	8	16
Simo Pulkki (I)	46	13	23	36	121	28	9	16	25	83	8	0	1	1	14
Darren Cotton 3	18	13	10	23	12	16	9	8	17	12					
Craig Britton	50	3	17	20	72	32	0	11	11	38	8	0	1	1	6
Russell Coleman	47	9	8	17	97	29	4	4	8	71	8	2	1	3	4
James Ellwood	45	6	9	15	35	31	4	4	8	31	6	0	2	2	2
Jason Buckman 5	52	5	10	15	50	32	1	6	7	40	8	0	0	0	2
James Morgan 5	14	4	10	14	54	6	2	5	7	38	6	2	4	6	12
Steven Maile	49	3	6	9	119	30	1	3	4	56	7	0	0	0	2
Kevin King	4	2	6	8	4	2	0	4	4	4					
Mark Williams 2	35	2	6	8	152	17	1	4	5	118	7	0	1	1	14
Rhys McWilliams	44	2	5	7	28	27	2	5	7	22	7	0	0	0	4
Grant Hendry	24	2	4	6	132	7	1	3	4	68	8	0	0	0	4
Julian Smith	25	0	4	4	2	14	0	3	3	0	7	0	0	0	2
Kent Nobes 1	3	2	1	3	4	3	2	1	3	4					
Bernie Bradford	47	2	1	3	34	28	2	1	3	24	8	0	0	0	8
Peter Morley	5	0	2	2	33	5	0	2	2	33					
Stephen Wall (N) 6	40	0	2	2	4	21	0	0	0	4	8	0	0	0	0
Craig Peacock	2	1	0	1	0	1	1	0	1	0					
David Whitwell (N)	26	0	1	1	4	23	0	1	1	4					
Jonathan Phillips 3	1	0	0	0	2	1	0	0	0	2					
James Ferrara	3	0	0	0	2	2	0	0	0	0					
Bench Penalties					12					12					0
TEAM TOTALS	52	280	405	685	1742	32	175	260	435	1243	8	31	43	74	186
Netminders	GPI	Mins	SOG	GA	Sv%	GPI	Mins	SOG	GA	Sv%	GPI	Mins	SOG	GA	Sv%
Stephen Wall 6	35	2036	966	76	92.1	18	1050	537	43	92.0	7	420	185	15	91.9
James Moore	7	305	126	13	89.7	4	181	70	7	90.0	1	60	42	5	88.1
David Whitwell	14	749	266	37	86.1	12	659	243	35	85.6					
Robert Amos	1	30	6	2	66.7	1	30	6	2	66.7					
TEAM TOTALS	52	3120	1364	128	90.6	32	1920	856	87	89.8	8	480	227	20	91.2

Also appeared: Euan King, James Archer, Kelly Herring,

Also played for: 1 Bracknell Bees, *Wightlink* Raiders; 2 Romford Raiders; 3 Cardiff Devils; 4 Basingstoke Bison; 5 Nottingham Panthers; 6 Newcastle Vipers.

Shutouts: Wall - league: 21 Feb at Slough Jets (30 saves).

Doug joins the 1,000-goal club

STEVE JUDGE

FORGET the pursuit of trophies and shoot the next player who claims there is no 'I' in team because to watch **Doug McEwen** is to see an ice hockey genius.

And that's not the only word with an 'I' in it that sums up the 40-year-old's inspirational talent. How about 'idol'? Even **Simon Cowell** would be lost for words if he ever saw McEwen perform. The only thing stopping him entering Britain's Hall of Fame is that there is no sign of him stopping yet.

Once again this season he produced moments of magic that few players in the English Premier League could dream of. But at Telford in an English Premier Cup game on 7 March 2004 he achieved something that even he could not have dreamed of in 1986 when he played his first match in this country with the old Pirates.

He scored his 1,000th goal and, typically of the man, he reached the magic millennium with his hat-trick goal. No sooner had the puck plunged into the net than his team-mates streamed on to the ice and presented him with a commemorative silver hockey stick to mark the occasion.

This was not the only silverware a Phantom was to get his hands on in an up-and-down season, though the team had to wait until the final weekend before beating the Isle of Wight and retaining their English Premier Cup.

Coach **Kevin King**'s hopes of building a side on defensive muscle rather than attacking flair were disrupted when **Pete Moriey** quit the team for personal reasons after a couple of weeks.

Back-to-back defeats by Romford and Chelmsford at the start of December led to the gassing of skilful Brit forward **Darren Cotton**; another defeat the following week by Milton Keynes all but ended their reign as league champions.

King's gamble on **Kent Nobes** backfired but the return of **James Morgan** from Nottingham proved a major boost. Three straight wins over fierce rivals, Lightning, lifted hopes for the playoffs, but then disaster struck.

Morgan broke his leg during the Planet Ice Challenge with Milton Keynes, the newly crowned league winners. **James Ellwood** also suffered knee ligament damage in the 2-1 reverse and both players were ruled out for the rest of the season.

Phantoms were beaten in a third competition by the men from Milton Keynes when Lightning knocked them out of the EPL Playoffs at the semi-final stage.

PLAYER AWARDS

Player of the Year	Doug McEwen
Players' Player	Stephen Wall
Best Forward	Doug McEwen
Best Defenceman	Simo Pulkki
Most Improved Player	James Ellwood
Best Young Player	Shaun Yardley

LEADING PLAYERS

Lewis Buckman born 19 May 1983

A hard-working two-way player capable of match-turning moments with a big forecheck or an incisive pass or a wrist shot. Also iced in the Elite League with Nottingham Panthers.

Antti Kohvakka born 4 January 1976

The Finn was the hero of the defensive line, and helped compatriot **Simo Pulkki** blossom. Not a big man, his secret was to keep things simple and make few mistakes.

Stephen Wall born 2 December 1981

Ended as the league's leading netminder after joining from Newcastle when last year's number one **David Whitwell** struggled with a knee injury. Shows great promise.

MAC THE MARKSMAN

The first goal that **Doug McEwen** scores in season 2004-05 will be his 1,000th in league, playoffs and officially recognised cup games.

The total referred to here was achieved in all competitive games.

At the end of 2003-04 McEwen, who has spent ten of his 18 seasons with Cardiff Devils, had a grand total of 999 goals and 2,105 points in 916 league, playoff and cup games.

FACT FILE 2003-04

English Premier League:	Runners-up
Playoffs:	Semi-finalists
Premier Cup:	Winners

HISTORY

Founded: 2002. The previous team at Peterborough was the **Pirates** 1982-2002.

Leagues: Phantoms English Premier Lge 2002-04. **Pirates** British National Lge 1997-2002; Premier Lge 1996-97; British Lge, Div One 1995-96, 1986-87, 1982-85; British Lge, Premier Div 1987-95, 1985-86.

Honours: Phantoms English Premier Lge 2002-03; Premier Cup 2003-04, 2002-03; **Pirates** British Lge, Div. One playoffs 1987-88; British Lge, Div. One 1986-87, 1984-85; Christmas Cup 1999.

PETERBOROUGH PHANTOMS *left to right, back row:* Rhys McWilliams, James Ferrara, Jason Buckman, Bernie Bradford, James Ellwood, Darren Cotton, Shaun Yardley; *middle row:* Andy Halifax, Rob Horspool (equipment), Lewis Buckman, Antti Kohvakka, Jesse Hammill, Simo Pulkki, Mark Williams, Russ Coleman, Jake Armstrong, Steve Maile, Bill Glover; *front row:* Bert Amos, James Moore, Doug McEwen, Rob Housden, Kevin King, Phil Wing (managing director), Jon Cotton, Craig Britton, David Whitwell, Stephen Wall.

Photo: Dave Page

ROMFORD RAIDERS

PLAYER	ALL COMPETITIONS					ENGLISH PREMIER LEAGUE					PLAYOFFS				
Scorers	GP	G	A	Pts	Pim	GP	G	A	Pts	Pim	GP	G	A	Pts	Pim
Juuso Vakkilainen (I)	46	60	59	119	130	31	50	45	95	81	6	4	6	10	35
Rob Douglas (I)	43	51	56	107	44	28	34	41	75	36	6	7	7	14	2
Danny Marshall	46	35	56	91	32	31	30	46	76	18	6	1	1	2	14
Elliot Andrews	40	21	32	53	10	26	17	22	39	6	6	2	3	5	2
James Austin (I)	43	20	26	46	106	28	17	20	37	94	6	0	0	0	6
Jamie Randall 4	47	9	24	33	4	32	7	22	29	4	6	0	0	0	0
Jani Keskinen (I)	18	11	18	29	12	7	4	13	17	10	6	3	3	6	0
Jon Beckett 3	20	9	13	22	22	11	6	11	17	4	6	1	2	3	16
Tyrone Miller	37	6	13	19	82	27	5	12	17	62	3	0	1	1	0
Darren Botha	40	4	15	19	47	27	4	11	15	39	4	0	2	2	4
Ben Pitchley	46	3	14	17	92	31	2	11	13	52	6	0	0	0	18
Grant Taylor	44	6	10	16	40	31	6	9	15	36	4	0	0	0	2
Stuart Low	42	5	10	15	22	30	5	9	14	18	4	0	0	0	0
David St Cyr (I)	12	0	7	7	58	12	0	7	7	58					
Hakan Nordlund (I)	3	3	3	6	6	3	3	3	6	6					
Rob Jenner	43	2	3	5	33	31	2	3	5	8	3	0	0	0	25
Tom Spinks	44	2	3	5	26	29	2	2	4	22	6	0	0	0	0
Aaron Atkins	4	1	2	3	0	3	1	2	3	0					
Mark Williams 1	8	1	2	3	36	8	1	2	3	36					
Chris Douglas (N)	46	0	3	3	0	31	0	3	3	0	6	0	0	0	0
Neil Adams 2	2	1	0	1	0	2	1	0	1	0					
Lachlan Coombe	7	1	0	1	16	5	1	0	1	16					
Tom Looker	16	0	1	1	6	15	0	1	1	6					
Anthony Childs	2	0	0	0	2	1	0	0	0	2					
Bench Penalties					12					6					4
TEAM TOTALS	48	251	370	621	838	32	198	295	493	620	6	18	25	43	128
Netminders	GPI	Mins	SOG	GA	Sv%	GPI	Mins	SOG	GA	Sv%	GPI	Mins	SOG	GA	Sv%
Glen Jackson	2	15	9	0	100	2	15	9	0	100					
Danny Kruse	1	20	11	1	90.9	1	20	11	1	90.9					
Chris Douglas (N)	45	2490	1493	153	89.8	30	1597	961	93	90.3	6	360	238	27	88.7
Tom Sliz	6	258	154	31	79.9	6	258	154	31	79.9					
Vicky Robbins	2	37	17	7	58.8	1	30	16	6	62.5					
TEAM TOTALS	48	2820	1684	192	88.6	32	1920	1151	131	88.6	6	360	238	27	88.7

Also appeared: Antony Peters, Ben King, Charlie Kaylor, James Warner, Phil O'Neil, Robert Cole, Sam Park, Tomas Pinewski.

Also played for: 1 Peterborough Phantoms; 2 Solihull Kings; 3 Chelmsford Chieftains; 4 Basingstoke Bison.

Shutouts: Douglas - league: 26 Oct v Slough Jets (31 saves)

All Competitions = league, playoffs and Premier Cup

Raiders of the lost chord

MICK CAHILL

Raiders' year resembled an orchestral piece played out of sequence. The crescendo came with a flying start when **Erskine Douglas**'s side briefly topped the English Premier League table. A smooth middle passage followed as they held third place for most of the season.

The slow movement came at the end. Raiders hit a barren spell and management had to handle falling gates and the aftermath of a rink fire that closed Rom Valley Way for three weeks, helping to banjax any chance of playoff success.

After opening with six straight wins, Raiders were leading at unbeaten Peterborough when netminder **Chris Douglas** - like father Erskine, back at Rom Valley Way - was crocked and had to retire from the contest.

Back-up **Tommy Sliz** gave a man-of-the-match performance but Phantoms eased to victory and repeated the dose at Romford the following night.

The highlights of a quiet mid-season were thrilling wins over Peterborough and Milton Keynes, but victory over the Lightning signalled the collapse of Raiders' campaign.

Thereafter - and this was still January - all but one of their successes came over basement boys, Telford and Solihull, and Invicta Dynamo of the English National League. Bizarrely, the one exception came in Raiders' playoff group at table-toppers Slough.

Offensively, Raiders were well served by Finnish newcomer, **Juuso Vakkilainen**, who rocketed to the top of the scoring charts but spent the second half of the season literally taking stick as rivals preyed on Romford's lack of physical presence.

The sadly under-used **James Austin**, fellow Canadian **Rob Douglas** and new signing **Elliot Andrews** always worked hard and skipper **Danny Marshall** produced his usual sparkling contribution.

In defence, Romford often looked rocky with Chris Douglas sometimes the only difference between defeat and victory. Canadian **David St Cyr** departed in mid-season and his import defenceman's slot was eventually filled by Finn **Jani Keskinen** who brought a cannon slapshot but little else.

Rookie **Thomas Spinks** made a good start in his first full season but returnee **Tyrone Miller** was probably Raiders' most effective blueliner, although he spent increasing time in the BNL with Bracknell Bees during the closing weeks.

PLAYER AWARDS

Player of the Year	Rob Douglas
Players' Player	Juuso Vakkilainen
Coach's Player	Rob Douglas
Internet Player	James Austin
Best Defenceman	Tyrone Miller
Best Forward	Juuso Vakkilainen
Most Improved Player	Thomas Spinks

LEADING PLAYERS

Chris Douglas *born 25 August 1979*

Not for the first time, he linked up with his father back at Romford. On his day, as good as any guardian in the league and usually better than most. Faced a barrage of rubber throughout the season as a leaky defence allowed too many shots on goal.

Danny Marshall *born 14 May 1977*

Team skipper ended the season second among the league's British scorers and continued to rewrite the record books at Rom Valley Way. Now chasing club legend **Gord Jeffrey** as their highest ever points grabber, the centreman has a long way to go, but he's only 27.

Juuso Vakkilainen *born 8 June 1980*

Signed from the French league, he became the latest Finn to delight the Romford faithful. Just beaten off by Chelmsford's **Kyle Amyotte** as the league's top scorer, he was a goal machine in the early months before the opposition wised up and made sure his threat was diminished - by fair means or foul.

FACT FILE 2003-04

English Premier League:	Third
Playoffs:	4th in qr-final grp
Premier Cup:	4th in qr-final grp

HISTORY

Founded: 1987. (Withdrew from British League, Div One midway through 1994-95 for financial reasons.)

Leagues: English (Premier) League 1995-2004, 1989-90; British League, Div One 1990-94 and 1988-89; British League, Div Two 1987-88.

Honours: English Premier Cup 2001-02; English National League, Premier Div playoffs 2000-01; British League, Div Two 1987-88.

SHEFFIELD STEELERS

PLAYER	ALL COMPETITIONS					ELITE LEAGUE					PLAYOFFS				
Scorers	GP	G	A	Pts	Pim	GP	G	A	Pts	Pim	GP	G	A	Pts	Pim
Mark Dutiaume (I)	62	36	55	91	77	53	34	54	88	69	5	1	0	1	4
Mike Peron (I)	59	28	48	76	124	49	24	42	66	104	6	3	6	9	12
Erik Anderson (I)	66	34	36	70	18	56	32	36	68	18	6	0	0	0	0
Brent Bobyck	65	18	37	55	62	55	16	35	51	60	6	2	1	3	0
Joel Irving (I)	60	24	30	54	58	50	23	26	49	50	6	1	3	4	4
Gerad Adams (I)	63	18	30	48	231	53	16	29	45	190	6	1	0	1	6
Ron Shudra	60	8	34	42	24	50	8	33	41	24	6	0	1	1	0
Steve Ellis (I)	62	20	14	34	22	52	19	14	33	18	6	0	0	0	2
Dion Darling (I)	65	10	24	34	144	55	8	22	30	120	6	2	2	4	20
Kevin Bolibruck (I)	49	9	22	31	64	39	9	18	27	40	6	0	2	2	12
Kirk DeWaele (I)	63	12	14	26	106	53	9	11	20	86	6	3	3	6	12
Marc Lefebvre (I)	64	7	17	24	143	54	6	15	21	139	6	1	1	2	4
Ryan Lake	65	6	7	13	122	55	5	6	11	95	6	1	1	2	27
Ben Bliss	62	5	1	6	20	52	4	1	5	14	6	0	0	0	2
Christian Bronsard (N) (I)	27	0	3	3	24	17	0	2	2	4	6	0	1	1	16
Chris Bailey 2	17	0	2	2	38	17	0	2	2	38					
Gavin Ferrand	37	1	0	1	36	29	1	0	1	36	5	0	0	0	0
Mark McCoy 1	2	0	1	1	0	2	0	1	1	0					
Pasi Raitanen (N) 3	9	0	1	1	0	9	0	1	1	0					
Steve Duncombe	36	0	1	1	4	30	0	1	1	4	4	0	0	0	0
Bench Penalties					37					10					27
TEAM TOTALS	66	236	377	613	1354	56	214	349	563	1119	6	15	21	36	148

Netminders	GPI	Min	SOG	GA	Sv%	GPI	Min	SOG	GA	Sv%	GPI	Min	SOG	GA	Sv%
Christian Bronsard (I)	27	1608	609	34	94.4	17	997	373	22	94.1	6	370	142	6	95.8
Pasi Raitanen	9	529	244	16	93.4	9	529	244	16	93.4					
Rob Dopson (I)	29	1708	827	63	92.4	29	1708	827	63	92.4					
Davey Lawrence	7	150	74	6	91.9	7	150	74	6	91.9					
Empty Net Goals			2	2				2	2				0	0	
TEAM TOTALS	66	3995	1756	121	93.1	56	3384	1520	109	92.8	6	370	142	6	95.8

Also appeared: Les Millie, Dan Hughes.

Also played for: 1 Basingstoke Bison; 2 London Racers; 3 Hull Stingrays, Newcastle Vipers.

Shutouts: Dopson - league: 21 Sept v Basingstoke Bison (16 saves)*,
10 Oct at Manchester Phoenix (22), 19 Nov v London Racers (23),
23 Nov v Manchester Phoenix (20), 29 Nov at Basingstoke Bison (32).
Lawrence (2) - league: 21 Sept v Basingstoke Bison (11 saves)*,
16 Jan at London Racers (3)*
Raitanen - league: 27 Dec v Nottingham Panthers (29 saves),
16 Jan at London Racers (23)*.
Bronsard - league: 14 Feb v Manchester Phoenix (19 saves),
22 Feb at Manchester Phoenix (15), 28 Feb at Nottingham Panthers (23),
5 Mar at Belfast Giants (25); playoffs: 28 March v Manchester Phoenix (14),
3 Apr v Cardiff Devils (20).

All Competitions = league, playoffs and Challenge Cup

SHEFFIELD STEELERS *left to right*, *back*: Norton Lea (owner), Dave Simms, Mike Peron, Gayle Cotton, Geoff Butcher (team doctor), Kevin Bolibruck, Marc Lefebvre, Gerad Adams, Andy Akers (equipment manager), John Collinge (equipment; *middle*: Mike Blaisdell (coach), Steve Ellis, Ben Bliss, Dion Darling, Gavin Ferrand; *front*: Brent Bobyck, Davey Lawrence, Kirk DeWaele, Christian Bronsard, Ryan Lake, Erik Anderson, Ron Shudra (and son), Joel Irving.

Photo: Dave Page

Only a double

SHARON HODKIN

Sheffield Steelers successfully lifted a second consecutive league trophy with a dominant display in the inaugural Elite League.

For a time it even looked as though the team could complete a second Grand Slam under coach **Mike Blaisdell**, but Panthers' overtime goal in the Challenge Cup final ended that hope.

Instead, the side had to be content with the league and playoff championship double. But as Blaisdell said: "If you'd told me at the start of the season we'd end with the league and playoff trophies, I would have been happy with that."

The coach dispensed with most of his highly paid stars from the Superleague era so it was a very different Steelers' side that started the new league. Only defenceman **Dion Darling** and forwards **Mark Dutiaume** and **Brent Bobyck** re-signed for the side while veteran defenceman **Ron Shudra** returned for his third stint and tenth season in a Steelers' shirt.

'Blaiser' bolstered his team with several British players, including the highly rated **Ryan Lake**, and two young Canadians, **Steve Ellis** and **Marc Lefebvre**.

The team signalled its intention from the start by remaining unbeaten for the first 11 games. An unprecedented six successive defeats followed and it took the signing of **Kevin Bolibruck** to return the club to its winning ways.

Sheffield was rocked in December by netminder **Rob Dopson**'s decision to return to Canada. **Pasi Raitanen** proved a good stand-in while Blaisdell trawled the globe for a permanent replacement. A month of searching found **Christian Bronsard** in Russia, putting the final piece in place for Sheffield's title charge.

The team finally secured the trophy when, after a 3-1 win in Belfast, their nearest challengers, Nottingham Panthers, lost in London.

But Panthers gained swift revenge when they took the Challenge Cup in Sheffield. Steelers had held Panthers to a 1-1 draw in the first leg in Nottingham but failed to capitalise on their home advantage in the return.

That was Sheffield's last defeat of the season as the team embarked on an unbeaten run that ended with them being crowned playoff champions. A 2-0 win over Cardiff Devils in the semi-final set up a second final against Panthers.

This time it was Steelers who won the showdown and the final trophy of the season, courtesy of a 2-1 victory in front of a capacity crowd in the National Ice Centre.

PLAYER AWARDS

Player of the Year	Mark Dutiaume
Players' Player	Mike Peron
Coach's Player	Ryan Lake
Away Player	Mike Peron

LEADING PLAYERS

Mark Dutiaume born 31 January 1977
The team's most influential forward was a regular match winner and finished the season as the club's leading goal and points scorer. His season came to a painful end when he suffered an eye injury in the playoff semi-final.

Mike Peron born 24 March 1976
The feisty forward was signed with high expectations and quickly won over the fans with his goals, great puck handling and no-nonsense approach, standing up to anyone who tried to stop him.

Dion Darling born 22 October 1974
Was Blaisdell's choice of captain when he returned to the club for a second season and proved a team leader on and off the ice. The cool defenceman was one of the main reasons for Steelers' miserly goals-against record.

FACT FILE 2003-04

Elite League	Winners
Playoffs	Champions
Challenge Cup	Finalists

HISTORY

Founded: 1991. Franchise purchased in August 2001 by **Norton Lea**. In May 2002, Lea set up a company, South Yorkshire Franchise Ice Hockey Club Ltd, to own both the team and the franchise.

Leagues: Elite League 2003-04; Superleague 1996-2003; British League, Premier Div 1993-96; British League, Div One 1992-93; English League 1991-92.

Honours: Elite League & playoffs 2003-04; Superleague Playoff Champions 2001-02, 2000-01 & 1996-97; Superleague 2002-03, 2000-01; Challenge Cup 2002-03, 2000-01, 1999-2000 & 1998-99; British League and Championship 1995-96 & 1994-95; *B&H* Autumn Cup 2000-01, 1995-96.

SLOUGH JETS

PLAYER	ALL COMPETITIONS					ENGLISH PREMIER LEAGUE					PLAYOFFS				
Scorers	GP	G	A	Pts	Pim	GP	G	A	Pts	Pim	GP	G	A	Pts	Pim
Adam Bicknell	47	22	32	54	114	31	20	18	38	68	7	1	3	4	18
Zoran Kozic 3	21	27	18	45	26	5	6	5	11	14	9	12	5	17	8
Jason Reilly	44	15	28	43	62	30	12	22	34	42	10	3	4	7	18
Matthew Foord	51	18	23	41	64	32	13	15	28	38	10	3	1	4	12
Matt Sirman (l)	30	20	14	34	36	14	11	7	18	4	9	2	3	5	0
Matt Towalski	42	12	13	25	68	25	4	6	10	12	9	5	4	9	24
Nicky Chinn 2	17	8	17	25	71	15	6	16	22	71					
Warren Rost	42	6	11	17	168	27	4	5	9	136	8	1	3	4	10
Terry Miles	39	10	5	15	75	20	4	1	5	22	10	3	3	6	10
Mike Timms	35	5	7	12	20	23	3	4	7	18	4	0	0	0	2
Adam Greener	46	5	7	12	309	27	2	3	5	182	10	1	3	4	85
Ricky Skene	42	3	8	11	75	27	2	7	9	59	10	1	0	1	16
Stuart Tait	38	1	10	11	50	21	0	7	7	38	10	0	1	1	8
Tom Long 1	29	4	6	10	12	13	3	4	7	2	10	1	2	3	4
Christian Babbage	44	6	3	9	24	27	4	3	7	22	8	2	0	2	0
Tom Boney	45	2	6	8	8	26	2	2	4	8	10	0	2	2	0
Brian McLaughlin 3	11	0	5	5	26	1	0	0	0	0	9	0	5	5	26
Adam Gray 1	24	1	3	4	76	11	0	0	0	22	9	1	2	3	32
Mike Plenty	33	0	4	4	16	16	0	2	2	4	10	0	0	0	10
Simon Smith (N)	46	0	4	4	6	29	0	3	3	2	10	0	1	1	2
Graham Bellamy	49	1	2	3	4	31	1	2	3	2	10	0	0	0	2
Robert Kowalenko	10	0	3	3	0	10	0	3	3	0					
Simon Greaves	7	0	2	2	8	7	0	2	2	8					
Tom Smith	12	1	0	1	0	10	0	0	0	0					
James Day	18	0	1	1	16	10	0	0	0	12	2	0	0	0	0
Dave Richards 1	20	0	1	1	68	13	0	1	1	62					
Carl Graham	22	0	0	0	22	20	0	0	0	22					
Tom Wills (N) 1	23	0	0	0	4	9	0	0	0	2	8	0	0	0	0
Bench Penalties					12					8					4
TEAM TOTALS	52	167	233	400	1440	32	97	138	235	880	10	36	42	78	291
Netminders	GPI	Mins	SOG	GA	Sv%	GPI	Mins	SOG	GA	Sv%	GPI	Mins	SOG	GA	Sv%
Tom Wills 1	9	540	283	29	89.8	3	180	86	10	88.4	2	120	69	8	88.4
Simon Smith	41	2421	1318	166	87.4	28	1642	885	119	86.6	8	480	268	24	91.0
Adam Dobson	2	95	64	11	82.8	2	95	64	11	82.8					
Empty Net Goals		4	2	2			3	2	2						
TEAM TOTALS	52	3060	1667	208	87.5	32	1920	1037	142	86.3	10	600	337	32	90.5

Also appeared: Kevin McGurk, Michael Gray, Ollie Medcalf, Will Sanderson.
Also played for: 1 Haringey Racers; 2 Basingstoke Bison, Nottingham Panthers, Bracknell Bees. 3 London Racers, Haringey Racers.

All Competitions = league, playoffs and Premier Cup

Chinn-less wonders

DICK BELLAMY

The last time the Hangar was full to capacity was when the Jets won promotion to the Premier Division of the *Heineken* League.

Nine long years passed before they did it again, for the English Premier League playoff finals against Milton Keynes Lightning. There was a real buzz in the rink for the first leg on 1 May, something no one had dared to forecast back in September.

Jets' 18th season - and their second in the EPL - was probably their most difficult one with no main sponsor and only one import for the last part of their campaign. Consequently, expectations were low, especially as their injury crisis dragged on and on, right from their opening challenge match against the Elite League's Cardiff Devils.

But player-coach **Warren Rost**'s team upset the odds with a superb playoff run all the way to the final, after finishing a lowly seventh in the league and making an early exit from the Premier Cup.

In the close season, **Scott Moody** left for Newcastle Vipers to protect his GB place, but several others declined better money offers to stay loyal to the club. Most of the British players returned and defenceman **Graham Bellamy** and forward **Rob Kowalenko** were added.

Ricky Skene re-signed in October after spells with Guildford Flames and in the USA, and **Mike Timms** came on a two-way deal with Guildford.

Rost's big coup was supposed to be the signing of GB veteran **Nicky Chinn**. Sadly, though he displayed match-winning capabilities, Chinn's prima-donna attitude did not endear him to either his team-mates or the fans. He left at the end of November, a month after import **Matt Sirman** returned from Canada.

With the injury crisis threatening to get out of hand, Jets brought in three players from the collapsed Haringey Racers and their parent club. Canadian goalie **Tom Wills** moved over from Ally Pally along with his former team-mate, **Zoran Kozic**, the Yugoslav international forward who at one time owned the Haringey team. A second Canadian, defenceman **Brian McLaughlin**, who previously skated at Romford and Chelmsford, joined when London Racers failed to reach the Elite League playoffs.

For the EPL playoffs, Rost was able to ice a fully fit squad for almost the only time in the season, and goalie **Simon Smith**, whose league form had been indifferent, was the key to Slough's opening 3-1 win in Peterborough.

After that, they never looked back.

PLAYER AWARDS

Player of the Year	**Zoran Kozic**
Players' Player	**Jason Reilly**
Coach's Player	**Simon Smith**
Captain's Player	**Terry Miles**
Best British Player	**Jason Reilly**

LEADING PLAYERS

Adam Greener *born 2 October 1981*

The Hampshire-born defenceman, a builder by trade, took more responsibility, playing on the first line. A hard-nosed, no-nonsense player he was always ready to step in and protect his younger team-mates.

Zoran Kozic *born 5 February 1970*

The Belgrade-born forward made his biggest impact in the playoffs, scoring 12 goals and 17 points. A former player with Yale University, he works as a banker in the City.

Simon Smith *born 31 July 1979*

Another who helped to turn round the team's fortunes in the playoffs when his man of the match-winning performances kept first choice **Tom Wills** on the bench for most games.

FACT FILE 2003-04

English Premier League	Seventh
Playoffs:	Finalists
Premier Cup	3rd in qr-final grp.

HISTORY

Founded: 1986.

Leagues: English Premier Lge 2002-04; British National Lge 1997-2002; Premier Lge 1996-97; British Lge, Premier Div 1995-96; British Lge, Div One 1986-95.

Honours: British National League 1998-99; *Benson and Hedges* Plate 1997-98; British League, Div One 1994-95 (and Playoffs), 1993-94 (south), 1989-90.

SLOUGH JETS *left to right, back:* Joe Gibson (equipment), Brian McLaughlin, Warren Rost, Adam Dobson, Graham Bellamy, Adam Greener, Matt Sirman, Jason Reilly, Michael Plenty, Stewart Tait, Zoran Kozic, Adam Gray, Tom Wills, Adam Bicknell, Tom Long, Matt Foord, Ricky Skene; *front (kneeling):* Simon Smith, Tom Boney, Matt Towalski, Chris Babbage, Jimmy Day, Mike Timms, Terry Miles.

SOLIHULL KINGS

PLAYER	ENGLISH PREMIER LEAGUE				
Scorers	GP	G	A	Pts	Pim
Kevin Conway	24	15	17	32	20
Joel Pickering	24	11	11	22	174
Mikka Kaski (I)	10	7	11	18	12
Andrew Howarth	30	9	8	17	61
Neil Adams 1	25	7	10	17	28
Nick Whyatt	31	5	9	14	48
Vitaly Koulikov	26	7	6	13	63
Jon Rodway	30	2	7	9	32
Andrew Ayers	18	3	5	8	20
Joe Wightman	21	3	5	8	22
Steve Rowlands	27	3	4	7	88
Daniel Scott 2	22	3	3	6	50
Richard Taylor	28	3	3	6	56
Tim Lockyer	19	2	3	5	30
Alex Jones	11	3	1	4	76
Gareth Owen	5	0	4	4	45
Liam Young	9	0	2	2	22
Barry Evans	30	0	2	2	28
Phil Knight	13	0	1	1	18
Matt Darnell	21	0	1	1	30
Ben Smith	6	0	0	0	34
Gareth Roddis	9	0	0	0	39
Ashley Jones	15	0	0	0	24
Daniel Page (N)	17	0	0	0	27
Bench Penalties					16
TEAM TOTALS	31	83	113	196	1063
Netminders	GPI	Mins	SOG	GA	Sv%
Rick Ashton	14	568	580	100	82.8
Ashley Cathcart	10	436	374	68	81.8
Daniel Page	16	592	552	104	81.2
Joel Pickering	1	20	26	5	80.8
Elliot Foley	10	244	224	61	72.8
TEAM TOTALS	31	1860	1756	338	80.7

Also appeared: Wayne Johnson
Also played for: 1 Romford Raiders; 2 Nottingham Panthers.

SOLIHULL KINGS *left to right, back row (standing)*: Andrew Howarth, Richard Taylor, Nick Whyatt, Barry Evans, Daniel Scott, Joel Pickering, Ben Smith, Stephen Rowlands, Mikka Kaski, Alex Jones, Jon Rodway; *front row*: Dan Page, Neil Adams, Kevin Conway, Andy Ayers, Elliot Folley; *inserts (clockwise from bottom left)*: Phil Knight, Joe Wightman, Matt Darnell, Vitaliy Koulikov, Ashley Jones, Tim Lockyer, Gareth Roddis.

One win Kings

ELAINE WITTERIDGE

When the old MK Kings decided to move to Hull, the Solihull Kings were created and entered in the English Premier League. Intended as a development team, they battled hard all season but gained only one win in their 32 games against more experienced sides. Sadly, a second win had to be forfeited.

After successfully securing *York Fitness* as their main sponsor, Kings appointed former Solihull and Birmingham player **Jon Rodway** to coach the new squad. He duly built the core of his team with local players, most of them coming up through Solihull's junior system.

To these he added MK Kings' returnees, **Andrew Howarth** and **Matt Darnell**, netminder **Rick Ashton** from Billingham, **Nick Whyatt** and **Joe Wightman** from Nottingham Lions and 16-year-old **Daniel Scott** on a two-way contract with Nottingham Panthers.

Then Rodway signed a couple of famous hockey names - Ukrainian **Vitaliy Koulikov**, the 17-year-old younger brother of former King, **Slava Koulikov**, and at the end of September, veteran and prolific scorer **Kevin Conway**. At the start, Koulikov was Kings' only import.

The first game, away to league title favourites Milton Keynes Lightning, gave a taste of the difficult task ahead, with the amateurs suffering a one-sided 16-0 defeat by the semi-pro side.

Apart from a narrow 3-1 loss to the powerful Peterborough Phantoms in early January, Kings stayed close only in games against Slough Jets, and local rivals, Telford Wild Foxes, sides also comprising aspiring youngsters and few imports.

By a quirk of the schedule Telford and Solihull met three times in four November weekends with Wild Foxes' first visit to Hobs Moat Road coming in the third game on the 30th. The fans were eagerly awaiting this confrontation as the first two games had ended in Telford victories, 8-1 and 9-6.

In the first, Kings' defenceman **Ashley Jones** had sustained a season-ending injury and netminder Rick Ashton had been released after the game, leaving Kings with a problem at the back for the rest of the season. (Forward **Joel Pickering** had to go between the pipes in one game!). So Kings were doubly delighted when they won, 9-7.

Unfortunately, it turned out to be their only win of the season. Though they achieved another two-goal victory in their second home game against Wild Foxes in February, the points were forfeited when they were found to have inadvertently iced a suspended player.

PLAYER AWARDS

Players' Player	**Joel Pickering**
Most Valuable Player	**Joel Pickering**
Coach's Award	**Miika Kaski**
Most Improved Player	**Nick Whyatt**

LEADING PLAYERS

Kevin Conway *born 13 July 1963*
The former GB international from Canada has been in the UK since the mid-1980s, and played two seasons with the old Telford Tigers. His experience on the young Kings was invaluable and he helped to keep morale high through their difficult season.

Andrew Howarth *born 18 May 1978*
The hard working, skilful winger is a product of the junior section and has played for the Blaze and the MK Kings in the BNL.

Joel Pickering *born 10 June 1979*
Another Solihull junior forward who played for the MK Kings, he has also lined up with the GB under-20s and Telford. He constantly frustrated the opposition with his intensity and never-say-die attitude.

FACT FILE 2003-04
English Premier League:	Ninth
Playoffs:	Did not qualify
Premier Cup:	Did not enter

HISTORY
Founded: 2003. The original Solihull team were the *Barons* who were formed in 1965, disbanded in 1996, and reformed again for two seasons in 2000-02. The *Blaze* played in Solihull from 1996 before moving to Coventry in 2000. *MK Kings* played in season 2002-03.

Leagues: *MK Kings* British National League 2002-03; *Barons* English Premier League 2000-02, British Lge, Div. One/Two 1993-96 & 1982-86; English Lge 1991-93; British Lge, Premier Div. 1986-91; Inter-City Lge 1978-82; Southern Lge 1972-78; *Blaze* British National League 1999-2000, English League 1997-99, Premier League 1996-97, .

Honours: *Blaze* English Lge, Premier Div 1998-99, 1997-98; *Barons* English League 1992-93, British Lge, Div One 1985-86, Div Two 1983-84, Southern League 1977-78.

SWINDON LYNX

PLAYER	ALL COMPETITIONS					ENGLISH PREMIER LEAGUE					PLAYOFFS				
Scorers	GP	G	A	Pts	Pim	GP	G	A	Pts	Pim	GP	G	A	Pts	Pim
Frank DeMasi (I)	46	50	51	101	137	31	38	36	74	81	6	5	3	8	6
Ken Forshee (I)	48	47	46	93	98	32	35	34	69	72	6	2	5	7	12
Robin Davison	23	9	38	47	20	13	5	28	33	8	4	1	4	5	10
Wayne Fiddes	46	6	30	36	77	32	4	26	30	30	6	2	1	3	31
Mike Smith	40	11	20	31	36	25	8	17	25	20	6	1	2	3	14
Alan Armour	43	15	15	30	66	29	9	8	17	42	6	0	4	4	16
Gareth Endicott	41	15	13	28	111	27	10	11	21	48	5	2	0	2	55
Richard Wojciak	42	12	10	22	44	27	10	7	17	24	6	0	1	1	18
Grant Bailey	22	8	14	22	63	20	8	13	21	53					
Michael Hargreaves	46	6	13	19	70	30	3	10	13	64	6	1	1	2	0
Shane Moore	45	3	13	16	130	30	2	9	11	100	6	1	0	1	14
Ian Clark	46	3	7	10	171	31	2	5	7	109	6	0	0	0	24
Lee Brathwaite	14	2	7	9	55	14	2	7	9	55					
Graham Newell	26	4	4	8	2	16	3	2	5	2	2	0	0	0	0
Andrew Shurmer 1	43	2	6	8	42	27	2	3	5	10	6	0	1	1	12
Shaun Littlewood	40	1	3	4	6	28	1	3	4	4	6	0	0	0	0
Nick Compton	24	1	2	3	0	15	1	2	3	0	2	0	0	0	0
Greg Martin	27	1	2	3	0	16	1	2	3	0	5	0	0	0	.0
Dan Shea (N)	47	0	2	2	6	32	0	2	2	4	5	0	0	0	0
Drew Chapman	1	0	1	1	4	1	0	1	1	4					
Joseph Dickens	34	0	1	1	6	25	0	0	0	2	4	0	0	0	0
Greg Rockman (N)	48	0	0	0	2	32	0	0	0	0	6	0	0	0	2
Bench Penalties					10					6					2
TEAM TOTALS	48	196	298	494	1156	32	144	226	370	738	6	15	22	37	216
Netminders	GPI	Mins	SOG	GA	Sv%	GPI	Mins	SOG	GA	Sv%	GPI	Mins	SOG	GA	Sv%
Greg Rockman	37	1909	1298	138	89.4	25	1330	886	100	88.7	6	273	194	14	92.8
Dan Shea	21	968	602	72	88.0	14	587	325	35	89.2	2	87	96	17	82.3
Empty Net Goals			3	2				3	2						
TEAM TOTALS	48	2880	1900	212	88.8	32	1920	1211	137	88.7	6	360	290	31	89.3

Also appeared: Aaron Nell, James Skaife, Tom Mills.

Also played for: 1 Oxford City Stars

Shutouts: Rockman - league: 30 Aug v Telford Wild Foxes (25 saves),
14 Sept at Telford Wild Foxes (32 saves);
playoffs: 20 Mar v Romford Raiders (34)

All Competitions = league, playoffs and Premier Cup

'Lipper' returns

DAVE LITTLEWOOD

Following several seasons of financial strife, the club came under new management whose first move was to bring back former player-coach **Daryl Lipsey** after a gap of eight years.

'Mr. Swindon Ice Hockey' had joined the old Wildcats in 1986-87 and filled various roles before leaving to join Manchester Storm in 1995-96. He signed a number of players from the previous season: **Gregg Rockman** in goal, **Lee Brathwaite** and **Wayne Fiddes** on defence, and up front **Ken Forshee**, **Robin Davison**, **Gareth Endicott** and **Grant Bailey**.

Frank DeMasi was brought in to try and fill the gap after the departure of player-coach **Merv Priest**. Also snapped up were former Swindon junior **Richard Wojciak**, who had been trying his luck across the pond, **Mike Smith**, and former favourite **Alan Armour**.

Two players new to Swindon were **Mike Hargreaves** from the Isle of Wight and **Ian Clark** from Haringey Racers. The team was supplemented with some promising juniors from the under-19 side, including **Shane Moore** who went on to play for GB's winning under-18 team, and back-up netminder **Dan Shea**.

Lynx were lying third at the end of October behind Milton Keynes and Peterborough but then they suffered two major setbacks. Davison's knee injury sidelined him for nearly three months, and worst of all, inspirational captain Brathwaite decided to retire after picking up another couple of injuries that threatened his career as a fire-fighter.

Lynx went 13 games without a win before beating Slough 3-2 on 24 January. This left them in sixth place and Lipsey's early objective of a top three spot had to be revised to finishing in the playoffs ahead of Slough. With crowds disappointingly down to the 300 level, financial restrictions prevented him from strengthening his squad.

With an end-of-season flourish, Lynx made it to the playoffs where they turned in some excellent performances in front of growing and enthusiastic crowds.

Despite losing 4-2 in the first game against group favourites, Peterborough, they bounced back with a superb 4-0 win over Romford. But then an 11-1 collapse at Peterborough and two defeats to the strengthened Slough Jets sealed their fate.

Brathwaite's long career in Swindon was recognised with a testimonial match against an Old Stars team.

PLAYER AWARDS

Players' Player	Ken Forshee
Best Forward	Frank DeMasi
Best Defenceman	Wayne Fiddes
Most Improved	Shane Moore
Best British Player	Shane Moore

LEADING PLAYERS

Frank DeMasi born 29 September 1975

Arrived in Swindon from the Belgian League after four seasons in the NCAA. Only 5ft, 6in tall, his accurate shooting helped him finish as the club's top points scorer.

Wayne Fiddes born 20 April 1979

The former Swindon junior had his work cut out when his blueline partner **Lee Brathwaite** retired. But with the increase in ice time he stepped up to be the number one defenceman and helped to develop a crop of juniors who played alongside him. Fourth in the team's scoring.

Gregg Rockman born 24 May 1982

In his second season in Swindon, the club's number one goalie was the man for the big occasion. Highlight was an unlikely 4-1 home win over high flying Peterborough when Lynx were outshot 40-13.

FACT FILE 2003-04

English Premier League: Sixth
Playoffs: Third in qr-final grp
Premier Cup: Fifth in qr-final grp

HISTORY

Founded: 2001. Previous clubs in the Link Centre were **Phoenix** 2000-01, **Chill** 1997-2000, **IceLords** 1996-97 and **Wildcats** 1986-96.

Leagues: **Lynx** and **Phoenix** - English (Premier) League 2000-04; **Chill** - English League 1997-2000; **IceLords** - Premier League 1996-97; **Wildcats** - British League, Div One 1986-96.

SWINDON LYNX *left to right, back row:* Nick Compton, Graham Newell, Andy Shurmer, Mike Smith, Shane Moore, Shaun Littlewood, Joe Dickens, Mike Hargreaves, Robin Davison, Ian Clark, Greg Martyn, Ray Taylor (asst coach), Hannah Boardman (physio), Daryl Lipsey (coach); *front row:* Dan Shea, Richard Wojciak, Ken Forshee, Wayne Fiddes, Lee Brathwaite, Grant Bailey, Frank DeMasi, Alan Armour, Gregg Rockman.

Photo: Ian Lewis

TELFORD WILD FOXES

PLAYER	ALL COMPETITIONS					ENGLISH PREMIER LEAGUE					PLAYOFFS				
Scorers	GP	G	A	Pts	Pim	GP	G	A	Pts	Pim	GP	G	A	Pts	Pim
Daniel Mackriel	40	25	36	61	183	28	19	28	47	126	5	2	5	7	12
Jared Owen	40	25	34	59	137	29	16	24	40	95	5	2	5	7	2
Tom Carlon 3	31	29	21	50	44	21	20	13	33	34	5	5	3	8	4
Adam Brittle 3	33	16	20	36	8	22	12	12	24	8	4	3	4	7	0
Claude Dumas	16	20	7	27	2	7	12	4	16	0	6	6	3	9	2
Dave Fielder	21	2	16	18	108	14	1	9	10	46	3	1	3	4	2
Michael Rodger (I)	25	11	6	17	22	18	7	4	11	20					
Ashley Stanton	43	3	10	13	116	31	3	8	11	72	6	0	0	0	10
Joe Miller	11	2	10	12	0	3	1	3	4	0	6	1	6	7	0
Daniel Croft	40	4	6	10	171	30	2	5	7	94	5	1	0	1	4
James Clarke	42	4	5	9	64	29	4	5	9	34	6	0	0	0	14
Jason Parry	33	3	6	9	71	19	2	2	4	59	6	0	0	0	6
Ryan Stanton	35	3	4	7	50	22	1	4	5	36	5	0	0	0	6
Gareth Davies	40	3	3	6	52	30	3	2	5	40	3	0	0	0	4
Matt Towe	21	2	4	6	2	18	1	4	5	2	1	0	0	0	0
Mark Hazlehurst	12	1	5	6	73	8	1	5	6	71	2	0	0	0	2
Stuart Bates	26	0	3	3	0	16	0	2	2	0	4	0	1	1	0
Daniel Brittle (N)	35	0	3	3	8	25	0	3	3	8	5	0	0	0	0
Mike Roden	33	2	0	2	226	20	2	0	2	130	6	0	0	0	12
Daniel Heslop (N)	40	0	2	2	26	28	0	2	2	24	6	0	0	0	2
Graham Oldham	1	1	0	1	0										
Simon James	32	1	0	1	4	21	0	0	0	0	3	1	0	1	2
Stuart Brittle 1	5	0	1	1	4	1	0	0	0	2	3	0	0	0	0
Marc Lovell 2	6	0	1	1	0	6	0	1	1	0					
Dean Tonks	21	0	1	1	2	18	0	1	1	2					
Jason Hewitt	1	0	0	0	46	1	0	0	0	46					
Bench Penalties					8					4					0
TEAM TOTALS	45	157	204	361	1427	31	107	141	248	953	6	22	30	52	84
Netminders	GPI	Mins	SOG	GA	Sv%	GPI	Mins	SOG	GA	Sv%	GPI	Mins	SOG	GA	Sv%
Daniel Heslop		34	1786	1466	180	87.7	24	1282	1060	128	87.9	5	244	187	27	85.6
Daniel Brittle		20	880	632	99	84.3	12	578	437	66	84.9	4	116	75	11	85.3
Steve Parry		1	34	15	3	80.0										
TEAM TOTALS		45	2700	2113	282	86.6	31	1860	1497	194	87.0	6	360	262	38	85.5

Also appeared: Andy Jaszczyk, Brian Worrall, Chad Briggs, Chris Morris, Dillan Leslie-Rowe, Jamie Burnett, Kevin Parton, Mark Thomas, Neil Brown, Rob Perks, Scott Williams, Tom Parker.

Also played for: 1 Hull Stingrays; 2 Manchester Phoenix; 3 Belfast Giants.

All Competitions = league, playoffs and Premier Cup

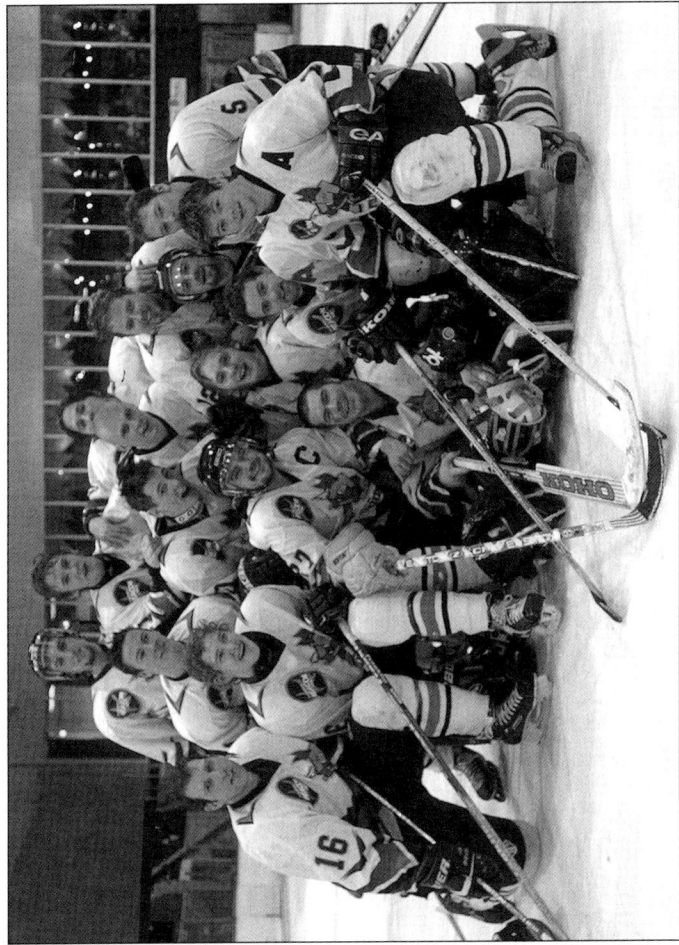

TELFORD WILD FOXES *left to right*, *back row*: Mike Rodger, Tom Carlon, Gareth Bates; *middle row*: Stuart Bates, Ryan Stanton, Mike Roden, Dave Fielder, James Clarke, Ashley Stanton; *front row*: Claude Dumas, Simon James, Daniel Croft, Daniel Heslop, Adam Brittle, Daniel Mackriel, Jason Parry.

Foxes in playoff hunt

DAVID HALL

Player-coach **Claude Dumas**, a Telford Tigers' legend, turned the amateur Wild Foxes into a disciplined team that enjoyed their best ever English Premier League campaign.

The club pulled off something of a coup when they signed the French-Canadian early in the New Year to replace **Dave Fielder**. The 37-year-old had retired from playing in the summer after 14 years in the British game, scoring over 2,000 points.

When the season got underway the young Shropshire side were the league's only outfit without imports, with a reputation for taking unnecessary penalties. Dumas brought leadership to the team and gave their talented home-bred players the confidence to take their game to a new level.

His first signing was GB under-20 international **Joe Miller**, 18, from Cardiff, who, along with local player **Tom Carlon**, 17, had helped the national team to a gold medal over Christmas.

DISCIPLINE AND SELF-BELIEF

By the end of the season Foxes were picking up points against some of the more fancied sides for the first time, with a 5-5 draw at Slough Jets and a 5-2 home win over *Wightlink* Raiders.

"We worked hard at doing the simple things well," said Dumas. "Not only did I want the players to believe in themselves but also to be disciplined on the ice. Going up against sides with four imports night after night is not easy, but everyone applied themselves and we got our reward."

That reward included the first ever playoff appearance for the Foxes and though they were unable to make much progress, they were not the whipping boys many might have imagined.

The two points they picked up in their six games came from their splendid 9-4 home win over Chelmsford Chieftains - though not the biggest win, it was definitely their most satisfying result of the season. And they ended the campaign with their heads high after losing to playoff champs, Milton Keynes, by only two goals.

Telford's youngsters were easy winners of the under-19 league championship, and Carlon and another GB junior international, **Adam Brittle**, signed two-way contracts with Elite League side, Belfast Giants, during the season. With top scorer **Danny Mackriel** still only 23, the future is looking bright.

PLAYER AWARDS

Player of the Year	**Tom Carlon**
Players' Player	**Daniel Croft**
Most Improved Player	**Simon James**

LEADING PLAYERS

Tom Carlon *born 18 February 1987*
Despite his tender years this 6ft, 3in forward proved to be at home in the EPL and looks destined for a long and successful career. Tasted gold medal success with GB under-18s and under-20s during the season.

Daniel Croft *born 11 June 1979*
Long-serving backbone of the side who never gives anything less than 100 per cent to the cause. In a young team, he is the player everyone looks to for inspiration and he rarely, if ever, lets them down.

Daniel Mackriel *born 16 July 1980*
The team's leading scorer and the coach's choice as his leading forward. Made his name with Telford as a youngster, and after spending time away has settled back with his home town team.

FACT FILE 2003-04

English Premier League: Eighth
Playoffs: Fourth in qr-final grp
Premier Cup: Fourth in qr-final grp

HISTORY

Founded: 2001. Previous teams in Telford were *Royals* 1997-2001 and *Tigers* 1985-97. The *Timberwolves* played six *B&H* Cup games in September 1999.
Leagues: *Wild Foxes* English Premier League 2002-04; English National League South 2001-02; *Royals* English (National) League 1997-2001; *Tigers* Premier League 1996-97, British League, Div One 1985-96.
Honours: None.

WHITLEY WARRIORS

PLAYER	ALL COMPETITIONS					ENGLISH NAT'L LEAGUE					ENGLISH LEAGUE CUP				
Scorers	GP	G	A	Pts	Pim	GP	G	A	Pts	Pim	GP	G	A	Pts	Pim
Andrew Tindale	20	24	24	48	20	14	18	19	37	16	6	6	5	11	4
Paul Graham	23	13	24	37	14	17	11	19	30	10	6	2	5	7	4
Lee Baxter	14	19	16	35	24	10	16	9	25	10	4	3	7	10	14
Bryan Dunn	18	10	15	25	115	13	6	7	13	107	5	4	8	12	8
Andrew Robinson	24	4	15	19	24	18	4	10	14	20	6	0	5	5	4
Raymond Haslam	24	6	10	16	51	18	4	8	12	24	6	2	2	4	27
Andrew Carter	4	7	3	10	8	4	7	3	10	8	0	0	0	0	0
David Barrett	24	1	9	10	78	18	1	8	9	56	6	0	1	1	22
Ben Campbell	21	5	4	9	2	15	2	4	6	0	6	3	0	3	2
Ian Emmerson	14	3	6	9	4	9	1	2	3	4	5	2	4	6	0
Robert Wilson	19	2	7	9	204	15	1	7	8	149	4	1	0	1	55
Stephen Winn	4	4	3	7	88	4	4	3	7	88	0	0	0	0	0
Garry Dowd	10	3	4	7	40	7	3	4	7	14	3	0	0	0	26
Adrian Huggins	22	2	4	6	6	18	1	4	5	6	4	1	0	1	0
Dale Howey	6	0	6	6	48	5	0	5	5	42	1	0	1	1	6
Phillip Atherton	15	3	2	5	12	11	0	2	2	10	4	3	0	3	2
Daniel Good	6	2	1	3	0	5	1	1	2	0	1	1	0	1	0
Shaun Kippin	18	2	1	3	26	14	2	1	3	22	4	0	0	0	4
Paul Sample	9	1	2	3	26	6	0	2	2	14	3	1	0	1	12
Paul Watson	10	2	0	2	2	7	2	0	2	0	3	0	0	0	2
Gareth Hughes	8	1	0	1	4	7	1	0	1	4	1	0	0	0	0
Ian Sproat	9	1	0	1	10	7	1	0	1	10	2	0	0	0	0
Gary Wood	8	0	1	1	4	5	0	0	0	0	3	0	1	1	4
Robert Cairns	2	0	0	0	6	2	0	0	0	6	0	0	0	0	0
Michael Christie	6	0	0	0	2	5	0	0	0	2	1	0	0	0	0
Alan Yarrow	6	0	0	0	108	5	0	0	0	98	1	0	0	0	10
Ryan Sample	7	0	0	0	22	5	0	0	0	8	2	0	0	0	14
Bench penalties					2					2					
TEAM TOTALS		115	157	272	950		86	118	204	730		29	39	68	220
Netminders	GPI	Mins	SOG	GA	Sv%	GPI	Mins	SOG	GA	Sv%	GPI	Mins	SOG	GA	Sv%
Calvin Khass	3	35	9	1	88.9	3	35	9	1	88.9					
Simon Burns	2	100	80	14	82.5	1	60	48	6	87.5	1	40	32	8	75.0
Stephen Hoult	23	1286	820	118	85.6	17	967	621	86	86.2	6	319	199	32	83.9
Nicholas Rowe	2	18	19	6	68.4	2	18	19	6	68.4					
Empty Net Goals		1	1	1								1	1	1	
TEAM TOTALS		1440	929	140	84.9		1080	697	99	85.8		360	232	41	82.3

Also appeared: Andrew Wile, John Shreeve, Paul Shreeve, Peter Zajac, Simon Day

Tam's plan lumbers Winn

DAVID HALL

A summer of speculation over a possible new Whitley Bay team - backed by **Tom Stewart's** EUNA Sports - left Warriors very little time to prepare for their assault on the English National League.

The wasted work on the new outfit, which was to have brought British National League hockey to Hillheads, was one of the reasons that Warriors failed to land a playoff slot for the first time in six years.

Coach **Peter Winn** had announced he was stepping down, but with no time left to appoint a new man he was persuaded to take up the reigns once more. He did well to put together a team in a couple of weeks that defeated Kingston 8-2 in the opening game.

However, despite just one defeat in their first four matches – a 7-6 loss at home to Sheffield – it was apparent that the squad was not going to challenge for the title; only one win from the next eight confirmed that.

The loss of key players **Gary Dowd** and **Lee Baxter** - who had to work away for much of the season - and university-bound **DJ Good** and **Dale Howey** didn't help the cause, either.

Then after an 8-1 loss at Bradford in November, Winn had to suspend four senior players for the following week's home clash with Billingham, and a young side lost 5-1.

Ironically, the best performance of the season followed when Whitley dented Nottingham's title hopes with a stunning 4-2 away success. Fans got a glimpse of the real Warriors over Christmas when both Nottingham and Blackburn were dispatched by a full strength side.

By now, however, Winn was finding it difficult to cope with coaching the seniors and running the junior programme. After a mid-week 6-4 success over Sunderland he stepped down to allow former Warriors' winger **Gary Wood** to take over.

Wood made an inauspicious start as Bradford completed an unlikely double with an 8-5 win that stunned the Hillheads crowd. The 41-year-old, who had come out of retirement earlier in the season to help Winn, had to wait until mid-February for his first victory when Blackburn were thrashed in the cup.

"It certainly wasn't the kind of introduction to coaching the first team I was looking for," he said, "but I couldn't fault the efforts of the lads in any of the games I took charge of.

"We ended the campaign with a young squad, quite often we didn't have a player over the age of 22, but they gave me everything they could."

PLAYER AWARDS

Player of the Year   **Stephen Hoult**

LEADING PLAYERS

Stephen Hoult *born 1 February 1985*
It was the teenage keeper's rookie season but he played like a veteran. Won a game at Nottingham almost single-handedly and was consistently the best performer in the side.

Andrew Robinson *born 5 Sept 1980*
Easily the most improved player on the roster. He was thrust into the role of senior defender and responded with some great performances that saw his season's points tally reach a career high.

Paul Sample *born 20 September 1983*
The defenceman [not to be confused with the Belfast forward of the same name - ed.] re-signed for the Warriors in January after 18 months out of the game and immediately showed what the team had missed. At 6ft, 3in he brought some much needed height to the Whitley back line, while his puck handling skills got the defence out of some tricky situations.

FACT FILE 2003-04

English National League:	6th in North
Playoffs:	Did not qualify
English Cup:	4th in North

HISTORY

Founded: 1956. Known as Newcastle Warriors in 1995-96, playing part of the season in Newcastle's *Telewest* Arena.

Leagues: English (National) League 1997-2004; Northern Premier League 1996-97; British League, Premier Division 1982-96; Northern League 1966-82.

Honours: English National League playoff champions 2000-02; English National League North and English Cup 2001-02; English League, Div One playoffs 1999-2000; Scottish Cup 1992; Northern League 1973-75; Icy Smith Cup 1972-73 & 1973-74.

WIGHTLINK RAIDERS

PLAYER	ALL COMPETITIONS					ENGLISH PREMIER LEAGUE					PLAYOFFS				
Scorers	GP	G	A	Pts	Pim	GP	G	A	Pts	Pim	GP	G	A	Pts	Pim
Jason Coles	52	55	54	109	134	31	28	28	56	106	8	9	8	17	6
Rob Lamey	53	48	57	105	59	31	29	32	61	41	8	8	9	17	0
Chris Crombie (I) 2	34	27	52	79	112	15	11	20	31	54	6	4	13	17	14
Scott Carter	52	18	31	49	46	32	10	22	32	20	8	1	4	5	4
Matt Cote	53	10	29	39	50	31	5	17	22	22	8	4	6	10	22
Kent Nobes (I) 1	16	19	16	35	32	15	18	15	33	30					
Andy Pickles	44	6	29	35	76	24	2	14	16	50	8	1	5	6	6
Anthony Blaize	53	5	20	25	56	31	4	16	20	20	8	0	0	0	20
Daniel Giden	54	13	9	22	24	32	10	7	17	14	8	2	0	2	4
Dean Phillimore	50	12	10	22	26	30	8	6	14	18	8	1	2	3	6
Andrew Robinson	53	9	9	18	111	31	4	8	12	81	8	2	0	2	20
Joe Baird	53	7	11	18	172	31	5	7	12	116	8	0	2	2	12
Steve Gannaway	52	0	13	13	40	30	0	8	8	20	8	0	2	2	12
Neil Leary	40	2	10	12	6	20	1	10	11	0	8	0	0	0	2
Damon Larter	45	2	7	9	24	25	0	4	4	20	8	0	1	1	0
Ashley Skinns	52	2	4	6	77	32	2	4	6	63	8	0	0	0	2
Richard Gutteridge	30	1	0	1	0	15	0	0	0	0	6	0	0	0	0
Steve Slater	7	0	1	1	2	5	0	0	0	0					
Toby Cooley (N)	54	0	1	1	8	32	0	1	1	4	8	0	0	0	0
Steve Gossett	10	0	0	0	22						7	0	0	0	22
Mike Barsdell	12	0	0	0	2	4	0	0	0	0	6	0	0	0	0
Bench Penalties					8					2					2
TEAM TOTALS	54	236	363	599	1087	32	137	219	356	681	8	32	52	84	154
Netminders	GPI	Mins	SOG	GA	Sv%	GPI	Mins	SOG	GA	Sv%	GPI	Mins	SOG	GA	Sv%
Toby Cooley	27	1492	868	86	90.1	15	807	482	46	90.5	3	180	83	8	90.4
Dave Hurst	30	1747	954	96	89.9	19	1112	583	67	88.5	5	300	165	17	89.7
Empty Net Goals			1	1				1	1						
TEAM TOTALS	54	3240	1822	183	89.9	32	1920	1065	114	89.3	8	480	248	25	90

Also played for: 1 Bracknell Bees, Peterborough Phantoms; 2 Bracknell Bees.

Shutouts: Hurst - league: 20 Sept v Solihull Kings (16 saves), 28 Sept at Slough Jets (31).
Cooley - league: 19 Oct v Swindon Lynx (33 saves), 7 Dec v Swindon Lynx (27). ·

All Competitions = league, playoffs and Premier Cup

Back to the future

CLARE WALL

The fans flooded back to Ryde Arena in 2003, restoring the great atmosphere that had been missing for a good few years. With the news that the team was on its own financially, they rallied round a squad picked by returning player-coaches, **Andy Pickles** and **Jason Coles**.

The hard-working pair chose players who would bring enthusiasm and grit to the Raiders. They also arranged a new deal with the club's former sponsors, *Wightlink*, the ferry company, which enabled them to bring back their old name, last used in **Dan Sweeney**'s glory days.

Much to the approval of the supporters, the new-look Raiders were hungrier and more determined than they'd been for some time.

Especially impressive were netminders **David Hurst** and **Toby Cooley**, with captain **Scott Carter** leading from the front. Additions to the squad included ex-Basingstoke Bison players, **Andrew Robinson**, **Dean Phillimore** and **Ashley Skinns**, who all showed promise, as did **Daniel Giden** and **Damon Larter**, both products of Raiders' junior development programme.

The team were fortunate to acquire the services of former Superleague defender, **Matt Coté**, who passed on many of his skills. His teammates were soon throwing themselves in front of every shot with the same disregard for their safety as the 38-year-old veteran.

The attack was not as effective. The Island side often outshot their opponents but they had trouble converting their chances.

One of Raiders' bogey teams was Telford Wild Foxes. They won all their home games against the Shropshire side but in Telford they were really pushed, with some of the games going to the wire. But the real thorn in their side was Chelmsford Chieftains, who beat the Raiders on three out of four occasions.

Like many English Premier League sides, they failed to gain a point off the Big Two, Milton Keynes and Peterborough. But they finished a respectable fifth, one better than the previous season, and then enjoyed good form in the playoffs, coming second in their group, before losing in the semis to Slough Jets.

Saving the best until last, Raiders pulled off their best results in the Premier Cup - a draw and a victory over Milton Keynes. But in the final they were outclassed by Peterborough and had to be content with winning the league's sportsmanship trophy for taking the fewest penalties.

PLAYER AWARDS

Player of the Year	**Matt Coté**
Players' Player	**Matt Coté**
Best Defenceman	**Matt Coté**
Best Forward	**Rob Lamey**
Most Improved Player	**David Hurst**
Best British Player	**Joe Baird**

LEADING PLAYERS

Matt Coté *born 19 January 1966*

The Bracknell Bees and Basingstoke Bison legend was a welcome addition and, as always, he held the fort impeccably. He adjusted well to the small ice of Ryde Arena and not only helped the team retain the third best defence in the league but also scored a number of goals.

David Hurst *26 November 1978*

The young goaltender from Slough made huge strides after playing roller hockey for a number of years. Sharing the duties with Cooley, both netminders stayed fresh and injury-free the whole season. Hurst was particularly impressive in away games and won acclaim from supporters at home and away.

Rob Lamey *born 4 September 1980*

He had played for the club in the latter half of 2002-03 and took some time to fit in. But from the outset of the 2003-04 season, he fired on all cylinders, scoring some brilliant goals. Undoubtedly the team's most influential forward and a great British talent.

FACT FILE 2003-04

English Premier League:	Fifth
Playoffs:	Semi-finalists
Premier Cup:	Finalists

HISTORY

Founded: 2003. The first club on the Island in 1991 was Solent Vikings, the second in 1992-99 was *Wightlink* Raiders. The name was changed to Isle of Wight Raiders in 1999-2003. **Leagues**: English (Premier) League 1991-2004. **Honours**: English Premier Cup 2001; English League 1993-97.

WIGHTLINK RAIDERS *left to right, back row:* Neil Leary, Ashley Skinns, Tony Blaize, Damon Larter, Daniel Giden, Andrew Robinson, Rob Lamey, Kent Nobes, Dean Phillimore; *front row:* Toby Cooley, Joe Baird, Jason Coles, Scott Carter, Andy Pickles, Steve Gannaway, Matt Cote, David Hurst.

LEAGUE ORGANISATION

Senior ice hockey in 2003-04 was run by three separate organisations, the first two under licence from the governing body, Ice Hockey UK.

The Elite Ice Hockey League Ltd (EIHL), a limited liability company, was run by its member clubs with each having one seat on the league's board of directors.

There were no restrictions on the origin of the players. The salary cap for each club was £7,000 per week, making £210,000 for a 30-week season. Team rosters were limited to 20 skaters plus two netminders with a maximum of 12 professional players. Two players had to be eligible to play for the GB under-20 team.

Each team was restricted to five work permit holders.

The **British National Ice Hockey League** Ltd (BNL), also a limited liability company, was run on similar lines to the Elite League, with each member club having a director on the board.

The clubs agreed that at least 50 per cent of each team's players on the ice should be British trained and eligible to play for the GB national team but clubs could sign as many International Transfer Card (ITC) holders as they wished.

The league imposed a wages' ceiling of £4,500 a week per club (over 30 weeks this amounted to £135,000), though this could be increased up to £6,750 (£202,500) provided the club paid a 20 per cent 'luxury tax' to the league.

The 'tax' is designed to help support and promote the smaller fan-based clubs and help them build upwards.

The league's policy on work permit players was to employ as few as possible.

The English Ice Hockey Association (EIHA) ran the **English Leagues** which comprise a wide range of clubs from the virtually amateur to those with budgets as large as the smaller BNL clubs. The teams with the most ice time and largest budgets competed in the Premier League and the remainder played in one of the National League's two regional conferences.

Each Premier League team could dress a maximum of four ITC holders per game and had to ice at all times at least three British trained players - defined as one who completed two years playing at under-19 level. National League teams were allowed one ITC-holding player or player-coach.

Players' wages were limited by what the club could afford.

IMPORTS

International Transfer Card (ITC) Holders

A signed International Transfer Card (ITC) is required by any player who has been a member of another national federation under the world governing body, the International Ice Hockey Federation (IIHF).

There are two types of ITC - 'limited' for one season, and 'unlimited' for players who intend to remain in this country. The latter are often dual national British-Canadians who are technically not imports.

Ice Hockey UK keeps records only of players needing 'limited' cards. These players are indicated by the letter 'I' appearing against their name in the *Annual*'s club pages. It was left to the clubs to decide how many of these players they wished to employ.

For season 2003-04 Ice Hockey UK issued 178 'limited' ITCs to the three leagues - 97 to the Elite (average 12 per team), 53 to the BNL (average 7.5), and 28 to the English Premier League (average 3).

■ For season 2004-05 the IIHF imposed a maximum of 11 ITC holders per team (reducing to 10 in 2005-06), but only the Elite League decided to employ this many.

Work Permit Holders

In addition to an ITC, work permits are required by players from outside the European Union area who do not qualify for an EU passport.

The government body, Work Permits UK, issues work permits only to 'established sports people whose employment will not displace or exclude resident workers.

'The overseas person should be internationally established at the highest level in their sport, and their employment should contribute to the development of the sport in this country'.

Each year the sport's representatives - Ice Hockey UK, the Elite League, the British National League and the Ice Hockey Players Association - meet to agree the criteria for Work Permit Holders in ice hockey.

For season 2003-04 the criteria were that players from North America must have played in a league at East Coast Hockey League (ECHL) level or above; Europeans had to have played on a team from a country which competed in the World Championships (elite group) in the previous season.

❏ For more on this topic, turn to our *Review of the Year* and go to www.icehockeyuk.co.uk.

ELITE LEAGUE

FINAL STANDINGS

		GP	W	L	D	OL	GF	GA	Pts	Pct.
(3-1)	Sheffield Steelers SHE	56	44	9	3	1	214	109	92	82.1
	Home	28	24	4	0	0	104	51	48	85.7
	Away	28	20	5	3	1	110	58	44	78.6
(4-3)	Nottingham Panthers NOT	56	34	16	6	2	209	158	76	67.8
	Home	28	16	8	4	1	109	86	37	66.1
	Away	28	18	8	2	1	100	72	39	69.6
*	Coventry Blaze COV	56	29	20	7	0	186	156	65	58.0
	Home	28	15	10	3	0	96	79	33	58.9
	Away	28	14	10	4	0	90	77	32	57.1
(1-2)	Belfast Giants BEL	56	27	22	7	1	218	185	62	55.3
	Home	28	14	9	5	1	109	87	34	60.7
	Away	28	13	13	2	0	109	98	28	50.0
*	Cardiff Devils CAR	56	23	27	6	3	155	163	55	49.1
	Home	28	14	11	3	2	77	76	33	58.9
	Away	28	9	16	3	1	78	87	22	39.3
#	Manchester Phoenix MAN	56	22	26	8	1	140	155	53	47.3
	Home	28	12	13	3	0	72	70	27	48.2
	Away	28	10	13	5	1	68	85	26	46.4
*	Basingstoke Bison BAS	56	20	31	5	3	146	195	48	42.8
	Home	28	9	16	3	2	80	99	23	41.1
	Away	28	11	15	2	1	66	96	25	44.6
#	London Racers LON	56	3	51	2	2	106	253	10	8.9
	Home	28	3	24	1	0	55	124	7	12.5
	Away	28	0	27	1	2	51	129	3	5.4

Figures in brackets are the last two seasons' Superleague positions.
* Previously competed in British National League.   # New club.
Scoring system: *two points for a win (W), one point for a draw (D) or overtime loss (OL).*
Pct. = *percentage of points gained to points available*

LEADING SCORERS

excluding playoffs	GP	G	A	Pts	Pim
Mark Dutiaume SHE	53	34	54	88	69
Jason Ruff BEL	52	35	50	85	134
Mark Cadotte NOT	56	30	47	77	40
Steve Gallace COV	55	29	45	74	56
John Craighead NOT	54	39	30	69	182
Erik Anderson SHE	56	32	36	68	18
Brad Kenny BEL	56	32	36	68	36
Kim Ahlroos NOT	56	29	38	67	34
Curt Bowen BEL	47	27	39	66	86
Mike Peron SHE	49	24	42	66	104

LEADING NETMINDERS

excluding playoffs	GPI	Mins	SoG	GA	Sav%
Rob Dopson SHE	29	1708	827	63	92.4
Curtis Cruickshank BAS	54	3103	2099	163	92.2
Jayme Platt MAN	55	3242	1667	141	91.5
Jody Lehman COV	56	3295	1661	149	91.0
Niklas Sundberg NOT	54	3160	1509	137	90.9
Jason Cugnet CAR	23	1400	645	59	90.9

Qualification: 1,120 minutes

FAIR PLAY

Team Penalties	GP	Pim	Ave
Manchester Phoenix	56	757	13.5
Coventry Blaze	56	932	16.6
London Racers	56	960	17.1
Basingstoke Bison	56	1024	18.3
Nottingham Panthers	56	1033	18.4
Sheffield Steelers	56	1119	20.0
Cardiff Devils	56	1240	22.1
Belfast Giants	56	1290	23.0
LEAGUE TOTALS		8355	18.6

SIN-BIN

Most Penalised Players	GP	Pim	Ave
Paxton Schulte BEL	54	352	6.52
Dennis Maxwell CAR	51	231	4.53
Gerad Adams SHE	53	190	3.58
Mike Ware CAR	47	167	3.55
Jason Bowen BEL	48	166	3.46

POWERPLAY

Powerplay percentages	Adv.	PPG	Pct.
Coventry Blaze	299	71	23.7
Belfast Giants	167	34	20.4
Nottingham Panthers	217	44	20.3
Sheffield Steelers	241	46	19.1
Manchester Phoenix	250	44	17.6
Cardiff Devils	229	39	17.0
Basingstoke Bison	217	30	13.8
London Racers	249	17	6.8
LEAGUE TOTALS	1869	325	17.4

Adv. - Times with man advantage (powerplay)
PPG - powerplay goals scored
Pct. - percentage of goals scored to powerplays.

TOP POWERPLAY GOAL SCORERS

John Craighead NOT, Steve Gallace COV 14; Erik Anderson SHE 11; Mike Peron SHE, Joel Poirier COV 10.

PENALTY KILLING

Penalty killing percentages	TSH	PGA	Pct.
Belfast Giants	273	39	85.7
Basingstoke Bison	245	37	84.9
Cardiff Devils	255	40	84.3
Nottingham Panthers	223	35	84.3
Sheffield Steelers	250	41	83.6
Coventry Blaze	215	36	83.3
Manchester Phoenix	189	35	81.5
London Racers	219	62	71.7
LEAGUE TOTALS	1869	325	82.6

TSH - times short-handed
PGA - powerplay goals against

TOP SHORT-HANDED GOAL SCORERS

Jason Ruff BEL, Mark Dutiaume SHE, Ivan Matulik CAR, Graham Schlender COV, Ashley Tait COV, all 3.

OVERTIME GAME WINNING GOALS

Ref	Team	Goal Scorer		Time
(1)	BEL	Todd Kelman		64.25
(2)	SHE	Kirk de Waele		61.27
(3)	COV	Joel Poirier	pp	60.22
(4)	MAN	George Awada		60.19
(5)	COV	Hilton Ruggles		63.05
(6)	NOT	Dave Struch		63.39
(7)	CAR	Kirk DeWaele		60.24
(8)	MAN	Miroslav Skovira	pp	62.53
(9)	SHE	Mark Dutiaume		63.57
(10)	BAS	Brad Schueller		60.13
(11)	COV	Steve Carpenter		63.03
(12)	LON	Lukas Filip		62.52
(13)	COV	Hilton Ruggles		64.57

NOTES ON RESULTS CHART

(See over)
* played at Deeside
London Racers played home games at Alexandra Palace until 31 October, then at Lee Valley.
Biggest win - 11-0 by Coventry at home to Manchester on 7 December.

OFFICIAL ELITE LEAGUE WEBSITE
www.eliteleague.co.uk

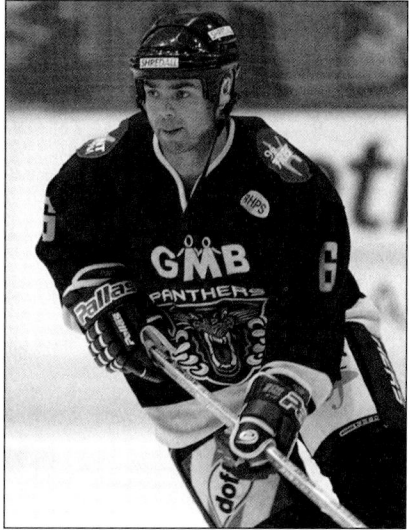

Clockwise from left: **DION DARLING**, Sheffield Steelers' All-Star defenceman; **KIM AHLROOS**, scorer of Nottingham Panthers' overtime winning Challenge Cup goal; **EVAN LINDSAY**, London Racers' goalie who had a shutout in their first win; **RYAN LAKE**, Sheffield Steelers' promising young British player.

Photos: Tony Boot, Roger Cook, Diane Davey.

ELITE LEAGUE

RESULTS CHART

	BAS	BEL	CAR	COV	LON	MAN	NOT	SHE
Bison	**	4-10C 14/9	2-3C 27/9	3-2C 20/9	3-1C 25/10	3-0 C 11/10	1-2C 18/10	4-6C 4/10
	**	7-2 1/11	3-5 21/12	2-3ot (5) 8/11	3-3ot 22/11	1-3 15/11	5-2 20/11	0-4 29/11
	**	2-8 27/12	3-3ot 17/1	2-5 13/12	5-4ot (10) 3/1	2-3 24/1	4-7 6/12	1-2ot (9) 9/12
	**	2-5 14/2	2-5 6/3	5-1 21/2	4-2 31/1	3-3ot 28/2	3-2 11/1	1-3 7/2
Giants	3-2otC (1) 28/9	**	6-3C 24/9	2-5C 13/9	5-1C 4/10	5-3C 19/9	3-3ot C 9/10	4-4ot C 11/10
	9-3 23/11	**	3-2 8/11	3-4ot (3) 29/10	6-3 21/10	6-4 11/12	4-3 19/12	1-5 23/1
	2-4 30/1	**	3-1 3/1	2-2ot 10/1	5-0 28/12	2-3 20/12	4-6 30/12	1-3 27/2
	7-2 12/3	**	5-3 4/3	2-2ot 13/3	7-1 8/2	5-5ot 6/2	4-6 22/2	0-4 5/3
Devils	1-1otC 5/10	2-3C 21/9	**	0-3C 22/11	2-1C 18/10	4-1C 13/9	2-1C 28/9	3-2C 1/11
	4-1 9/11	2-3 26/10	**	4-6 29/11	6-5 18/12	2-3ot (8) 27/11	1-5 7/12	3-4ot (7) 15/11
	2-3 28/12	3-3ot 14/12	**	4-2 14/2	4-2 4/1	1-1ot 15/1	1-4 8/2	2-4 20/12
	5-4 18/1	3-2 24/1	**	3-2 28/2	6-1 7/3	3-1 19/2	1-6 13/3	3-2 11/1
Blaze	2-2otC 19/10	7-3C 5/10	1-4C 12/10	**	2-1C 21/9	2-2otC 27/9	1-4C 14/9	6-1C 26/10
	2-5 30/11	5-1 18/1	4-3 23/11	**	7-1 2/11	11-0 7/12	2-2ot 9/11	1-4 16/11
	4-2 20/12	4-2 25/1	5-2 22/2	**	2-1 14/12	3-1 28/12	3-6 1/2	2-6 4/1
	3-5 29/2	4-2 7/3	4-3ot (13) 14/3	**	6-4 11/1	0-2 6/3	0-5 15/2	3-5 8/2
Racers	1-4 C 10/10	3-6C 26/9	3-5C 19/9	4-4ot C 24/10	**	3-6C 3/10	2-3 5/10	1-6C 12/9
	3-4 23/1	2-6 31/10	3-0 30/1	3-6 14/11	**	1-3 9/1	1-3C 17/10	1-4 19/12
	3-4 20/2	2-9 21/11	1-2 6/2	0-5 5/12	**	0-2 24/2	2-3 28/11	0-7 16/1
	4-0 2/3	3-8 13/2	1-5 17/2	0-4 2/1	**	2-7 5/3	3-2ot (12) 27/2	3-6 12/3
Phoenix	1-2 C 26/10	0-2C 17/10	5-2C 19/10	4-3C 24/9	4-0C 14/9	**	2-3C 21/9	0-0ot C 10/10
	0-1 5/12	7-2 9/11	3-2 2/11	3-3ot 26/12	5-4ot (4)* 4/11	**	0-2 4/1	2-5 14/12
	1-3 8/2	3-4 11/1	1-1ot 29/2	1-4 21/1	3-1 18/1	**	2-3 28/1	3-2 2/1
	6-0 15/2	5-4 1/2	0-3 12/3	3-1 13/2	5-3 14/3	**	3-8 3/3	0-2 22/2
Panthers	2-1 C 13/9	1-1ot C 30/9	4-6 C 25/10	2-4C 4/10	3-0C 29/10	1-1ot C 21/10	**	5-5ot C 20/9
	2-6 16/11	5-3 30/11	2-2ot 14/11	7-2 1/11	9-3 10/12	4-2 22/11	**	5-4ot (6) 8/11
	4-2 2/1	4-7 7/2	3-2 13/12	3-5 24/1	5-1 20/12	5-1 31/1	**	3-7 26/12
	6-2 20/1	7-4 14/3	3-2 10/1	3-4ot (11) 19/2	4-1 14/2	7-5 21/2	**	0-3 28/2
Steelers	6-0 C 21/9	2-5C 19/10	5-2C 14/9	3-2C 18/10	7-3 C 28/9	3-2ot (2)C 5/10	4-1C 27/9	**
	3-1 10/1	3-2 7/12	4-2 30/11	1-2 21/12	3-0 19/11	3-4 25/10	2-4 2/11	**
	5-1 11/2	3-1 21/1	6-4 25/1	4-2 17/1	4-2 7/1	2-0 23/11	5-0 27/12	**
	5-1 14/3	3-1 21/2	2-1 15/2	4-2 31/1	4-2 10/3	1-0 14/2	7-4 6/3	**

ELITE INTERNATIONALS

MATT MYERS, Cardiff Devils *left* and **PAUL SAMPLE**, Belfast Giants, scored for Britain on their senior World Championship debuts.

Photos: Dave Page

Two-horse race

Another season, another league, but **Sheffield Steelers** were the champions again. Last year's Superleague winners captured the first Elite League title by 16 points over their fierce rivals, **Nottingham Panthers**.

The new league was a mixture of three arena teams from the defunct Superleague, three former BNL clubs, and two new teams, London Racers and Manchester Phoenix. The latter arose from the ashes of the bankrupt Storm.

In truth, only two - Steelers and Panthers - were ever likely to win the league. Their big crowds and experienced management meant the others were always trying to catch up.

Steelers' coach **Mike Blaisdell** once again showed himself to be the master of finding Canadians and motivating them into British league winners. Panthers' **Paul Adey** went for a more cosmopolitan roster and couldn't achieve the same consistency as his rival.

Coventry Blaze finished a creditable third while regularly icing more home-grown players, including several British internationals, than any other side. Blaze also boasted the league's only English coach in **Paul Thompson**.

Belfast Giants lost their coach **Dave Whistle** and his promoted assistant **Rob Stewart** could only guide the Superleague playoff champs to fourth while piling up the Elite League's highest penalty total. Their notorious enforcer, **Paxton Schulte**, took a quarter of his entire team's penalties in his last season in the UK.

Giants' loss was **Cardiff Devils'** gain. 'Whis' replaced **Glen Mulvenna** at the season's mid-point and took the team - who returned to the top level after a two-season break - from bottom of the pile to fifth while using a respectable quota of native Brits.

Manchester Phoenix struggled under player-manager-coach **Rick Brebant**, but the appointment after Christmas of Glaswegian **Paul Heavey** changed their fortunes and they reached the sixth and last playoff place.

Seventh-placed **Basingstoke Bison** might not have given Phoenix such a close race had it not been for their netminder **Curtis Cruickshank**. A 24-year-old minor leaguer from Ottawa, his save percentage of 92.2 was the best among goalies who played the full season.

London Racers, which the league liked to promote as a replacement for the **Phil Anschutz**-owned London Knights, attracted barely 500 fans a game and were forced to change venues in mid-season. They also went through three coaches with the first, Canadian politician **Gary Carr**, quitting before the season even started. Unsurprisingly, Racers won only three games, the worst record of any leading club in recent years.

Like Superleague, the new circuit was heavily dependent on overseas players. The top British points scorer, **Ashley Tait** of Panthers, finished 15th overall and all the first choice goalies were imports.

PLAYOFFS

The league's top six teams were split into two groups for the playoffs: group A contained the teams finishing first, fourth and sixth and group B the teams who came second, third and fifth.

Each team played the others in their group twice (home and away) with the top two teams in each group qualifying for the finals weekend in Nottingham.

In the semi-finals the winner of group A played the runner-up in group B and the runner-up in group B met the winner of group A.

The first semi-final comprised the group winners that finished higher in the league table.

QUALIFYING ROUND

Group A	GP	W	L	D	OL	GF	GA	Pts
Sheffield Steelers	4	2	0	2	0	11	5	6
Manch'ter Phoenix	4	2	1	1	0	6	6	5
Belfast Giants	4	0	3	1	0	5	11	1
Group B								
Nott'ham Panthers	4	3	1	0	0	12	6	6
Cardiff Devils	4	3	1	0	0	12	8	6
Coventry Blaze	4	0	4	0	0	10	20	0

RESULTS

Group A	BEL	MAN	SHE
Belfast Giants	-	1-2	3-3ot
Manchester Phoenix	3-0	-	1-1ot*
Sheffield Steelers	3-1	4-0	-
Group B	CAR	COV	NOT
Cardiff Devils	-	4-1	1-0
Coventry Blaze	4-7	-	2-4
Nott'ham Panthers	3-0	5-3	-

* at iceSheffield

SEMI-FINALS

3 April 2004 at Nottingham's National Ice Centre
Sheffield-Cardiff   **2-0** (1-0,0-0,1-0)
Nottingham-Manchester   **6-1** (1-1,2-0,3-0)

FINAL

4 April 2004 at the National Ice Centre
Sheffield-Nottingham   **2-1** (0-0,2-1,0-0)

SHEFFIELD STEELERS win Elite League Playoff Championship

Steelers trap trophy two

Sheffield Steelers completed the league and playoff double when they edged Nottingham Panthers 2-1 in the final. The game also completed the bitter enemies' domination of the league's three major competitions.

The victory enabled Steelers' coach **Mike Blaisdell** to hoist his 14th major trophy, a modern era, and very possibly an all-time record for a coach in the UK.

He praised his players for sticking to his strictly defensive game plan against the sharp shooting, fast skating Panthers forwards. "We played the neutral zone trap as well as any other team has ever played it in this country," he told the *Sheffield Star.* "We strapped four guys across the blue line and it worked."

This system had already brought Steelers the league title but it was even more important in the final when they had to manage without the league's top forward, **Mark Dutiaume**, who was struck in the eye by an errant high stick in the semi-final. "His loss made us stronger and more focused," said Blaisdell.

Though Steelers' netminder **Christian Bronsard** kept a clean sheet against Cardiff in the first semi, Devils' coach **Dave Whistle** professed himself content with his unfancied team's workrate against a superior side. Bronsard's opposite number, **Jason Cugnet**, looked shaky on both Steelers' efforts.

Manchester Phoenix, who had battled hard just to reach the playoffs, let alone the final four, were comprehensively thrashed by Panthers, despite scoring the first goal. Colourful forward, **John Craighead**, had a hat-trick.

The quarter-final groups worked out neatly. Panthers and Steelers were kept apart and the split couldn't have been better geographically if it had been designed that way.

The surprise was the failure of Coventry Blaze, third place league finishers, to make the semis. They completely lost their form, failing to win a game. Belfast Giants, too, were unable to rise to the challenge of the new season.

Manchester happily jumped into the gap, beating Giants home and away and pulling off one the season's biggest upsets when they held Steelers 1-1 at 'home'.

When the *MEN* Arena was unavailable, Phoenix took a lot of flak from their fans for agreeing to stage their home game in the new iceSheffield rink across the way from the *Hallam FM* Arena. The gamble paid off as Steelers perhaps took the encounter too lightly.

PLAYOFF SEMI-FINALS
National Ice Centre, Nottingham
Saturday 3 April 2004

SHEFFIELD STEELERS	2	(1-0-1)
CARDIFF DEVILS	0	(0-0-0)

Scoring
1-0 SHE Lefebvre   13.02
2-0 SHE Peron (Darling)   sh   54.50
Netminding
Bronsard SHE   4-6-10 20   *save %*: 100.0
Cugnet CAR   7-11-6 24   *save %*: 91.7
Penalty minutes:
Steelers 16, Devils 22 (Hill 10 min- misc.)
Goals/powerplays: Steelers 0/5, Devils 0/6.
Men of the Match: Lefebvre SHE, Myers CAR.
Referee: Simon Kirkham.   *Attendance*: 6,572
Linesmen: Joy Tottman, Lee Young.

NOTTINGHAM PANTHERS	6	(1-2-3)
MANCHESTER PHOENIX	1	(1-0-0)

Scoring:
0-1 MAN Awada (Anderson)   1.01
1-1 NOT Craighead (Cadotte, Carlsson)   4.54
2-1 NOT Clarke (Jinman, Cadotte)   29.18
3-1 NOT Struch (Clarke, Jinman) pp   34.44
4-1 NOT Cadotte   41.24
5-1 NOT Craighead (Salonen)   sh   43.18
6-1 NOT Craighead (Jinman, Cadotte)   45.26
Netminding
Sundberg NOT   9-8-8 25   *save %*: 96.0
Platt MAN   8-9-6 23   *save %*: 73.9
Penalty minutes: Panthers 14, Phoenix 12
Goals/powerplays: Panthers 1/6, Phoenix 0/7.
Men of the Match:
Craighead NOT, Lankshear MAN.
Referee: Moray Hanson   *Attendance*: 6,572
Linesmen: Tom Darnell, Matt Folka.

PLAYOFF FINAL
National Ice Centre, Nottingham
Sunday, 4 April 2004

SHEFFIELD STEELERS	2	(0-2-0)
NOTTINGHAM PANTHERS	1	(0-1-0)

Scoring:
1-0 SHE Adams (Bolibruk)   20.56
1-1 NOT Cadotte (Jinman, Struch) pp   31.41
2-1 SHE DeWaele (Peron)   33.39
Netminding
Bronsard SHE   4-7-7 18   *save %*: 94.4
Sundberg NOT 10-8-5 23   *save %*: 91.3
Penalty minutes: Steelers 8, Panthers 8.
Goals/powerplays: Steelers 0/2, Panthers 1/2.
Men of the match: Adams SHE, Jinman NOT.
Referee: Nigel Boniface   *Attendance*: 6,724
Linesmen: Marco Coenen, Michael Hicks.

THE FINAL FOUR
CARDIFF DEVILS
Jason Cugnet, Mike Brabon; Jeff Burgoyne, Jason Stone, Jason Becker, Ed Patterson, Matt Myers, Doug McEwen, David James, Phil Manny, Russ Romaniuk, Phil Hill, Jonathan Phillips, Jeff Brown, Ivan Matulik, Mike Ware (capt), Neil Francis, James Manson, Dennis Maxwell.
Coach: Dave Whistle. *Manager*: Shannon Hope.
MANCHESTER PHOENIX
Jayme Platt, Dave Clancy; Mike Lankshear, Dwight Parrish, Carl Greenhous, Mark Thomas, Marc Lovell, Jason Hewitt, Aaron Davies, Chad Brandimore, Mike Morin, David Kozier, Petteri. Lotila, Darcy Anderson, Mikka Skytta, George Awada (capt), Rick Brebant.
Coach: Paul Heavey. *Manager*: Rick Brebant.
NOTTINGHAM PANTHERS
Niklas Sundberg, Geoff Woolhouse; Robert Stancok, Briane Thompson (capt), Kristian Taubert, Calle Carlsson; David Clarke, Kim Ahlroos, David Struch, Marc Levers, Mikko Koivunoro, Joel Salonen, Mark Cadotte, Paul Moran, Daniel Scott, Lewis Buckman, Lee Jinman, John Craighead.
Coach: Paul Adey. *Manager*: Gary Moran.
SHEFFIELD STEELERS
Christian Bronsard, Davey Lawrence; Ron Shudra, Gerad Adams, Steve Duncombe, Ryan Lake, Marc Lefebvre, Mike Peron, Mark Dutiaume, Gavin Farrand, Erik Anderson, Kevin Bolibruck, Kirk DeWaele, Ben Bliss, Dion Darling (capt), Joel Irving, Steve Ellis, Brent Bobyck.
Coach: Mike Blaisdell. *Manager*: Scott Neil.

LEADING PLAYOFF SCORERS

	GP	G	A	Pts	Pim
Lee Jinman NOT	6	2	10	12	4
Mark Cadotte NOT	5	3	6	9	6
Mike Peron SHE	6	3	6	9	12
John Craighead NOT	6	5	1	6	8
Kirk DeWaele SHE	6	3	3	6	12
Ed Patterson CAR	5	3	2	5	4
Mike Ware CAR	5	3	1	4	6
David Clarke NOT	4	2	2	4	4

LEADING PLAYOFF NETMINDERS

	GPI	Mins	SoG	GA	Sv%
Christian Bronsard SHE	6	370	142	6	95.8
Niklas Sundberg NOT	6	360	163	9	94.5
Jason Cugnett CAR	5	300	129	9	93.0

CHALLENGE CUP

The first round of Elite League games counted towards the Challenge Cup (see Elite League Results Chart) with the top four teams meeting in the semi-finals on a home-and-away basis. The leading team played the fourth placed side, and the runner-up met the team finishing third.

The final was also played over home and away legs, the team finishing higher in the preliminary round receiving choice of home leg.

QUALIFYING ROUND STANDINGS

	GP	W	L	D	OTL	GF	GA	Pts
Belfast Giants	14	9	2	3	0	58	40	21
Sheff'd Steelers	14	8	3	3	0	54	38	19
Cardiff Devils	14	8	5	1	0	39	38	17
Nott'ham Panthers	14	6	4	4	0	35	32	16
Coventry Blaze	14	6	5	3	0	44	35	15
Basingstoke Bison	14	5	6	2	1	32	40	13
M'chester Phoenix	14	4	6	3	1	31	33	12
London Racers	14	0	13	1	0	23	60	1

SEMI-FINALS

First semi-final, first leg, 14 January 2004
BELFAST-NOTTINGHAM   **2-4** (1-3,1-1,0-0)
Scoring: BEL Ruff 1+1; Kelman 1g; Johnson, C Bowen, J Bowen 1a. NOT Jinman, Ahlroos, Moran 1+1; Thompson 1g; Taubert, Craighead, Salonen 1a.
First semi-final, second leg, 17 January 2004
NOTTINGHAM-BELFAST   **7-3** (3-0,4-1,0-2)
Scoring: NOT Cadotte, Jinman 2+2; Ahlroos 1+1; Struch, Stancok 1g; Clarke 3a; Thompson, Koivunoro 2a; Salonen 1a.

NOTTINGHAM PANTHERS win 11-5 on agg.

Second semi-final, first leg, 29 January 2004
CARDIFF-SHEFFIELD   **1-3** (1-1,0-1,0-1)
Scoring: CAR Romaniuk 1g; Sacratini 1a. SHE Adams, Bliss, Peron 1g; Lefebvre, Bolibruck, Dutiaume 1a.
Second semi-final, second leg, 1 February 2004
SHEFFIELD-CARDIFF   **1-1** (0-1,0-0,1-0)
Scoring: SHE Ellis 1g. CAR Maxwell 1g; Patterson, Brown 1a.

SHEFFIELD STEELERS win 4-2 on aggregate.

FINAL

First leg, 9 March 2004
NOTTINGHAM-SHEFFIELD   **1-1** (0-0,1-1,0-0)
Scoring:
1-0 NOT Clarke (Moran, Struch)   33.57
1-1 SHE Dutiaume (Adams)   36.06
Netminding:
Sundberg NOT 12-7-10 29   save % 96.5
Bronsard SHE   9-7- 5 21   save % 95.2
Goals/powerplays: Panthers 0/3, Steelers 0/4.
Penalty minutes: Panthers 50 (Craighead 2+10 roughing + game misc), Steelers 16.
Referee: Simon Kirkham.   Attendance: 4,915
Linesmen: Marco Coenen, Michael Hicks.

Second leg, 17 March 2004
SHEFFIELD-NOTTINGHAM   **2-3ot**
   (0-2,1-0,1-0,0-1).
Scoring:
0-1 NOT Salonen (Jinman, Thompson)   pp   6.59
0-2 NOT Craighead (Stancok, Koivunoro) pp   8.05
1-2 SHE Anderson (Irving, Brebant)   38.54
2-2 SHE Anderson (Bolibruck)   pp   49.22
3-2 NOT Ahlroos (Koivunoro, Thompson)   60.53
Netminding:
Bronsard SHE   9- 8- 7-1 25   save % 88.0
Sundberg NOT   7-10-14-0 31   save % 93.5
Goals/powerplays: Steelers 1/5, Panthers 2/4.
Penalty minutes: Steelers 12, Panthers 10.
Referee: Moray Hanson.   Attendance: 6,724
Linesmen: Marco Coenen, Matt Folka.

Nottingham Panthers win Challenge Cup
4-3 on aggregate

It was Ahlroos on the night

Kim Ahlroos' overtime goal in the home of their deadly rivals gave Panthers their first trophy win since the 1998 Benson and Hedges Cup.

The team and their coach were ecstatic. "We will look back on winning this - in Sheffield of all places - with fond memories for the rest of our lives," said coach **Paul Adey**.

His opposite number, **Mike Blaisdell**, admitted that his players were tired, especially when the game went into overtime. "I goofed by putting out players who had given their all," he said. "Panthers looked fresh by comparison."

Steelers have won this trophy four times in the seven years it has been competed for. This was Panthers' first cup victory.

■ The NIC management had to apologise to the Steelers when ugly scenes ensued after water was poured on them by two fans at the end of the first leg in Nottingham.

NOTTINGHAM PANTHERS

As in the Elite League playoffs, except Lewis Buckman and Daniel Scott.

FINDUS BRITISH
NATIONAL LEAGUE

FINAL STANDINGS

		GP	W	L	D	OL	GF	GA	Pts	Pct
(3-7)	**Fife Flyers** FIF	36	23	7	3	3	135	97	52	72.2
(5-3)	**Guildford Flames** GUI	36	24	9	0	3	136	88	51	70.8
(7-6)	**Edinburgh Capitals** EDI	36	19	13	2	2	143	117	42	58.3
*	**Bracknell Bees** BRK	36	16	13	6	1	116	103	39	54.2
(/-8)	**Newcastle Vipers** NEW	36	17	16	1	2	109	135	37	51.4
(1-2)	**Dundee Stars** DUN	36	14	15	3	4	112	140	35	48.6
(6-9)	**Hull Stingrays** HUL	36	4	25	3	4	71	142	15	20.8

* played in Superleague 2003-04.
Hull Stingrays previously known as Hull Thunder.
Figures in brackets are the league positions in each of the last two seasons.
Scoring system: *two points for a win (W), one point for a draw (D) or overtime loss (OL).*
Pct. *- percentage of points gained to points available.*

LEADING SCORERS

	GP	G	A	Pts	Pim
Tony Hand EDI	36	21	63	84	38
Adrian Saul EDI	35	31	32	63	22
Steven Kaye EDI	35	29	33	62	42
Dan Goneau FIF	33	22	37	59	42
Matt Beveridge NEW	36	18	32	50	32
Nathan Rempel BRK	35	28	21	49	28
Karry Biette FIF	33	23	25	48	81
Scott Allison BRK	35	20	27	47	114
Milos Melicherik GUI	36	19	28	47	48
Dino Bauba DUN	35	17	30	47	122
Jonathan Weaver NEW	35	21	22	43	26
Patric Lochi DUN	34	20	23	43	55
Martin Cingel EDI	33	18	25	43	76

LEADING NETMINDERS

	GPI	Mins	SoG	GA	Sv%
Steve Briere FIF	36	2210	1170	96	91.8
Scott Hay BRK	28	1694	893	79	91.1
Stevie Lyle GUI	36	2179	965	86	91.1
Ladislav Kudrna EDI	36	2156	1209	114	90.6
Anders Hogberg HUL	20	1231	677	63	90.5

Qualification: 720 mins

SIN-BIN

Players' Penalties	GP	Pim	Ave
Paul Berrington DUN	28	131	4.68
Daryl Lavoie BRK	19	81	4.26
Jason Shymr DUN	35	142	4.06
Brent Pope HUL	33	122	3.70
Dino Bauba DUN	35	122	3.48

OFFICIAL BRITISH NATIONAL LEAGUE
WEBSITE
www.britnatleague.net

OVERTIME GAME WINNING GOALS
(See Results Chart over)

Ref	Team	Scorer	Time
(1)	BRK	Darren Hurley (Lavoie)	64.00
(2)	NEW	Rob Wilson (Beveridge)	60.42
(3)	GUI	Melicherik (Michnak, Parlatore) pp	62.51
(4)	EDI	Tony Hand (Kaye, Lynch)	65.39
(5)	BRK	Dave Matsos (Meyer, Chinn)	60.22
(6)	FIF	John Haig (Biette)	61.07
(7)	EDI	Adrian Saul (Lynch, Krajicek)	61.31
(8)	BRK	Scott Allison (Chinn, Soucy)	69.20
(9)	BRK	Scott Allison (Rempel)	63.17
(10)	EDI	Miroslav Droppa (Hand)	62.43
(11)	HUL	Nikolaev (Koulikov, Timchenko) pp	260.25
(12)	DUN	Derek DeCosty (Smith)	68.54
(13)	GUI	Scott Levins (Konder)	67.34
(14)	BRK	Nathan Rempel (Aldridge)	67.08
(15)	NEW	Longstaff (Ferone, Beveridge)	68.36
(16)	GUI	Ryan Vince (Plant, Konder) pp	63.01
(17)	NEW	Longstaff (Beveridge, Campbell) pp	60.36
(18)	GUI	Ryan Vince (Smerciak, Palov)	62.13
(19)	FIF	Paul Spadafora (Walker, Biette)	60.27

LEAGUE PLAYERS OF THE MONTH
October
Domenic Parlatore, Guildford
November
Greg Kuznik, Fife
December
Daniel Goneau, Fife
January
Information not available
February
Mark Morrison, Fife
March
Scott Allison, Bracknell

FAIR PLAY

Team Penalties	GP	Pim	Ave
Edinburgh Capitals	36	312	8.67
Hull Stingrays	36	432	12.0
Guildford Flames	36	559	15.5
Newcastle Vipers	36	593	16.5
Fife Flyers	36	601	16.7
Bracknell Bees	36	659	18.3
Dundee Stars	36	782	21.7
LEAGUE TOTALS	252	3938	15.6

Flyers leave it late

Fife Flyers, who at one time looked like running away with the league, eventually clinched the title on the last weekend of the season.

Mark Morrison's team enjoyed an eight-point lead at the end of December and were 13 points clear of *Guildford Flames*. But the southern club almost obliterated that lead with a remarkable run of 16 wins in 21 games.

The title's destination came down to Flyers' game at last placed Hull Stingrays on 28 February. The Scots leapt into a 3-0 lead and held off a spirited fightback by **Rick Strachan**'s strugglers. The 3-3 tie gave them the precious point they needed and **Paul Spadafora** delighted the large crowd of travelling supporters with the game winner 27 seconds into sudden death.

Canadian keeper **Steve Briere**, who had the league's best save percentage, was the key to Flyers' second league title, along with his countryman, **Dan Goneau**, who ended fourth in league scoring, and defender **Greg Kuznik**.

The league's unsung success story was **Tony Hand**'s *Edinburgh Capitals* who chalked up their best record since the glory days of their predecessors, Murrayfield Racers.

Apart from their irreplaceable player-coach (Hand was the league's top scorer yet again), Capitals built their success around their returning Czechs, netminder **Ladislav Kudrna** and defender **Jan Krajicek**.

After some fine seasons in the Superleague, a lot was expected of *Bracknell Bees* in the 'lower' league. But new coach **Mike Ellis** and his equally new team struggled with injuries to key players all year long, starting with GB netminder **Stephen Murphy** and ending with his fellow international, forward **Greg Owen**.

Newcastle Vipers lost their best player, Geordie **David Longstaff**, in a gym accident before their campaign even started. Later on, a financial scare caused more disruption in the ranks. So it was little surprise when Vipers failed to realise their potential and came in fifth.

Severe cost-cutting by *Dundee Stars* and the consequent loss of their leading light, Tony Hand, left the club floundering in sixth place. Since their Double win in their first season, 2001-02, Stars have lost over a third of their followers.

Under new owners **Mike** and **Sue Pack**, *Hull Stingrays* were determined to be financially responsible and finish the season, even it meant all they could show for a season's effort was last place. After years of watching mismanaged teams, that must have felt like a sweet victory to Hull's long-suffering fans.

BRITISH NATIONAL LEAGUE

RESULTS CHART

	BRK	DUN	EDI	FIF	GUI	HUL	NEW
Bees	**	2-3 8/11	1-3 26/10	5-1 2/11	2-3 6/12	4-1 16/11	2-3 29/11
	**	3-2 4/2	1-4 10/1	5-0 18/1	4-3ot (9) 25/1	7-3 21/12	4-0 1/2
	**	7-0 14/2	3-3ot 28/2	1-1ot 22/2	2-5 29/2	2-2ot 7/2	9-2 12/2
Stars	3-2 25/10	**	6-3 21/12	3-5 28/12	5-4 13/12	4-2 30/11	5-0 2/11
	3-3ot 15/11	**	1-7 7/1	2-4 21/1	1-7 1/2	1-1ot 3/1	8-3 23/11
	2-3ot (5) 14/12	**	1-3 18/1	5-4ot (12) 8/2	3-4ot (18) 22/2	2-1 15/2	6-4 29/2
Capitals	4-1 20/12	3-5 16/11	**	4-3ot (4) 30/11	2-3 2/11	8-3 8/11	2-5 6/12
	5-3 11/1	6-8 4/1	**	4-4ot 1/2	2-4 14/12	6-2 13/12	5-4ot (7) 28/12
	5-6ot (14) 15/2	4-7 17/1	**	7-5 29/2	2-4 20/1	7-2 24/2	9-1 24/1
Flyers	4-4ot 13/12	4-1 29/11	6-0 15/11	**	4-2 1/11	4-1 25/10	2-4 8/11
	5-2 3/1	6-5ot (6) 23/12	4-1 16/12	**	4-2 2/12	4-3 17/1	4-0 20/12
	5-1 24/2	1-3 10/1	4-3 27/12	**	4-3 7/2	5-1 21/2	1-2 14/2
Flames	2-0 29/11	6-0 20/12	4-6 25/10	4-3ot (3) 9/11	**	9-1 11/11	3-2 15/11
	1-2 26/12	4-2 24/1	4-3 7/12	2-4 4/1	**	6-1 28/1	5-3 18/1
	6-1 8/2	4-3ot (16) 21/2	1-2ot (10) 31/1	4-2 15/2	**	3-0 11/2	5-2 28/2
Stingrays	5-6ot (1) 1/11	4-4ot 9/11	2-4 22/11	1-3 7/12	1-5 26/10	**	1-3 10/1
	0-1ot (8) 4/1	4-2 6/12	0-3 29/11	3-6 25/1	1-0 28/12	**	4-3ot 31/1
	2-3 24/1	6-1 25/2	1-5 8/2	3-4ot (19) 28/2	2-3ot (13) 14/2	**	2-4 22/2
Vipers	3-6 5/11	5-3 7/12	5-4ot (2) 1/11	1-4 21/12	7-4 3/1	4-2 31/10	**
	5-5ot 17/1	6-2 11/1	0-2 7/2	1-5 7/1	0-3 14/1	4-2 14/12	**
	4-3ot (17) 21/2	5-0 25/1	3-2 11/2	4-6 19/2	5-4ot (15) 18/2	2-1 26/12	**
	BRK	DUN	EDI	FIF	GUI	HUL	NEW

Second figure is date of game.

PLAYOFFS

The top six league clubs competed in the Playoffs in a double round-robin tournament played over three weeks after the end of the league season.

The top four teams after the first round progressed into the semi-finals with the first-placed team playing the fourth and the second against the third, home and away. (The teams finishing first and second in the round robin stage had choice of home date.)

The final was also played over home and away legs, the team finishing highest in the league receiving choice of home date.

The playoff winner received the **John Brady Bowl**, named in memory of the former manager of Kirkcaldy ice rink who was influential in creating the league.

QUARTER-FINAL STANDINGS

	GP	W	L	D	GF	GA	Pts
Guildford Flames	10	6	2	2	33	16	14
Fife Flyers	10	6	3	1	31	22	13
Bracknell Bees	10	5	4	1	28	25	11
Edinburgh Capitals	10	4	5	1	31	42	9
Newcastle Vipers	10	3	6	1	21	31	7
Dundee Stars	10	2	6	2	29	37	6

QUARTER-FINAL RESULTS

	BRK	DUN	EDI	FIF	GUI	NEW
Bees	-	7-3	2-1	2-4	2-5	3-1
Stars	2-2	-	10-4	2-4	2-2	2-1
Capitals	4-6	5-4	-	4-2	1-0	7-4
Flyers	3-0	4-0	5-2	-	2-2	6-2
Flames	1-4	4-1	6-0	6-1	-	4-2
Vipers	1-0	4-3	3-3	2-0	1-3	-

SEMI-FINALS

First semi-final
Game One   27 Mar   **Fife-Bracknell**   **1-2**
Game Two   28 Mar   **Bracknell-Fife**   **3-2**
BRACKNELL BEES won 5-3 on aggregate

Second semi-final
Game One   27 Mar   **Guildford-Edinburgh 6-2**
Game Two   28 Mar   **Edinburgh-Guildford 3-4**
GUILDFORD FLAMES won 10-5 on aggregate

CHAMPIONSHIP FINALS
First leg, Saturday 3 April

BRACKNELL BEES	4	(1-3-0)
GUILDFORD FLAMES	5	(1-3-1)

Scoring:
1-0 BRK Soucy (unassisted)   7.29
1-1 GUI Kohut (Vince, Michnac)   8.37
2-1 BRK Allison (Rempel)   pp   20.09
2-2 GUI Vince (Konder, Smerciak)   pp   25.10
2-3 GUI Levins (Melicherik, Kohut) pp   29.57
3-3 BRK Ellis (Allison, Rempel)   30.10
3-4 GUI Melicherik (Kohut, Cross)   32.06
4-4 BRK Matsos (Chinn, Soucy)   pp   33.41
4-5 GUI Dixon (Smerciak, Vince)   pp   57.02
Netminding
Shots: Hay BRK 8-13- 4 25   save% 80.0
Shots: Lyle GUI 9-13-11 33   save% 87.9
Penalty minutes: Bees 8, Flames 24 (Marple 2+10 misc. check-behind).
Referee: Andy Carson.   *Attendance*: 2,213
Linesmen: Alice Stanley, Marco Coenen.

Second Leg, Sunday 4 April

GUILDFORD FLAMES	4	(1-1-2)
BRACKNELL BEES	3	(2-1-0)

Scoring:
0-1 BRK Allison (Rempel)   0.25
0-2 BRK Aldridge (Soucy)   pp   8.10
1-2 GUI Levins (Dixon)   9.17
1-3 BRK Richardson (Allison, Meyers)   20.18
2-3 GUI Kohut (Melicherik)   37.17
3-3 GUI Smerciak (Konder)   52.38
4-3 GUI Melicherik (Vince, Dixon) en   59.31
Netminding:
Shots: Lyle GUI 10- 7-3 20   save% 85.0
Shots: Hay BRK 10-17-7 34   save% 91.2
Penalty minutes: Flames 14, Bees 24 (Allison 2+10misc. check-behind).
Referee: Andy Carson   *Attendance*: 2,069
Linesmen: Lee Young, Joy Tottman.

GUILDFORD FLAMES are champions
9-7 on aggregate.

PAST PLAYOFF WINNERS

2002-03	Coventry Blaze
2001-02	Dundee Stars
2000-01	Guildford Flames
1999-2000	Fife Flyers
1998-99	Fife Flyers
1997-98	Guildford Flames
1996-97	Swindon IceLords (Premier Lge)
	Fife Flyers (Northern Premier Lge)

THE FINALISTS

BRACKNELL BEES
Stephen Murphy, Scott Hay; Adam Hyman, Danny Hughes, Ross McDougall, Nathan Rempel, Mark Richardson, Corey Lyons, Scott Allison, David Matsos (capt). Tyrone Miller, Danny Meyers, JP Soucy, Nicky Chinn, Mike Ellis, Ryan Aldridge, David Poulton, Luke Reynolds.   *Manager/Coach*: Mike Ellis.

GUILDFORD FLAMES
Joe Dollin, Stevie Lyle; Peter Michnac, Stan Marple, Marian Smerciak, Neil Liddiard, Ryan Vince, Michael Timms, Tony Redmond, Milos Melicherik, Paul Dixon (capt), Jozef Kohut, Peter Konder, Scott Levins, Mark Galazzi, Nick Cross.   *Manager/Coach*: Stan Marple.

LEADING PLAYOFF SCORERS

	GP	G	A	Pts	Pim
Milos Melicherik GUI	14	10	12	22	18
Jozef Kohut GUI	13	11	9	20	12
Ryan Vince GUI	14	7	12	19	18
Nathan Rempel BRK	14	10	8	18	8
Tony Hand EDI	11	2	14	16	2
Karry Biette FIF	12	7	8	15	22
Martin Cingel EDI	12	9	5	14	32
Scott Allison BRK	13	3	11	14	79
Peter Konder GUI	14	3	10	13	6
Todd Dutiaume FIF	12	5	8	13	12
Patric Lochi DUN	10	6	6	12	8
Jason Shmyr DUN	10	4	8	12	26

LEADING PLAYOFF NETMINDERS

	GPI	Mins	SoG	GA	S%
Scott Hay BRK	13	746	423	28	93.4
Steve Briere FIF	12	720	383	27	93.0
Pasi Raitanen NEW	10	600	373	29	92.2

WACKY PLAYOFF SCHEDULE

The wackiest example of scheduling to come our way in quite a while was the visit of Bracknell Bees to Murrayfield on a Tuesday, followed the very next night by Edinburgh Capitals going south to **John Nike**'s sporting palace. Total crowds at the two games? 931.

Slovaks catch fire for Flames

Guildford Flames needed late goals by their new Slovakian forwards, **Jozef Kohut, Marian Smerciak** and **Milos Melicherik**, to beat off their local rivals, Bracknell Bees, and capture their second playoff trophy in four attempts.

The victory by **Stan Marple**'s team meant the awards were spread among three different teams for the first time since 1998-99.

This year, thankfully, the league reverted to the usual practice of two-game, aggregate-goal contests in the playoff semis and final. But they found another way to infuriate their fans.

The first round - with only one league team, Hull Stingrays, eliminated - squeezed in 30 games over three weeks. To do this, 12 of the contests were played in mid-week, although this is a league that prides itself - indeed, fights endless battles with other clubs over the issue - on playing only at weekends.

Moreover, with two of the six playoff teams in southern England and three in Scotland, the time spent travelling was enormous. The fans showed their disapproval by staying away, with crowds down by ten per cent over 2003.

In the semi-finals, both Fife and Edinburgh were beaten by one goal at home, though in Capitals' case it scarcely mattered as they'd already been hammered 6-2 at the Spectrum.

Bracknell's **Scott Hay** stood on his head in Kirkcaldy to keep the Fifers out, facing 38 shots, while **Steve Briere** had a quiet time handling only 26 from Bees. **Nathan Rempel** did the damage early on, putting **Mike Ellis'** team 2-0 up after 21 minutes. Only the former New York Ranger **Dan Goneau**, in his first game back from injury, got on the scoreboard for Flyers.

In another close fought thriller the next day, it was Rempel again. He scored the insurance goal at 57.40 after **JP Soucy** had beaten Briere for the winner.

Tony Hand and his Capitals fell asleep for five minutes in the middle period of their first leg at Guildford, allowing four goals. **Peter Michnac** (22.56), **Peter Konder** (23.52), Smerciak (26.34) and Melicherik (28.16) were all on target as Flames built a 5-0 lead from which Edinburgh never recovered.

So to the final, a local derby that is probably the BNL's equivalent of the Steelers-Panthers' battles in whatever they're calling the other league this year. Both legs attracted record crowds and the fans were rewarded with some sparkling play.

Bees, the underdogs, lost the first leg at home, but young **Mark Richardson** gave them hope when his goal early in the fifth period handed them a 7-6 lead. But then the Slovaks caught fire for Flames.

FINDUS CUP

All British National League teams were eligible to compete in the qualifying round of this competition, the first of the season.

After each team played the other home and away, the top four teams were drawn into the semi-finals which were also played over two legs.

The final and third place playoff were one-game contests played at Newcastle's Telewest Arena.

QUALIFYING ROUND STANDINGS

	GP	W	L	D	GF	GA	Pts
Guildford Flames	12	7	4	1	45	33	15
Newcastle Vipers	12	7	5	0	49	39	14
Bracknell Bees	12	5	3	4	36	29	14
Fife Flyers	12	5	5	2	32	41	12
Hull Stingrays	12	4	6	2	37	39	10
Dundee Stars	12	5	7	0	28	42	10
Edinburgh Capitals	12	3	6	3	28	32	9

Tied teams separated by results between them

QUALIFYING ROUND RESULTS

	BRK	DUN	EDI	FIF	GUI	HUL	NEW
Bracknell	-	5-2	2-2	5-0	4-4	1-1	0-4
Dundee	2-5	-	4-3	0-3	2-4	2-4	4-0
Ed'burgh	0-1	0-2	-	4-4	3-4	0-2	5-2
Fife	1-5	4-2	2-2	-	4-2	3-2	4-6
Guildf'd	4-1	3-4	5-1	1-2	-	8-3	4-2
Hull	5-5	1-2	3-4	5-3	4-1	-	4-6
N'castle	4-2	10-2	1-4	7-2	3-5	4-3	-

SEMI-FINALS
FIRST SEMI-FINAL
16 Nov Newcastle-Fife   3-2 (0-0,3-2,0-0)
22 Nov Fife-Newcastle   2-1ot (1-0,0-0,1-1,0-0)
Vipers won 5-4 *on aggregate after penalty shootout (2-1).*
*(Winning penalty shot - **Simon Leach**)*

SECOND SEMI-FINAL
22 Nov Bracknell-Guildford   1-5 (1-0,0-2,0-3)
23 Nov Guildford-Bracknell
               2-5ot (0-1,0-1,1-3,1-0)
Flames won 7-6 *on aggregate*
*(Overtime game winner - **Nick Cross** 62.24)*

THE WINNING TEAM
NEWCASTLE VIPERS
Tommi Satosaari, Rory Dunn; Rob Wilson, Richie Thornton, Scott Moody, Paul Ferone, Matt Beveridge, Jonathan Weaver, Simon Leach, Stephen Wallace, David Longstaff, Paul Graham, Robert Wilson, Andrew Thornton, Karl Culley, Martin King, Rob Trumbley (capt), Stuart Potts, Scott Campbell, Kevin Bucas.
Manager/Coach: Clyde Tuyl.

THIRD PLACE PLAYOFF
29 December at Telewest Arena, Newcastle
FIFE-BRACKNELL   **2-6**   (1-0.1-3,0-3)
Scoring: FIF S King, Dutiaume 1g; D King, Haig, Goneau 1a. BRK Matsos 3g; Meyers 1+1; Owen, Richardson 1g; Rempe 3a; Sheptak 2a; McDougall, Lavoie, Allison, Hyman, Aldridge 1a.
Penalty minutes: Flyers 2, Bees 2.
Shots on Goal: Briere/Arthur FIF   36
                Annetts/Wride BRK   20
Referee: Michael Evans.   *Attendance*: 3,300
Linesmen: MacPhee, Von Haselberg.

FINAL
29 December at Telewest Arena, Newcastle
GUILDFORD-NEWCASTLE 1-6   (0-2,1-2,0-2)
Scoring:
0-1 NEW Longstaff (Beveridge, Wilson)   9.36
0-2 NEW Potts (Wilson, Beveridge) pp   16.13
1-2 GUI Vince (Smerciak, Konder)   20.42
1-3 NEW Campbell (Ferone, Graham)   25.02
1-4 NEW Ferone (Potts, Wallace)   26.39
1-5 NEW Trumbley (Beveridge, Weaver) pp   40.48
1-6 NEW Wallace (Weaver)   52.42
Penalty minutes: Flames 8, Vipers 22.
Netminding:
Shots: Lyle GUI   7- 7- 7 21   *save %*: 71.4
Shots: Satosaari NEW 10-14-14 38   *save %*: 97.4
Referee: Moray Hanson.   *Attendance*: 3,300
Linesmen: Young, Tottman.

PAST FINALISTS
2003 **Newcastle Vipers** beat Coventry Blaze 3-0 at the *Telewest* Arena, Newcastle.
2002 **Fife Flyers** beat Coventry Blaze 6-3 at the National Ice Centre, Nottingham.

SLOVAKIAN STARS

Defenceman **JAN KRAJICEK** *left* returned to Edinburgh Capitals; **MILOS MELICHERIK** spread the eastern exodus south and became Guildford Flames' top scorer.

Photos: Chris Valentine

LEADING CUP SCORERS

	GP	G	A	Pts	Pim
Jonathan Weaver NEW	15	10	16	26	31
Marc West NEW	13	7	19	26	14
Ryan Vince GUI	15	12	8	20	22
Todd Dutiaume FIF	15	7	13	20	10
Dan Goneau FIF	12	9	10	19	24
Slava Koulikov HUL	12	6	13	19	10
Daryl Lavoie BRK	15	2	17	19	53
Paul Ferone NEW	14	7	11	18	100
Ratislav Palov GUI	15	7	11	18	6
Tony Hand EDI	12	5	13	18	16

LEADING CUP NETMINDERS

	GPI	Mins	SoG	GA	S%
Ladislav Kudrna EDI	12	720	380	29	92.4
Stephen Murphy BRK	12	684	303	24	92.1
Tommi Satosaari NEW	15	910	536	44	91.8

SIN-BIN

Player Penalties	GP	Pim	Ave
Paul Spadafora FIF	7	82	11.71
Jason Shmyr DUN	11	84	7.64
Paul Ferone NEW	14	100	7.14

Lobby strikes for Vipers

David Longstaff made a surprise return to Newcastle Vipers' line-up for the cup final and scored the first goal in Vipers' 6-1 rout of Guildford Flames.

This was Lobby's first game back after he dropped weights on both feet, breaking his ankles, during a summer gym session. "I probably came back two weeks early," he told the Newcastle *Evening Chronicle*, "but I felt with **Marc West** leaving the team they would need a little help." Canadian West had returned home unexpectedly, promising to return for the final. He never did.

Longstaff, 29, beat Flames' netminder **Stevie Lyle** with a fake, similar to the penalty shot he took against **Mike Torchia** when Vipers knocked out Flames in last year's cup semi. "To be honest, I thought he knew that move," grinned 'Lobby' afterwards.

Vipers played a strong, physical game, intimidating Flames' European influenced side, though Slovakian **Marian Smerciak** scored their only goal early in the second stanza. Guildford's coach, **Stan Marple**, described his team's play as "an embarrassment".

Vipers' owner **Darryl Illingworth** was delighted when his team retained the cup, especially as he'd had to ask them to take a pay cut only a few weeks earlier. "They've overcome all that and not only beaten Guildford but slaughtered them," he said.

Clockwise from left above: Bracknell Bees' defenceman **DANNY MEYERS** made his GB debut; **GREG OWEN**, Bees' leading British scorer, missed his national call-up through injury; in the English Premier League, **GARY CLARKE** was the top British marksman again; and defender **MATT COTÉ** helped to revive *Wightlink* Raiders' fortunes.

Photos: Dave Page, Bob Swann, Chris Valentine.

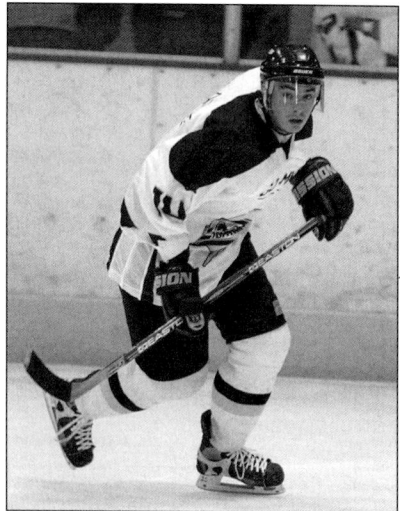

ENGLISH LEAGUES

The English leagues - the Premier and the National - comprise the sport's third tier and are designed for clubs with low budgets whose chief aim is developing local players.

The Premier League was first established in 1997-98 to accommodate the non-Superleague clubs who were unable to afford the increasing cost of competing in the British National League (BNL). The low budget teams now compete in the National League's north and south conferences. There is no automatic promotion to the BNL from the English leagues.

In the Premier League, teams met four times, twice at home and twice away. The National League sides played each other twice, once home and once away.

LEADING SCORERS

Premier League	GP	G	A	Pts	Pim
Kyle Amyotte CHE	31	56	46	102	112
Juuso Vakkilainen ROM	31	50	45	95	81
Gary Clarke MIL	32	55	32	87	18
Andrew Power CHE	30	36	46	82	120
Nick Poole MIL	32	32	50	82	28
Danny Marshall ROM	31	30	46	76	18
Rob Douglas ROM	28	34	41	75	36
Frank DeMasi SWI	31	38	36	74	81
Ken Forshee SWI	32	35	34	69	72
Doug McEwen PET	32	31	37	68	73
National League North					
John Ross SHE	18	30	41	71	14
Peter Founds FLI	18	32	38	70	30
Mark Stokes FLI	17	28	34	62	34
Les Millie SHE	18	33	25	58	120
Bobby Haig BLA	18	30	28	58	22
National League South					
Dan Prachar OXF	16	22	28	50	10
Andrew Campbell BAS	16	27	21	48	37
Anthony Page BAS	14	16	24	40	0
Garry Dodds INV	16	17	22	39	28
Joe Johnston STR	15	17	19	36	6

FINAL STANDINGS

Premier League	GP	W	L	D	GF	GA	Pts
MK Lightning MIL	32	28	4	0	200	60	56
P'boro' Phantoms PET	32	25	5	2	175	87	52
Romford Raiders ROM	32	21	9	2	198	131	44
Ch'ford Chieftains CHE	32	18	11	3	211	149	39
Wightlink Raiders WIG	32	16	13	3	137	114	35
Swindon Lynx SWI	32	14	16	2	144	137	30
Slough Jets SLO	32	9	20	3	97	142	21
Telford Wild Foxes TEL	32	4	27	1	112	194	9
Solihull Kings SOL	32	1	31	0	83	343	2
National Lge North							
Flintshire Freeze FLI	18	15	2	1	151	73	31
Sh'ffield Scimitars SHE	18	15	3	0	168	43	30
Nottingham Lions NOT	18	12	6	0	105	71	24
Blackburn Hawks BLA	18	11	6	1	120	71	23
Billingham Eagles BIL	18	8	8	2	93	72	18
Whitley Warriors WHI	18	8	10	0	86	99	16
Kingston Jets KIN	18	8	10	0	72	86	16
Bradford Bulldogs BRD	18	4	14	0	79	144	8
Grimsby Buffaloes GRI	18	4	14	0	56	198	8
Sun'land Chiefs SUN	18	3	15	0	64	137	6
National Lge South							
Invicta Dynamo INV	16	15	1	0	121	28	30
Oxford City Stars OXF	16	12	3	1	132	62	25
MK Thunder MIL	16	9	5	2	62	42	20
Bas'stoke Buffalo BAS	16	9	6	1	113	57	19
Str'tham Redskins STR	16	9	7	0	88	57	18
Bracknell Hornets BRK	16	8	7	1	84	64	17
P'boro' Islanders PET	16	2	13	1	57	112	5
Solent Sharks GOS	16	2	13	1	41	186	5
Slough H Hawks SLO	16	2	13	1	42	132	5

Positions of teams tied on points decided on the results of the games between them

LEADING NETMINDERS

Premier League	GPI	Mins	SoG	GA	Sv%
Stephen Wall PET	18	1050	537	43	92.O
Allen Sutton MIL	15	900	306	25	91.8
Barry Hollyhead MIL	17	1019	411	35	91.5
Toby Cooley WIG	15	807	482	46	90.5
Chris Douglas ROM	30	1597	961	93	90.3
National Lge North					
Matt Compton FLI	15	829	550	49	91.1
Darren Maynard SHE	14	653	233	24	89.7
National Lge South					
Ian Rowlands INV	8	413	201	10	95.O
Carl Ambler INV	11	547	265	18	93.2

Qualification: one-third of team's games

FAIR PLAY

Premier League	GP	Pims	Ave
Romford Raiders	32	620	19.4
Wightlink Raiders	32	681	21.3
Milton Keynes Lightning	32	683	21.3
Chelmsford Chieftains	32	698	21.8
Swindon Lynx	32	738	23.1
Slough Jets	32	880	27.5
Telford Wild Foxes	31	953	30.7
Solihull Kings	31	1063	34.3
Peterborough Phantoms	32	1243	38.8

PAST (PREMIER) LEAGUE WINNERS

2002-03	Peterborough Phantoms
2001-02	Invicta Dynamos
2000-01	Swindon Phoenix
1999-00	Chelmsford Chieftains
1998-99	Solihull Blaze
1997-98	Solihull Blaze
1996-97	Wightlink Raiders
1995-96	Wightlink Raiders
1994-95	Wightlink Raiders
1993-94	Wightlink Raiders
1992-93	Solihull Barons
1991-92	Medway Bears
1990-91	Oxford City Stars
1989-90	Bracknell Bees
1988-89	Humberside Seahawks

Early strike by Lightning

Milton Keynes Lightning brought the first league title to the Planet Ice rink for ten years, edging out the defending champions, **Peterborough Phantoms**, by four points.

Despite the narrowness of their win, Lightning had clinched first place by 17 January after winning the first two games against their big rivals. Their high-scoring forward, **Gary Clarke**, was the league's leading British marksman, closely followed by their Canadian player-coach **Nick Poole**. Their stingey defence was backed by goalie **Allen Sutton** who was runner-up in the save percentages.

Phantoms' key players came from opposite ends of the experience range - veteran **Doug McEwen**, who scored his 1,000th goal in British ice hockey during the season, and promising 22-year-old netminder **Stephen Wall** who had the league's best save percentage.

Kevin King's side may well have left the league title in the penalty box as his players spent more time in the sin-bin than any other team, averaging nearly two periods a game.

Romford Raiders, inspired by their Finnish newcomer, **Juuso Vakkilainen**, challenged for the title early on, only to crumble in the second half, partly when their opponents learned how to close down the sharpshooting forward.

Chelmsford Chieftains also had plenty of firepower in the league's best marksman, **Kyle Amyotte**, and finished one place higher than last year.

Wightlink Raiders, under the new ownership of players **Andy Pickles** and **Jason Coles**, also moved up one place, thanks to one of the league's tightest defences. Credit here goes to veteran international defender **Matt Cote**, signed from 'sister' club, Basingstoke Bison, and goalies **Toby Cooley** and **Dave Hurst**.

Swindon Lynx were rejuvenated when their old coach **Darryl Lipsey** returned to the town after a eventful spell in the Superleague. But Lynx finished sixth, two places lower than in 2002-03, after injuries to key players **Robin Davison** and **Lee Brathwaite**, and a strict budget imposed by a watchful new management.

Injuries and financial restrictions were a familiar story at **Slough Jets**. Player-coach **Warren Rost** signed three players from the London/Haringey Racers late on but they arrived too late to lift Jets above seventh place.

The young **Telford Wild Foxes** also left it late before bringing in former Telford Tigers' legend, **Claude Dumas**, to play and coach. Foxes only finished off the bottom due to the dismal performances of the outclassed **Solihull Kings**.

RESULTS CHART

	CHE	HAR see note below	MIL	PET	ROM	SLO	SOL	SWI	TEL	WIG
CHE	**	10-3 23/11	4-5 31/8	4-6 11/10	3-6 21/9	4-2 7/9	15-1 7/12	7-2 9/11	8-3 28/9	3-2 2/11
	**		6-4 19/10	3-3 25/1	5-11 8/11	6-3 18/1	17-4 1/2	10-2 4/1	11-4 26/10	5-4 22/2
HAR	7-7 12/10	**				3-4 5/10	7-2 25/10	6-8 28/9		2-10 14/9
MIL	3-1 20/9	5-3 13/9	**	2-1 20/12	10-1 4/10	6-0 30/11	16-0 30/8	9-1 27/9	5-2 1/11	3-2 26/10
	8-2 18/10	11-1 9/11	**	2-4 14/2	10-1 22/11	5-1 31/1	12-0 12/10	6-0 16/11	9-3 17/1	6-3 6/12
PET	7-6 14/9	6-2 7/9	1-3 14/12	**	6-3 27/9	9-1 21/9	10-4 2/11	5-4 5/10	5-1 19/10	3-2 12/10
	1-4 6/12		5-4 22/2	**	4-2 16/11	4-2 9/11	19-1 3/1	7-4 21/12	9-3 28/12	6-1 18/1
ROM	5-5 5/10	9-1 19/10	0-4 2/11	6-8 28/9	**	10-1 14/9	12-1 9/11	5-1 31/8	9-2 14/12	7-2 7/9
	8-8 21/12		7-4 18/1	5-2 7/12	**	5-0 26/10	12-4 17/1	5-6 12/10	5-2 22/2	4-5 8/2
SLO	3-5 27/9	5-9 20/9	0-4 8/11	2-3 25/10	5-6 20/12	**	5-1 13/9	5-4 11/1	7-4 4/10	0-5 28/9
	4-3 17/1		2-5 29/11	0-3 21/2	2-9 3/1	**	8-3 6/12	4-5 8/2	5-5 28/2	4-4 18/10
SOL	7-14 16/11		3-11 14/9	2-14 4/10	3-11 6/9	1-5 19/10	**	1-16 7/9	9-7 30/11	1-7 5/10
	5-9 14/12		0-15 28/9	1-3 4/1	6-13 7/2	4-6 22/2	**	1-7 26/10	0-5 * 8/2	4-5 15/2
SWI	6-4 4/10	4-3 6/9	1-4 25/10	4-1 20/9	1-4 13/9	5-5 1/11	18-1 18/10	**	5-0 30/8	3-3 22/11
	8-6 6/3		2-5 15/11	1-5 8/11	3-5 10/1	3-2 24/1	11-5 28/2	**	5-4 11/10	4-7 3/1
TEL	5-9 7/2	8-9 15/11	1-5 5/10	4-6 6/9	2-5 18/10	1-5 12/10	8-1 8/11	0-7 14/9	**	5-6 21/9
	8-9 21/2		3-9 4/1	2-7 13/12	3-4 25/1	3-5 7/12	9-6 23/11	4-5 2/11	**	5-2 29/2
WIG	3-10 6/9	7-2 27/9	1-3 11/10	1-5 13/9	5-8 25/10	3-1 15/11	16-0 20/9	2-0 19/10	5-1 10/1	**
	6-5 27/12	4-2 8/11	2-3 23/11	3-3 1/11	8-4 13/12	4-2 21/12	7-3 29/11	5-0 7/12	6-3 24/1	**
	CHE	HAR	MIL	PET	ROM	SLO	SOL	SWI	TEL	WIG

* Game forfeit for icing an suspended player. Actual result 6-4 to Solihull.

Haringey Racers *withdrew from competition after game on 25 October 2003. All results were officially expunged and are shown here for information only.*

PREMIER LEAGUE PLAYOFFS

At the end of the league games, the top eight teams in the Premier League qualified for the Playoffs.

The league winner was placed in group A along with the fourth, fifth and eighth placed teams, with the remaining sides going into group B. Each team played the other in their group home and away and the top two in each group met in the semi-finals.

In the semi-finals, the winner of one group played the runner-up in the other group, home and away, and the final was also played over two legs.

QUARTER-FINAL STANDINGS

Group A	GP	W	L	D	GF	GA	Pts
M Keynes Lightning	6	5	0	1	32	10	11
Wightlink Raiders	6	3	1	2	27	18	8
Chelmsford Chieftains	6	1	4	1	27	42	3
Telford Wild Foxes	6	1	5	0	22	38	2
Group B							
Slough Jets	6	4	1	1	27	15	9
P'boro Phantoms	6	3	1	2	28	15	8
Swindon Lynx	6	2	4	0	15	31	4
Romford Raiders	6	1	4	1	18	27	3

QUARTER-FINAL RESULTS

Group A	CHE	MIL	TEL	WIG
Chelmsford Chieftains	-	2-7	9-7	2-2
M Keynes Lightning	7-3	-	10-1	4-2
Telford Wild Foxes	9-4	1-3	-	3-4
Wightlink Raiders	10-7	1-1	8-1	-
Group B	PET	ROM	SLO	SWI
P'borough Phantoms	-	5-2	1-3	11-1
Romford Raiders	5-5	-	4-6	3-4
Slough Jets	2-2	3-4	-	8-2
Swindon Lynx	2-4	4-0	2-5	-

SEMI-FINALS

FIRST SEMI-FINAL

17 Apr M Keynes-Peterboro'	1-1
18 Apr Peterboro'-M Keynes	2-4

MILTON KEYNES LIGHTNING won 5-3 on aggregate.

SECOND SEMI-FINAL

17 Apr *Wightlink*-Slough	3-4
18 Apr Slough-*Wightlink*	3-2

SLOUGH JETS won 7-5 on aggregate

FINAL

First leg, 1 May 2004

SLOUGH JETS	0	(0-0-0)
MILTON KEYNES LIGHTNING	7	(0-5-2)

Scoring:

0-1 MIL	Jamieson (Skinnari)	21.22
0-2 MIL	Howard (Irvine, Wales)	31.20
0-3 MIL	Poole (Clarke)	32.34
0-4 MIL	Wales (Skinnari, McEwen)	32.59
0-5 MIL	Clarke (Poole) sh	33.58
0-6 MIL	Carr (Skinnari)	44.10
0-7 MIL	Clarke (Irvine, McKenzie)	53.47

Penalty minutes: Jets 18, Lightning 18.

Netminding

Shots:	Smith SLO	34	save %	79.4
	Hollyhead MIL	24	save %	100.0

Referee: Glen Meier.   *Attendance:* 990.
Linesmen: Colcuc, Hewitt.

Second leg, 2 May 2004

MILTON KEYNES LIGHTNING	5	(1-1-3)
SLOUGH JETS	2	(1-0-1)

Scoring

0-1 SLO	Greener (Bicknell, Rost)	4.38
1-1 MIL	Randall	15.12
2-1 MIL	McKenzie (Jamieson)	34.18
2-2 SLO	Towalski (Sirman, Kosic) pp	48.53
3-2 MIL	Clarke (Randall)	55.04
4-2 MIL	Carr	56.41
5-2 MIL	Griffiths (Skinnari, Jamieson)	59.07

Penalty minutes: Lightning 75 (Irvine 2+2+10 roughing + 2+5+game roughing, Wales 2+2+10 roughing, Jamieson 2+2+10 roughing), Jets 75 (Gray 2+2+10 roughing, Greener 2+2+10 roughing, Bicknell 2+2+10 roughing).

Netminding

Shots:	Hollyhead MIL	35	save %: 94.3
	Smith SLO	34	save %: 85.3

Referee: Glen Meier.   *Attendance:* 2,075.
Linesmen: Colcuc, Hewitt.

MILTON KEYNES LIGHTNING
are Playoff champions, *12-2 on aggregate.*

THE WINNING TEAM
MILTON KEYNES LIGHTNING
Barry Hollyhead, Allen Sutton; Chris McEwen, James Pease, Michael Wales, Phil Wooderson, Leigh Jamieson, Gary Clarke, Kurt Irvine, Dean Campbell, Adam Carr, Geoff O'Hara, Ross Bowers, Tom Griffiths, Dwayne Newman (capt), Bari McKenzie, Mikko Skinnari, Greg Randall, Simon Howard, Nick Poole.
Coach: Nick Poole. *Manager:* John Jamieson.

LEADING PLAYOFF SCORERS

	GP	G	A	Pts	Pim
Gary Clarke MIL	10	13	10	23	16
Zoran Kozic SLO	9	12	5	17	8
Jason Coles WIG	8	9	8	17	6
Rob Lamey WIG	8	8	9	17	0
Chris Crombie WIG	6	4	13	17	14
Nick Poole MIL	10	5	11	16	6

LEADING PLAYOFF NETMINDERS

	GPI	Mins	SoG	GA	Sv%
Barry Hollyhead MIL	7	420	188	12	93.6
Greg Rockman SWI	6	273	194	14	92.8
Stephen Wall PET	7	420	185	15	91.9
Simon Smith SLO	8	480	268	24	91.0

Qualification: 200 minutes

PAST PLAYOFF WINNERS

Clarke strikes thrice and Lightning strike twice

Milton Keynes Lightning completed the league and playoff double with a comfortable two-legged victory over surprise finalists, Slough Jets.

A hat-trick from their leading scorer, **Gary Clarke**, and a pair from **Adam Carr**, plus a shutout in Slough by **Barry Hollyhead**, helped Lightning to retain their playoff title with a comfortable 12-2 aggregate win.

Their cause was also aided by a goal and three points from defender **Leigh Jamieson** who returned to his home town after winning two major awards for his play in the Elite League.

A season-high crowd of 2,075 watched the title-winning game in the Planet Ice rink.

In truth, the championship was decided - as was the league - by the results between **Nick Poole**'s team and their bitter rivals, Peterborough Phantoms. In the playoff semis, Phantoms were again struck down by Lightning.

Jesse Hammill's goal after only two minutes of the second leg in Milton Keynes gave Phantoms a 2-1 lead. But this only stung Lightning into action and by the mid-point they were 3-2 up on goals from **Greg Randall** (2) and **Bari McKenzie**. The clincher into an empty net came from MK's prolific goalgetter, **Gary Clarke**.

In the first leg, **Lewis Buckman** of Phantoms had cancelled out **Dean Campbell**'s opener.

There was plenty of drama in the other semi where the upstart Jets faced *Wightlink* Raiders. Jets had flown from a lowly seventh place league finish to the top of their playoff group after reinforcing their injury-hit line-up with Yugoslav international goal sniper **Zoran Kozic** and Canadian defender **Brian McLaughlin**.

Raiders started as slight favourites with the first leg being played in their own compact Ryde Arena. But Jets took the play to their opponents right from the opening face-off and were 2-0 up after only six minutes through **Matt Towalski** and **Jason Reilly**.

After **Adam Gray** stretched the lead to 3-0 early in the second, Jets allowed Raiders back into the game. The home side battled hard and when the clock read 52.16, **Scott Carter** equalised. Then it was the Zoran Kozic show.

The Yugoslav had a penalty shot saved by **Toby Cooley**, only to gain his revenge with Jets' leg-winning fourth goal at 56.45.

Fortunes fluctuated in a nail-biting second leg. Raider **Rob Lamey** levelled the aggregate score on a powerplay late in the first period, and in the 29th minute he gave the visitors a one-goal lead.

But that was Raiders' last gasp. After another from Kozic, **Ricky Skene** equalised at 41.15 and **Adam Bicknell** hit the winner at 56.48.

PREMIER CUP

In this invitational tournament played during the league season, the top eight Premier League teams were joined by three sides from the National League.

In the preliminary round, the 11 teams competed in two geographically divided groups, each team playing the other in its own group once at home and once away.

The top two teams in each group met in the semi-finals - also home and away - and a two-legged final decided the cup's destination.

QUARTER-FINAL STANDINGS

Group A	GP	W	L	D	GF	GA	Pts
P'boro' Phantoms	8	7	1	0	60	15	14
MK Lightning	8	6	1	1	55	21	13
Sheffield Scimitars	8	2	4	2	27	42	6
Telford Wild Foxes	8	1	5	2	28	50	4
Blackburn Hawks	8	0	5	3	28	70	3
Group B							
Wightlink Raiders	10	7	1	2	54	29	16
Ch'ford Chieftains	10	8	2	0	45	32	16
Slough Jets	10	4	4	2	34	34	10
Romford Raiders	10	4	5	1	35	34	9
Swindon Lynx	10	3	5	2	37	44	8
Invicta Dynamo	10	0	9	1	20	52	1

SEMI-FINALS
FIRST SEMI-FINAL
3 Apr	MK Lightning-*Wightlink*	2-2
10 Apr	*Wightlink*-MK Lightning	9-6

Wightlink *Raiders* won 11-8 on aggregate
SECOND SEMI-FINAL
11 Apr	Chelmsford-Peterborough	1-2
12 Apr	Peterborough-Chelmsford	5-3

***Phantoms* won 7-4 on aggregate**

FINAL
First leg, 24 April 2004
Wightlink-Peterborough   1-3
Second leg, 25 April 2004
Peterborough-*Wightlink*   4-1
PETERBOROUGH PHANTOMS
won Premier Cup 7-2 on aggregate

NATIONAL LEAGUE PLAYOFFS

The top four teams in each group of the National League qualified for the Playoffs, in which they met the other teams in their group once at home and once away. The winning team in each group played again, home and away, to decide the Championship.

FIRST ROUND STANDINGS

North	GP	W	L	D	GF	GA	Pts
Sheffield Scimitars	6	5	0	1	31	5	11
Blackburn Hawks	6	3	2	1	16	16	7
Flintshire Freeze	6	1	4	1	20	32	3
Nottingham Lions	6	1	4	1	13	27	3
South							
Invicta Dynamo	6	5	0	1	37	14	11
Basingstoke Buffalo	6	3	3	0	22	23	6
Oxford City Stars	6	3	3	0	24	31	6
M Keynes Thunder	6	0	5	1	13	28	1

FINAL
First leg, 16 May 2004
INVICTA-SHEFFIELD   **3-4**   (1-3,1-1;1-0)
Scorers: INV Beerling, Carey, Smith 1g; Korff 2a; Martin, Copeland 1a. SHE Millie 2g; Oliver 1+1; C Ashton 1g; Ross 2a; Abel, Ashton, Hardy 1a.
Penalty minutes: Dynamo 12, Scimitars 16.
Netminding: Rowlands INV *shots*: 32, *save %*: 87.50; Jones SHE *shots*: 31, *save %*: 90.32.
Referee: Matt Thompson.   *Attendance*: 486.

Second leg, 22 May 2004
SHEFFIELD-INVICTA   **4-2**   (0-0,3-1,1-1)
Scorers: SHE Ross, Oliver 1+2; Millie 1+1; S Ashton 1g; Abel 2a. INV Smith 2g; Copeland, Beerling 1a. *Penalty minutes*: Scimitars 57 (Abel 2+10 xchecking + 5+game roughing), Dynamos 49 (Baxter 5+game roughing, Parrish 10-misc.abuse). *Netminding*: Jones SHE *shots*: 24, *save %*: 91.67, Rowlands INV *shots*: 35, *save %*: 88.57.
Referee: M Litchfield.   *Attendance*: 2,046.

SHEFFIELD SCIMITARS
are Playoff champions 8-5 on aggregate

SHEFFIELD SCIMITARS

left to right, back row: Paul Jones, Simon Lavis, Dave Briggs, Les Millie, Gavin Farrand, Rob Fleming, James Goodman, Ross Burberry, Neil Abel, Andy Chapman, Carl Ashton, Shaun Ashton, Steve Bingham, Simon Butterworth, Jon Woolhouse, Matt Darlow; *front row:* Danny Wood, John Wigston, Richie Oliver, Ryan Johnson, Dean Smith, Bob Clegg (manager), John Ross, Richard Clegg (coach), Andy Kelly, Neil Hardy, Andrew Hancock, Darren Maynard.

LEADING PLAYOFF SCORERS

	GP	G	A	Pts	Pim
John Ross SHE	8	5	13	18	2
Les Millie SHE	8	9	5	14	39
Paul Hume INV	8	5	6	11	8
Simon Beere BAS	6	9	1	10	12
Peter Carey INV	8	7	3	10	6
Jamie Smith INV	7	6	4	10	24
Richard Oliver SHE	6	4	6	10	2
Bobby Haig BLA	6	3	7	10	0

LEADING PLAYOFF NETMINDERS

	GPI	Mins	SoG	GA	Sv%
Paul Jones SHE	7	413	157	9	94.27
Colin Downie BLA	3	180	108	7	93.52
Carl Ambler INV	5	296	148	10	93.24

Qualification: 160 minutes

Clegg bows out on top

Richard Clegg celebrated his last season as coach of Sheffield Scimitars in the best possible way as he guided his team to the English National League Playoff Championship for the first time in their history.

Scimitars, who lost out on the league's northern title by one point, toppled Invicta Dynamos, the league's southern champs, 4-3 at home to take the playoff trophy 8-5 on aggregate.

Les Millie inflicted the most damage on Dynamos with three goals in the two legs, while his team-mate, **Ritchie Oliver**, added two more.

The playoff triumph completed a memorable year for Scimitars which had begun in the summer of 2003 when the club moved into their sparkling new home at iceSheffield, just along the road from Sheffield Arena.

Holding a slim 4-3 lead from the first leg in Gillingham, Scimitars outshot Dynamos 23-12 in the first two periods of the return and **John Ross**, Millie and Oliver gave the home team a commanding 7-3 aggregate lead by the halfway mark.

Jamie Smith pulled two back for Invicta but **Shaun Ashton** wrapped up the title on a powerplay three minutes from time.

SCOTTISH COMPETITIONS

CALEDONIAN CUP

The competition was created in 2001 to find the best senior team in Scotland. It replaced the Scottish Cup (formed 1986) which is now competed for by the Scottish National League sides.

The BNL's Newcastle Vipers were invited to enter the Cup when Superleague's Scottish Eagles collapsed in 2002.

Each team plays the others home and away with rosters being restricted to 50 per cent home-grown players in accordance with the guidelines of the British National League.

All four teams qualified for the semi-finals which were one-game affairs pitching first versus fourth and second against third. The final was played over two legs, home and away.

FIRST ROUND STANDINGS

	GP	W	L	D	GF	GA	Pts
Fife Flyers	6	4	1	1	38	27	9
Edinburgh Capitals	6	4	1	1	29	23	9
Newcastle Vipers	6	2	3	1	27	33	5
Dundee Stars	6	0	5	1	22	33	1

SEMI-FINALS

First semi-final
13 Jan   Fife Flyers-Dundee Stars   6-3
Second semi-final
3 Feb   Edinburgh-Newcastle   4-3

FINAL

First leg, 3 April 2004
Fife Flyers-Edinburgh Capitals   6-3
Second leg, 4 April 2004
Edinburgh Capitals-Fife Flyers   6-7

FIFE FLYERS retain Caledonian Cup
13-9 on aggregate

PAST WINNERS
2002-03	Fife Flyers
2001-02	Dundee Stars

Briere stops Caps

Games between Fife Flyers and Edinburgh Capitals, Scotland's oldest established sides, are guaranteed to be drama-packed. And the 2004 final of the Caledonian Cup was no exception.

A 31-save performance from Flyers' **Steve Briere**, missed chances, empty net goals and dodgy ref'ing, all made the Scottish fans forget the big games which were being staged elsewhere on the same weekend.

Although the teams had qualified in February, the two-legged final was arranged at the last minute after both clubs were knocked out of the British National League playoffs.

The fun began in the ancient Kirkcaldy rink on Saturday night in front of a large crowd determined to enjoy their last game of the season. They weren't disappointed as after slipping badly behind, Flyers eventually woke up in the final ten minutes and scored three goals to take a 6-3 lead into Murrayfield the next night.

There, Capitals quickly swung the game their way, **Steve Kaye** (2), **Adrian Saul** and **Martin Cingel** pulling the aggregate score back to 8-7 after 31 minutes. But that was as close as the home team came. Edinburgh's **Tony Hand** (2) was the only one to beat the on-form Briere while **Karry Biette** completed his hat-trick and three other Flyers scored to retain the trophy.

Capitals' bench coach, **Jock Hay**, was upset at the defeat. "The refereeing was awful," he told the *Edinburgh Evening News*. "They had too many men on the ice at least six times and there were other things going on." But he conceded: "We had enough chances to win the game but we made too many errors."

SCOTTISH NATIONAL LEAGUE

	GP	W	L	D	GF	GA	Pts
Camperdown Stars	14	11	2	1	90	42	23
Paisley Pirates	14	9	4	1	91	39	19
Edinburgh Capitals	14	9	4	1	64	47	19
Kirkcaldy Kestrels	14	8	4	2	73	44	18
Dumfries Vikings	14	8	6	0	93	72	16
Kil'nock Avalanche	14	5	9	0	59	88	10
Elgin Tornadoes	14	2	12	0	49	105	4
Dundee Tigers	14	1	12	1	30	112	3

YOUTH INTERNATIONALS

UNDER-19 HOME INTERNATIONAL

Players born 1 January 1985 or later

Nottingham Arena, 6 April 2003

ENGLAND UNDER-19	3	(1-0-2)
SCOTLAND UNDER-19	1	(1-0-0)

Scorers: **England** Wood 2g; Thompson 1g; Jamieson, Butterworth 1a. **Scotland** Campbell 1g; Forsyth 1a.
Penalty minutes: England 6, Scotland 2. *Shots on Goal*: Shea/Craze ENG 22, Arthur SCO 30. *Referee*: James Ashton. *Attendance*: 1,913.

Wood gives England late win

The 7th annual battle between the 'auld enemies' was won by England for the sixth time. Scotland's lone victory came in 2000.

Sheffield's **Greg Wood** sealed the latest Sassenach success with two goals seven minutes apart in the last period.

Six of the English players and five Scots played for the under-18 and under-20 GB teams that won gold in the World Championships.

THE TEAMS
ENGLAND UNDER-19
Nathan Craze CAR, Dan Shea SWI; Leigh Jamieson BEL (capt), Steve Pritchard, Liam Telfer, Andy Thornton BIL, Ricky Deacon CAR, Luke Boothroyd, David Phillips, Kevin Phillips HUL, Ross Bowers MIL, Simon Butterworth, Steve Duncombe, Chance Farrand, Greg Wood SHE, Shaun Thompson SLO, Shaun Littlewood, Shane Moore SWI.
Coaches: Mark Beggs SWI, Mick Mishener.
Manager: Barry Knock.
SCOTLAND UNDER-19
Craig Arthur FIF, Daryl Findlay KIL; Scott McKenzie, Chad Reekie CHE, Alan Crane, Mark Gallacher, Corrie Telfer DUM, Euan Forsyth, Scott McAndrew, Lee Mitchell, Tom Muir FIF, Iain Beattie, Chris Blackburn, Ross Dalgleish, Grant McPherson MUR, Alain Campbell, Stuart McCaig, Ryan McNeil, Paul McPhail PAI, Bari McKenzie MIL.
Coach: Kevin King PET.
Manager: Graham Grubb FIF.

ENGLAND UNDER-16

Players born 1 January 1988 or later

NEW YORK INTERNATIONAL CUP
Albany, New York, 27-31 December 2003

England-Middlesex Islanders	6-1 (0-1,3-0,3-0)
England-Jaahonka FIN	6-0 (1-0,3-0,2-0)
England-Assabet Valley	6-0 (2-0,3-0,1-0)
England-Long Island	7-2 (2-0,4-2,1-0)
Semi-final England-Assabet	7-0 (1-0,3-0,3-0)
Final England-Albany	3-0 (2-0,1-0,0-0)

ENGLAND UNDER-16 win Cup

CHRIS VERWIJST TOURNAMENT
Tilburg, Netherlands, 19-21 March 2004

England-Austria	2-2 (1-1,1-0,0-1)
England-France	5-4 (1-0,0-3,4-1)
England-Eaglebrook USA	4-4 (0-1,0-2,4-1)
England-Slovenia	1-5 (0-0,1-3,0-2)
3rd place playoff	
England-Austria	3-7 (1-0,0-4,2-3)

ENGLAND UNDER-16 finish 4th

LEADING UNDER-16 SCORERS

Both competitions	GP	G	A	Pts	Pim
Matt Towe	11	12	10	22	4
Robert Dowd	11	11	6	17	14
Danny Wood	11	5	9	14	0
James Ferrara	11	2	9	11	10
Craig Peacock	11	1	10	11	4
Dean Tonks	11	5	3	8	8
Ben O'Connor	4	6	1	7	4

ENGLAND UNDER-16
Martin Clarkson CAR, Joe White INV; Michael Farn BIL, David Savage GUI, Chad Briggs, Danny McAleese SHE, Nick Compton, Graham Newell SWI, Tom Parker TEL; Robert Dowd BIL, Nathan Miller HUL, #James Ferrara, Craig Peacock PET, Dean Tonks, Andrew Turner, Danny Wood SHE, Richard Westgarth SUN, Greg Martyn SWI, Tom Mills SWI, Matt Towe TEL; *Ben O'Connor (London, Ontario).
Coaches: Warren Rost SLO, Robert Wilkinson, Paul Simpson. *Manager*: Bob Wilkinson.
* Captain in New York. # Captain in Tilburg.

ENGLAND UNDER-14

Players born 1 January 1990 or later

Windsor, Ontario, 27-30 December 2003
RIVERSIDE BANTAM TOURNAMENT
England-Riverside Rangers	4-0
England-Tecumseh Eagles	9-1
England-Lasalle Sabres	3-0

Final
England-Belle River Rink Rats	0-3

***ENGLAND UNDER-14** finished 2nd.*

Füssen Ice Arena, Germany, 15-17 April 2004
FÜSSEN INTERNATIONAL CUP
England-Ahmat	1-2
England-HC Femme	3-2
England-EHC Olten	1-2
England-Füssen	5-3
England-Sterzing	1-8

3rd place playoff
England-EHC Olten	2-2

***ENGLAND UNDER-14** finished 3rd after penalty shoot-out.* ***Matt Davies** scored winning penalty shot.*

ENGLAND UNDER-14

Ben Bowns, Jonathan Tindall SHE; Chris Arnone BLA, James Francis (capt) GUI, Stephen Lee HUL, Richard Bentham NOT, Joe Graham SHE, Danny Lamb SUN; Jimmy Moutrey BIL, Matt Davies HUL, David Coffey MIL, Robert Farmer, Robert Lachowicz, James Neil NOT, Tom Squires SHE, Jamie Line SWI, Jamie Tinsley, Callum Watson WHI.
Coach: Dave Graham.
Manager: Stacey Davies.

ENGLAND UNDER-13

Colisee Pepsi, Quebec, 13-18 February 2004

WORLD PEE-WEE TOURNAMENT
13 Feb	England-Campus	6-4
18 Feb	England-Moncton Wildcats	3-5

ENGLAND UNDER-13

Charles Kaylor ROM, Ben Bowns SHE; Andy Finn BIL, Josh Batch, Declan Finn CHE, Georgina Farman HUL, Josh Wilson SHE, Danny Goldthorpe SLO, Ross Hanlon SUN; Ben Davies CAR, Richard Haggar HUL, Robert Farmer (capt), Jack Prince NOT, Callum Fowler ROM, Ashley Calvert SHE, Tom Squires SHE, Shannon Taylor SWI, Nathan Salem SUN, Callum Watson WHI.
Coach: Marty Parfitt.
Manager: John Ramsden.

Tindall leads under-14 defence

Nick Compton of Swindon and Sheffield's **Jonathan Tindall** won honours when England sent teams to Europe and North America at three different age levels.

Compton, 15, of the under-16s, was voted to the All-Star team on defence in the Chris Verwjist tournament in Tilburg. Under-14 Tindall was selected as the best netminder in Füssen, Germany.

The under-16s must have embarrassed a few Americans in New York at Christmas-time when **Warren Rost**'s team won an international event in the state capital of Albany.

They didn't just win, they slaugtered their opponents. Goalies **Martin Clarkson** (Cardiff) and **Joe White** (Invicta) shared three shutouts and allowed only three goals in five games. England then whitewashed their hosts in the final.

This was the second successive North American event in which Rost, player-coach of Slough Jets, has guided his team to success. The under-16s won Ontario's Riverside Midget tournament in 2002.

The under-14s entered the Riverside competition this time, at Bantam level, and finished as runners-up only after facing a hot goalie in the final.

Coach **Dave Graham**, the former GB international netminder, was especially proud of his defence. Tindall and his Sheffield team-mate **Ben Bowns** (he also played for the under-13s) conceded only one goal before the final.

Tindall was his side's hero again in Füssen where he saved every penalty in the playoff shootout against Swiss club, Olten. Combined with **Matt Davies's** successful shot, England finished a satisfying third out of 12 teams. Nottingham's **James Line** scored five goals in the six Füssen games.

The under-13s had surprised their hosts last year in Canada when they carried off the trophy in the unofficial world pee-wee championship in Quebec. Their reward was promotion to a higher level where they faced stronger teams. But England held their own and were knocked out only by the team that eventually won their group.

With only two games in the official tournament, the squad had plenty of time to spare in the home of hockey. They didn't waste it, arranging no less than eight friendlies and winning half of them.

Richard Haggar of Hull scored most points (13) from the ten games played. His five goals were equalled by Nottingham's **Jack Prince**, who was runner-up with 11 points. Swindon's **Shannon Taylor** had ten points (four goals).

ENGLAND UNDER-19 *above*

left to right, back row: David Phillips, Steve Duncombe, Ross Bowers, Leigh Jamieson, Chance Ferrand, Shaun Littlewood; *middle row:* Luke Boothroyd, Shaun Thompson, Simon Butterworth, Kevin Phillips, Dan Shea, Greg Wood, Liam Telfer, Steven Pritchard; *front row:* Nathan Craze, Ricky Deacon, Andy Thornton, Shane Moore.   *Photo:* Diane Davey

ENGLAND UNDER-13

left to right, back row: Josh Wilson, Neville Moralee (EIHA), John Ramsden (manager), Simon Manning (asst coach), Marty Parfitt (coach), Georgina Farman; *middle row:* Josh Batch, Richard Haggar, Declan Finn, Andy Finn, Ross Hanlon, Ashley Calvert, Callam Watson, Jack Prince; *front row:* Charles Kaylor, Ben Davies, Callum Fowler, Shannon Taylor, Robert Farmer, Tom Squires, Nathan Salem, Danny Goldthorpe, Ben Bowns.

WOMEN'S ICE HOCKEY

PREMIER LEAGUE STANDINGS

	GP	W	L	D	GF	GA	Pts
Sund'land Scorpions SUN	18	16	2	0	123	30	32
Slough Jets SLO	18	11	4	3	108	55	25
Guildford Lightning GUI	18	10	4	4	57	28	24
Kingston Diamonds HUL	18	9	5	4	79	51	22
Cardiff Comets CAR	18	9	5	4	52	39	22
Sheffield Shadows SHE	18	9	6	3	74	39	21
Brack'll Queen Bees BRK	18	8	6	4	80	51	20
Swindon Top Cats SWI	18	3	14	1	49	97	7
Flintshire Furies FLI	18	3	15	0	44	115	6
B'stoke Lady Bison BAS	18	0	17	1	27	188	1

Tied teams separated by results in the games between them.

LEADING SCORERS

	GP	G	A	Pts	Pim
Louise Wheeler SLO	15	45	25	70	16
Nicola Bicknell SLO	17	32	38	70	14
Lynsey Emerson SUN	17	28	20	48	20
Claire Oldfield SUN	18	26	22	48	10
Emily Turner SHE	17	28	8	36	6
Leen de Decker HUL	16	17	15	32	6
Jayne McClelland SUN	18	10	20	30	2

LEADING NETMINDERS

	GPI	Mins	SoG	GA	Sv%
Laura Saunders GUI	13	660	263	21	92.0
Bev Hutchinson SUN	18	833	268	26	90.3

Qualification: 360 minutes

CHAMPIONSHIP PLAYOFFS
iceSheffield, 29 May-1 June 2004
Premier League

Final	**Sunderland**-Guildford	2-0

Goal scorers: Emmerson, Lewis.

3rd place	Slough-Kingston	4-2
Semi-finals	Sunderland-Kingston	3-2
	Guildford-Slough	3-1

Division One

Final	**Solihull**-Whitley Bay	9-2

Louise a jolly good scorer

Louise Wheeler retained her Premier League scoring title with a staggering 45 goals in 15 games for Slough Jets, but her team lost out to Sunderland Scorpions who topped the league for a record sixth time.

Scorpions added the championship playoffs when goalie **Bev Hutchinson** achieved a 19-save shutout over the third placed Guildford Lightning in the final.

Solihull Vixens won the Division One championship playoffs and were promoted to the Premier League along with Telford Wrekin Raiders who won Divison One North.

Basingstoke Lady Bison, who gained only one point in the Premier League and conceded nearly 200 goals, accepted relegation to Division One South.

☑ This was the 21st season of the Women's League. So that makes something else the women can do better than their menfolk!

WOMEN'S WORLD CHAMPIONSHIPS
Div II Vipiteno-Sterzing, Italy, 14-20 March 2004

	GP	W	L	D	GF	GA	Pts
Denmark	5	4	0	1	24	7	9
Italy	5	4	1	0	24	7	8
Slovakia	5	3	1	1	28	7	7
Netherlands	5	2	3	0	8	14	4
Australia	5	1	4	0	6	32	2
Britain	5	0	5	0	6	29	0

Denmark promoted to Division I in 2005, **Australia** and **Britain** relegated.

BRITAIN'S RESULTS
14 Mar **Britain-Denmark**   2-3 (0-1,2-1,0-1)
   GB goal scorers: Maitland, Turner.
   Netminding: Robbins 93.33%.
15 Mar **Italy-Britain**   10-2 (2-1,3-1,5-0)
   GB goal scorers: Taylor, Bicknell.
   Netminding: Robbins 90.9%, Herring 60%.
17 Mar **Britain-Netherlands**   0-1 (0-1,0-0,0-0)
   Netminding: Robbins 97.37%
18 Mar **Slovakia-Britain**   11-0 (4-0,3-0,4-0)
   Netminding: Herring 86.54%, Robbins 80.95%
20 Mar **Australia-Britain**   4-2 (1-0,0-0,3-2)
   GB goal scorers: Oldfield, Taylor.
   Netminding: Robbins 93.45%.

Vicky keeps Robbin 'em
Basingstoke keeper **Vicky Robbins** faced a torrent of rubber as Britain lost all five of their World Championship games, dooming them to relegation.

The 24-year-old Robbins, a veteran of all Britain's World Championship sides since 1999, turned in a spectacular display, kicking out 215 of the 234 shots aimed at her for a remarkable 91.88 save percentage.

But her acrobatics could not save her country who lost to Denmark, the only team they had taken a point off in 2003, in their opening game.
▪ GB's relegation to Div III last year was avoided when the IIHF re-organised the groups.

BRITAIN
Vicky Robbins BAS, Kelly Herring PET; Lauren Halliwell BLA, Ami Merrick CAR, Louise Fisher, Alex von Haselberg GUI, Gillian Wyatt SHE, Nicola Bicknell SLO, Fiona King (capt), Katherine Wiggins, Hannah Young GUI, Eleanor Maitland KIL, Kirstin Beattie MUR, Angela Taylor PAI, Emily Turner SHE, Claire Oldfield, Helen Stowe, Gemma Watt SUN, Becky Kasner WHI. *Head Coach*: Reg Wilcox. *Asst. coach*: Jo Abbs. *Manager*: Ian Turner.

HOME INTERNATIONAL
Lagoon Ice Rink, Paisley, 10 April 2004

SCOTLAND	0	(0-0-0)
WALES	**7**	(3-1-3)

Scoring:
0-1 WAL Brunning (Cheetham, Dodwell)   4.20
0-2 WAL Brunning (Cheetham, Williams)   12.30
0-3 WAL Williams (A Merrick)   16.38
0-4 WAL Lawton (Pugsley)   30.50
0-5 WAL A Merrick (Kowalyshen)   47.55
0-6 WAL Brunning (Dodwell, Cheetham)   53.15
0-7 WAL Langford (McMullen, Hargreaves)   55.11
Penalty minutes: Scotland 16, Wales 8.
Referee: R Cowan. *Linesmen*: Foster, Jess.

Hat-trick for number 99
Heather Brunning, wearing shirt 99, scored a hat-trick for Wales as her team won their second home international in two years.

Goalie **Emma Hayman** kept the Scots at bay in the first game between two home countries since the Welsh upset England in May 2002.
▪ This was Wales' second shutout of the year as they whitewashed a Northern Select 3-0 at Nottingham on 1 February 2004.

THE TEAMS
WALES
Emma Hayman, Sue Hart; Helen Pugsley, Lorraine McMullan, Sophie Lawton HUL, Laura Merrick, Oenone Dodwell BAS, Becci Hargeaves (capt), Ami Merrick, Sam Cheetham BRK, Laura Burns, Bethan Williams, Elaine Langford, Sarah Audsley BAS, Deborah Warwick SOL, Kara Kowalyshen, Heather Brunning BRK.
Coaches: Mike Pugsley, Sam Hart.
Manager: Helen Jefferies
All Cardiff Comets, except where shown.
SCOTLAND
Sarah Gibson DUM, Katie Worthing PAI; Gill MacDiarmid EDI, Fiona Letton CAM, Eleanor Maitland KIL (capt), Gemma Watt PAI, Leanne Hogan ABE, Kirsty McMillan MUR, Pamela Edwards EDI, Kelly Grindrod AYR, Kirsten Beattie MUR, Mo Muir DUM, Lisa Piper AYR, Amanda Webster DUM, Natasha Duff AYR, Jennifer Kirk FIF, Angela Taylor PAI, Fiona Vorel BAS, Becky Kasner WHI, Debbie McCready PAI.
Coach: Stuart Wilson.
Asst coach: Colette Cowie.

FIRST GAMES

The £15.7m IceSheffield complex was the only new rink to open in 2003, as we reported in last year's Annual.

The building is situated only a few hundred yards from the Sheffield Steelers' home arena and has two ice pads, both Olympic size, with one seating 1,500 and the other 500.

IceSheffield replaced the city's old Queen's Road rink and is now the home of the Sheffield Scimitars who play in the northern section of the English National League.

Details follow of the first game that Scimitars played in the rink. This was the first league game staged there, though the venue hosted a junior tournament in the summer of 2003.

Scimitars mauled by Lions

7 September 2003, English National League (North), IceSheffield

SCIMITARS-NOTTINGHAM LIONS   5-6

Fittingly, the great Sheffield-Nottingham rivalry was chosen to open the new iceSheffield centre.

Scimitars, the defending league champs, were delighted to be opening the new season in a state-of-the-art rink after years in gloomy Queens Road. They out-shot Lions 35-29 and **John Ross**, their top scorer in 2002-03, had two goals, including the first senior league goal in the new building. But it wasn't enough.

Stewart Bliss and **Stefan Dodwell** with two goals apiece and a fine display from netminder **Adam White** helped Lions to upset Scimitars, fighting back from 5-3 down at the end of the second period to win 6-5.

Former Steelers forward, **Les Millie**, celebrated the occasion in his own way by being thrown out halfway through the game.

The contest was the first in the National League for the Lions who were previously in the Premier League.

Game Summary

Scoring

1-0	SHE	Ross (Oliver)	1.59
1-1	NOT	S Dodwell	9.04
2-1	SHE	S Ashton (C Ashton)	23.22
2-2	NOT	Bliss (S Dodwell, Mercer)	23.51
2-3	NOT	N Dodwell (Robson)	26.50
3-3	SHE	Ross (Smith) pp	30.20
4-3	SHE	C Ashton pp	33.47
5-3	SHE	Abel (Smith)	37.24
5-4	NOT	Colegate (Mercer)	43.45
5-5	NOT	Bliss (S Dodwell)	50.12
5-6	NOT	S Dodwell (Wilcox)	56.25

Shots on Goal

Maynard SHE   13- 3-13 29
White NOT   11-13-11 35

Penalty minutes: Sheffield   40   (Millie 2+10-+game), Nottingham 18.

Referee: T Young.   *Attendance*: 321

Linesmen: Cranstone, Doubleday.

SHEFFIELD SCIMITARS

Darren Maynard, Matt Darlow; Andrew Hancock, Alan White, Rob Flemming, John Wigston, Neil Abel (capt), Shaun Ashton, Stephen Duncombe, Paul Lofthouse, James Goodman, Ross Burberry, Andy Kelly, Richard Oliver, John Ross, Andy Chapman, Jon Woolhouse, Dean Smith, Steve Bingham, Gavin Farrand, Carl Ashton, Les Millie.

NOTTINGHAM LIONS

Adam White, Daniel Kemp; Ben Cheshire, Chris Wilcox, Chris Colegate, Stewart Bliss, Stefan Dodwell (capt), Lee Mercer, David Radford, Paul Whitby, Jon Bell, Craig Poynter, Oscar Wightman, Adam Robson, Nicky Dodwell.

• Scimitars went on to win the English National League Playoff Championship. Full details and team pic are in the *English Leagues* section.

• The first game played at iceSheffield by Scimitars' Elite League neighbours, Sheffield Steelers, came on 4 November 2003 when Edinburgh Capitals of the British National League lost a challenge game 6-4. **Joel Irving** had a hat-trick and five points for Steelers.

The game marked the return to the Steel City of former Steeler **Tony Hand**, who was Capitals' player-coach. It was arranged by **Scott Neil**, who doubled as general manager of the Steelers and the Capitals.

HALL OF FAME

Mike Blaisdell

Canadian **Mike Blaisdell** has won more trophies at the top level than any other coach in Britain. The Elite League and playoff double which his Steelers captured in 2003-04 brought his tally to a remarkable 13 since he took up coaching in 1993 with Nottingham Panthers.

The baker's dozen include Steelers' Grand Slam of four titles in 2000-01 and two more league trophies, plus three Benson and Hedges cups with Panthers.

He has been honoured four times by the British Ice Hockey Writers Association with their Coach of the Year award, three of them coming in the last four seasons.

A hard-nosed forward from Moose Jaw, Saskatchewan on the Canadian prairies, 'Blaiser' plugged his way through over 300 NHL games and represented his country before coming to England in 1990 and playing three seasons with Durham Wasps.

A master motivator and a shrewd judge of talent, he guided Panthers to the Benson and Hedges in only his second season behind the bench. Since he joined Steelers from their deadly rivals in the middle of 1999-2000, the club have won at least one piece of silverware each season.

He revamped the squad on his arrival, bringing in forwards like **Rick Brebant** and **Scott Allison**, goalies **Mike O'Neill** and **Mike Torchia**, and making hard man, **Dennis Vial**, captain. They rewarded him by winning the Grand Slam.

His signing of netminder **Joel Laing** was another of his master-strokes, though he cheerfully admitted it was a happy accident. He was able to build his 2002-03 squad around his fellow native of Saskatchewan as Laing chalked up a record ten shutouts and the team captured the league and Challenge Cup.

In the previous season, with the club only belatedly recovering from mismanagement by its former owner, he had literally days to put together a team on a drastically slimmed-down budget. He succeeded so well that Steelers carried off the Superleague Playoff championship.

Mike returned to Canada in the summer of 2004 to take up the post of assistant coach with his old Canadian junior team, Regina (Saskatchewan) Pats.

Rick Brebant

In season 2002-03, centreman **Rick Brebant** became one of only two players to score more than 1,000 goals at the highest level of British ice hockey. The achievement took the native of Elliot Lake, Ontario 16 seasons and just over 800 games in major competitions since he left Canada in 1987.

Brebant, 40, closed his British career with 2,407 points (1,017 goals), though he sneaked another 27 (two goals) this past season when, as coach of Manchester Phoenix, he helped out his new team in 33 league games.

He played on seven different sides (two in Manchester) throughout his long career and his fierce competitiveness was a major influence on their success. His teams won seven playoff championships, seven league titles and six cups. Two of his clubs - Durham Wasps and Sheffield Steelers - won the Grand Slam.

He led the league three times in points and the playoffs twice. He was top goal scorer in the British League, Premier Division with 146 in his second season with Wasps, 1988-89.

Between 1994 and 2002, he was capped 32 times for Britain scoring ten goals and 23 points. The 1994 championships in the World A Pool were among the highlights of his career. "My favourite goal was a short-handed one for Britain against Canada's NHL goalie [Quebec's **Stephane Fiset**]," he recalled.

Before joining Phoenix for his final season here, he spent four years with Sheffield Steelers, winning eight trophies in the most consistent spell of success of any British club in recent times. His coach, **Mike Blaisdell**, described him as "one of the most intense guys I've ever come across. I've always respected the way he's the first on the puck. It doesn't matter if the biggest guy in the league is coming into the corner to kill him, he'll go in every time."

Neil Morris, the owner of the Phoenix, was equally glowing in his praise when he signed the stocky forward. "He's one of the hardest working, grittiest, skilful and most driven players I've ever had the privilege to watch," he said.

Billy Brennan

Defenceman **Billy Brennan** competed for Britain in six World Championships and also became a respected coach.

He made his debut in the Canadian dominated, professional Scottish National League at the age of 17 while still a schoolboy at Glasgow's St Mungo's Academy. He played ten games for Ayr Raiders in his first season, 1951-52, helping them to win the league and Autumn Cup.

His coach was the Canadian **Keith Kewley** whom he cites as the major influence on his career. When Kewley moved to Bill's home town of Paisley the folowing year, he took the youngster with him, converting him into a winger and establishing him with the Pirates.

Only two years later he was selected for Britain. He was captain of the 1962 (Pool A) squad and player-coach in 1965 and 1966, coming out of retirement for his final one in 1971. Unusually, he played on the wing in his first and last championships but on defence for the other four.

William Patrick Brennan was born on 13 January 1934 and developed his skating and hockey skills as a 13 year-old at the old Paisley rink in East Lane.

His club career was played entirely in Scotland. With the collapse of the Pirates, in 1961 he took over as player-coach of the newly formed amateur side, Paisley Mohawks, and moulded them into Grand Slam winners in the old Northern League.

An innovative coach, he introduced an off-ice fitness programme for his players, using the ice-time for skills and tactical development. He took Mohawks on several European tours in the 1960s, helping their development by matching them against strong opposition.

A number of his players went on to achieve international recognition themselves, including his younger brother **Alastair Brennan** - who was inducted into the Hall of Fame in 1990 - **Billy Miller**, **Alistair McRae** and the late **Jackson McBride**.

A draughtsman by profession, he worked for 23 years with Babcock & Wilcox, before moving back north in 1975 to Aberdeen as sales and projects manager with a Norwegian engineering company, retiring as their UK managing director in 1999.

Though Bill had retired from the sport in 1973, he became involved again in 1992 when a new rink opened in Aberdeen and he was invited to help with the creation of the ice hockey programme.

David S Gordon

Charlie Knott

Charles J Knott Jr , known affectionately as 'CJ', was managing director of the Southampton ice rink and the successful Vikings for 11 years in the 1950s and 1960s.

A keen advocate of the home-bred player, he promoted amateur hockey at Southampton with a dash of showmanship, publicising the city as 'the Heart of English Ice Hockey'.

When he took charge of the Southampton ice rink, his first team in 1952-53 consisted entirely of home-grown players. The new Southampton Vikings joined the Southern Intermediate League and were an instant success, drawing capacity crowds and winning the league title in their first season.

The fans were also treated to visits from England, Scotland, Sweden, the USA and Czechoslovakia as well as foreign club sides. Vikings won Southampton's BIHA Cup five times and the Southern Cup on three occasions. Several Vikings represented their country in the World Championships.

The British Ice Hockey Association, the sport's governing body at the time, made him an England selector in 1959 and a year later appointed him to their ruling council in recognition of his enthusiasm for British players. He also acted as Britain's official delegate to the 1961 World Championships in Switzerland.

Always approachable and immaculately attired in an evening suit, he was often seen chatting to his customers or aspiring young players. **Roy Saunders**, one of the surviving members of the 1950s team, recently recalled him as "the finest gentleman I've ever met".

Charlie's brief reign in ice hockey ended sadly in the summer of 1963 when the family sold the rink and the adjacent speedway and greyhound stadium to the Rank Organisation. It took 13 long years before the Vikings were revived and he returned to head the club's management committee for a season.

Charles, who died last year, aged 88, was best known in sporting circles as a successful amateur bowler with Hampshire County Cricket Club between 1938 and 1954. Cricket commentator, **John Arlott**, once declared that Charlie was the finest amateur bowler to play for Hampshire.

When he was inducted into the Hall of Fame earlier this year, his widow, Iris, said she was delighted that a man famous for playing a gentlemen's game should be honoured for his part in organising one of the roughest games.

Martin Harris/Stewart Roberts

MIKE BLAISDELL

CHARLIE KNOTT JR

RICK BREBANT

BILL BRENNAN

HALL OF FAME MEMBERS

The current Hall of Fame was established in 1986 by the British Ice Hockey Writers' Association.

In addition to the members profiled above, the Association have inducted the following: 2003 - Stephen Cooper, Frederick Meredith. 2002 - Ian Cooper, Chris Kelland, Norman de Mesquita. 2001 - Jim Lynch. 2000 - *Vic Batchelder, Gary Stefan. 1999 - Les Anning, Shannon Hope, Gordon Latto, Roy Shepherd. 1998 - *Earl Carlson. 1997- John Lawless. 1996 - Johnny Murray. 1995 - Alex Dampier. 1994 - *Mick Curry, *Jack Wharry. 1993 - Willie Clark, Nico Toemen, Ian Wight. 1992 - Frank Dempster, *Alec Goldstone, Lawrie Lovell. 1991 - Jack Dryburgh, John Rost, Glynne Thomas. 1990 - Alastair Brennan, *Sir Arthur Elvin MBE, *Willie Kerr Sr. 1989 - George Beach, *Bill Booth, *Art Hodgins, Peter Johnson, Alfie Miller. 1988 - Pat Marsh, Johnny Carlyle, *Percy H Nicklin, *J F J (Icy) Smith, *Alan Weeks. 1987 - *Ernie Leacock, Tom (Red) Imrie, Terry Matthews, Derek Reilly, Les Strongman. 1986 - *J F (Bunny) Ahearne, *Robert (Bobby) Giddens, Roy Halpin, *Harvey (Red) Stapleford, *Sam Stevenson.

* deceased

British ice hockey's original Hall of Fame was created in 1950 by Canadian journalist and player **Bob Giddens**, the editor/publisher of Ice Hockey World, the sport's major British publication from 1935 to 1958.

The members of this Hall are listed in The Ice Hockey Annual 2000-01.

Biographies of all Hall members can be found on the BIHWA website at www.bihwa.co.uk.

TRIBUTES

Frank Boucher

Francis George Boucher found fame on both sides of the Atlantic, coaching Canada to Olympic gold in Switzerland in 1948 and Wembley Lions to the English National League title four years later.

Frank - described by one of his players as 'a real prince among men' - came from a famous hockey family: he was the son of **George 'Buck' Boucher** and a nephew of New York Rangers' illustrious **Frank Boucher**, after whom he was named. Both are in the Hockey Hall of Fame. Another uncle, **Bobby Boucher**, also played in the NHL

Weighing in at only 140 lb and standing at 5ft 6in, Frank Boucher never reached the NHL like his father and uncles, but played in the American Hockey League.

His great claim to fame came in the 1948 Winter Olympics when he coached Canada, represented by the RCAF Flyers, to the World and Olympic Championships in St Moritz. On their way to the titles, the Canucks beat Britain, captained by **Archie Stinchcombe**, 3-0.

The following season, 1949-50, he came to England and spent four seasons on defence with Wembley Lions. With Frank as player-coach, they won the ENL in 1951-52. A left-hand shot, he accumulated 26 goals and 116 points in 184 games, with a meagre 40 minutes in penalties.

During World War Two he enlisted with the Royal Canadian Air Force and served in England with no.6 bomber group. This allowed him to play hockey when the sport resumed at Wembley in December 1945.

He died of pneumonia on 11 December 2003, aged 85, leaving a daughter. His wife predeceased him.

Martin C Harris/Phil Drackett

'Dorry' Boyle

Scotland and GB international, **Dorrington (Dorry) Boyle**, was the first home-grown player to sign for Edinburgh Royals in the Canadian-dominated Scottish National League of the Fifties. Equally at home as a centreman or on defence, 'Dorry' played 103 games for Royals over two seasons in 1953-55, scoring 12 goals and 29 points.

Born at Paisley on 16 December 1932, he began his international career with the Scotland under-18s in May 1950, travelling to Richmond where they beat the English 4-1. But there was little international competition in this country in the Fifties and he had to wait until 1960 before being selected to play for Scotland's senior team in their annual clash with the English. He turned out three times, scoring a goal and four points.

This led to him being capped for Great Britain 12 times in the 1963 and 1965 World Championships in Sweden and Finland. He scored three points (two goals), all in Stockholm.

After his two seasons with Royals, he signed for Paisley Mohawks who won section B of the Scottish League for three successive years from 1963.

Dorry died in 2003, aged 71.

Martin C Harris/Stewart Roberts

Nancy Chisholm

Nancy Chisholm, who died on 8 October 2003 aged 49, served for 17 years as treasurer of the Scottish Ice Hockey Association. She had been in poor health for some time and was believed to have suffered a heart attack in the night at her home in Glasgow.

Nancy first became involved with the sport as a teenager, selling copies of the old *Ice Hockey Herald* at Scottish rinks, and then helped her local team, Glasgow Dynamos, at the Crossmyloof arena.

A librarian who worked in Glasgow's world famous Mitchell Library, she was a valued member of the Scottish IHA, taking on various other jobs including those of general secretary and player registration secretary.

Frank Dempster

Mike Cook

The chairman of the Lee Valley Lions Supporters Club who worked alongside coach **Steve James** in the team's heyday of the 1980s, died in March 2004. He was 67.

With the help of his family, he ran the T-Stop hockey shop selling merchandise on match nights. As an employee of the Lee Valley Park Regional Authority he also worked for the club behind the scenes.

Perhaps most memorably, he was the prime mover in twinning the Supporters Club with the Booster Club of NHL team, Hartford Whalers.

Dan 'Heavy' Evason

A former coach of Peterborough Pirates, **Dan Evason**, died suddenly on 6 March 2004. He was 41.

A immensely popular character who insisted on being known only as 'Heavy', he joined Pirates in the summer of 1993. At the time, the team were feeling the pressure of playing in the Premier Division of the British League and their finances were not good. Then the rink was closed for ten weeks when 'bumps' appeared in the ice surface.

'Heavy' waded in with a will, leading a team of volunteers to rebuild the ice. **Ian McFarlane**, a director of the Pirates at the time, recalled: "He was a very jovial chap, heavy by name and by physique. I remember he was always singing, you could hear him all over the rink. He was a great guy and made an ideal Santa Claus that Christmas."

The disruption and the cancellation of so many training sessions left Pirates vulnerable to injury and next to bottom of the table. After 30 games they had a 5-23-2 W-L-D record and an even worse financial position and were left with no option but to cancel Evason's contract in February 1994.

He returned to Canada and devoted his time and considerable energy to the sport. He coached numerous junior teams and was a scout for the Western (major junior) Hockey League's Kamloops Blazers.

But his passion was for the Special Olympics (for people with intellectual disabilities). He was chairman of the host committee for the 2006 Special Olympics Summer Games which had been awarded to his home town of Brandon, Manitoba.

The mayor of Brandon, **Dave Burgess**, paid personal tribute when Heavy died after collapsing while playing in a recreational game. "It's really very upsetting to hear of somebody of such quality to be lost."

Simon Potter/Stewart Roberts

Geoff Kellond

Geoff Kellond was a referee and linesman for many years at all levels, but he was probably best known as the proprietor of Ultraworld, the sports equipment business.

Born in Montreal on 1 January 1939, he played hockey in Ottawa as a youngster, before moving west to Vancouver. He came to England in 1976 to work for *Xerox*.

When the Oxford ice rink opened in 1984 Geoff, who lived at nearby Thame, became involved with the organisation of the youth hockey programme. This eventually led to his appointment as a referee in which role he reached Division One of the Heineken-sponsored British League. He later became a supervisor of match officials.

In the mid-1980s he put some money into a newly formed sports equipment business which blossomed into Ultraworld. As the UK agent for the *Easton* brand he provided an equipment repair service at several World Championships and two Winter Olympic tournaments.

Geoff was able to enjoy his 40th wedding anniversary with his wife Jenny, and his daughter Lisanne's wedding, before he succumbed to bone cancer on 1 November 2003. He also left two sons.

Fred Kentner

Canadian **Fred Kentner** was Fife Flyers' leading scorer in 1953-54, his only season in the UK. The Acton, Ontario-born forward, then aged 24, finished 22nd overall in Scottish tournaments that year with 36 goals and 65 points in 60 games. Flyers finished seventh and last in all three major competitions.

Before coming to Scotland, Fred had a brief spell with Washington (DC) Lions of the Eastern Hockey League. After retiring from the sport he ran a small construction company and raised show poultry. His chickens won many prizes in Canada and the USA.

He passed away on 27 March 2004, aged 73.

Martin C Harris/Denis Gibbons

Charles (Herbie) Little

Cdr. **Charles Herbert (Herbie) Little** CD, MA, FRCGS, FAMF, Isabel La Catolica Order (Spain), died on 10 January 2004, aged 96.

While attending Brasenose College, Oxford as a Rhodes scholar, he captained the Oxford University team in Davos, Switzerland that won the Spengler Cup twice in the early 1930s.

Cdr. Little, who was raised in Mount Forest, Ontario, enjoyed a productive life encompassing many and varied fields of endeavour.

During World War II he became the first Canadian Director of Naval Intelligence and was one of a very few Canadians to handle Ultra decrypts. He served in the Royal Canadian Navy until 1958 and he was awarded the Admirals' Medal in 1991.

On retirement he joined the (Canadian) Federal Public Service serving in a number of capacities including the bilingual chief editor of the Royal Commission on Pilotage.

GRAHAM NURSE

Sad news arrived as we were going to press of the passing of **Graham Nurse**, a stalwart of the Altrincham and Manchester clubs for over 30 years. He was 57. We will have a full tribute to a great friend of the sport in our next edition.

In a life-time of service to his family, friends, community and church among his most distinguished contributions were his works with the Canadian Authors' Association (National President 1972-75, appointed Honorary President in 2001); the Canadian Writers' Foundation (longest serving president from 1978 to 2001; thereafter appointed Honorary President); and All Saints' Anglican Church Warden and Lay Reader.

He published ten historical works, a book of poetry and numerous articles, and was a long time contributor to the Canadian Geographical Society Journal (Fellow 1969).

A former member of the Rideau (Ottawa) Club, Royal Ottawa Golf Club and Rideau Curling Club, he authored definitive club histories and contributed many years of active involvement on various committees.

He was awarded the Queen's Jubilee Medal in 1977.

His contribution to Oxford University's ice hockey team was remembered at the Centenary Varsity Match in 2000. Aged 92, he crossed the Atlantic to present the Patton Trophy to the captain of his old team.

He left three sons and daughter. His wife predeceased him.

Davey Mason

Former Murrayfield Racers and Great Britain defenceman, **Davey Mason**, died after falling from a boat in the Mediterranean. The tragedy happened on 2 January 2004 in Limasol, Cyprus.

A civil engineer from Inverness, Davey, 49, had gone on holiday with his daughter Karen and was about to take a ride on a high speed banana fun boat when he suffered a fatal heart attack.

A one-club man, Mason served with Murrayfield from the early Seventies until retiring during the 1982-83 season. During his time with the Racers, they twice won the Grand Slam of British Championship (Icy Smith Cup), Northern League and Spring Cup (league playoffs)

His steady play on the blue line for Scotland during five consecutive winters from 1975, attracted the attention of the GB selectors and he went to Barcelona in 1979 and Beijing in 1981. He scored a goal in Spain.

Martin C. Harris

Ray Milton

Raymond Bernard Milton was one of the last surviving players who competed in the 1936 Winter Olympics in Germany. He represented Canada where the team won a silver medal behind Britain's gold. He was captain of the 1939-40 Allan Cup champions, Canada's most important senior competition.

He died peacefully at his home in Stouffville, Ontario, aged 91, on 17 September 2003, leaving Jeanne, his wife of 66 years, five children, 14 grandchildren and three great-grandchildren.

Mark McKendrick

Mark McKendrick, reserve netminder for Murrayfield Racers and Glasgow Saints between 1988 and 1991, died of leukaemia on 4 February 2004, at the young age of 33.

Mark, born on 14 March 1970, came to the attention of the ice hockey world when he was selected to represent Scotland's under-17 team at the 1986 Sport Goofy youth tournament held at Dundee and organised by **Tom Stewart**.

During the 1988-89 season he appeared in nine games for Racers in the Premier Division of the British League when Racers were runners-up.

Two years on, Mark dressed for three matches with Glasgow Saints in their one and only campaign in Division One of the league.

Martin C. Harris

Andy Port

Former Hull forward, **Andy Port**, died in tragic circumstances, aged only 27.

Andy played for the Kingston junior club before turning professional at the age of 17 with Humberside Hawks in the Premier Division of the British League. A talented player, he also turned out for Milton Keynes Kings, Solihull Barons and Peterborough Pirates.

Peter Johnson, coach of the Kingston juniors, paid a personal tribute to Andy: "He was an excellent player who even had trials for Britain, he was that good. He was a really nice, polite lad. I never had any problems with him."

Port was rushed from a house in New George Street, Hull, to Hull Royal Infirmary by ambulance at about 4.00 p.m. on 14 June 2004. He was dead on arrival. A post mortem was held and a police spokesman said it was being treated as a suspected drugs-related death.

John (Scotty) Reid

John Reid won four trophies with Fife Flyers in the post-war era and in 1958-60, as player-coach of Whitley Bees, he led them to a hat-trick of Nothern Tournament titles

Though raised in Oshawa, Ontario, Reid was born in Glasgow, earning him the nickname 'Scotty' which stuck for the rest of his life.

He returned to Britain in 1947 and played 42 games with Wembley Lions. A right-winger who later dropped back to defence, he was selected to play for an England select side against a touring Czech club from Prague.

After 223 games with Fife in which he scored 89 goals and 150 points plus 369 penalty minutes, he moved to the Continent, playing and coaching in Austria and Switzerland.

Back in this country in the 1960s he overcame failing eyesight to turn out for teams in Glasgow and Whitley Bay, his last game coming in 1968 for the Warriors.

Scotty died in Whitley Bay on 17 January 2004, aged 80, following a stroke on Boxing Day. He left a wife, Margaret, who was born in the town, and two sons.

Martin C. Harris/David Hall

Vic Shettler

Vic Shettler, captain of Wembley Lions of the English National League during season 1948-49, died on 13 February 2004 in his home town of Winnipeg, aged 81.

He played 53 games on Lions' blue-line, scoring six goals and 24 points, before returning home on the *Queen Mary*. For many years he was coach and manager of the Manitoba Old Timers and served as a member of the Manitoba Hockey Foundation.

Vic had come to Britain after spells in the minor leagues with Washington Lions and Baltimore Clippers. During World War 2 he spent four years on corvettes and destroyers on Atlantic convoy escort duty.

Martin C Harris

Danny Wong

Danny Wong, a popular Chinese-Canadian defenceman with Streatham, died in Regina, Saskatchewan on 14 June 2004. He was 67.

Wong partnered Scotsman **Tom (Red) Imrie** on Streatham's blue-line and helped the London club to win the old British National League and Autumn Cup in season 1959-60. Five years later, he rejoined Imrie for a few weeks with Wembley Lions.

Hailing from Heward, a small farming community just south of Regina, he played briefly for Trois Rivieres of the Quebec Hockey League in 1955-56 and for Saskatoon Quakers of the Western Hockey League a year later.

A self-employed real estate salesman, married to Margaret, a Londoner from Harrow, he returned to this country a third time in February 1986 at the invitation of his old club, now known as the Redskins. Pursuing a youth policy, mixed with three imports, he guided the cash-strapped Redskins to eighth place in the Premier Division of the *Heineken* League.

He was a lifelong friend of Wembley immortal **George Beach**, another Regina native. "Danny never smoked, never drank and had an unblemished career as a sportsman and a citizen that his family can be proud of," said George.

Phil Drackett/Martin C Harris

TRIBUTES

ALEX DAMPIER

Alex Dampier, a Canadian defenceman who came to Scotland in the late 1970s, returned to Canada in the summer of 2004. He was inducted into the British Ice Hockey Hall of Fame in 1995 for his services to the sport.

*A player's coach, he trained **Tony Hand**, the finest player this country has ever produced, and guided the two most successful club sides of the modern era - Nottingham Panthers and Sheffield Steelers - as well as Great Britain in their best spell of modern times .*

Your editor's fondest memory of him is of Britain's first game in the 1993 World Championships against Poland when he successfully queried the legality of a Polish stick. GB scored on the powerplay, beat the Poles and went on to win promotion to the A Pool.

Alex's decision to return home to Canada in 2004 was partly prompted by his increasing disillusion with what he saw as the bland professionalism of the sport. His preference was for the enthusiastic amateur.

*Like those fun times he recalls below in an interview with **Mick Holland** of the* Nottingham Evening Post *(extracts from which are reproduced here with their kind permission), 'Damps' will be greatly missed.*

Fifteen years ago, Nottingham Panthers beat the odds - and the best England and Scotland could throw at them - to win the *Heineken* British Championships at Wembley.

The man who masterminded that memorable victory over Ayr Bruins in 1989, coach **Alex Dampier**, left England in the summer of 2004 with his family to return to Canada after 26 eventful and successful years here, first as player and then coach.

SEEN IT DONE IT, BOUGHT THE T-SHIRT

And if there is anyone in the British game that you could hang the cliché on, 'seen it done it, bought the T-shirt,' it's the rugged 52-year-old from Thunder Bay.

While on holiday in Edinburgh, Damps' discovered Murrayfield Racers and in 1979 became their player-coach as a no-nonsense defenceman.

It was a love affair with the British game that brought him to Nottingham in 1985, where he led Panthers to their first trophies in the modern era. Then on to Sheffield in 1992 to win the Steelers' first grand slam, then Newcastle and back to Nottingham in 1999 for a couple of seasons.

In between times, he had two spells coaching the Great Britain senior team, culminating in him leading them to promotion to Pool A in 1994 and unforgettable meetings with ice hockey's big boys, Canada and Russia.

Goalies figure largely in Dampier's all-time list of favourites. He names **David Graham**, the giant north-easterner who backstopped Panthers to that Wembley triumph in 1989 as his best.

Dampier said: "More recently, Panthers had **Trevor Robins**, who came from nowhere to set a new standard for goaltenders over here, and there was **Rob Dopson** who starred for Ayr and Sheffield. But Davie worked so hard at his game. He was a great team player and very valuable in the dressing room and on the ice. He could be nasty, too, as anyone who skated near him could vouch for."

One goalie he'll never forget was Durham's **Keith Franklin**, a roly-poly figure who later became a referee. Dampier explained: "Murrayfield were at Durham one night in a big playoff game and we were leading 4-1, which was an experience in itself. The late **Micky Curry** was ref'ing and he was taking some awful stick from the crowd when someone insulted his wife. Micky did no more than climb over the boards into the crowd and clobber this bloke while the crowd looked on in amazement.

RINK THREW REF OUT

"The rink staff threw Micky out and I stood there wondering what was happening when big Keith, not so long before a Durham player, skated onto the ice in his striped shirt pulling on the ref's red arm-bands. I said that him ref'ing was unacceptable and asked him who I appealed to. He replied: 'Me, let's get on with it,' and we lost 5-4."

Among Dampier's favourite defencemen are **Terry Kurtenbach** and **Selmar Odelein**. "Terry was not very big for a D-man but he was so strong, smart and a great guy," said Dampier. "His contribution to the development of the Nottingham kids cannot be under-estimated."

Selmar, who played for Panthers and Steelers, was a great leader with an immense presence and would do anything to help the Brits. "Anyone who beats up **Mike Rowe**, who bullied the young opposition while playing for Whitley, deserves the praise of everyone."

Former *Heineken* League Player of the Year **Dan Dorion** was one of Dampier's favourite forwards. "He took the league apart for Panthers one season," said Dampier. "Then it got to his head and the next season we released him - just before I left the club.

"**Simon Hunt**, who was just turned 16 in that playoff final victory, was another Panthers player who you could guarantee would stir things up - the fans, the opposition - he didn't give a monkey's." ➤

-158-

Alex Dampier with some of his former players, *left to right* **Marc Twaite**, **John Bremner**, **Gavin Fraser**, **Nigel Rhodes**, Alex, **John Hobson**, **Dave Hutchinson**, **Mark Goldby**, **Simon Hunt**.
Photo courtesy: Nottingham Evening Post

➤ Dampier also played a big part in the development of Britain's most famous home-bred player Tony Hand (now MBE) whom he first saw as a 12-year-old in Edinburgh. "Tony was exceptional as a kid and he still is. He's one of the best players, skill-wise to play in this country," Dampier added.

Without doubt, though, it is Panthers' first trophy in the modern era - the *Norwich Union* Cup in 1986 - that takes prominence in the Damps' memory bank. "We had a bunch of young lads, experienced Brits and three imports dedicated to winning the trophy," he said. "They were fun times then and even though some of the players had jobs outside of hockey, they were all very professional. Unfortunately, a lot of the fun has gone out of hockey now.

"Imagine saying to Canada's tough guy: 'How's your wife and my kids?' That's exactly what **David Longstaff** shouted across the bench when GB played Canada in Pool A in 1994. Then 'Lobby' ducked and the player thought it was **Nicky Chinn**. He spent the rest of the game trying to get Nicky to fight and we couldn't stop laughing."

Newcastle Vipers' owner **Darryl Illingworth** said that the club wouldn't be in such a strong position without the influence of their former coach Alex Dampier. "Alex's knowledge of the hockey scene played a big part in our setting up," Illingworth said. "When we got the green light from the British National League, we had a very short time frame to get a team together and Alex convinced me that it could be done."

The Vipers were formed in June 2002 and by mid-August they were playing their inaugural game. Dampier was coach for the first season in the yellow and black, guiding the side to a memorable *Findus* Cup triumph over Coventry Blaze. Last season, family commitments limited his hands-on involvement with the club.

"On behalf of everyone involved with the club, I'd like to thank Alex for the work he did in getting the club off the ground," said Illingworth. "We wish Alex and his family all the best for their future back home."

*- **Miles Starforth**, Newcastle Evening Chronicle*

INTERNATIONAL ROUND-UP

HONOURS ROLL-CALL 2003-04

World Champions
CANADA
Division I
BELARUS (Group A)
SLOVENIA (Group B)
Division II
CHINA (Group A)
LITHUANIA (Group B)
Division III
ICELAND

World Junior U20 Champions
USA

World Junior U18 Champions
RUSSIA

Continental Cup
SLOVAN BRATISLAVA (Slovakia)

Stanley Cup
TAMPA BAY LIGHTNING

IIHF SUPER SIX
First step towards a World Club Championship

A new Europe-wide competition to replace the European League was created in the summer of 2004.

Teams from Russia, Sweden, Finland, Czech Republic, Slovakia and Germany will meet in the IIHF Super Six to decide the champion club of Europe. The inaugural event is to be played on 13-16 January 2005 in St. Petersburg, Russia.

The organisers hope that one day the winners might challenge the Stanley Cup champions.

The top teams in the six leading European nations (decided on the basis of the IIHF's world rankings) will play a total of seven games in the 12,300-seat St Petersburg Ice Palace, the state-of-the-art arena which hosted the 2000 World Championship.

The competing sides are: HC Zlin (Czech Republic), Karpat Oulu (Finland), Frankfurt Lions (Germany), Avangard Omsk (Russia), Dukla Trencin (Slovakia), HV71, Jonkoping (Sweden).

"This competition opens new territory in international ice hockey", said IIHF President René Fasel. "It is something that European club hockey and the fans have been missing since the European League folded four years ago.

"Further down the line there is a desire to match the best club team of Europe against the Stanley Cup champion for world club supremacy. Many fans are still talking about the great games between CSKA Moscow and the Montreal Canadiens in the 1970s and 1980s and the potential of games like these is even bigger today".

The Super Six is being marketed by sports promotions company, Telesport Moscow. Their CEO, **Peter Makarenko**, said: "It makes great sporting sense that the best teams on both continents can one day play in a world club final just like they do in soccer. But first we must establish the IIHF Super Six and make this a great tournament."

The following total prize money will be distributed among the teams:
2005 - 600,000 Swiss francs (about £260,000)
2006 - 700,000 Swiss francs (£300,000)
2007 - 800,000 Swiss francs (£350,000)

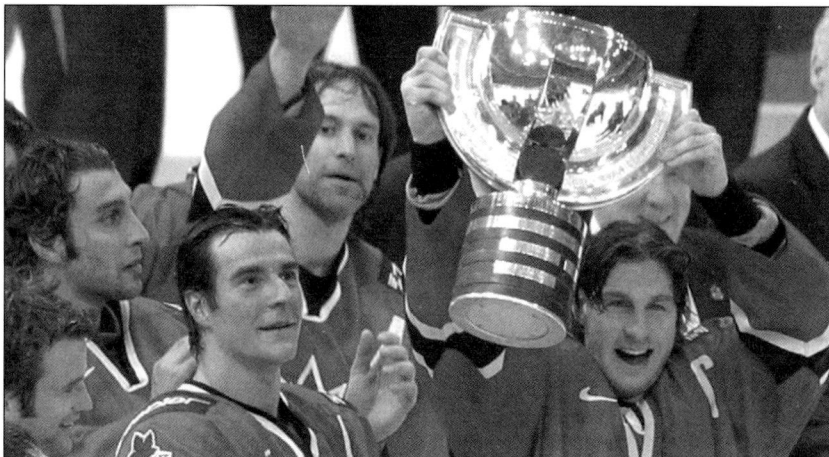

CANADA WINS WORLD CHAMPIONSHIP

Canadian captain **RYAN SMITH** *right* raises the World Championship trophy as his team celebrates their 23rd world title.

Photo: Roger Cook

CONTINENTAL CUP 2003
Pavlas' hat-trick for Bratislava

Slovan Bratislava won the seventh Continental Cup on their opponents' ice. With the help of a **Petr Pavlas** hat-trick, the Slovakian champs beat HC Gomel of Belarus 6-2 in the final on 11 January 2004 in the Belarussian city.

The gold medal game, which has attracted disappointing crowds in the past, was packed to the rafters, with the organisers claiming they could have sold 100,000 tickets. Unfortunately, the arena was built to accommodate only 3,700. Bratislava overcame the odds in the semi-final when they unexpectedly triumphed 5-3 over Russian elite side, Severstal Cherepovets.

Despite Gomel's defeat, the fans gave them a standing ovation for their overall performance in Europe's only club tournament which included a 3-2 defeat of the Swiss champions, HC Lugano.

Keramin Minsk, Belarus' other entrant in the six-team Super Final, finished fifth, completing the best spell for Belarussian hockey since their national team upset Sweden in the 2002 Olympics.

X For only the second time in the Modern Era, no British clubs competed in the Continental Cup. Britain entered the Europe-wide tournament 19 times, starting in 1983 when Dundee Rockets played in the competition's forerunner, the European Cup. Cardiff Devils missed the inaugural Continental Cup in 1997 when the IIHF decreed that the Wales National Ice Rink was not up to international standards.

WORLD CUP OF HOCKEY 2004
Russian team a shambles

Russia was the last of the six participating nations to name its team on 31 May 2004 for the second World Cup of Hockey.

The competition, organised jointly by the NHL, the NHL Players Association and the IIHF, is the only one (apart from the Winter Olympics) in which all NHL professionals are free to compete for their home country.

The Cup arose from the enormously successful series between the Soviet Union and Canadian teams from the NHL and World Hockey Association (WHA) in the early 1970s. Originally named the Canada Cup, it was first played in 1976. After five tournaments, it was re-named the World Cup in 1996, the last time it was held. The USA upset Canada two games to one in the final.

These two teams were to be joined by Slovakia, the 2003 world champs, the Czech Republic, Sweden, Finland, Germany and Russia in the 2004 World Cup which was to be played in Europe and North America between 30 August and 14 September. As this coincided with the printing of the *Annual*, we will be bringing you the results in our next edition.

Meanwhile, the Russians were having problems in putting a team together after their disastrous World Championship showing under their 74-year-old coach, **Viktor Tikhonov**. The old boy who had coached so many of those wonderful Soviet Union sides during the Cold War era was sacked after the championships and replaced at the end of May by former national team defenceman, **Zinetula Bilyaletdinov**.

Better known as Coach Bill, the youngster - he's 49 - was a controversial choice as he was fired as coach of Moscow Dynamo in January. But he has experience as an assistant on the benches of two NHL franchises and was head coach of HC Lugano in the Swiss A League.

Three days after this announcement, the Russian Federation's president, **Alexander Steblin**, revealed their roster, all bar four of whom play in the NHL. Fifteen of the 26-man squad played in the 2002 Winter Olympics and nine were at the 1996 World Cup.

But the big shock came two weeks later when Stanley Cup winning goalie, **Nikolai Khabibulin**, pulled out of the line-up. "We have no chance of winning based on the preparation of our team," he said. "I had a similar experience before the 1996 World Cup. Frankly, I don't see any point in my participation in this tournament."

The problem appears to be at the top where Steblin, a former KGB agent, insists on having total control of the team. Two former respected NHL and Soviet Union players - **Slava Fetisov**, who is Russia's sport minister, and **Igor Larionov** - were keen to have some input but the Russian Federation declined their offers of help. Many players would have preferred Larionov as coach or GM.

In another knock at the Federation, Khabibulin added: "I can't understand how people can declare a roster for such a tournament without having seen a single NHL game." The goalie's agent said his player was not informed before the team was announced and he didn't believe any of the players had been contacted.

A second netminder, **Evgeni Nabokov** of San Jose Sharks, pulled out with a knee injury, and other, uninjured players were said to be seriously considering their participation, including Detroit centreman, **Sergei Fedorov**, **Alexei Zhamnov** (Philadelphia) and **Valeri Bure** (Dallas).

IIHF
Darryl Easson

Former Nottingham Panther, **Darryl Easson**, joined the IIHF's staff on 1 December 2003 as sport development manager of youth hockey. Easson, a British-Canadian, was the technical director of Ice Hockey UK for several years after retiring as a player.

GERMAN DEL
McIntyre sued by German club

Ian McIntyre, who played in Superleague with Cardiff Devils and London Knights, was sued by Iserlohn Roosters after suddenly quitting the German club in October 2003.

The 29-year-old forward, who followed Belfast Giants' coach, **Dave Whistle**, to Iserlohn, was allowed to leave the team for personal reasons. Whistle had been sacked days earlier after Roosters lost the fifth of their nine games under his guidance.

Roosters announced that they would take legal action to prevent McIntyre from icing in any other IIHF-recognised league. Their general manager, **Karsten Mende**, declared in a release:

"He has betrayed our trust. He has let down his team-mates, he has lied to the club and thus to the fans. He will have to bear the consequences of this unacceptable behaviour."

McIntyre, a native of Montreal, joined Mission de Saint-Jean of the Quebec Senior Pro League. "It has always been my goal to finish my career in Quebec," McIntyre told the German website, *prohockey.de*.

National post for Poss

American **Greg Poss**, the coach of Nürnburg Ice Tigers in the DEL, has been appointed coach of the German national team, succeeding **Hans Zach**. Poss was assistant coach of the USA at the 2004 World Championships.

Poss spent six seasons coaching Iserlohn Roosters before joining the Ice Tigers. His successor at Iserlohn was, briefly, **Dave Whistle**.

Zach, an intense coach who emphasised defence, took Germany from 20th to eighth in the world rankings. The younger Poss is expected to be more offensive minded but he said: "It's not necessarily about the change. Any system will work if the players do it."

SWISS NATIONAL A LEAGUE
McSorley is coach of the year

GB's **Chris McSorley** was voted coach of the year after steering his club side, Geneva Servette-Eagles, to third place in the Swiss National A league. Eagles won 26 and drew six of their 48 games, finishing behind only the wealthier clubs in Lugano and Bern.

Canadian McSorley, who coached Superleague's London Knights for two years, told the *Annual*: "I'm pretty proud of it...not too many non-Swiss nationals get this one."

Eagles went further into the playoffs than they have for 30 years, eventually being knocked out, four games to three, in the semi-finals by the eventual champions, SC Bern.

In McSorley's first season in Switzerland, Eagles won promotion out of the B League, and last year they finished sixth in the A league.

In the summer of 2004, the coach was offered, and signed a lucrative new contract by Eagles' owner, **Phillip Anschutz**, to stay with the team for another three years.

Bern are biggest Euro draw

SC Bern of the Swiss National A League were the undisputed leaders in European league crowds for the third consecutive year.

Bern, one of the richest clubs in Europe's wealthiest league, have increased their average attendances each year and are the first to break the 13,000-mark since the IIHF started collating the figures in 1999.

Russian club, Lokomotiv Yaroslavl, filled its arena almost to NHL-level capacity.

The leading clubs (last season's placing in brackets) with percentage of arena capacity:

1 (1)	SC Bern	13,034	79.8%
2 (2)	Cologne Eagles	12,887	69.6%
3 (3)	Hamburg Freezers	11,351	88.9%
4 (4)	Vastra Frolunda		
	(Gothenburg, Sweden)	10,942	90.8%
5 (5)	Jokerit Helsinki	9,093	66.5%
6 (6)	Lokomotiv Yaroslavl	8,824	97.5%
7 (10)	HC Pardubice (Czech.)	8,200	88.2%

RUSSIAN LEAGUE
Another Russian player killed

Russian ice hockey star **Sergei Zemchyonok** was shot dead in the hallway of his block of flats in the Urals city of Magnitogorsk after he returned home from training on Monday evening. No motive for the killing has yet been suggested.

The murder of another high-profile star shows Russian sport has a rotten core. Much of the money on which it runs is from shady business and contract killings, robbery and extortion have become the norm.

Zemchyonok has become the latest victim of a corrupt and often violent system. The 24-year-old netminder was one of the stars of the modern game. He kept goal for Metallurg when they won the Russian championship and the European League in 1999, and when they won the European championship again in 2000.

But now he will be remembered along with a too-long list of others:

Valentin Sych: president of the Ice Hockey Federation - shot dead in 1997.

Larisa Nechayeva: financial director of Moscow Spartak - gunned down the same year.

Sergei Latushko: 18-year-old European junior boxing champion - killed near Moscow almost a year ago.

Other top Russian sportsmen have gone to play abroad - less for the financial gain than to escape the web of corruption which is strangling sport at home.

BBC News Online, October 2003

OBITUARY
Ivan Hlinka

Ivan Hlinka, one of the greatest players in the history of Czechoslovak and Czech ice hockey, died in a car crash on 16 August 2004.

Hlinka was coach of the Czech national team and was about to start preparations for the 2004 World Cup of Hockey. He was driving to play golf with his star forward, **Jaromir Jagr**, near the Czech city of Karlovy Vary (Karlsbad) when an oncoming truck crossed the central reservation and hit his Skoda Superb head-on. The truck's brakes were reported to be faulty.

Jagr paid tribute to his coach: "He was a charismatic leader and a hero for our generation." At the recent World Championships in his home country, Hlinka had been named as the best Czech player of all time.

He was replaced as coach by **Vladimir Ruzicka** who said: "Ivan was simply irreplaceable for us. We all idolised him."

This would have been Hlinka's second spell behind the bench. In 1998 he led the Czech Republic to its greatest achievement, the gold medal at the 1998 Olympic Games. A year later, the Czechs won the World Championship.

As a player, Hlinka represented Czechoslovakia in 256 national team games while capturing the World Championship gold medal three times in the Seventies. He also played in the 1972 and 1976 Winter Olympics.

He had an impressive career in the NHL. He was in the first wave of Europeans to leave his Communist country, joining the Vancouver Canucks in 1981 and helping them to their first Stanley Cup final.

And he was the NHL's first European coach when he led the Pittsburgh Penguins during the 2000-01 season. A year later, he was the GM of the Czech Olympic team in Salt Lake City.

Hlinka also played in the inaugural Canada Cup in 1976 when the Czechs took the silver medal behind Canada.

He was inducted to the IIHF Hall of Fame in 2002.

WORLD CHAMPIONSHIPS

Prague & Ostrava, Czech Republic,
24 April-9 May 2004

FINAL
9 May, Sazka Arena, Prague
SWEDEN-CANADA   3-5   (2-1,1-2,0-2)

BRONZE MEDAL
9 May, Sazka Arena, Prague
SLOVAKIA-USA   0-0ot   (0-0,0-0,0-0,0-0)
USA won after penalty shootout (winning penalty shot - Andy Roach)

SEMI-FINALS
8 May, Sazka Arena, Prague
SLOVAKIA-CANADA   1-2   (0-0,1-1,0-1)
USA-SWEDEN   2-3   (0-2,1-1,1-0)

WORLD RANKINGS
1 CANADA (2004 World Champions),
2 Sweden, 3 Slovakia, 4 Czech Republic, 5 Finland, 6 USA, 7 Russia, 8 Germany, 9 Switzerland, 10 Latvia, 11 Austria, 12 Ukraine, 13 Belarus, 14 Denmark, 15 Japan, 16 Slovenia. This system was introduced in 2004 and is based on points gained in the last four World Championships (currently 2001-2004) and the last Olympics (2002).

WINNING TEAM
CANADA
J-S Giguere (Anaheim), Marc Denis (Columbus), Roberto Luongo (Florida); Eric Brewer, Steve Staios (Edmonton), Jay Bouwmeester (Florida), Willie Mitchell, Nick Schultz (Minnesota), Scott Niedermayer (New Jersey), Derek Morris (Phoenix), Jamie Heward (Zurich); Rob Niedermayer (Anaheim), Dany Heatley (Atlanta), Patrice Bergeron, Glen Murray (Boston), Danny Briere, JP Dumont (Buffalo), Justin Williams (Carolina), Brenden Morrow (Dallas), Shawn Horcoff, Ryan Smith (Edmonton), Jeff Friesen (New Jersey), Matt Cooke, Brendan Morrison (Vancouver), Jeff Shantz (Langnau).
Head Coach: Mike Babcock (Anaheim).
General Manager: Jim Nill (Detroit).

Warrior wins world
Coached by Whitley Warrior-for-a-year, **Mike Babcock**, Canada won their second successive World Championship with their second straight defeat of Sweden in the final.

The triumph was Canada's 23rd world title, bringing them level with Russia (Soviet Union).

Atlanta Thrashers' forward **Dany Heatley** was the Canadian hero, scoring a goal and an assist in the final. The championship's leading points scorer, he was voted the MVP and Best Forward, and won a berth on the All Star team, the first player to win this triple honour.

His performance was the more remarkable for coming after the Ferrari he was driving in Atlanta crashed in September 2003, killing his passenger, Thrasher team-mate, **Dan Snyder**.

Under septuagenarian coach, **Viktor Tikhonov**, Russia finished tenth, only the second time since the Soviet Union first entered the tournament in 1954 that they failed to reach the last eight.

☑ Staged in Prague's new Hala-Sazka arena which seats 16,300, the championships set a new attendance record of 552,097.

ALL-STAR TEAM
Selected by the media.

Goal	**Henrik Lundqvist** SWE
Defence	**Dick Tarnstrom** SWE, **Zdeno Chara** SVK
Forwards	**Dany Heatley** CAN, **Jaromir Jagr** CZE, **Ville Peltonen** FIN.

LEADING SCORERS

	GP	G	A	Pts.	Pim
Dany Heatley CAN	9	8	3	11	4
Ville Peltonen FIN	7	4	6	10	2
Jaromir Jagr CZE	7	5	4	9	6
Martin Rucinsky CZE	7	5	4	9	6
Oli Jokinen FIN	7	5	3	8	6

LEADING NETMINDERS

	GPI	Mins	SoG	GA	Sv%
Jan Lasak SVK	9	539	195	9	95.4
Tomas Vokoun CZE	6	380	126	7	94.4
Ty Conklin USA	5	300	152	10	93.4

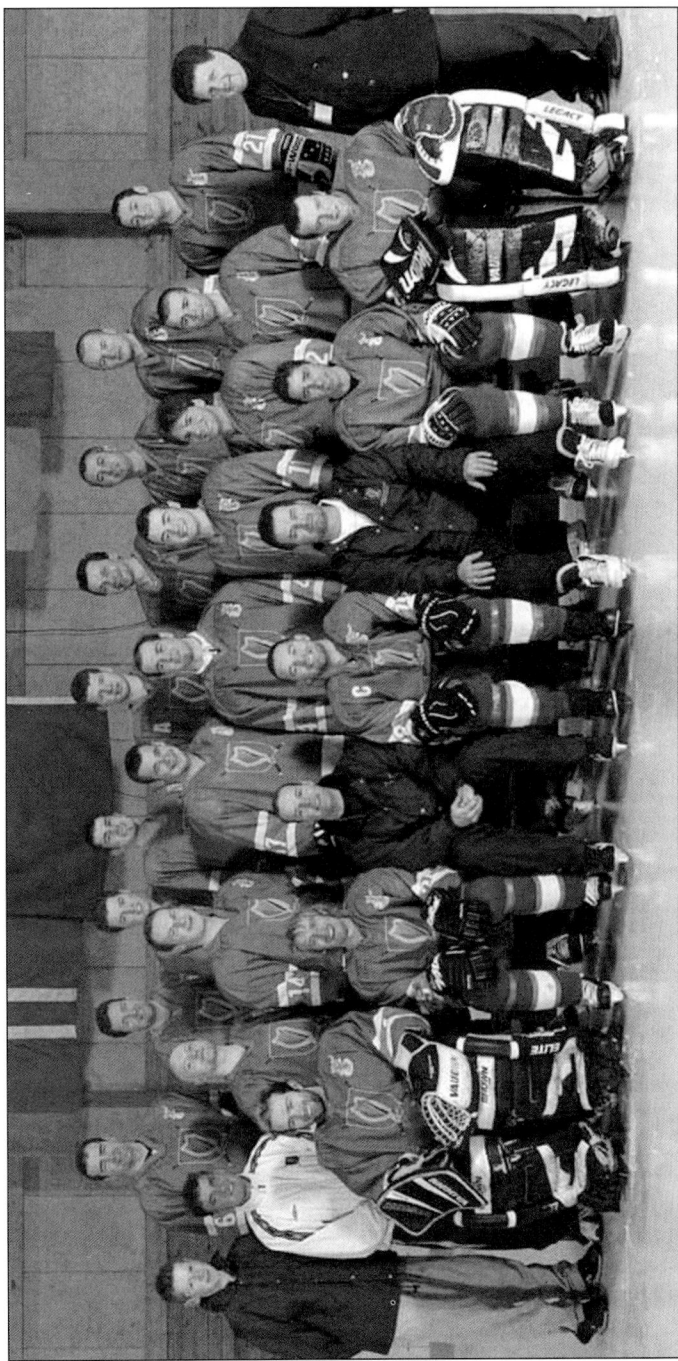

IRELAND *left to right, back row:* Cliff Saunders, John White, Stephen Cooper, Phillip Darcy, O'Connor Lyne, Dimitriy Slavashevskiy, Anthony Griffin, David Kelly, Willie Morrison; *middle row:* Dean Kelly (stick boy), John Crawley (equipment), Davie Morrison, Trevor Kennedy, James Healey, Garrett MacNeill, Dave Gibson, Larry Jurovich, Robert Leckey, Michael Higgins (GM); *front row (seated):* Kevin Kelly, Stevie Hamill, Greg Fitzgerald (head coach), Mark Bowes, Jim Graves (asst. coach), Gary McKeag, Dermot Carney.

DIVISION III

Reykjavik, Iceland, 16-21 March 2004

	GP	W	L	D	GF	GA	Pts
Iceland ISL	4	3	0	1	46	8	7
Turkey TUR	4	3	1	0	26	14	6
Mexico MEX	4	2	1	1	29	8	5
Ireland IRL	4	1	3	0	23	23	2
Armenia ARM	4	0	4	0	2	73	0

Iceland are promoted to Division II in 2005.

IRELAND'S WORLD RANKING: 44th

RESULTS

	ISL	TUR	MEX	ARM
IRL	1-7	4-7	3-8	**15-1**
ISL		7-5	2-2	30-0
TUR			3-2	11-1
MEX				17-0

IRELAND'S LEADING SCORERS

	GP	G	A	Pts	Pim
Larry Jurovich	4	4	4	8	2
Willie Morrison	4	4	3	7	2
Mark Bowes	4	1	4	5	6
Dimitriy Slavashevskiy	4	3	1	4	29

IRELAND'S NETMINDING

	GPI	Mins	SoG	GA	Sv%
Dermot Carney	1	40	16	1	93.75
Kevin Kelly	4	200	109	22	79.82
TEAM TOTALS	4	240	125	23	81.60

IRELAND'S MVP
Willie Morrison

IRELAND

Dermot Carney, Kevin Kelly; James Healey, David Kelly, Trevor Kennedy (Belfast), Robert Leckey (Dundonald), Garrett MacNeill, Cliff Saunders, Dimitriy Slavashevskiy; Mark Bowes (capt), Stephen Cooper, Phillip Darcy, Dave Gibson (Dundonald), Stevie Hamill (Dundonald), Larry Jurovich, O'Connor Lynne, Gary McKeag (Dundonald), Davie Morrison (Belfast), Willie Morrison (Dundonald), John White.
all Dublin Flyers except where noted.
Head coach: Greg Fitzgerald. *Asst coach*: Jim Graves. *Manager*: Michael Higgins.

Hats off to Willie

Teenager **Willie Morrison** scored a hat-trick as Ireland thrashed Armenia 15-1 in the Emerald Isle's first ever senior World Championship, writes **Wayne Hardman**.

The victory - Ireland's only one of the tournament - came, fittingly, on St Patrick's Day, 17 March 2004.

Morrison, 19, who was voted his team's most valuable player, is one of three hockey playing brothers. Davie was also on the team while Mark played in the Elite League with Belfast Giants.

Canadian coaches **Greg Fitzgerald** and **Jim Graves** (a former goalie with Ayr Bruins who was more recently with the Giants) brought together players from both sides of the border as well as from North America and Minsk, Belarus.

Many of them were first capped for their country as juniors when Ireland competed in the European under-18 championships in 1999 and the World under-20s in 2001. With no league hockey in Ireland apart from the Giants, several players joined the Dumfries club, Solway Sharks.

Ireland was admitted to the IIHF in 1997 after representations from **Cliff Saunders** and **Mark Bowes**, the president and secretary of the Irish Ice Hockey Association - and the only IIHF delegates still playing at senior level.

The sport was played in the Dublin area for around 20 years until the last rink closed in 2000. That left the island with only two ice venues, both in the north at Belfast: the Odyssey Arena, and the Dundonald Ice Bowl in a suburb of the city.

Before the championships, the Ireland players were able to have a few practices at the Odyssey and a couple of games in Scotland.

DIVISION I

Group A, Oslo, Norway, 12-18 April 2004
See next page.

Group B, Gdansk, Poland, 12-18 April 2004
1 Slovenia, 2 Italy, 3 Poland, 4 Estonia, 5 Romania, 6 (South) Korea.
Slovenia promoted to World Championships in 2005, Korea relegated to Division II.

DIVISION II

Group A, Jaca, Spain, 12-18 April 2004
1 China, 2 Croatia, 3 Australia, 4 Spain, 5 Israel, 6 Luxembourg.
China promoted to Division I in 2005, Luxembourg relegated to Division III.

Group B, Elektrenai, Lithuania, 12-18 April 2004
1 Lithuania, 2 Serbia & Montenegro, 3 DPR (North) Korea, 4 Bulgaria, 5 New Zealand, 6 South Africa.
Lithuania promoted to Division I in 2005, South Africa relegated to Division III.

DIVISION I

GROUP A
Oslo, Norway, 12-18 April, 2004

FINAL STANDINGS

	GP	W	L	D	GF	GA	Pts
Belarus BLR	5	5	0	0	34	9	10
Norway NOR	5	3	1	1	31	14	7
Netherlands NED	5	2	2	1	21	22	5
Hungary HUN	5	2	2	1	20	24	5
Britain GB	5	1	3	1	18	18	3
Belgium BEL	5	0	5	0	7	44	0

As Hungary and Netherlands tied 4-4, their positions were decided by goal difference.

GB'S WORLD RANKING: 25th*

Belarus are promoted to the World Championships in 2005; **Belgium** are relegated to Division II.

RESULTS

	BLR	NOR	NED	HUN	BEL
GB	**4-5**	**4-4**	**1-4**	**3-5**	**6-0**
BLR		5-2	7-2	7-1	10-0
NOR			8-0	6-4	11-1
NED				4-4	11-2
HUN					6-4

GB's BEST PLAYERS
1 ASHLEY TAIT
2 David Clarke
3 Jonathan Phillips
selected by the GB Supporters Club

FAIR PLAY CUP

Penalty minutes per team
Norway 60, Hungary 62, Belgium 76, Belarus 77, **Britain 91**, Netherlands 102.

The IIHF world rankings are now based on the past four years' results - 100 per cent of 2004, 75 per cent of 2003, and 50 per cent and 25 per cent of the first two years respectively.

GB have dropped four places since 2003 because the points they received for their bronze medal in 2000 no longer count, while they finished fifth in the two most recent tournaments which have the heaviest weightings.

BRITAIN'S SCORING

All points scorers	GP	G	A	Pts	Pim
David Clarke	5	4	3	7	2
Steve Thornton	5	1	5	6	6
Colin Ward	5	3	0	3	2
Ashley Tait	5	2	1	3	2
Paul Dixon	4	1	2	3	4
Jeff Hoad	4	1	2	3	4
Matt Myers	5	1	2	3	2
Rob Wilson	5	0	3	3	4
Jonathan Phillips	5	2	0	2	10
Danny Meyers	5	1	1	2	2
Colin Shields	5	0	2	2	6
Paul Moran	5	1	0	1	2
Paul Sample	5	1	0	1	4
David Longstaff	1	0	1	1	0
Ryan Lake	5	0	1	1	0
Leigh Jamieson	5	0	1	1	4
TEAM TOTALS	5	18	24	42	91

BRITAIN'S NETMINDING

	GPI	Mins	SoG	GA	Sv%
Joe Watkins	3	179	97	9	90.72
Mark Cavallin	2	120	70	8	88.57
TEAM TOTALS	5	299	167	17	89.82

BRITAIN

Goal: *Mark Cavallin (EV Ravensburg, GER), Joe Watkins (Bakersfield Condors USA).
Defence: #Leigh Jamieson (Belfast), *Mike Ellis, #Danny Meyers (Bracknell), Paul Dixon (Guildford), *Brent Pope (Hull), #Scott Moody, *Rob Wilson (Newcastle).
Forwards: #Paul Sample, #*Colin Ward (Belfast), #Matt Myers, Jonathan Phillips (Cardiff), Russ Cowley, Ashley Tait (Coventry), David Longstaff (Newcastle), David Clarke, #Paul Moran (Nottingham), #Ryan Lake (Sheffield), *Jeff Hoad (EC Bad Tolz GER), Colin Shields (Un of Maine USA), *Steve Thornton, capt (SC Brunico ITA).
Head coach: Chris McSorley (Geneva, SWI).
Asst coaches: Roger Hunt (Dundee), Rick Strachan (Hull).
General manager: Gary Stefan (BNL).

* dual national (7)   # new cap (8)

BRITAIN'S GAME SUMMARIES

12 April 2004, Jordal Amfi Arena, Oslo, Norway

BRITAIN-HUNGARY   3-5 (1-1,0-1,2-3)

Scoring:

1-0	GB	Ward (Dixon)		3.28
1-1	HUN	Ladanyi (Vas, Peterdi)		11.49
1-2	HUN	Ladanyi		21.41
2-2	GB	Thornton (Clarke, Longstaff)	pp	41.51
2-3	HUN	Kovacs (Szelig)		52.47
3-3	GB	Clarke	pp	58.46
3-4	HUN	Palkovics (Groschl)		59.06
3-5	HUN	Peterdi (Horvath)	eng	59.35

Netminding:

Watkins GB	11-14-11 36	save %:	86.1
Budai HUN	11- 8 -11 30	save %:	90.0

Penalty minutes: GB 6, Hungary 20.
Goals/powerplays: GB 2/8, Hungary 0/2.
GB Man of Match: Shields.
Referee: Rudolf Lauff (Slovakia)
Attendance: 624

Britain's first game blues continued with this heart-breaking last minute loss. GB have won only two opening games since their classic win over Poland in 1993.

Adding to their woes, **David Longstaff**, the inspirational Geordie forward and dressing room leader, twisted his thumb against the boards and was ruled out of the rest of the tournament.

Coach **Chris McSorley** said: "We had chances but the other teams here are better oiled. But our newcomers gave us energy and depth and we will improve the more we play."

There was little to choose between the teams in a scrappy game with passes going astray on both sides. Unusually, Britain enjoyed the man advantage four times in the second period but as this was their first full game together as a team, they were unable to capitalise.

Referee **Rudolf Lauff** who officiated Britain's game against Hungary, was involved in a nasty incident in a Slovakian playoff game in March 2004 between Slovan Bratislava and HKm Zvolen.

He was attacked by HKm Zvolen defenceman **Martin Mraz** who slashed him with a two-hander, then when the ref fell to the ice, he jumped on him and punched him repeatedly until some players intervened.

Mraz, 23, was suspended for 18 playing months, effectively more than two years.

They compensated with two powerplay goals in the last session which brought them level at 3-3. Unwisely, your reporter gathered up his papers at this point, smugly feeling this was a fair result. So imagine my surprise when with 54

seconds left Britain gave the puck away and Palkovics, one of Hungary's most dangerous forwards, beat Watkins from close range.

Naturally, McSorley substituted his keeper with an extra attacker as the clock counted down, but the pressure move backfired and Peterdi slid the puck into the unguarded net.

Gloom descended on the bench and among the 100-odd GB fans as Hungary chalked up their second win in two championships. Britain won in 1992 and 1999 and the teams drew 3-3 in 1991.

Glasgow-born forward **Colin Shields** was the man of the match despite having flown the Atlantic the day before after playing for the University of Maine in the NCAA Frozen Four final in Boston.

X Longstaff's freak accident was his third in two years. He needed treatment for blood clots (DVT) in his left leg which forced him to miss part of the 2002 championships in Hungary, and he dropped weights on his ankles in a gym accident in August 2003, missing most of the season.

As the ligaments of his thumb were badly damaged, the medics prescribed urgent surgery and 'Lobby' flew home two days after the game.

13 April 2004, Jordal Amfi Arena, Oslo, Norway

NORWAY-BRITAIN   4-4 (1-2,0-1,3-1)

Scoring:

0-1	GB	Tait (Clarke, Hoad)		1.10
1-1	NOR	Thoresen (Ygranes)		5.00
1-2	GB	Ward (Wilson)	pp2	19.59
1-3	GB	Dixon (Thornton)	pp	32.12
2-3	NOR	Jakobsen (Thoresen, Vikingstad)		41.13
3-3	NOR	Trygg (Olsen)		41.32
4-3	NOR	Vikingstad (Nilsen)	pp	46.15
4-4	GB	Clarke (Wilson, Thornton)	pp	56.02

Netminding:

Wiberg NOR	9- 4- 2 15	save %:	73.3
Cavallin GB	11-13-20 44	save %:	90.9

Penalty minutes: Norway 16, GB 18.
Goals/powerplays: Norway 1/8, GB 3/6.
GB Man of Match: Thornton.
Referee: V Bulanov (Russia).
Attendance: 2,815

Oh no, not again! Late opposition goals robbed Britain of a point just when the game looked to be in the bag

GB shocked the half-full arena by winning the first two periods even though **Mark Cavallin**, replacing **Joe Watkins** in goal, faced a barrage of shots from the Norwegians who had possession for much of the contest but couldn't convert their chances.

The game took a dramatic turn early in the last period as Norway scored twice in 19 seconds to

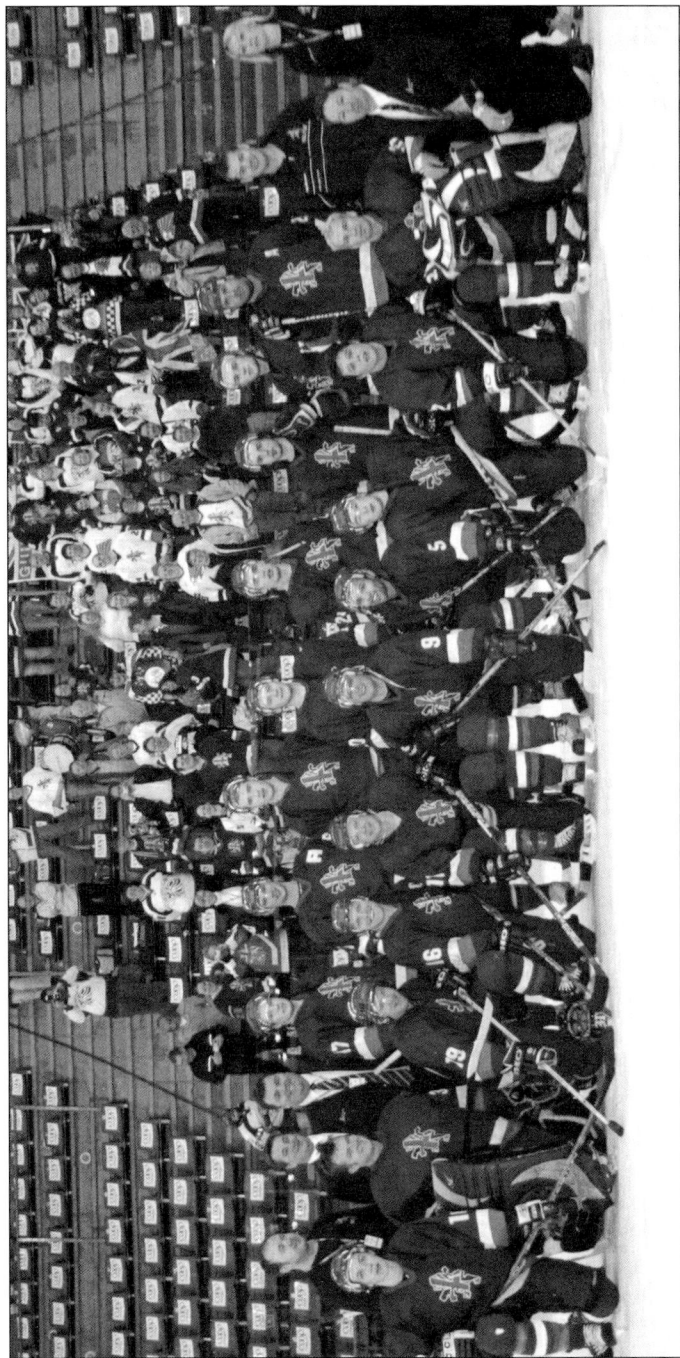

BRITAIN *left to right, back row:* Keith Warner (physio), Rick Strachan (asst. coach), Roger Hunt (asst. coach), Russ Cowley, Ashley Tait, Leigh Jamieson, Jonathan Phillips, Matt Myers, Colin Shields, Danny Meyers, Rob Wilson, Paul Dixon, Clare Goodwin (physio); *front row:* Ryan Lake, Joe Watkins, Jeff Hoad, Steve Thornton, Colin Ward, Scott Moody, David Clarke, Paul Sample, Paul Moran, Mark Cavallin, Chris McSorley (head coach).

Photo: Diane Davey

tie the score and Vikingstad gave them the lead on the powerplay while Shields was off for tripping.

David Clarke tipped in **Rob Wilson**'s blueline equaliser with four minutes left, a goal that McSorley mistakenly described as "the winning goal". He swiftly corrected himself but against this calibre of opponent, that must have been how it felt.

He singled out defenders **Paul Dixon** and Wilson for praise and said he was "gratified" by the team's continuing improvement, especially the home-grown players who scored three of GB's goals. The powerplay shone, scoring on 50 per cent of their chances.

This was the first point Britain have taken off Norway in three straight championships. The Norwegians also beat GB in Pool A in 1994.

☑ Forward **Jeff Hoad** joined the team after missing the Hungary game due to commitments to his German club.

15 April 2004, Jordal Amfi Arena, Oslo, Norway

BELARUS-BRITAIN   5-4 (2-0,2-2,1-2)

Scoring:

1-0	BLR	Strakhau (Yesaulau)		7.11
2-0	BLR	Kalyuzhny (Tsyplakov, Salei)	pp	13.01
2-1	GB	Clarke		24.07
3-1	BLR	Skabelka (Antonenko, Stas)		28.03
4-1	BLR	Tsyplakov (Kalyuzhny, Kastsitsyn)	pp	31.03
4-2	GB	Hoad	ps	39.29
5-2	BLR	Tsyplakov (Alekseev)	sh	46.08
5-3	GB	Moran (Myers, Thornton)	pp	47.16
5-4	GB	Phillips (Dixon, Shields)	pp	56.25

Netminding:

Mezin BLR   6-16-12 34   *save %*: 88.2
Watkins GB 17-18-12 47   *save %*: 89.4

Penalty minutes: Belarus 45 (Erkovich 5+game - cross-check), GB 45 (Pope match - att to injure)
Goals/powerplays: Belarus 2/9, GB 2/10
GB Man of Match: Hoad.
Referee: Chris Savage (Canada)
Attendance: 693

Britain gave their best performance of the tournament but it wasn't quite enough to beat the team that finished 14th in the world last year. McSorley said he was proud of his team who showed great spirit in fighting back from 4-1 down at the mid-point.

In fact, they came desperately close to equalising in the final minute after the coach withdrew Watkins in favour of an extra forward, and **Steve Thornton**'s shot hit the post.

As this was Britain's third game in four days, McSorley gave plenty of ice-time to his new caps, especially on defence where Britain have few experienced players. "I was pleased with them," he said. "They rose to the occasion."

The game was marred by some puzzling refereeing decisions, one leading to the second Belarussian goal after 13 minutes. Defender Dixon was banished to the sin-bin for 'interference' when he slid helplessly into the keeper and Kalyuzhny scored on the resulting powerplay.

Britain got more into the game as it went on, holding their own 2-2 in the middle period (Hoad converted a penalty shot awarded after he had been brought down) and winning the last 2-1, both powerplay goals.

McSORLEY WALK-OUT

"If you're not going to do your job, I'm not going to do mine." **Chris McSorley**, *walking out in protest at a controversial decision from Canadian referee Chris Savage in the Belarus game.*

Their third goal came from **Paul Moran**, his first in the championships, which was particularly pleasing for his watching parents, Gary and Audrey.

There was controversy in the 32nd minute when McSorley staged a protest walk-out after Erkovich struck **Jonathan Phillips** with his stick. Incensed that the Belarussian received a lesser penalty than **Brent Pope** who foolishly took retribution by punching Erkovich, McSorley retreated to the sidelines for ten minutes, telling the Canadian official: "If you're not going to do your job, I'm not going to do mine."

He later explained: "There was no way the game should have re-started with the teams even-handed. I felt I had to make a protest to take the pressure off our team."

Pope was banned for two games for his action, ruling him out of the rest of the championships, and Erkovich was suspended for one game.

This was Belarus's second victory over GB in three championships.

• **Frederick Meredith**, the IIHF's tournament supervisor, told the *Annual* that the Directorate had reviewed the video of the Erkovich incident and were satisfied that the cross-check was in Phillips' chest and not his head or throat.

However, he said they took a dim view of Pope's action as he came across the ice some moments afterwards and punched the Belarussian from behind.

16 April 2004, Jordal Amfi Arena, Oslo, Norway

NETHERLANDS-BRITAIN   **4-1 (0-0,2-0,2-1)**

Scoring:
1-0	NED	Oort (Bultje, Livingston) pp	21.46
2-0	NED	Hartogs	25.30
3-0	NED	Oort (Jacobs) sh	40.53
4-0	NED	Eimers (Oort) pp	53.14
4-1	GB	Sample (Wilson, Lake)	55.52

Netminding:
Nijland NED   7-11-10 28   save %: 96.4
Cavallin GB   12- 6- 8 26   save %: 84.6
Penalty minutes: NED 16, GB 16 (Phillips 10 m.).
Goals/powerplays: N'lands 2/2, GB 0/6.
GB Man of Match: Moran.
Referee: Brent Reiber (Switz.) *Attendance:* 610

There's always one championship game that's a real stinker - usually one against a nation GB ought to beat. Well, this was it.

"Pitiful", one disgusted fan called their performance. What's more, it was GB's first defeat by the Dutch in the modern era.

While the Dutch have obviously come on a bundle since then, Britain had good reasons for their poor display: they played their hearts out against Belarus, believing they had a chance of a point; several players were missing due to injuries and suspension; and the team were playing their fourth game in five days. "We lack conditioning so some of the [older] guys   had little left in the tank," McSorley pointed out.

The coach also said that a couple of players were under-achieving, though he preferred to emphasise the continuing improvement of his younger charges. "The kids provided the team's energy," he said. Though he named no names, he certainly meant man of the match Moran, **Ryan Lake** - with his first championship point - and **Paul Sample** with GB's only goal and his first in the championships.

Britain's hospital list lengthened when .Thornton, their joint leading points scorer (with Clarke), injured his hip in the last period, ruling him out of the final game.

He joined four others on the sidelines: Longstaff who had flown home for treatment to his thumb, and three defencemen from the already weak blueline corps - **Mike Ellis** (leg), Dixon (pulled hamstring against the Netherlands) and Pope (suspended).

The only good news was that relegation didn't beckon as GB's last opponents were the inept Belgians who had managed only six goals in three games.

18 April 2004, Jordal Amfi Arena, Oslo, Norway

BRITAIN-BELGIUM   **6-0 (4-0,1-0,1-0)**

Scoring:
1-0	GB	Meyers	0.20
2-0	GB	Tait (Hoad, Jamieson) sh	9.58
3-0	GB	Clarke (Tait, Thornton) pp	11.50
4-0	GB	Myers (Meyers)	16.01
5-0	GB	Phillips (Clarke) sh	20.52
6-0	GB	Ward (Myers, Shields)	50.08

Netminding:
Watkins   GB   5-5- 6 16 *save %:* 100.0
Steylen/Cremer BEL 16-8-12 36 *save %:* 83.3
Penalty minutes: GB 6, Belgium 10.
Goals/powerplays: GB 1/5 Belgium 0/3.
GB Man of Match: Tait.
Referee: Rudolf Lauff (Slovakia)
Attendance: 630

Thornton was back in the side, albeit only for the opening minutes, as Britain, theoretically, faced relegation for the first time since Bratislava in 1995.

The nerves were steadied with a fluky goal after only 20 seconds when the puck deflected high into the air and the Belgian goalie lost sight of it. When Clarke made it 3-0 after 12 minutes,

---

Paul Dixon, who pulled a hamstring in the disaster against the Netherlands, pointed out that he played 70 games with Guildford Flames during the season.

---

everyone could relax, especially as Steylen, the Belgian's first choice netminder, was having a stinker.

He was replaced in the second period by Cremer but within a minute, Phillips beat him to make it 5-0.

The first five goals were all scored by home-grown players as McSorley rested most of his tired and battered dual nats. Moran impressed on defence and Watkins needed only 16 saves for his shutout.

"Our national programme has a long way to go," said McSorley afterwards. "There are not enough home-grown players in the Elite League so I'm pleased they have agreed to impose a limit on their overseas contingent next season."

As this limit is as high as eleven imports, it is debatable how much difference this will make. In his fourth campaign with GB, McSorley is learning just how many obstacles are thrown in front of the national team. Frankly, it's a miracle that he stays so positive.

The old story

STEWART ROBERTS

With their rivals continuing to improve, Britain had to be content with fifth place in Division 1A, the same as last year, leaving them ranked a lowly 25th in the world.

It may seem remarkable to some fans that GB can't beat even small nations like Hungary or the Netherlands, but as coach Chris McSorley said: "The other teams here are better oiled."

And he didn't just mean on the ice. Ice Hockey UK have so little money (partly due to their on-going dispute with the professional teams) that the biggest backers of the British squad were their fans, through the well organised GB Supporters Club.

Britain could afford just one warm-up game, against the Netherlands, and they struggled to a 4-4 draw. That was a bad omen because in their last meeting in 2000, Britain had shutout the Dutch 9-0.

But McSorley stressed how well the team coped with the unique pressures of playing five games in seven days against well-drilled opponents. Belgium were the only weak link.

Almost a third of the team changed from the 2003 squad with the coaching staff keen to blood more home-grown players. There were eight new caps - all home-grown except Belfast Giants' forward **Colin Ward** - and exactly half of the 22-man team were aged under 25. But McSorley was frustrated by their limited experience.

"I couldn't use some of the kids on our special teams because they don't play on them with their clubs," he said. Some of the senior players looked jaded and became injury-prone.

Guildford's Paul Dixon, one of GB's most reliable defencemen, missed the Belgium game with a pulled hamstring. "I played around 70 games for the Flames last season," he said. "Injuires are bound to happen."

Nottingham's David Clarke, playing in his fifth World Championship though still only 22, was Britain's top scorer with four goals and seven points and, in this reporter's opinion, was the team's best player. The GB Supporters Club voted him a close second to another Brit forward, Coventry's **Ashley Tait**.

Both goalies gave steady performances with Joe Watkins ending as runner-up in the save percentages to the Belarussian keeper. Joe also enjoyed a 16-shot shutout against Belgium.

• Britain played three friendlies during the season, but decided to ice teams composed mostly of hopeful young Brits rather than the side that travelled to Norway.

This upset Dundee Stars who pulled out of their scheduled international saying they couldn't sell tickets for a GB team that was not the full World Championship side.

Only **David Clarke, Paul Moran** and **Brent Pope** of the Oslo squad played in Kirkcaldy on 4 November when GB edged Fife Flyers 6-5 with the winning goal coming from Edinburgh's **Iain Robertson.** Clarke scored a hat-trick with the other goals coming from Pope and **Slava Koulikov.**

Pope and GB assistant coach **Rick Strachan** were playing for Hull Stingrays on 17 December when their team lost 4-2 to GB. This time **Mike Ellis, Danny Meyers, Jonathan Phillips, Matt Myers, Ryan Lake** and Moran turned out for the national team. GB's goals came from **Marc Levers, Stephen Wallace, Stuart Potts** and Phillips. 'Strachs' scored for Hull.

A Britain Select side also formed the opposition at iceSheffield on 3 March for **Mike Blaisdell's** testimonial match.

ASHLEY TAIT *centre* is presented with his trophy as GB's Best Player by **Allan Petrie** *left*, the chairman of the GB Supporters Club. *Photo*: Diane Davey

BRITAIN'S RECORD 1989-2003

2003 Division I/B, Zagreb, Croatia
Coach: **Chris McSorley** (Geneva)
France 2-2, Italy 2-4, Estonia 3-4, Croatia 7-1, Norway 2-3.
World Ranking: 21st. *Group standing*: 5th

2002 Divison I/B,
Szeskesfehervar and Dunaujvaros, Hungary.
Coach: **Chris McSorley** (Geneva)
Denmark 3-5, Hungary 1-4, Romania 5-2, China 8-3, Norway 1-2.
World Ranking: 20th. *Group standing*: 4th

2001 Pool B, Ljubljana, Slovenia
Coach: **Chris McSorley** (London)
Estonia 6-2, Croatia 10-1, Slovenia 3-3, China 12-1, Kazakhstan 11-2.
World Ranking: **18th**. *Group Standing*: 2nd.

2000 Pool B, Katowice, Poland
Coach: **Peter Woods** (Superleague)
Estonia 5-6, Slovenia 3-3, Netherlands 9-0, Poland 6-4, Denmark 5-4, Kazakhstan 3-1, Germany 0-5.
World Ranking: 19th. Group standing: 3rd

1999 Pool B, Copenhagen, Denmark
Coach: **Peter Woods** (Superleague)
Slovenia 2-1, Kazakhstan 1-0, Germany 2-3, Estonia 6-2, Poland 4-3, Hungary 4-2, Denmark 5-5.
World Ranking: 18th Group standing: 2nd

1998 Pool B, Ljubljana/Jesenice, Slovenia.
Coach: Peter Woods (Superleague).
Ukraine 1-6, Denmark 7-1, Estonia 4-5, Slovenia 3-5, Poland 4-3, Norway 3-4, Netherlands 10-3.
World Ranking: 22nd Group standing: 6th

1997 Pool B, Katowice/Sosnowiec, Poland
Coach: **Peter Woods** (Basingstoke)
Poland 3-4, Kazakhstan 2-4, Netherlands 8-2, Denmark 9-1, Austria 2-2, Switzerland 2-3, Belarus 2-6.
World Ranking: 18th Group standing: 6th

1996 Pool B, Eindhoven, Netherlands
Coach: **Peter Woods** (Basingstoke).
Latvia 5-6, Switzerland 2-7, Poland 4-2, Netherlands 6-2, Japan 3-3, Denmark 5-1, Belarus 4-2.
World Ranking: 16th

1995 Pool B, Bratislava, Slovakia.
Coach: **George Peternousek** (unatt.)
Slovakia 3-7, Romania 0-2, Netherlands 3-2, Denmark 2-9, Japan 3-4, Poland 4-3, Latvia 4-8.
World Ranking: 19th

1994 Pool A, Bolzano, Italy.
Coach: **Alex Dampier** (Sheffield)
Russia 3-12, Germany 0-4, Italy 2-10, Canada 2-8, Austria 0-10, Norway 2-5.
World Ranking: 12th

1993 Pool B, Eindhoven, Netherlands.
Coach: **Alex Dampier** (Sheffield).
Poland 4-3, Denmark 4-0, Japan 5-4, Bulgaria 10-0, Netherlands 3-2, Romania 10-4, China 14-0.
World Ranking: 13th

1992 Pool C, Hull, England.
Coach: **Alex Dampier** (Nottingham).
Australia 10-2, S Korea 15-0, Belgium 7-3, N Korea 16-2, Hungary 14-3.
World Ranking: 21st

1991 Pool C , Copenhagen, Denmark.
Coach: **Alex Dampier** (Nottingham).
China 5-6, N Korea 7-2, Denmark 2-3, Belgium 11-0, Hungary 3-3, Bulgaria 4-5, S Korea 7-1, Romania 6-5.
World Ranking: 21st

1990 Pool D, Cardiff, Wales.
Coach: **Alex Dampier** (Nottingham)
Australia 14-0, 13-3; Spain 13-1, 17-3.
World Ranking: 26th

1989 Pool D, Belgium.
Coach: **Terry Matthews** (Whitley Bay).
New Zealand 26-0, Romania 6-6, Belgium 5-6, Spain 8-4.
World Ranking: 27th

CAVALLIN Mark   b. 20-Nov-71

Club	Year	Comp	GP	GPI	Mins	GA	GAA
Sco	2002	EC	3	3	178	9	3.03
Sco	2003	WC	4	3	180	8	2.67
GER	2004	WC	5	2	120	8	4.00
		Totals	**12**	**8**	**478**	**25**	**3.14**

CLARKE David   b. 5-Aug-81

Club	Year	Comp	GP	G	A	Pts	PIM
Pet	2000	WC	7	0	0	0	2
New	2001	WC	5	2	0	2	6
Lon	2002	WC	5	0	1	1	10
Gui	2002	EC	6	2	1	3	18
Gui	2003	WC	5	0	0	0	8
Not	2004	WC	5	4	3	7	2
		Totals	**33**	**8**	**5**	**13**	**46**

COWLEY Russell   b. 12-Aug-83

Club	Year	Comp	GP	G	A	Pts	PIM
Cov	2002	EC	3	2	0	2	2
Cov	2003	WC	5	0	0	0	0
Cov	2004	WC	5	0	0	0	4
		Totals	**13**	**2**	**0**	**2**	**6**

DIXON Paul   b. 4-Aug-73

Club	Year	Comp	GP	G	A	Pts	PIM
Dur	1995	WC	5	1	1	2	2
Dur	1995	OQ	2	0	0	0	0
Dur	1996	WC	7	1	1	2	14
New	1996	OQ	2	0	1	1	0
New	1997	WC	7	0	1	1	0
New	1998	WC	4	0	2	2	2
New	1999	WC	7	0	1	1	0
Gui	1999	WCQ	3	0	0	0	2
Gui	2000	WC	7	0	2	2	0
Gui	2001	WC	5	1	2	3	0
Gui	2002	WC	5	0	3	3	2
Gui	2004	WC	5	1	2	3	4
		Totals	**59**	**4**	**16**	**20**	**26**

HOAD Jeff   b. 26-Jan-73

Club	Year	Comp	GP	G	A	Pts	PIM
Bel	2002	WC	5	3	1	4	6
Lon	2002	EC	6	3	1	4	2
Lon	2003	WC	5	2	2	4	4
GER	2004	WC	4	1	2	3	4
		Totals	**20**	**9**	**6**	**15**	**16**

JAMIESON Leigh   b. 30-Jul-85

Club	Year	Comp	GP	G	A	Pts	PIM
Bel	2004	WC	5	0	1	1	4

LAKE Ryan   b. 30-Aug-83

Club	Year	Comp	GP	G	A	Pts	PIM
She	2004	WC	5	0	1	1	0

LONGSTAFF David   b. 26-Aug-74

Club	Year	Comp	GP	G	A	Pts	PIM
Whi	1994	WC	6	0	0	0	6
Whi	1995	WC	7	6	1	7	8
New	1995	OQ	1	0	0	0	0
She	1996	WC	7	1	2	3	10
She	1996	OQ	5	1	3	4	6
She	1997	WC	7	1	2	3	8
She	1998	WC	7	4	3	7	8
She	1999	WC	7	2	2	4	4
She	2000	OQ	3	0	1	1	2
She	2000	WC	7	2	3	5	14
She	2001	WC	5	3	7	10	4
Dju	2002	WC	3	1	4	5	2
New	2002	EC	3	0	3	3	4
New	2003	WC	5	3	6	9	2
New	2004	WC	5	0	1	1	0
		Totals	**78**	**24**	**38**	**62**	**78**

MEYERS Danny   b. 2-Mar-83

Club	Year	Comp	GP	G	A	Pts	PIM
Brk	2004	WC	5	1	1	2	2

MYERS Matthew   b. 6-Nov-84

Club	Year	Comp	GP	G	A	Pts	PIM
Car	2004	**WC**	5	1	2	3	2

MOODY Scott   b. 6-Sep-79

Club	Year	Comp	GP	G	A	Pts	PIM
Slo	2002	EC	8	0	0	0	0
Slo	2003	WC	4	1	0	1	2
New	2004	WC	5	0	0	0	4
		Totals	**17**	**1**	**0**	**1**	**6**

MORAN Paul   b. 3-Aug-74

Club	Year	Comp	GP	G	A	Pts	PIM
Not	2004	WC	5	1	0	1	2

PHILLIPS Jonathan   b. 14-July-82

Club	Year	Comp	GP	G	A	Pts	PIM
Car	2002	EC	9	0	0	0	8
Car	2003	WC	5	0	1	1	6
Car	2004	WC	5	2	0	2	10
		Totals	**19**	**2**	**1**	**3**	**24**

TAIT Ashley   b. 9-Aug-75

Club	Year	Comp	GP	G	A	Pts	PIM
Not	1995	WC	2	0	0	0	4
Not	1995	OQ	3	1	1	2	0
Not	1996	WC	7	1	1	2	10
Kin	1998	WC	7	2	0	2	4
Not	1999	WCQ	4	0	0	0	4
Not	2000	OQ	3	0	0	0	6
Not	2000	WC	7	3	4	7	10
Not	2001	WC	5	2	4	6	4
Not	2002	WC	5	1	1	2	0
Cov	2002	EC	3	1	1	2	2
Cov	2003	WC	5	0	3	3	0
Cov	2004	WC	5	2	1	3	2
		Totals	**56**	**13**	**16**	**29**	**46**

THORNTON Steve   b. 8-Mar-73

Club	Year	Comp	GP	G	A	Pts	PIM
Car	1999	WC	7	2	1	3	0
Car	1999	WCQ	4	0	1	1	2
Car	2001	WC	5	2	8	10	6
Bel	2002	EC	3	1	0	1	4
Bel	2003	WC	5	1	9	10	0
	2004	WC	5	1	4	5	6
		Totals	**29**	**7**	**23**	**30**	**18**

WARD Colin   b. 5-Sep-70

Club	Year	Comp	GP	G	A	Pts	PIM
Bel	2004	WC	5	3	0	3	2

WILSON Rob   b. 18-Jul-68

Club	Year	Comp	GP	G	A	Pts	PIM
She	1998	WC	7	1	4	5	10
She	1999	WC	7	1	3	4	6
New	2001	WC	5	6	7	13	2
Man	2002	WC	5	1	2	3	4
Man	2002	EC	3	1	0	1	2
Man	2003	WC	5	2	3	5	6
New	2004	WC	5	0	3	3	4
		Totals	**37**	**12**	**22**	**34**	**34**

WATKINS Joe   b. 27-Oct-79

Club	Year	Comp	GP	GPI	Mins	GA	GAA
Bas	1999	WCQ	1	0	0	0	0.00
Bas	2000	WC	6	4	240	10	2.50
Brk	2002	WC	4	2	120	6	6.00
Brk	2002	EC	6	6	370	29	4.70
Brk	2003	WC	4	2	119	5	2.52
USA	2004	WC	5	3	180	9	3.00
		Totals	**26**	**17**	**1029**	**59**	**3.44**

Summary of GB records of all players having iced in the modern era are listed on pages 175/6

Forwards & Defencemen

	Years	GP	G	A	Pts	PIM
ADEY Paul	1995-2001	55	28	24	52	65
BAILEY Chris	2003	4	0	0	0	25
BENNETT Ivor	1989	4	0	1	1	2
BERRINGTON PAUL	2002-03	10	2	3	5	8
BIDNER Todd	1993	4	1	1	2	4
BISHOP Mike	1995-2000	36	5	8	13	109
BOBYCK Brent	1999-2000	7	0	1	1	0
BOE Vince	1999-2000	11	0	3	3	22
BREBANT Rick	1994-2002	32	10	13	23	78
CAMPBELL Scott	1999-2003	13	0	1	1	60
CHARD Chris	1995	1	0	0	0	0
CHINN Nicky	1993-2000	40	6	8	14	109
CLARKE David	2000-2004	33	8	5	13	46
CONWAY Kevin	1992-1999	58	33	33	66	54
COOPER Ian	1989-2000	80	30	31	61	128
COOPER Stephen	1989-2000	61	11	27	38	54
COTE Matt	1994-2000	29	0	2	2	16
COWLEY Russell	2003-04	10	0	0	0	4
CRAPPER Jamie	1990-1992	17	12	8	20	34
CRANSTON Tim	1993-1997	39	11	13	24	91
DIXON Paul	1995-2004	59	4	16	20	26
DURDLE Darren	1996-2000	22	3	6	9	36
EDMISTON Dean	1991-1992	12	3	4	7	15
ELLIS Mike	2000-2004	27	1	4	5	18
FERA Rick	1993-1994	17	7	17	24	34
GALAZZI Mark	2003	4	0	0	0	25
GARDEN Graham	1995-2000	27	5	5	10	28
HAND Paul	1989-1992	18	7	5	12	41
HAND Tony	1989-2002	59	40	79	119	34
HARDING Mike	1999-2000	7	1	3	4	4
HOAD Jeff	2002-2004	14	6	5	11	14
HOPE Shannon	1992-1998	53	1	8	9	88
HORNE Kyle	2001-2003	10	0	2	2	4
HUNT Simon	1995-1996	11	3	1	4	26
HURLEY Darren	1999-2003	36	9	8	17	138
IREDALE John	1989-1993	24	6	8	14	12
JAMIESON Leigh	2004	5	0	1	1	4
JOHNSON Anthony	1990-1993	28	15	13	28	20
JOHNSON Shaun	1992-2001	16	2	7	9	6
JOHNSON Stephen	1990-1993	23	10	12	22	6
JOHNSTONE Jeff	1999-2000	14	4	3	7	6
KENDALL Jason	2000	3	0	0	0	0
KELLAND Chris	1990-1994	31	10	8	18	44
KIDD John	1989	4	2	1	3	0
KINDRED Mike	1995	5	0	1	1	2
KURTENBACH Terry	1993-1996	29	1	7	8	6
LAKE Ryan	2004	5	0	1	1	0
LAMBERT Dale	1993	4	0	0	0	4
LARKIN Bryan	1997	7	0	1	1	6

Forwards & Defencemen

	Years	GP	G	A	Pts	PIM
LATTO Gordon	1976-89	21	2	2	4	10
LAWLESS John	1990-1991	12	5	10	15	22
LEE Phil	1989-1990	8	2	0	2	0
LIDDIARD Neil	2000-2002	28	4	4	8	55
LINDSAY Jeff	1995-1996	22	0	1	1	22
LITTLE Richard	1996-1997	10	5	2	7	18
LONGSTAFF David	1994-2004	75	24	35	59	74
MacNAUGHT Kevin	1990-1992	17	14	16	30	16
MALO Andre	1993-2000	37	2	7	9	40
MARSDEN Doug	1997	7	0	1	1	8
MASON Brian	1990-1994	34	10	10	20	37
McEWEN Doug	1993-2001	49	13	13	26	32
MOODY Scott	2003-04	9	1	0	1	6
MORAN Paul	2004	5	1	0	1	2
MORGAN Neil	1995-1998	35	11	11	22	16
MORIA Steve	1995-2000	49	22	13	35	30
MORRIS Frank	1994-1995	13	1	1	2	10
MORRISON Scott	1993-1995	25	15	8	23	16
MULVENNA Glen	2000	7	0	0	0	18
MYERS Danny	2004	5	1	1	2	2
MYERS Matthew	2004	5	1	2	3	2
NEIL Scott	1981-1993	37	23	12	35	18
NELSON Craig	2002	5	0	0	0	10
ORD Terry	1989	4	0	1	1	0
O'CONNOR Mike	1992-1994	22	4	5	9	52
OWEN Greg	2003	5	0	0	0	20
PAYNE Anthony	1995	6	1	0	1	0
PENNYCOOK Jim	1977-89	23	10	9	19	4
PENTLAND Paul	1989	4	0	0	0	0
PHILLIPS Jonathan	2003-04	10	2	1	3	16
PICKLES Andy	2001	5	0	1	1	2
PLOMMER Tommy	1995-1996	7	3	0	3	4
POPE Brent	2003-04	8	0	0	0	37
POUND Ian	1995	7	0	0	0	10
PRIEST Merv	1996-2000	30	6	7	13	30
REID Alistair	1989	4	1	2	3	0
RHODES Nigel	1989	4	2	0	2	0
ROBERTSON Iain	1991-1995	27	4	3	7	2
SAMPLE Paul	2004	5	1	0	1	4
SAUNDERS Lee	1995-1996	8	0	1	1	0
SCOTT Patrick	1993-1997	31	10	9	19	24
SHIELDS Colin	2001-2004	20	12	8	20	16
SMITH Damian	1992-1995	14	3	4	7	10
SMITH David	1995	5	1	0	1	0
SMITH Paul	1981-89	11	0	1	1	13
SMITH Peter	1989-1991	14	7	2	9	10
SMITH Stephen	1989	4	2	1	3	2
STEFAN Gary	1990-1992	17	12	10	22	28
STONE Jason	1998	6	0	0	0	0

Forwards & Defencemen

	Years	GP	G	A	Pts	PIM
STRACHAN Rick	1995-2002	66	7	10	17	20
TAIT Ashley	1995-2004	53	12	15	27	44
TASKER Michael	2001-2002	10	2	3	5	8
THOMPSON Paul	1998	6	1	1	2	8
THORNTON Steve	1999-2004	26	6	23	29	14
WAGHORN Graham	1991-1996	19	1	3	4	16
WARD Colin	2004	5	3	0	3	2
WEAVER Jonathan	1998-2003	31	10	10	20	8
WEBER Randall	1998	7	0	2	2	6
WILSON Rob	1998-2004	34	11	22	33	32
WISHART Gary	2002	5	0	2	2	4
YOUNG Scott	1999-2002	16	5	4	9	56

GOALKEEPERS

	Years	GP	GPl	Mins	GA	GAA
CAVALLIN Mark	2003-04	9	5	300	16	3.20
COWLEY Wayne	1999-2000	10	3	160	10	3.75
FOSTER Stephen	1995-2000	31	16	855	61	4.28
GRAHAM David	1989-1991	10	6	330	18	3.27
GRUBB Ricky	1995	1	1	40	5	7.50
HANSON Moray	1989-1994	9	6	317	32	6.06
HIBBERT Jim	2000	1	1	20	3	9.00
LYLE Stevie	1995-2002	39	26	1495	63	2.53
McCRONE John	1989-1994	23	19	957	57	3.57
McKAY Martin	1990-1994	15	8	418	28	4.02
MORRISON Bill	1995-1999	33	17	1000	38	2.28
MURPHY Stephen	2001-2003	10	2	90	3	2.00
O'CONNOR Scott	1992-2003	9	5	198	4	1.21
SMITH Jeff	1990	3	1	60	2	2.00
WATKINS Joe	1999-2004	20	11	659	30	2.73

2004 players shown in bold
Detailed records are in The Ice Hockey Annual 2003-04

BRITAIN v HUNGARY

COLIN WARD *right* scores GB's first goal on his debut in the World Championships.
Colin Shields rushes to congratulate him. Ward retired at the end of the tournament.

GB'S PLAYING RECORD IN OLYMPIC, WORLD AND EUROPEAN CHAMPIONSHIPS

OPPONENTS	GP	W	L	D	GF	GA	Win%
Australia	4	4	0	0	46	8	100.0
Austria	14	5	7	2	37	60	42.9
Belarus	3	1	2	0	10	13	33.3
Belgium	14	11	2	1	110	31	82.1
Bulgaria	7	1	5	1	28	34	21.4
Canada	13	1	12	0	12	106	7.7
China	6	3	3	0	42	29	50.0
Czechoslovakia*	7	4	3	0	15	17	57.1
Croatia	2	2	0	0	17	2	100.0
Denmark	16	7	6	3	66	73	53.1
Estonia	5	2	3	0	24	19	40.0
Finland	2	2	0	0	13	8	100.0
France	20	8	10	2	86	79	45.0
Germany	13	4	8	1	26	49	34.6
Holland	13	11	2	0	78	40	84.6
Hungary	18	8	9	1	52	67	47.2
Italy	10	4	5	1	43	59	45.0
Japan	5	2	2	1	16	15	50.0
Kazakstan	5	3	1	1	18	8	70.0
Latvia	7	3	3	1	28	26	50.0
New Zealand	1	1	0	0	26	0	100.0
North Korea	3	2	1	0	24	9	66.7
Norway	14	4	9	1	39	69	32.1
Poland	15	10	4	1	63	54	70.0
Romania	13	8	4	1	60	43	65.4
Russia	1	0	1	0	3	12	0.0
Slovakia	2	0	2	0	4	14	0.0
Slovenia	6	3	1	2	21	16	66.7
South Korea	3	2	1	0	28	10	66.7
Spain	5	4	1	0	46	17	80.0
Sweden	8	3	5	0	15	39	37.5
Switzerland	18	3	12	3	46	90	25.0
Ukraine	2	0	1	1	3	8	25.0
USA	7	0	4	3	17	37	21.4
Yugoslavia	4	0	2	2	11	33	25.0
Totals	286	126	131	29	1173	1194	49.1

* Great Britain have not played the Czech Republic

WORLD JUNIOR CHAMPIONSHIPS

U20 CHAMPIONSHIPS

Division II, *Kaunas & Elektrenai, Lithuania, 5-11 January 2004.*

Age limit is under 20 years on 1 January 2004

GROUP STANDINGS

Group B	GP	W	L	D	GF	GA	Pts
Britain	**5**	**5**	**0**	**0**	**38**	**5**	**10**
Korea	5	4	1	0	45	7	8
Croatia	5	2	3	0	18	18	4
Serbia & Montenegro	5	2	3	0	15	21	4
Lithuania	5	2	3	0	12	25	4
South Africa	5	0	5	0	4	56	0

Britain promoted to Division I in 2005, **South Africa relegated** to Division III.

BRITAIN UNDER-20

Alan Levers COV, Davey Lawrence SHE; James Hutchinson BAS, Leigh Jamieson BEL, Adam Radmall COV, Paddy Ward DUN (capt), Euan Forsyth FIF, Kevin Phillips HUL, Steve Duncombe SHE; Mark Richardson BRK, Joe Miller, Matt Myers CAR, Lee Mitchell, Adam Walker FIF, Adam Carr MIL, Stephen Wallace NEW, Simon Butterworth SHE, Matt Towalski SLO, Adam Brittle, Tom Carlon TEL.
Head coach: Roger Hunt (Dundee). *Asst coach*: Mick Mishener. *Manager*: Jim Laing.

RESULTS

	KOR	CRO	SCG	LTU	RSA
GB	2-0	8-1	7-1	7-3	14-0
KOR		7-2	9-1	13-1	16-1
CRO			1-3	3-0	11-0
SCG				1-2	9-2
LTU					6-1

GB UNDER-20'S LEADING SCORERS

	GP	G	A	Pts	Pim
Stephen Wallace	5	12	3	15	8
Matt Myers	5	3	6	9	6
Adam Carr	5	5	3	8	8
Adam Brittle	5	3	4	7	4
Mark Richardson	5	1	5	6	4
James Hutchinson	4	1	4	5	2
Adam Walker	5	4	0	4	0
Paddy Ward	5	1	3	4	0

GB UNDER-20'S NETMINDING

	GPI	Mins	SoG	GA	Sv%
Davey Lawrence	4	240	47	2	95.7
Alan Levers	1	60	17	3	82.4
GB TOTALS	**5**	**300**	**64**	**5**	**92.2**

GB UNDER-20'S GAME SUMMARIES

5 Jan **LITHUANIA-BRITAIN 3-7** (0-2,2-3,1-2)
GB scorers: Brittle 2g; Wallace 1+2; Towalski, Jamieson 1+1; Carr, Carlon 1g; Hutchinson 4a; Myers, Richardson 1a. *Penalty minutes*: Lithuania 14, GB 18. *Netminder*: Levers.

6 Jan **BRITAIN-S AFRICA 14-0** (3-0,6-0,5-0)
GB scorers: Carr, Wallace 3+1; Myers 2+1; Butterworth 2g; Richardson 1+2; Hutchinson, Brittle, Walker 1g; Mitchell, Miller, Carlon 1a. *Penalty minutes*: GB 2, S Africa 6. *Netminder*: Lawrence.

8 Jan **BRITAIN-SERBIA 7-1** (1-0,3-0,3-1)
GB scorers: Wallace 3g; Walker 2g; Ward 1+1; Duncombe 1g; Brittle, Myers 3a; Phillips 2a; Carr, Richardson 1a. *Penalty minutes*: GB 18, Serbia 36. *Netminder*: Lawrence

9 Jan **BRITAIN-KOREA 2-0** (1-0,1-0,0-0)
GB scorers: Wallace 2g; Lawrence, Ward 1a. *Penalty minutes*: GB 14, Korea 20. *Netminder*: Lawrence

11 Jan **CROATIA-BRITAIN 1-8** (0-1,1-3,0-4)
GB scorers: Wallace 3g; Butterworth, Towalski, Walker 1g; Myers, Carr 1+1; Jamieson, Richardson, Ward, Lawrence, Brittle, Carlon. *Penalty minutes*: Croatia 26, GB 12. *Netminder*: Lawrence

BRITAIN UNDER-18 *left to right*, *back row*: Nicky Watt, Mark Richardson, Bari McKenzie, Adam Walker, Tom Carlon, David Phillips, Luke Boothroyd, George Murray, Kurt Reynolds, Lewis Day; *front row*: Nathan Craze, Chad Reekie, Matt Towe, Greg Wood, Lee Mitchell, Kevin Phillips, Shane Moore, Alain Campbell, Simon Butterworth, Joe Dollin.

Under-20s win Hunt for gold

At last! Britain's under-20s won the gold medal in their group and promotion to Division I for the first time since they entered the championships 20 years ago.

And they did it in style, winning all five games. **Stephen Wallace** was the top goal scorer, **Davey Lawrence** had two shutouts, and no GB player took more than four minor penalties.

Lawrence, who dressed in half-a-dozen Steelers' games during the season, allowed only two goals and made up for it by assisting on two.

Rookie coach, **Roger Hunt** of Dundee Stars, was naturally delighted at his charges' disciplined and entertaining performance, pointing out that, like the seniors, they had very little preparation.

CHAMPIONSHIP AWARDS
Best Forward
STEPHEN WALLACE, GB
Best Goaltender
DAVEY LAWRENCE, GB
Best GB Player
STEPHEN WALLACE
GB Supporters Club Player
PADDY WARD

"The boys only came together for one challenge game against Edinburgh Capitals the week before we flew out. The experience of having 11 guys from the previous campaign certainly worked for us," he said.

Britain won silver last year and their optimism that they could do better this time was quickly proved right as they walloped their hosts, Lithuania, 7-3, in their opening game.

The victory was all the sweeter for being played in front of a noisy, partisan 2,000 crowd and it set the teenagers up for the rest of the tournament.

Only Korea proved a tough nut to crack in the penultimate game, but some shrewd scouting by Hunt and his assistant **Mick Mishner** paid off handsomely with a 2-0 shutout.

Hunt, who assisted **Chris McSorley** with the senior team coaching in April, took two players to Oslo - Cardiff's **Matt Myers** and Belfast's **Leigh Jamieson**. Some felt they should have taken more, but apart from these two only a handful of the under-20s had Elite League experience and that was mostly brief. There is a wide gap in standards between Division II of the under-20s and Division I of the seniors.

Hunt's reward for his team's success will be a much bigger challenge next term. But he will have the help of 12 of this year's gold medal winners and for the first time since 1989, the games will be at home, in Sheffield.

U18 CHAMPIONSHIPS

Division II, Group B, Kaunas & Elektrenai, Lithuania, 1-7 March 2004

Age limit is under 18 years on 1 January 2004

GROUP STANDINGS

Group B	GP	W	L	D	GF	GA	Pts
Britain	5	5	0	0	30	6	10
Estonia	5	4	1	0	35	6	8
Croatia	5	3	2	0	17	14	6
Lithuania	5	1	3	1	10	15	3
Serbia & Montenegro	5	1	4	0	12	26	2
Australia	5	0	4	1	5	42	1

Britain promoted to Division I in 2005, **Australia relegated** to Division III.

BRITAIN UNDER-18

Nathan Craze CAR, Joe Dollin GUI; Chad Reekie CHE, Luke Boothroyd, David Phillips, Kevin Phillips (capt) HUL, Shane Moore SWI, Kurt Reynolds (Sault Ste. Marie, USA); Nicky Watt BAS, Mark Richardson BRK, Lee Mitchell, Adam Walker FIF, Bari McKenzie MIL, Alain Campbell PAI, Simon Butterworth, Greg Wood SHE, Tom Carlon, Matt Towe TEL, Lewis Day (Okanagan, CAN), George Murray (Znojemsi Orli, CZE).
Head coach: Mike Urquhart. *Assistant coach:* Peter Russell. *Manager:* Tony Hall.

CHAMPIONSHIP AWARDS
Best Defenceman
KEVIN PHILLIPS, GB
Best Netminder
NATHAN CRAZE, GB

RESULTS

	EST	CRO	LTU	SCG	AUS
GB	2-1	7-1	2-1	5-3	14-0
EST		5-1	4-2	10-0	15-1
CRO			4-1	5-1	6-0
LTU				4-3	2-2
SCG					5-2

GB UNDER-18'S LEADING POINTS SCORERS

	GP	G	A	Pts	Pim
Tom Carlon	5	10	4	14	12
Mark Richardson	5	2	8	10	10
Nicky Watt	5	6	0	6	20
Alain Campbell	5	1	5	6	4
Adam Walker	5	2	2	4	4
Lewis Day	5	2	2	4	20
Simon Butterworth	5	2	1	3	2
Kurt Reynolds	4	1	2	3	10
Kevin Phillips	5	0	3	3	8

GB UNDER-18'S NETMINDING

	GPI	Mins	SoG	GA	Sv%
Nathan Craze	5	280	99	6	93.94
Joe Dollin	1	20	2	0	100.O
GB TOTALS	5	300	101	6	94.06

GB UNDER-18'S GAME SUMMARIES

1 Mar **AUSTRALIA-BRITAIN 0-14**

(0-5,0-3,0-6)
GB scorers: Lewis, Walker, Richardson, Watt 2+1; Campbell 1+4; Carlon 1+2; Murray, D Phillips, Butterworth 1+1; Wood 1g; K Phillips 2a; Moore, Towe, Reekie 1a.
Penalty minutes: Australia 16, GB 14. *GB Man of Match*: David Phillips. *Shots on Goal*: Phillips/Bonnici AUS 53, Craze/Dollin GB 10.

2 Mar **BRITAIN-SERBIA 5-3** (1-0,2-1,2-2)
GB scorers: Carlon 3g; Watt, Walker 1g; McKenzie, Campbell, Day 1a.
Penalty minutes: GB 30, Serbia 20. *GB Man of Match*: Craze. *Shots on Goal*: Craze GB 19, Lukovich SCG 30.

4 Mar **BRITAIN-LITHUANIA 2-1** (1-0,0-0,1-1)
GB scorers: Carlon, Watt 1g; Richardson 1a.
Penalty minutes: GB 26, Lithuania 12. *GB Man of Match*: Kevin Phillips. *Shots on Goal*: Craze. GB 18, Jaksys LTU 25.

5 Mar **CROATIA-BRITAIN 1-7** (0-1,0-4,1-2)
GB scorers: Carlon 2+2; Watt 2g; Reynolds 1+2; Butterworth, McKenzie 1g; Richardson 4a; K Phillips, Walker 1a.
Penalty minutes: Croatia 24, GB 38 (Watt 10-misconduct). *GB Man of Match*: Carlon. *Shots on Goal*: Filipec CRO 31, Craze GB 24.

7 Mar **BRITAIN-ESTONIA 2-1** (0-0,0-0,2-1)
GB scorers: Carlon 2g; Richardson 2a.
Penalty minutes: GB 16, Estonia 12. *GB Man of Match*: Craze. *Shots on Goal*: Craze GB 30, Eerme EST 19.

Another gold

In a first for the sport in Britain, the GB under-18s made it a Double Gold Medal win in the junior World Championships.

Mike Urquhart's team won all five games in their Division II group only two months after the under-20s wiped the board in their tournament.

Goalies **Nathan Craze** and **Joe Dollin** conceded only six goals in four games and kept a clean sheet in the fifth, against Australia.

Hull teenager **Kevin Phillips** was voted the championship's best defenceman and Telford's **Tom Carlon** topped the tournament scoring in goals and points. **Simon Butterworth**, **Lee Mitchell**, **Mark Richardson**, **Adam Walker** and Carlon can proudly display two gold medals as they iced at both age levels.

'ROOS BOUNCED IN FIRST GAME

In any world championship, it's always good to get a win under your belt in the first game and GB did this in spades as they whitewashed the Aussies while pouring 53 shots on their net.

None of the other contests was anything like as easy, as they came up against a string of East European nations. The 2-1 win over the hosts, Lithuania, was probably the most satisfying, as it had been for the under-20s. (Not for the first time, both junior championships were held in the same country.)

That was until the last game against Estonia, who had knocked the under-20s out of first place last year.

With the gold up for grabs, Estonia poured rubber on Craze but the Welsh keeper kicked out everything. His opposite number **Kristjan Eerme** was unbeatable, too, until Carlon finally beat him 45 seconds into the last session off a pass from Richardson. The pair combined for a second time moments after **Aleksandr Polozov** had equalised in the 55th minute.

This is the fourth time Britain have won gold at this level since they first entered the championships in 1979, a run of 26 years. The trick, of course, is staying up the following year.

This team may well have benefited from the unexpected experience they gained last year when an administrative cock-up pushed them up into Division I. **George Murray**, **Kurt Reynolds**, Butterworth, Craze, Phillips, Richardson and Walker all played in the higher division in 2003.

NORTH AMERICAN LEAGUES

NATIONAL HOCKEY LEAGUE
STANLEY CUP

Winners   TAMPA BAY LIGHTNING
Finalists   CALGARY FLAMES
Series score: 4-3
Game scores (Lightning first):
1-4h, 4-1h, 0-3a, 1-0a, 2-3ot-h, 3-2ot-a,2-1h

PRESIDENT'S TROPHY (*most league points*)
DETROIT REDWINGS (Western Conference)
Runners-up
TAMPA BAY LIGHTNING (Eastern Conference)

FIRST ALL-STAR TEAM
Goal	**Martin Brodeur**, New Jersey
Defence	**Scott Niedermayer**, New Jersey
	Zdeno Chara, Ottawa
Centre	**Joe Sakic**, Colorado
Right Wing	**Martin St Louis**, Tampa Bay
Left Wing	**Markus Naslund**, Vancouver

AWARD WINNERS
Art Ross Trophy (Most Points)
Martin St Louis, Tampa Bay Lightning
Maurice 'Rocket' Richard Trophy (Most Goals)
Jarome Iginla, Calgary Flame/**Ilya Kowalchuk**, Atlanta Thrashers/**Rick Nash**, Columbus Blue Jackets *
Hart Memorial Trophy (Most Valuable Player)
Martin St Louis, Tampa Bay Lightning
James Norris Mem'l Trophy (Best Defenceman)
Scott Niedermayer, New Jersey Devils
Vezina Trophy (Best Goaltender)
Martin Brodeur, New Jersey Devils
William Jennings Trophy (Fewest Goals Against)
Martin Brodeur New Jersey Devils
Lester B Pearson Trophy (Players' Player)
Martin St Louis, Tampa Bay Lightning
Calder Memorial Trophy (Rookie of the Year)
Andrew Raycroft, Boston Bruins
Lady Byng Mem'l Trophy (Most Sportsmanlike)
Brad Richards, Tampa Bay Lightning
Jack Adams Award (Coach of the Year)
John Tortorella, Tampa Bay Lightning
Conn Smythe Trophy (Playoffs MVP)
Brad Richards, Tampa Bay Lightning
Frank J. Selke Trophy (Defensive Forward)
Kris Draper, Detroit Redwings
Bill Masterton Memorial Trophy (Most Dedicated)
Bryan Berard, Chicago Blackhawks

* *shared*

STANLEY CUP
Stan gets a tan

NORMAN DE MESQUITA

It was one of the most unlikely finals in the recent history of the Stanley Cup.

Two goals by Ukrainian **Ruslan Fedotenko** sparked Tampa Bay Lightning to a 2-1 win over Calgary Flames in game seven, bringing the venerable trophy to the Sunshine State of Florida for the first time.

Lightning had won the NHL's Eastern Conference and ended as runners-up to Detroit Redwings overall, but their Cup success was a surprise as they had reached the playoffs on only two previous occasions in their 12 seasons.

> 'The Lightning winning the Cup using an offensive scheme instead of the neutral zone trap could be the dawn of a new era in the NHL. But it won't be because 28 teams saw the Calgary Flames make it to the final by doing anything and everything to slow down their opposition. And they got away with it.'
>
> **Mike Brophy**, The Hockey News

As for the Flames... you could have got 200-1 against them appearing in the final. **Darryl Sutter**'s team qualified for the post-season only in the last week of league play. Their amazing form lasted all the way to overtime in game five of the final when Russian **Oleg Saprykin** scored to give them a 3-2 series lead.

With game six to be played in Calgary, the experts forecast a home success, but this time **Martin St. Louis** (who admitted to taking oxygen in the high altitude) scored in sudden-death and Lightning went on to make home ice tell in a game seven thriller.

It was a series which promised much but only half fulfilled expectations. Tampa's coach **John Tortorella** is a firm believer in attacking hockey and in the first two games of the final, attack was their watchword. But then Flames decided that they had to be more physical and defensive. Lightning responded in kind and, as a result, games three, four and five were more reminiscent of the defence-orientated 2003 final.

Just in time to save the series as a spectacle, Tampa reverted to their attacking philosophy and

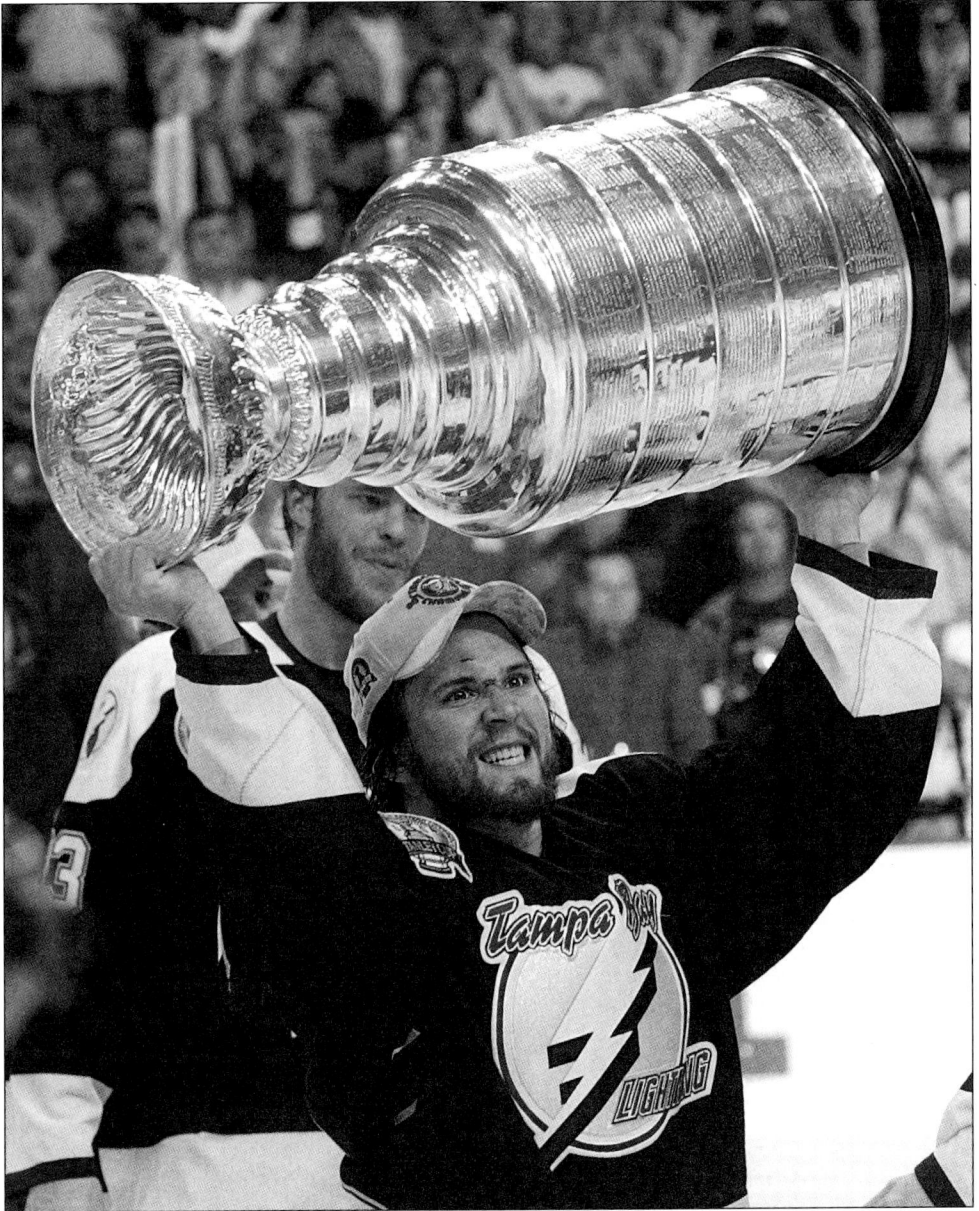

MARTIN ST LOUIS of Tampa Bay Lightning with the Stanley Cup, the oldest trophy competed for by North American sport teams.   *Photo*: Bruce Jessop/IHA (www.ihahockey.de)

were duly rewarded. It was the first final in which the lead never changed hands and the team which scored first won every game.

Brad Richards, who broke the Cup record for game winning goals with seven, won the Conn Smythe Trophy as the playoff MVP. A remarkable statistic reveals that whenever he scored a goal (in both the regular season and playoffs) Lightning won the game.

Both teams benefited from superior goaltending from the final's first all-European duo. Tampa's Russian **Nikolai Khabibulin** just about outplayed Finn **Miika Kiprusoff**.

The continuing theme throughout the playoffs was the fall of the giant and the success of the underdog. Flames were the first team to beat three division winners - Vancouver, Detroit and San Jose - on their way to the final.

The defending champion New Jersey Devils found the absence of their captain **Scott Stevens** too much to bear and the highly-fancied Toronto Maple Leafs also suffered from injuries to key players. In the second round, as in 2003, Philadelphia Flyers were too strong for the Leafs.

In another 2003 replay Ottawa Senators, favourites to emerge from the East, were beaten by the Leafs in the first round and, as a result, **Jacques Martin** lost his job as coach.

It was thought that Detroit had made all the right personnel moves to win the Cup again but they found Flames' sheer enthusiasm too much.

• Calgary is Canada's first Stanley Cup finalist since Vancouver Canucks lost a seven-game thriller to New York Rangers in 1994. Montreal Canadiens in 1993 were Canada's last champions, defeating Los Angeles Kings.

MINOR LEAGUES
PLAYOFF WINNERS
American League (AHL) - Calder Cup
Milwaukee Admirals

East Coast League (ECHL) - Kelly Cup
Idaho Steelheads

Central League (CHL) - President's Cup
Laredo Bucks

United League (UHL) - Colonial Cup
Muskegon Fury

South East Hockey League (President's Cup)
Huntsville Channel Cats

WHA2
Jacksonville Barracudas

Canadian (Major Junior A) League (CHL) Memorial Cup
Kelowna Rockets

NHL AWARDS
St Louis marches into history

STEWART ROBERTS

His team listing states that Tampa Bay Lightning forward **Martin St Louis** is 5ft 9in tall. The 28-year-old admits to only 5ft 8in. Whatever, surely an athlete that, er, stocky, couldn't amount to much in today's giant-size NHL. Think again.

The **John Lawless** look-alike swept the board at the end-of-season awards night, joining the greats of the game by collecting more trophies than anyone since **Wayne Gretzky** in 1987.

First was the Stanley Cup in which he finished as runner-up in the scoring with 24 points (nine goals) in 23 games. Then there was the Art Ross Trophy for most points during the season, the Hart Trophy as the League's most valuable player and the Lester B Pearson Award as Players' Player. He was also voted onto the first All-Star team.

The right-winger probably had a job getting all this lot out of the door (they don't believe in small trophies in North American sports) and he could certainly be forgiven if he suddenly found difficulty in getting the upper part of his body through the exit.

Not a bit of it. "I don't know if this means I'm the best player in the NHL," he said. "There are a lot of good players. And Tampa is a good organisation who believed in me."

They certainly did. The other remarkable thing about St Louis, who hails from Laval, Quebec, is that he was never drafted. He signed his first NHL contract as a free agent five years after he was passed over in his draft year. His career took off when he joined Lightning in July 2000.

"I don't worry about people's opinion," he said. "It doesn't feel any better now because they didn't think I could play then. It still feels as good."

St Louis joined an elite club. The only other players to win a Stanley Cup, the scoring title and the league MVP in the same season were **Guy Lafleur**, **Bobby Orr**, **Jean Beliveau**, **Gordie Howe**, **Bill Cowley**, **Howie Morenz** and Gretzky.

It was a good night for the Lightning. Their coach, **John Tortorella**, won the Jack Adams Award as the Coach of the Year and **Brad Richards**, the Cup's leading points scorer, added the Lady Byng Trophy for sportsmanship to his Conn Smythe Trophy as the Cup's MVP.

Like his trophy-laden forward, Tortorella, who deserves much of the credit for Lightning's amazing season, would only say: "This award is not about one guy. It's about an organisation."

HALL OF FAME

The following were due to be inducted into the Hockey Hall of Fame in November 2004:

RAY BOURQUE

Blueliner played all bar 15 months of his 22 -year NHL career with Boston Bruins, winning five Norris Trophies as the league's best defenceman. His only Stanley Cup came with Colorado Avalanche in his last season, 2000-01. The league's all-time highest scoring defenceman with 410 goals and 1,579 points in 1,612 games.

PAUL COFFEY

His career ran on similar lines to Bourque's of whom he was a contemporary. He won three Stanley Cups with **Wayne Gretzky**'s great Edmonton Oilers teams of the 1980s and collected a fourth when he moved to Pittsburgh Penguins. Won the Norris Trophy three times and with 1,531 points is the all-time second highest scoring defenceman behind Bourque .

PLEASE DON'T TRY THIS AT HOME

Quad City (Illinois) Mallards of the United Hockey League held a special promotional night when their big rivals, Flint (Michigan) Generals, came to town.

They decided to use the occasion and their home crowd to try and break the world record for the most people sitting on whoopee cushions at one time.

Mallards' GM **Howard Cornfeld**, who had been feuding all season with his opposite number on the Generals, handed out 5,000 cushions and at a break in the game around the halfway mark, he ordered the fans to sit.

The game attracted 5,327 fans thus breaking the old record of 1,372 cushions, set at the Brighton [England] Comedy Festival in October 2003.

But Cornfeld's plan to put Generals off their game backfired as Flint won 6-5 after a shootout. "Howard can suck on that," said their GM.

LARRY MURPHY

The third defenceman to be inducted though he never won a Norris Trophy. He was on four Stanley Cup winners in Pittsburgh and Detroit and is the fifth highest scoring blueliner with 1,216 points.

CLIFF FLETCHER

One of the league's most experienced and respected managers and a former member of the Hall's selection committee. Won the Stanley Cup with Calgary Flames in 1989 and has tasted league success with Flames and Toronto Maple Leafs. He was GM of Team Canada in the 1981 Canada Cup.

HERITAGE HOCKEY CLASSIC

Record crowd at NHL's first outdoor game

STEWART ROBERTS

If you, like me, have ever enjoyed playing pond hockey in a British winter... you'll have hardly any idea what it's like to take part in the first regular season NHL game to be staged outdoors.

On November 22 2003, the temperature at Edmonton's Commonwealth Stadium was 20 degrees Celsius below freezing, 28 below with the wind chill factor. How cold is that? Well, the ice in NHL arenas is usually kept at around six below.

The cold didn't bother the Oilers or their opponents, the Montreal Canadiens. "There was a little shortness of breath because of the cold air, that's all," said Edmonton forward, **Jason Chimera**.

Canadiens' goalie, **Jose Theodore**, was more worried about what his mother thought. "When I was 11 or 12 years old," he recalled, "my mom always said, 'Put a tuque [a Canadian woolly hat] on or you'll catch a cold.' I wanted to make sure she's not going to say anything when I go back home, so I put a tuque on." *Over* his mask.

PRAGUE (AP) -- Three hundred players in the NHL this season were born and trained in Europe, the most ever.

The Czech Republic had 76 players in the NHL, the most of any European country according to [the 30 April 2004] announcement by the International Ice Hockey Federation.

Russia had 65 and Sweden had 53. Yugoslavia, France and Ireland had one player each.

Last season, 294 European-born players were in the NHL. There were 1,018 players who appeared in at least one NHL game this season, also a record.

You could say, as Monty Python might have done, that it was 'sheer luxury' for the players. Not only were the millionaires whizzing around the ice at high speed but when they weren't, they had nice, heated benches to sit on. There was even provision for the goalies to come off during the commercial breaks and warm their extremities.

Meanwhile, the poor old punters were wrapped in parkas, fleeces and even sleeping bags. The Mexican Wave was unusually popular. No wonder there were plenty of empty seats in the last period.

But we heard of no complaints from the crowd. Indeed, a streaker wore nothing but a T-shirt.

(When he was arrested, one wag quipped: "They couldn't charge him for lack of evidence.")

But there were some whingers among the teams. Oilers' coach, **Craig MacTavish**, moaned about the bad bounces due to the chipped ice from the extreme cold. , "It was a great day but they got the better of the bounces," he said. Not often he gets the chance to use that one for real, eh?

There was a wimpy Czech, too. "I didn't like to be on the bench before," admitted Canadiens' **Richard Zednik**, "but now I was excited to come back and sit."

LOCKOUT? THANK GOODNESS

"Some of these [European NHL] guys are so glad to get back to their home towns and get a year off the bad coaching and brutality of the NHL. They're looking forward to [the lockout]." *Rich Winter, NHL player-agent. Toronto Globe and Mail.*

The point of this seemingly crazy exercise - apart from Canadiens beating Oilers 4-3 - was to set an NHL attendance record and get some positive publicty. Both were comfortably achieved as a crowd of 57,167 watched the Heritage Hockey Classic, more than double the previous NHL record of 28,183. The 50-50 Draw paid out $75,000, probably another record.

The game itself was definitely not a classic. Frankly, the view was more attractive than the action. With the rink surrounded by snow and ice - the stands began several metres away - the bright TV lights and only faint lines in the ice, the arena took on a surreal Christmas card look.

The MegaStars game was more entertaining. The Oilumni beat Les Anciens Canadiens 2-0 in a well played 'friendly' with both rosters stuffed with hockey greats from the past. **Grant Fuhr** and **Bill Ranford** shared the 26-shot shutout.

Former Oilers' teammates, **Mark Messier** and **Wayne Gretzky**, were reunited on the ice for probably the last time. Messier played truant from the New York Rangers to join the fun in his home town and even helped to clear the ice with a shovel after the first period.

"That's the way we did it when I was growing up," he explained. "And that's how this whole weekend is supposed to be, getting back to the grass-roots."

No 99, who retired in 1999, was not feeling quite so energetic. When Canadiens' legend **Guy Lafleur** told the post-game press conference: "I felt like a ten-year-old but with the legs of a 50-year-old", Gretzky shot back: "Maybe 60. Our team will need a whole year to rest."

☑ Both games were screened in the UK via the digital TV channel, NASN.

LEAGUE TRAGEDIES

Todd Bertuzzi

The nastiest attack by one player on another since the **Marty McSorley-Donald Brashear** incident came on 8 March 2004.

The old story of retribution was behind the sucker-punch that Vancouver's **Todd Bertuzzi** landed on Colorado's **Steve Moore**, leaving the centreman unconscious with a broken neck and a concussion. It ended Moore's season and possibly his career, and left super-star Bertuzzi suspended until reinstated by league. commissioner, **Gary Bettman**.

The ban cost Bertuzzi over US$500,000 of his $6.8 million annual salary while the Canucks were fined $250,000. He missed 20 games of the regular season and without him, Canucks were knocked out of the Stanley Cup playoffs in the first round. He was left off Canada's roster for the World Cup and reportedly put his house on the market for Can$2.5 million.

HOCKEY THE MOST DEMANDING SPORT

'More than any other sport, hockey demands that a player work hard, skate hard, hit hard and think hard. You can float through some other sports, like baseball, basketball and even some positions in [American] football, but you can't float through the NHL without the standings reflecting it.

'In hockey you have to be determined to be successful. If you're not determined, you're defeated before you start because too many other teams are determined.' *Dave Anderson, veteran sports columnist in the New York Times.*

The nastiness apparently stemmed from Moore's unpunished borderline hit on **Markus Naslund** two games earlier that left the Vancouver captain concussed.

Six days later in Vancouver - and after a re-match had gone off without any problems - Bertuzzi chased Moore in the third period of a game that Avalanche were winning 8-2. He struck him from behind with a roundhouse right, knocking him clean off his feet. Both players fell down and others then piled in.

On 26 August 2004 in a Vancouver court, Bertuzzi pleaded not guilty to charges of assault causing bodily harm. The trial was expected to last three weeks.

Opinion in Canada is divided over the case with hockey people insisting that the league has taken the appropriate action against the player and that legal intervention from outside the sport is unnecessary. His boss at the Canucks, GM **Brian Burke**, described Bertuzzi as "a fine person and an excellent hockey player."

Dany Heatley

The NHL lost three personalities in car crashes in 2003-04. Legendary USA Olympic coach **Herb Brooks** died in his minivan, and former Chicago Blackhawk **Keith Magnusson** was killed when a car driven by another former NHLer veered into oncoming traffic. (See *Obituaries* later in this section.)

On 29 September 2003, in the second of the three tragedies, **Dany Heatley**, an exciting 23-year-old forward with Atlanta Thrashers, lost control of his Ferrari and crashed into a brick wall, ripping the sports car almost in half. His passenger was his team-mate **Dan Snyder**, who suffered critical brain injuries and never recovered, dying a few days later, aged 25.

Heatley suffered only minor injuries and helped by the compassion and forgiveness of Snyder's parents, he made a remarkably swift recovery. Thrashers also rallied round.

Though Heatley faced possible criminal charges, as well as having to cope with the mental and physical trauma from the accident, he was the best player in the World Championships in Prague.

NHL OWNERS PLEAD POVERTY

According to figures distributed to owners this summer, the record losses posted by the NHL teams were an increase of 35 percent from the US$218 million in operating losses incurred by the league last year.

The losses are blamed on soaring player salaries and the lack of a salary cap, without which the NHL spent 76 percent of US$1.93 billion in revenue on players' salaries and benefits.

Commented **Bill Daly**, the NHL's chief legal officer: "This is a level at which no business can survive. The league will lose teams and players will lose jobs if we can't fix this."

sportbusiness.com, September 2003

X Heatley was indicted in July 2004 with vehicular homicide, reckless driving and four other charges. The district attorney said his car was travelling at between 100 and 130 kmh (60 to 80 mph). The speed limit was 56 kmh. Heatley had consumed alcohol but was not intoxicated at the time of the accident.

Though Heatley could be sentenced to up to 20 years in prison, the judge has wide discretion in such cases and probation was one option.

NHL cough up $1.2 million for death

The cost of a tragic accident during an NHL game in 2002, which left a 13-year-old girl dead, was made public in April 2004 - with the league contributing heavily to a US$1.2 million pay-out.

The parents of **Brittanie Cecil**, killed when a puck hit her during a Columbus Blue Jackets' game, sued the NHL, the club and the arena who jointly paid $705,000 to the girl's mother, and $470,000 to her father.

Lawyers had taken action against the three parties following the incident, as well as the hospital which treated their daughter.

The legal papers had been kept private following the settlement in February 2003, until Columbus' WBNS-TV won the right for the details to be made public.

sportbusiness.com

New shutout record

Phoenix Coyotes' goalie, **Brian Boucher**, broke the league's shutout record on 8 January 2004 in Minnesota.

Bill Durnan, Turk Broda, John Vanbiesbrouck, J S Giguerre? - they're history. Boucher, 27, went without conceding a goal for five straight games - 325 minutes, 45 seconds. He blanked the Los Angeles Kings (4-0), Dallas Stars (6-0), Carolina Hurricanes (3-0), Washington Capitals (3-0) and the Minnesota Wild (2-0). All except the first were achieved on the road.

He entered the fifth game, in Minnesota, needing to keep a clean sheet for 43:37 to beat Durnan's mark of 309:21 and four shutouts, set way back in 1949 with Montreal Canadiens.

"I did look up at the clock," he admitted. "But once I saw it was four minutes into the third, I knew I could breathe easy as far as the streak was concerned. That's probably the first time [in the streak] that I counted down. I hate to do that but I don't know if anyone could ignore it."

Richard Park of the Wild thought he'd beaten the new Mr Zero midway through the game but his shot ricocheted off the goalie's right leg. He was wide-eyed in disbelief. "That's a goal 9.9 times out of ten," he said. "I got off the shot I wanted, but it's remarkable the swagger he's got in the net, the confidence."

The remarkable run ended on 11 January in front of over 18,000 noisy fans in Coyotes' beautiful new arena. The streak-ending goal was a flukey one. Just 6:16 into the game against Atlanta Thrashers, a slap shot from **Randy Robitaille** hit Coyotes' defenceman **David Tanabe** in the chest, and the puck deflected past Boucher's glove hand before he could snag it.

"It was a nice run, something I'll never forget but I think it's good for our team that it's over,"

STANLEY CUP LOST AND FOUND

Fort St John, British Columbia (AP), Aug 22 2004.
The Stanley Cup spent Sunday night in luggage limbo. The fabled trophy disappeared during an Air Canada flight from Vancouver to Fort St. John over the weekend when Vancouver airline officials removed it from the plane because of weight restrictions.

Walter Neubrand, keeper of the Cup, was delivering the trophy to **Jake Goertzen**, head scout for the Stanley Cup champion Tampa Bay Lightning. As the two waited by the baggage claim, it didn't take long for them to realize something was wrong.

"We were waiting for it to come out," Goertzen said. "Everybody's bag was there, except the Cup."

After a call to Vancouver, they learned the 35-pound Cup was sitting in the Vancouver airport's luggage area 750 miles away. It was too heavy to fly.

Fitness gym owner **Brent Lock**, who had planned to view the Cup Sunday night, said he doesn't understand how Air Canada could have left it behind. "It's not like it's a brown paper bag; it's the holy grail," he said. "It's probably the most important non-religious artifact in Canada."

said a visibly relieved Boucher. "We don't have to worry about it or answer any more questions about it."

The final tally was 332 minutes and one second, and 147 failed shots on his net since the streak began on December 31.
• Boucher's achievement set two new modern day NHL standards - for shutouts and scoreless minutes. The NHL's modern era began with the introduction of the red line in 1943-44.

Ottawa's **Alex Connell** set the all-time shutout record with six in 1927-28, in the days when forward passing was not permitted in the attacking zone.

Boucher's scoreless span ranks third, behind Montreal's **George Hainsworth** who went more than 343 minutes without allowing a goal in 1928-29, and Connell who went more than 460 minutes in 1927-28.
• Boucher's red-and-white striped goalie pads are in the Hockey Hall of Fame in Toronto. It's just as well. Equipment man **Stan Wilson** had been after the American goalie to break in a new pair of pads for ages. Apparently, the ones he made history with were ready to fall apart!

Igor Larionov

One of the all-time great Russian players, **Igor Larionov**, has retired from the Detroit Red Wings at the age of 43 after 27 years as a pro.

Igor, who started out in 1977 with the Russian club side, Khimik Voskresensk, was rated as one of the finest playmakers produced in Europe. Thanks to his 'sixth sense' skill which led him to be compared with **Wayne Gretzky**, he enjoyed a long career on CSKA Moscow, which doubled as the famous Red Army national team.

"I can instinctively see the ice and see a situation developing three or four moves before it actually happens," he said from his home in New Jersey. "I have always liked chess and I think this helped me on the ice."

Though he didn't play in the NHL until he was 29, he finished up with 475 assists in 921 games with Red Wings and five other teams. He had around 200 assists with his Russian teams, mostly in the days when they didn't count the second assist.

His favourite memory is of the classic 1987 Canada Cup final between Canada and the USSR. "We lost that series," he recalled. "but hockey was the true winner. That was the way the game should be played."

Although he has sworn never to coach in his retirement, he wants to remain involved in the sport and has firm views of what he believes is wrong with the game.

"We must bring back the attention to puck control, skating and thinking," he said. "There is so little creativity in the game today. All the emphasis is on playing the trap and it really takes the excitement away from the game for players and fans."

Meanwhile, Igor is taking a year off to indulge some of his pet projects, including his own wine label. He is marketing a thousand bottles of Australian wine under the label 'Triple Overtime'. "I developed a taste for wine during my season with Lugano [1992-93] in the Swiss League," he grinned.

Larionov played at the highest level on both sides of the Atlantic during his remarkable career. Just a few highlights:
☑ Won two Olympic gold medals, three Stanley Cups (all Detroit), four world Championships and the 1981 Canada Cup.
☑ Won an Olympic bronze in 2002 and played in the 1996 World Cup.
☑ Played 457 games in the Soviet league, winning eight national titles.
☑ One of only a dozen players to win the triple of Olympic gold, the Stanley Cup and the World Championship.
*- Interview courtesy of **Szymon Szemberg**, IIHF*

QUOTES

"The irony is that we could have a $20 million roster and do just as good a job. They're taking the skill out of the game, so why have skill players?" *Mike Modano, whose Dallas team has a $70 million payroll.*

"We feel sorry for the guys coming into this league. You can't enjoy this any more. All creativity...is gone. I don't want to be a part of this for many years." *Teemu Selanne, Colorado's Finnish forward, bemoaning the state of play in the NHL.*

"I fully expect that what is coming in hockey [the threatened lockout of the players] is going to have a (harmful) impact on all of sport - on TV, on fan loyalty, on merchandise sales, just generally on the state of sports." *David Stern, commissioner of the NBA, on the forthcoming negotiations on the NHL/NHLPA's Collective Bargaining Agreement. Stern and NHL commissioner Gary Bettman were colleagues at the NBA.*

NEW YORK'S SANTA WARS

During a promotion that gave a free ticket to anyone dressed as Santa, the [NHL's] New York Islanders decided to bring all the Santas onto the ice. That's when two ripped off their suits to reveal [New York] Rangers' jerseys. And that's when they were pounced on by other Santas. And that's when the rest of the Santas started running around the ice. It took almost ten minutes to calm everyone down. The players were in the locker room the whole time, but when Islanders' forward **Aaron Asham** was told about the melée, he smiled and said: "Awesome."

- from www.jerkoftheweek.com

"I'm ashamed of the fact that we have lost so much money here, and I say that knowing we're probably operating the business better than at any time in the history of this franchise." *Tim Leiweke, president of Los Angeles Kings, admitting that the Anschutz Corporation had lost US$100 million since purchasing the Kings in 1995. [A shade more than Mr A blew on London Knights then - ed.]*

"In the second game you couldn't have found him with a pair of binoculars and a bloodhound." *Brian Burke, Vancouver Canucks' GM, agreeing that Fedor Fedorov, the brother of Sergei Fedorov, should remain with Canucks' AHL team.*

"It's insane, to be honest with you. It's tough just to get one. I've had one in the past two years, and I play on a pretty good team." *Manny Legace, Detroit Redwings' goalie, on Brian Boucher's shutout records.*

"Sometimes things just happen instinctively - you don't really think about the game. That's when you play your best, when you're not thinking out there. When you let in a goal, you try just to forget about it and you try and stop the next one, then the next one after that." *Brian Boucher, attempting to give reporters the secret of his amazing shutout success.*

'... with the payroll approaching US$90 million, these [New York] Rangers, dollar for dollar, are the worst team in any sport in any era.' *Dave Anderson, New York Times' columnist, after Rangers' 4-1 loss to Montreal Canadiens left them in 25th place in the 30-team league and effectively knocked them out of the Stanley Cup playoffs for the seventh consecutive season.*

'New Mexico Scorpions (CHL) are composed of Navajo Indians from Santa Fe who can't shoot, can't check, can't pass, but in between periods they will be selling jewellery'. *Highly non-PC advert which Scorpions were forced to withdraw and apologise for.*

The Jagr Trade - what they said

"This is an immensely unpopular move made by an immensely unpopular chief executive [**Glen Sather**]. The Rangers can't keep the puck out of their own net and their response is to add yet another offensive-minded forward whose best days are behind him." *Larry Brooks, beat reporter for the New York Post, after Rangers signed Jaromir Jagr from Washington Capitals.*

"When all about you are doubting whether you have any intelligence or not, it's nice to know that somebody thinks you're still capable of doing something." *Glen Sather, Rangers' GM/coach, after he received firm backing from the club's owner.*

'**Glen Sather**, 60, has three more seasons remaining on the seven-year deal he signed to become the Rangers' president and general manager in June 2000. Sather's salary is believed to be $4 million a season, with another $1 million in bonuses and options.' *New York Times.*

"He is, I don't know how else to say this, a beautiful player." *Mark Messier, Rangers' forward, on his new team-mate.*

WORLD HOCKEY ASSOCIATION
1970s league to be revived?

The NHL's *bête noire* of the 1970s was revived at the end of 2003 with NHL Hall of Famer, **Bobby Hull** as commissioner.

The brainchild of Ontario businessman, **Al Howell**, the WHA intend to have eight franchises in North America for 2004-05 with expansion to Europe in 2005-06.

Apart from hoping to attract NHLers who could be locked out, the WHA are keen to make several rule changes. Hull said: "We have to get families back in the game, get back where on Saturday night everything stops for hockey."

Bobby, like his son **Brett Hull**, is scornful of the NHL's attempts to cut down on the obstruction offences which prevent the game's most gifted stars from shining.

"The game was great for 75 years and they didn't have to change any rules," he said. "Now they've had to change because they're not playing the game the way it should be played. They're not allowing talented players to play. That's why they're having problems.

"We're going to have a gun and shoot style of hockey, and we're also going to get the goaltender's equipment down so a guy can see a bit of webbing when he comes in on the net."

Just like 30 years ago, the NHL ignored the WHA - publicly. But NHL commissioner **Gary Bettman** gave away the old league's true feelings at the time of the launch when he announced that the NHL would be taking "a good look at the game" during the February All-Star break.

It was thought he would like to introduce any rule changes as soon as the league re-starts after the labour dispute is over. "I have a vision," he said, "where we can in effect put everything behind us at one time."

■ *No sniggering, please, we're French-Canadian* Quebec decided to call its WHA franchise, Nordiks. We are assured that this is pronounced Nor-deeks, the same as the more famous and much missed Quebec team, the Nordiques.

■ "When we drop the puck on the ice for the opening game, people might say it's not a real puck." *Allan Howell, co-founder of the revived World Hockey Association, accepting the scepticism of many Canadian hockey fans.*

OBITUARIES
Herb Brooks

The mastermind of America's Miracle on Ice and one of the more colourful and inspirational characters in hockey history, **Herb Brooks** died in a single-car accident in his home state of Minnesota on 11 August 2003. He was 66. State Patrol investigators believed it was most likely that he fell asleep at the wheel.

Brooks was best known throughout the world for coaching the USA to a wildly improbable 4-3 semi-final victory over the Soviet Union which led to them winning the 1980 Olympics at Lake Placid, New York.

HERB BROOKS SAID -

"Don't dump the puck in, that went out with short pants."

"Coaching is like being king. It prepares you for nothing."

The gold medal inspired scores of young Americans to take up the sport. In the following two decades the NHL expanded by 85 per cent in the USA (from 13 teams to 24) and the number of players registered with USA Hockey shot up by more than 200 per cent.

"Herb Brooks is synonymous with American hockey, and those of us lucky enough to be around him learned something from him every day," said Pittsburgh Penguins' GM, **Craig Patrick**, who was Brooks' assistant on the 1980 team. "Herbie loved the game, he lived the game."

Patrick later hired Brooks to coach the New York Rangers and the Penguins. Brooks coached 507 NHL games with Rangers, Penguins, Minnesota and New Jersey between 1981 and 2000, as well as 40 playoff contests.

Born and raised in St Paul, Minnesota, Brooks was a big-hearted, brilliant, quirky, sometimes cranky, always curious man. He was an outstanding player at the University of Minnesota and was the last player cut from the 1960 USA Olympic squad which also won a gold medal. But he made the 1964 and 1968 teams.

He was an outspoken critic of the passive, trapping systems that have come to dominate the NHL. He brought the European style to North America and used it to beat the Soviets at their own game. "Don't dump the puck in," he would say. "That went out with short pants."

Instead, he and Patrick developed their own style of play, taking the best from both continents. "We were more of a European team on offence and more of a North American-Canadian team on defence," he said.

Brooks worked for Patrick at the Penguins from 1995 until his death, most recently as the team's director of player development.

He coached the French team at the 1998 Olympics in Nagano and returned to Team USA in 2002, taking them to a silver medal in the Salt Lake City Olympics.

He was inducted into the USA Hockey Hall of Fame in 1990 and the IIHF Hall of Fame in 1999.

with grateful acknowledgements to The Hockey News.

Keith McCreary/Keith Magnuson

Their day started with a funeral and ended with a death. It could not have been worse for former NHLers **Keith Magnuson** and **Rob Ramage**.

On 15 December 2003, Magnuson, 56, and Ramage, 44, had flown into Toronto, rented a Chrysler Intrepid, then drove up to Bolton for the funeral of their friend and the chairman of the NHL Alumni Association executive, **Keith McCreary**. No one could have anticipated that by day's end the alumni association would also be mourning the loss of its past chairman, Magnuson.

Ramage, the group's vice-chairman, was hospitalised with a broken leg and is facing a charge of impaired driving causing death.

"It's almost incomprehensible to think we were burying our chairman (McCreary). Keith Magnuson was our past chairman and Rob Ramage is our vice-chairman," said alumni president **Brian Conacher**. "To have anything happen to all three is devastating."

Ramage and Magnuson were two of more than 1,000 friends and family who arrived in Bolton at Holy Family Church to pay their respects to McCreary, a co-founder of the alumni group, who died of cancer on 9 December 2003.

After the funeral they shared memories of McCreary with dozens of former NHLers including Conacher, **Ron Ellis**, **Rick Vaive**, **Gary Leeman**, **Paul Henderson**, **Jocelyn Lemieux**, **Dean Prentice** and **Mike Gartner**.

The two former captains - Ramage led the Toronto Maple Leafs in the late 1980s, and Magnuson wore the 'C' for the Chicago Blackhawks in the late 1970s - went on to the reception at the Glen Eagle Golf Club.

Luke Ursa, who runs the Glen Eagle clubhouse, said there was a lunch, an alcoholic and non-alcoholic punch and cash bar. "From what I know, the bar didn't do much business," he said. "A lot of the guys were out-of-towners and had to catch planes."

That included Ramage and Magnuson. "Rob and Keith were going to come by our office at 4 or 4:30 p.m.," said alumni president Conacher, who left the reception at 1 p.m. "They called at around 3:30 p.m. to say they would be a little late. They never made it," said Conacher, a former Leaf himself.

At 5 p.m. with Ramage behind the wheel, the Chrysler smashed into oncoming traffic, killing Magnuson and leaving a trail of devastation.

- Toronto Sun

George Plimpton

The urbane and witty American writer died at his home in Manhattan on 26 September 2003, aged 76. He will be best remembered by hockey fans for his book 'Open Net' which described his stint playing in goal for Boston Bruins during an exhibition game.

Plimpton wrote many other sporting books 'from the inside', among them boxing (Shadow Box'), baseball ('Out of My League'), American football ('Paper Lion') and golf ('The Bogey Man'). He also tried his hand as a circus aerialist and a percussionist in a symphony orchestra, and had several cameo roles in movies.

As a 'participatory journalist,' he believed that it was not enough for writers of non-fiction to simply observe; they needed to immerse themselves in whatever they were covering to understand fully what was involved. The results were both comic and instructive.

George Ames Plimpton was born in New York on 18 March 1927, the son of a successful corporate lawyer who became the American ambassador to the United Nations. His grandfather, George A Plimpton, had been a publisher. The family traced its roots in America to the Mayflower.

Perhaps his unusual career was best summarised by a cartoon that once appeared in *The New Yorker* magazine. In it, a patient looks at the surgeon preparing to operate on him and demands: "How do I know you're not George Plimpton?"

- from the New York Times

■ The last time we looked 'Open Net' was still available from amazon.com. Highly recommended - ed.

Ice hockey in the UK

The sport first became prominent in the UK in the 1930s with the opening of large indoor arenas at Wembley, Harringay and Earls Court (Empress Hall). Teams were manned almost entirely by Canadian professionals, several of whom went on to compete in the National Hockey League.

The 1930s also produced what is considered to be the game's finest hour. In February 1936, Britain upset the ice hockey world in Garmisch-Partenkirchen, Bavaria by winning the Triple Crown of Olympic, World and European titles. Their five victories included a 2-1 defeat of Canada, the reigning world champions.

The players - though born in Britain, all but two lived in Canada where they had learned the game - were hand-picked by the Canadian coach, **Percy Nicklin**, and **John F (Bunny) Ahearne**, the secretary of the British Ice Hockey Association.

The World and European Championships were held in London the following year when Britain retained their European title and were runners-up in the world, a feat they repeated in 1938. They remained among the leading five nations in the world until 1951 and won four European crowns.

The 13 seasons either side of World War Two (1935-54) are often referred to as the sport's golden era. As well as the national team's successes, two professional leagues, the English National League and the Scottish National League, drew large crowds to arenas in London, Brighton, Nottingham and Scotland.

The two leagues merged in 1954 into a British National League but rising wages and falling crowds caused it to fold in 1960 and the sport went into decline. It only achieved wide popularity again in 1982 when the British League was re-formed with teams staffed mostly by home-grown players and a strict limit on imported professionals. This is generally seen as the start of the game's modern era.

With a new generation of fans, the Whitbread Company agreed to sponsor the league under the *Heineken* banner. The (*Heineken*) British Championships, 1983-1996, were televised and drew capacity crowds to Wembley Arena.

This success, coupled with the promise of more arenas like the new ones in Sheffield and Manchester, prompted a revival of the professional game. The Superleague, which was formed in 1996, again relied heavily on overseas players and although at first the crowds continued to increase, many clubs eventually found the league too expensive and it collapsed in 2003.

The national team have recently experienced difficult times due to the the absence of opportunities for native talent in the professional Superleague and the addition of half-a-dozen former Soviet countries to the World Championship roster.

In 1993 under coach **Alex Dampier**, Britain were promoted to the elite A Pool but since then, despite the appointment of one of Europe's leading coaches in **Chris McSorley**, they have tumbled to 25th in the world.

Roll of Honour (Modern Era)

Winners and runners-up in all major domestic club competitions since the start of the Modern Era.
*Compiled exclusively for the Annual by **Gordon Wade** with contributions from **Martin Harris**.*
The Roll of Honour for the years before season 1982-83 is in The Ice Hockey Annual 1998-99.

SEASON	COMPETITION	WINNER	RUNNER-UP	NOTES
2003-04	Elite League Playoff Ch'ship	Sheffield Steelers	Nottingham Panthers	Won 2-1 at Nottingham
	Elite League	Sheffield Steelers	Nottingham Panthers	New 8-team league
	Challenge Cup	Nottingham Panthers	Sheffield Steelers	Won 4-3 on agg. (1-1h,3-2ot a)
	British Nat'l Lge Ch'ship	Guidford Flames	Bracknell Bees	Won 9-7 on agg. (5-4a,4-3h)
	British National League	Fife Flyers	Guildford Flames	7-team league
	Findus Cup	Newcastle Vipers	Guildford Flames	Won 6-1 at Newcastle
	Eng Premier Lge Ch'ship	Milton Keynes Lightning	Slough Jets	Won 12-2 on agg. (7-0a, 5-2h)
	Eng Premier League	Milton Keynes Lightning	Peterborough Phantoms	9-team league
	Eng Premier Cup	Peterborough Phantoms	*Wightlink* Raiders	Won 7-2 on agg. (3-1a,4-1h)
	Eng Nat'n'l Lge Ch'ship	Sheffield Scimitars	Invicta Dynamo	Won 8-5 on agg. (4-3a,4-2h)
	Eng Nat'n'l Lge, North	Flintshire Freeze	Sheffield Scimitars	
	Eng Nat'n'l Lge, South	Invicta Dynamo	Oxford City Stars	
	Caledonian Cup	Fife Flyers	Edinburgh Capitals	Won 12-10 on agg. (6-7h, 6-3a)

ROLL OF HONOUR

SEASON	COMPETITION	WINNER	RUNNER-UP	NOTES
2002-03	+ Superleague Playoff Ch'ship	Belfast Giants	London Knights	Won 5-3 at Nottingham
	+ Superleague	Sheffield Steelers	Belfast Giants	Only five teams in league
	+ Challenge Cup	Sheffield Steelers	Nottingham Panthers	Won 3-2 at Manchester
	British Nat'l Lge Ch'ship	Coventry Blaze	Cardiff Devils	Won 5-3 on agg. (3-2a,2-1h)
	British National League	Coventry Blaze	Dundee Stars	10-team league
	Findus Cup	Newcastle Vipers	Coventry Blaze	Won 3-0 at Newcastle
	Eng Nat'l Lge, Premier Div Ch'ship	Milton Keynes Lightning	Peterborough Phantoms	Won 16-4 on agg. (10-0h,6-4a)
	Eng Nat'l Lge, Premier Division	Peterborough Phantoms	Milton Keynes Lightning	12-team league
	Eng Nat'l Lge, Premier Cup	Peterborough Phantoms	Milton Keynes Lightning	Won 7-6 on agg. (2-4a,5-2h)
	Eng Nat'l Lge, Div. One Ch'ship	Basingstoke Buffalo	Altrincham Aces	Won 10-9 on agg. (4-5a,6-4h)
	Eng Nat'l Lge, Div. One North	Sheffield Scimitars	Altrincham Aces	Aces' last season
	Eng Nat'l Lge, Div. One South	Basingstoke Buffalo	Bracknell Hornets	
	Caledonian Cup	Fife Flyers	Dundee Stars	Won 9-7 on agg. (5-3h,4-4a)
2001-02	+ Superleague Playoff Ch'ship	Sheffield Steelers	Manchester Storm	Won 4-3 (ps) at Nottingham
	+Sekonda Superleague	Belfast Giants	Ayr Scottish Eagles	7-team lge; Giants' 2nd season
	+ Challenge Cup	Ayr Scottish Eagles	Belfast Giants	Won 5-0 at Belfast
	British Nat'l Lge Ch'ship	Dundee Stars	Coventry Blaze	Won 8-7 on agg. (7-4a, 1-3h)
	British National League	Dundee Stars	Coventry Blaze	12-team lge; Stars' first season
	Findus Cup	Fife Flyers	Coventry Blaze	Won 6-3 at Nottingham
	Eng Nat'l Lge, Premier Div Ch'ship	Invicta Dynamos	Isle of Wight Raiders	Won 6-3 on agg. (2-1a, 4-2h)
	Eng Nat'l Lge, Premier Division	Invicta Dynamos	Solihull Barons	8-team league
	Eng Nat'l Lge, Premier Cup	Romford Raiders	Invicta Dynamos	Won 9-7 on agg. ((5-3h, 4-4a)
	Eng Nat'l Lge, Div. One Ch'ship	Whitley Warriors	Basingstoke Buffalo	Won on agg. 12-7 (6-6a, 6-1h)
	Eng Nat'l Lge, Div. One North	Whitley Warriors	Altrincham Aces	
	Eng Nat'l Lge, Div. One South	Basingstoke Buffalo	Flintshire Freeze	
	Eng Nat'l Lge, Cup	Whitley Warriors	Telford Wild Foxes	Won 10-8 on agg. (2-5a, 8-3h)
	Caledonian Cup	Dundee Stars	Fife Flyers	Won 8-4 on agg. (3-2a, 5-2h)
2000-01	+= Superleague Playoff Ch'ship	Sheffield Steelers	London Knights	Won 2-1 at Nottingham
	+ Sekonda Superleague	Sheffield Steelers	Caridff Devils	9-team lge; won by 19 points but censured for breaking wage cap.
	B&H Autumn Cup	Sheffield Steelers	Newcastle Jesters	Won 4-0 at Sheffield
	+Challenge Cup	Sheffield Steelers	Ayr Scottish Eagles	Won 4-2 at Belfast
	Findus British Nat'l Lge Ch'ship	Guildford Flames	Basingstoke Bison	Won 12-4 on agg. (7-2a, 5-2h)
	Findus British Nat'l Lge	Guildford Flames	Basingstoke Bison	10-team league
	Benson and Hedges Plate	Basingstoke Bison	Guildford Flames	Won 3-2 at Sheffield
	ntl Christmas Cup	Guildford Flames	Fife Flyers	Won 7-3 on agg. (4-1h,3-2a)
	Eng Nat'l Lge, Premier Div Ch'ship	Romford Raiders	Chelmsford Chieftains	Won 11-4 on agg. (7-2, 4-2)
	Eng Nat'l Lge, Premier Division	Swindon Phoenix	Chelmsford Chieftains	9-team league
	Eng Nat'l Lge, Premier Cup	Isle of Wight Raiders	Swindon Phoenix	Won 5-2 on agg. (3-2a, 2-0h)
	Eng Nat'l Lge, Div. One Ch'ship	Whitley Warriors	Billingham Eagles	Won 14-7 on agg. (4-6h,10-1a)
	Eng Nat'l Lge, Div. One North	Billingham Eagles	Whitley Warriors	
	Eng Nat'l Lge, Div. One South	Basingstoke Buffalo	Flintshire Freeze	
	Scottish Cup	Fife Flyers	Edinburgh Capitals	Won 7-4 at Kirkcaldy.
1999-00	+= Superleague Playoff Ch'ship	London Knights	Newcastle Riverkings	Won 7-3 at Manchester
	+ Sekonda Superleague	Bracknell Bees	Sheffield Steelers	8-team league
	B&H Autumn Cup	Manchester Storm	London Knights	Won 4-3 (ps) at Sheffield.
	+Challenge Cup	Sheffield Steelers	Nottingham Panthers	Won 2-1 at London Arena
	British National Lge Ch'ship	Fife Flyers	Basingstoke Bison	Won best-of-five series 3-0.
	British National Lge	Fife Flyers	Guildford Flames	10-team league
	Benson and Hedges Plate	Basingstoke Bison	Slough Jets	Won 5-1 at Sheffield
	ntl Christmas Cup	Fife Flyers	Basingstoke Bison	Won 6-5 on agg. (3-3,3-2)
	Eng. Lge, Premier Div. Ch'ship	Chelmsford Chieftains	Swindon Chill	Won 7-4 on agg. (5-2,2-2)
	English Lge, Premier Div.	Chelmsford Chieftains	Isle of Wight Raiders	5-team league
	Data Vision Millennium Cup	Chelmsford Chieftains	Swindon Chill	Won 10-7 at Swindon.
	English Lge, Div. One Ch'ship	Whitley Warriors	Billingham Eagles	Won 14-10 on agg. (7-4,7-6)
	English Lge, Div One North	Billingham Eagles	Whitley Warriors	
	English Lge, Div One South	Haringey Greyhounds	Basingstoke Buffalo	
	Scottish Cup	Fife Flyers	Paisley Pirates	Won 9-4 at Kirkcaldy

SEASON	COMPETITION	WINNER	RUNNER-UP	NOTES
1998-99	+=Superleague Playoff Ch'ship	Cardiff Devils	Nottingham Panthers	Won 2-1 at Manchester
	+*Sekonda* Superleague	Manchester Storm	Cardiff Devils	8-team league
	B&H (Autumn) Cup	Nottingham Panthers	Ayr Scottish Eagles	Won 2-1 at Sheffield
	+Challenge Cup	Sheffield Steelers	Nottingham Panthers	Won 4-0 at Sheffield
	British National Lge Ch'ship	Fife Flyers	Slough Jets	Won 6-5 (ps) at Hull
	British National League	Slough Jets	Basingstoke Bison	9-team league
	Benson and Hedges Plate	Guildford Flames	Telford Tigers	Won 4-3 at Sheffield
	Vic Christmas Cup	Peterborough Pirates	Basingstoke Bison	Won 5-3 on agg. (2-1,3-2)
	Eng. Lge, Premier Div. Ch'ship	Solihull Blaze	Milton Keynes Kings	Won 5-3 on agg. (3-0,2-3)
	English Lge, Premier Div	Solihull Blaze	Milton Keynes Kings	9-team league
	English Cup	Milton Keynes Kings	Solihull Blaze	Won 13-9 on agg. (7-6,6-3)
	English Lge, Div. One Ch'ship	Whitley Warriors	Billingham Eagles	Won 14-10 on agg. (7-4,7-6)
	English Lge, Div One North	Billingham Eagles	Altrincham Aces	
	English Lge, Div One South	Cardiff Rage	Basingstoke Buffalo	
	Scottish Cup	Fife Flyers	Edinburgh Capitals	Won 6-4 at Kirkcaldy.
1997-98	+Superleague Playoff Ch'ship	Ayr Scottish Eagles	Cardiff Devils	Won 3-2ot at Manchester
	+Superleague	Ayr Scottish Eagles	Manchester Storm	8-team league
	B & H (Autumn) Cup	Ayr Scottish Eagles	Cardiff Devils	Won 2-1 at Sheffield
	+*The Express* Cup	Ayr Scottish Eagles	Bracknell Bees	Won 3-2 at Newcastle
	British National Lge Ch'ship	Guildford Flames	Kingston Hawks	Won 5-1 at Hull
	British National League	Guildford Flames	Telford Tigers	New 9-team league
	Southern Premier League	Guildford Flames	Slough Jets	4 BNL teams plus Cardiff Rage
	Northern Premier League	Fife Flyers	Paisley Pirates	Remaining 5 BNL teams
	Benson & Hedges Plate	Slough Jets	Telford Tigers	Won 4-3 at Sheffield
	Upper Deck Christmas Cup	Telford Tigers	Guildford Flames	Won 10-7 on agg. (5-5, 5-2)
	Eng. Lge, National Div Ch'ship.	Solihull Blaze	Chelmsford Chieftains	Won 18-6 on agg. (9-5,9-1)
	English Lge, National Div.	Solihull Blaze	Whitley Warriors	8-team league
	English Lge, Div One North	Solihull Blaze	Whitley Warriors	
	English Lge, Div One South	Invicta Dynamos	Chelmsford Chieftains	
	Scottish Cup	Fife Flyers	Paisley Pirates	Won 5-1 at Kirkcaldy
1996-97	+Superleague Playoff Ch'ship	Sheffield Steelers	Nottingham Panthers	Won 3-1 at Manchester
	+Superleague	Cardiff Devils	Sheffield Steelers	New 8-team league
	B & H (Autumn) Cup	Nottingham Panthers	Ayr Scottish Eagles	Won 5-3 at Sheffield
	Premier League Playoffs	Swindon IceLords	Fife Flyers	Won 5-0 at Manchester
	(Southern) Premier League	Swindon IceLords	Solihull Blaze	New 8-team league
	Northern Premier League	Fife Flyers	Paisley Pirates	New 7-team league
	English League Championship	*Wightlink* Raiders	Chelmsford Chieftains	Won 10-6 on agg. (5-2,5-4)
	English League, South	Romford Raiders	Chelmsford Chietains	
	English League, North	Kingston Jets	Altrincham Aces	
	Scottish Cup	Paisley Pirates	Fife Flyers	Won 8-4 at Kirkcaldy
	British Jnr Championship	Sunderland Arrows	Fife Flames	Won 3-2 at Manchester
1995-96	British Championship	Sheffield Steelers	Nottingham Panthers	Won on 2-1 PS (3-3ot) at Wembley.
	British League, Premier Div.	Sheffield Steelers	Cardiff Devils	
	British League, Div One	Manchester Storm	Blackburn Hawks	
	Promotion Playoffs	Manchester Storm	Milton Keynes Kings	Two playoff group winners
	B & H (Autumn) Cup	Sheffield Steelers	Nottingham Panthers	Won 5-2 at Sheffield
	English League Championship	*Wightlink* Raiders	Durham City Wasps	Won 15-8 on agg. (8-0,7-8)
	English League, South	Oxford City Stars	*Wightlink* Raiders	
	English League, North	Humberside Jets	Altrincham Aces	
	Autumn Trophy	Dumfries Border Vikings	Chelmsford Chieftains	Won 23-0, second leg not played.
	British Jnr Championship	Guildford Firestars	Fife Flames	Won 3-2 at Wembley

SEASON	COMPETITION	WINNER	RUNNER-UP	NOTES
1994-95	British Championship	Sheffield Steelers	Edinburgh Racers	Won 7-2 at Wembley
	British League, Premier Div.	Sheffield Steelers	Cardiff Devils	
	British League, Div One	Slough Jets	Telford Tigers	
	Promotion Playoffs	Slough Jets	Whitley Warriors	Two playoff group winners
	B & H (Autumn) Cup	Nottingham Panthers	Cardiff Devils	Won 7-2 at Sheffield
	English League Championship	*Wightlink* Raiders	Sunderland Chiefs	Won 11-5 on agg. (7-2,4-3)
	English League, South	*Wightlink* Raiders	Peterborough Patriots	
	English League, North	Sunderland Chiefs	Nottingham Jaguars	
	Autumn Trophy	Solihull Barons	Swindon Wildcats	Won 19-16 on agg. (7-6,12-10)
	Scottish Cup	Fife Flyers	Paisley Pirates	Won 11-2 at Kirkcaldy
	British Jnr Championship	Fife Flames	Durham Mosquitoes	Won 5-1 at Wembley
1993-94	British Championship	Cardiff Devils	Sheffield Steelers	Won 12-1 at Wembley
	British League, Premier Div.	Cardiff Devils	Sheffield Steelers	Fife Flyers later placed 2nd
	British League, Div One	M Keynes Kings (N)	Slough Jets (S)	No playoff. Kings most points.
	Promotion Playoffs	Milton Keynes Kings	Peterborough Pirates	Two playoff group winners
	B & H (Autumn) Cup	Murrayfield Racers	Cardiff Devils	Won 6-2 at Sheffield
	English League Championship	*Wightlink* Raiders	Nottingham Jaguars	Won 17-7 on agg. (6-4,11-3)
	English League	*Wightlink* Raiders	Sunderland Chiefs	
	Autumn Trophy	Telford Tigers	Medway Bears	Won 11-7 on agg. (8-3,3-4)
	Scottish Cup	Fife Flyers	Murrayfield Racers	Won 6-5 at Kirkcaldy
	British Jnr Championship	Fife Flames	Swindon Leopards	1-1ot at Wembley. Trophy shared.
1992-93	*British Championship	Cardiff Devils	Humberside Seahawks	Won 7-4 at Wembley
	*British League, Premier Div	Cardiff Devils	Murrayfield Racers	
	*British League, Div One	Basingstoke Beavers	Sheffield Steelers	
	*Promotion Playoffs	Basingstoke Beavers	Sheffield Steelers	Two group winners
	B & H (Autumn) Cup	Cardiff Devils	Whitley Warriors	Won 10-4 atSheffield
	English League Championship	Solihull Barons	Guildford Flames	Won 16-13 on agg. (6-7,10-6)
	English League, Conference A	Solihull Barons	Bristol Bulldogs	
	English League, Conference B	Guildford Flames	Chelmsford Chieftains	
	BL Entry Playoffs	Trafford Metros	Chelmsford Chieftains	Also EL PO. Two group winners
	Autumn Trophy	Milton Keynes Kings	Solihull Barons	Won 11-4 at Sheffield
	Scottish Cup	Murrayfield Racers	Whitley Warriors	Won 8-7 at Murrayfield
	British Jnr Championship	Durham Mosquitoes	Fife Flames	Won 5-2 at Wembley
1991-92	*British Championship	Durham Wasps	Nottingham Panthers	Won 7-6 at Wembley
	*British League, Premier Div.	Durham Wasps	Nottingham Panthers	
	*British League, Div One	Fife Flyers	Slough Jets	
	*Promotion Playoffs	Bracknell Bees	Fife Flyers	Two group winners
	Autumn Cup	Nottingham Panthers	Humberside Seahawks	Won 7-5 at Sheffield
	English League	Medway Bears	Sheffield Steelers	No championship playoff.
	BL Entry Playoffs	Medway Bears	Sheffield Steelers	Also EL PO. Two group winners.
	Autumn Trophy	Swindon Wildcats	Milton Keynes Kings	Won 3-2 on PS (5-5ot) at Sheffield.
	Scottish Cup	Whitley Warriors	Ayr Raiders	Won 7-4 at Murrayfield
	British Jnr Championship	Fife Flames	Durham Mosquitoes	Won 3-2 at Wembley
1990-91	*British Championship	Durham Wasps	Peterborough Pirates	Won 7-4 at Wembley
	*British League, Premier Div.	Durham Wasps	Cardiff Devils	
	*British League, Div One	Humberside Seahawks	Slough Jets	
	*Promotion Playoffs	Humberside Seahawks	Bracknell Bees	Two group winners
	Norwich Union (Autumn) Cup	Durham Wasps	Murrayfield Racers	Won 12-6 at Whitley
	English League	Oxford Stars	Milton Keynes Kings	First Division
	BL Entry Playoffs	Lee Valley Lions	Milton Keynes Kings	Also EL PO. Two group winners.
	Autumn Trophy	Chelmsford Chieftains	Oxford City Stars	League format.
	Scottish Cup	Murrayfield Racers	Ayr Raiders	Won 9-4 at Murrayfield
	British Jnr Championship	Fife Flames	Romford Hornets	Won 5-0 at Wembley

ROLL OF HONOUR

SEASON	COMPETITION	WINNER	RUNNER-UP	NOTES
1989-90	*British Championship	Cardiff Devils	Murrayfield Racers	Won 6-5 PS (6-6 ot) at Wembley.
	*British League, Premier Div.	Cardiff Devils	Murrayfield Racers	
	*British League, Div One	Slough Jets	Cleveland Bombers	
	*Promotion Playoffs	Cleveland Bombers	Slough Jets	Div One top four
	Norwich Union (Autumn) Cup	Murrayfield Racers	Durham Wasps	Won 10-4 at Basingstoke
	English League	Bracknell Bees	Romford Raiders	First Division
	BL Entry Playoffs	Basingstoke Beavers	Romford Raiders	Also EL playoffs
	Autumn Trophy	Humberside Seahawks	Bracknell Bees	Won 23-17 on agg. (15-9,8-8)
	Scottish Cup	Murrayfield Racers	Cardiff Devils	Won 13-4 at Murrayfield
	British Jnr Championship	Nottingham Cougars	Fife Flames	Won 3-1 at Wembley
1988-89	*British Championship	Nottingham Panthers	Ayr Bruins	Won 6-3 at Wembley
	*British League, Premier Div.	Durham Wasps	Murrayfield Racers	
	*British League, Div One	Cardiff Devils	Medway Bears	
	*Promotion Playoffs	Cardiff Devils	Streatham Redskins	Premier winner v last in Div One.
	Norwich Union (Autumn) Cup	Durham Wasps	Tayside Tigers	Won 7-5 at NEC, Birmingham
	English League	Humberside Seahawks	Bracknell Bees	First Division
	Autumn Trophy	Cardiff Devils	Medway Bears	Won 15-8 on agg. (9-4,6-4)
	Scottish Cup	Murrayfield Racers	Ayr Bruins	Won 9-5 at Murrayfield
	British Jnr Championship	Durham Mosquitoes	Dundee Bengals	Won pen shots at Wembley (5-5)
1987-88	*British Championship	Durham Wasps	Fife Flyers	Won 8-5 at Wembley
	*British League, Premier Div.	Murrayfield Racers	Whitley Warriors	
	*British League, Div One	Telford Tigers (S)	Cleveland Bombers (N)	Won 21-14 on agg. (12-10, 9-4)
	Promotion Playoffs	Peterborough Pirates	Telford Tigers	Premier winner v last in Div One
	British League, Div Two	Romford Raiders	Chelmsford Chieftains	
	Norwich Union (Autumn) Cup	Durham Wasps	Murrayfield Racers	Won 11-5 at Kirkcaldy
	Autumn Trophy	Cardiff Devils	Trafford Metros	Won 11-10 on agg. (7-5,4-5)
	Scottish Cup	Murrayfield Racers	Fife Flyers	Won 9-6 at Murrayfield
	British Jnr Championship	Nottingham Cougars	Fife Flames	Won 4-2 at Wembley
1986-87	*British Championship	Durham Wasps	Murrayfield Racers	Won 9-5 at Wembley
	*British League, Premier Div.	Murrayfield Racers	Dundee Rockets	
	*British League, Div One	Peterborough Pirates	Medway Bears	
	British League, Div Two	Aviemore Blackhawks	Cardiff Devils	Won playoff 10-9 at Cardiff
	Norwich Union (Autumn) Cup	Nottingham Panthers	Fife Flyers	Won 5-4ot at NEC, Birmingham
	Scottish Cup	Murrayfield Racers	Dundee Rockets	Won 7-6 at Kirkcaldy
	British Jnr Championship	Durham Mosquitoes	Murrayfield Ravens	Won 11-1 at Wembley
1985-86	*British Championship	Murrayfield Racers	Dundee Rockets	Won 4-2 at Wembley
	*British League, Premier Div.	Durham Wasps	Murrayfield Racers	
	*British League, Div One	Solihull Barons	Lee Valley Lions	
	British League, Div Two	Medway Bears	Grimsby Buffaloes	Won playoff 26-4 at Medway
	Norwich Union (Autumn) Cup	Murrayfield Racers	Durham Wasps	Won 8-5 at Murrayfield
	Scottish Cup	Dundee Rockets	Murrayfield Racers	Won 7-3 at Dundee
	British Jnr Championship	Streatham Scorpions	Fife Flames	Won 7-0 at Wembley
1984-85	*British Championship	Fife Flyers	Murrayfield Racers	Won 9-4 at Wembley
	*British League, Premier Div.	Durham Wasps	Fife Flyers	
	*British League, Div One	Peterborough Pirates	Solihull Barons	
	British League, Div Two	Oxford Stars	Aviemore Blackhawks	Won playoff 6-1 at Oxford
	Bluecol Autumn Cup	Durham Wasps	Fife Flyers	Won 6-4 at Streatham
1983-84	*British Championship	Dundee Rockets	Murrayfield Racers	Won 5-4 at Wembley
	*British League, Premier Div.	Dundee Rockets	Durham Wasps	
	*British League, Div One	Southampton Vikings	Crowtree Chiefs	
	British League, Div Two	Whitley Braves	Streatham Bruins	Won playoff 14-9 on agg (6-7, 8-2)
	Autumn Cup	Dundee Rockets	Streatham Redskins	Won pen shots at Streatham (6-6)
1982-83	*British Championship	Dundee Rockets	Durham Wasps	Won 6-2 at Streatham
	British League Section A	Dundee Rockets	Murrayfield Racers	)
	Section B	Durham Wasps	Cleveland Bombers	)Div One - interlocking schedule
	Section C	Altrincham Aces	Blackpool Seagulls	)
	British League, Div Two	Solihull Barons	Grimsby Buffaloes	Won Play-off 8-5 at Solihull

= Sponsored by *Sekonda*   * Sponsored by *Heineken*   + All-professional competition

GOVERNING BODIES

ICE HOCKEY UK LTD

Chairman: Neville Moralee.
Administrator: Gill Short, 47 Westminster Buildings, Theatre Sq, Nottingham NG1 6LG.
Tel: 0115-924-1441. **Fax:** 0115-924-3443.
e-mail: hockey@icehockeyuk.co.uk
website: www.icehockeyuk.co.uk
The Board of Directors of the sport's national governing body are: **Neville Moralee** (chairman & EIHA), **Stuart Robertson** (vice-chairman & Scottish IHA), **Danny Carroll** (treasurer), **Bob Wilkinson** (EIHA), **Alan Gray** (SIHA), **John Lyttle** & **Andy Gibson** (N Ireland IHF), **Eamon Convery** & **Mike Cowley** (Elite Lge), **Tom Muir** (BNL), **Warren Rost** (IHPA).

ELITE ICE HOCKEY LEAGUE LTD

Chairman: Eamon Convery.
Secretary: To be appointed.
Director of Hockey: Andy French.
Tel/fax: 01633-440631.
e-mail: andyhockey.french@btopenworld.com
Regd. Address: EIHL Ltd, Phoenix House, Mansfield Road, Sutton-in-Ashfield, Nottingham NG17 4HD.
Tel: 01623-551150. **Fax:** 01623-440483.
website: www.eliteleague.co.uk

BRITISH NAT. ICE HOCKEY LGE LTD

Chairman: Tom Muir.
Secretary: To be appointed.
e-mail: enquiries@britnatleague.net
website: www.britnatleague.net

ENGLISH ICE HOCKEY ASSOCIATION

Chairman: Ken Taggart.
Gen Secretary: Bill Britton, 7 Laughton Avenue, West Bridgford, Notts NG2 7GJ.
Tel/Fax: 0115-923-1461
website: www.eiha.co.uk
The EIHA is managed by an Executive Committee comprising: **Ken Taggart** (chairman), **Tony Oliver** (deputy chairman), **Bill Britton** (secretary), **Neville Moralee** (treasurer), **Bob Wilkinson**, **Alan Moutrey**, **Irene Jones**.

N IRELAND ICE HOCKEY FED.

Chairman: John Lyttle.
Secretary: Lorna Taylor.
Address: 1st floor, 201 Upper Newtownards Road, Belfast BT4 3JD.
Tel: 012890-654040. **Fax:** 012890-651700.

SCOTTISH ICE HOCKEY ASSN.

Chairman: Frank Dempster.
Secretary: Mrs Pat Swiatek, 71 Prestwick Road, Ayr KA5 7LQ.
Tel/Fax: 01292-284053
website: www.siha.net

SCOTTISH NATIONAL LEAGUE
Secretary: Sandra Edgar, 5 St Anne's Road, Dumfries DG2 9HZ. **Tel:** 01387-264010.
e-mail: sedgar5701@aol.com

WOMEN'S ICE HOCKEY LEAGUE

Chairman: Bill Britton.
Secretary: Sylvian Clifford, 14 Windrush Drive, Springfield, Chelmsford CM1 7QF.
Tel/Fax: 01245-259181.
e-mail: sylvian.clifford1@btopenworld.com
website: www.eiha.co.uk

ICE HOCKEY PLAYERS ASSN (GB)

Executive Director: Joanne Collins, 25 Caxton Ave, Addlestone, Weybridge, Surrey KT15 1LJ.
Tel: 01932-843660. **Fax:** 01932-844401.
e-mail: ihpa@virgin.net
website: www.ihpa.co.uk

USEFUL ADDRESSES

BRITISH ICE HOCKEY WRITERS' ASSN

Chairman/Secretary: Stewart Roberts, 50 Surrenden Lodge, Surrenden Road, Brighton BN1 6QB. **Tel/fax:** 01273-597889.
e-mail: stewice@aol.com
website: www.bihwa.co.uk

GB SUPPORTERS CLUB

Secretary: Annette Petrie, 65 Leas Drive, Iver, Bucks SL0 9RB. **Tel/Fax:** 01753-710778.
e-mail: gbsc@blueyonder.co.uk.
website: www.gbsc.co.uk/

CLUB DIRECTORY 2004-05

ABERDEEN

Rink Address: Linx Ice Arena, Beach Leisure Centre, Beach Esplanade, Aberdeen AB2 1NR.
Tel: 01224-655406/7. **Fax**: 01224-648693.
Ice Size: 184 x 85 feet (56 x 26 metres).
Spectator Capacity: 1,200
Club Secretary: Collette Cowie, 18 Woodhill Terrace, Bridge of Don AB15 5LE.
Tel: 01224-312250.
e-mail: collette.cowie@gpcp.co.uk
Juniors and recreational teams only 2004-05

AYR/PRESTWICK

Rink closed until further notice.
Arena Address: Centrum Arena, Ayr Road, Prestwick KA9 1TR.
Tel: 01292-671600. **Fax**: 01292-678833.
Ice Size: 200 x 103 feet (61 x 31.5 metres).
Spectator Capacity: 2,745.

BASINGSTOKE

Rink Address: Planet Ice Basingstoke Arena, Basingstoke Leisure Park, Worting Road, Basingstoke, Hants RG22 6PG.
Tel: 01256-355266. **Fax**: 01256-357367.
Ice Size: 197 x 98 feet (60 x 30 metres)
Spectator Capacity: 1,600.
Senior Teams: Bison (Elite League) and Buffalo (Eng Nat Lge South).
Bison's contact: Mark Bernard at the rink.
Tel: 01256-346159. **Fax**: 01256-357367
Bison's Colours: *home*: White, Red & Silver; *away*: Red & Silver.
website: www.bstokebison.co.uk

BELFAST

ODYSSEY ARENA
Address: Queen's Quay, Belfast BT3.
Tel: 02890-766000. **Fax**: 02890-766044.
Ice Size: 197 x 98 feet (60 x 30 metres).
Spectator Capacity (for ice hockey): 7,100.
Team: Giants (Elite League).
Communications to: John Elliott.
Club Address: Belfast Giants Ltd, Unit 3, Ormeau Business Park, 8 Cromac Avenue, Belfast BT7 2JA.
Tel: 028-9059-1111. **Fax**: 028-9059-1212.
e-mail: office@belfastgiants.co.uk
Colours: *home*: White, Red & Teal; *away*: Teal, White & Red.
website: www.belfastgiants.co.uk

DUNDONALD INTERNATIONAL ICE BOWL
Address: 111 Old Dundonald Road, Dundonald, Co Down, N Ireland.
Tel: 02890-482611. **Fax**: 02890-489604.
Ice Size: 197 x 98 feet (60 x 30 metres).
Spectator Capacity: 1,500.
Junior and recreational teams only 2004-05

BILLINGHAM

Rink Address: Billingham Forum Leisure Centre, Town Centre, Billingham, Cleveland TS23 2OJ. **Tel/Fax**: 01642-551381.
Ice Size: 180 x 80 feet (55 x 24 metres)
Spectator Capacity: 1,200.
Senior Team: Eagles (Eng Nat Lge North).
Club Secretary: Brian McCabe, 7 Cranstock Close, Wolviston Court, Billingham, Cleveland TS22 5RS. **Tel/Fax**: 01642-534458.
e-mail: bmccabe_1@hotmail.com
Colours: *Home*: White, Red & Black; *away*: Black & Red.

BLACKBURN

Rink Address: Blackburn Arena, Lower Audley, Waterside, Blackburn, Lancs BB1 1BB.
Tel: 01254-668686. **Fax**: 01254-691516.
Ice Size: 197 x 98 feet (60 x 30 metres)
Spectator Capacity: 3,200.
Senior Team: Hawks (English Nat Lge North)
Club Secretary: Mark Halliwell c/o the arena.
e-mail: mark@blackburnicearena.co.uk
Colours: Pacific Teal, Grey, Black & White.
website: www.blackburnhawks.com

BRACKNELL

Rink Address: John Nike Leisuresport Complex, John Nike Way, Bracknell, Berks RG12 4TN.
Tel: 01344-789006, **Fax**: 01344-789201.
Ice Size: 197 x 98 feet (60 x 30 metres)
Spectator Capacity: 3,100.
Senior Teams: Bees (British National League) and Hornets (English Nat Lge South).
Bees' Club Secretary: Jane McDougall c/o rink.
Tel: 01344-789209. **Fax**: 01344-789022
e-mail: bracknellbees@nikegroup.co.uk
Bees' colours: *home*: White, Gold & Black; *away*: Black, Gold & White.
website: www.beesprohockey.co.uk

BRADFORD

Rink Address: Great Cause, Little Horton Lane, Bradford, Yorks BD5 0AE.
Tel: 01274-729091. **Fax**: 01274-778818.
Ice Size: 180 x 80 feet (55 x 24 metres)
Spectator Capacity: 700.
Senior Team: Bulldogs (English Nat Lge North).
Club Secretary: Barbara Brown, 43 North Road, Wibsey, Bradford, W Yorks BD6 1RJ.
Tel/fax: 01274-676414.
e-mail: babsbrown@hotmail.com
Colours: White, Green & Black.

BRAEHEAD (GLASGOW)

No senior ice hockey 2004-05.
Arena Address: Braehead Arena, Kings Inch Road, Glasgow, G51 4BN
Tel: 0870 444 6062.
Ice Size: 197 x 98 feet (60 x 30 metres).
Spectator Capacity (for ice hockey): 4,000.

BRISTOL

Rink Address: John Nike Leisuresport Bristol Ice Rink, Frogmore Street, Bristol BS1 5NA.
Tel: 0117-929-2148. **Fax**: 0117-925-9736.
Ice Size: 180 x 80 feet (55 x 24 metres).
Spectator Capacity: 650.
Club Secretary: Mary Faunt, c/o the rink.'
Juniors only 2004-05.

CAMBRIDGE UNIVERSITY

Home ice 2004-05: Planet Ice Peterborough Arena. (see Peterborough entry)
Communications to: Prof Bill Harris, Dept of Anatomy, Cambridge University, Downing St. Cambridge CB2 3DYUK.
Phone: 01223-333772. **Fax**: 01223-333786.
e-mail: harris@mole.bio.cam.ac.uk
Colours: Light Blue & White.
website: www.cam.ac.uk/societies/cuihc
Recreational.

CARDIFF

Rink Address: Wales National Ice Rink, Hayes Bridge Road, Cardiff CF1 2GH.
Tel: 02920-397198, **Fax**: 02920-397160.
Ice Size: 184 x 85 feet (56 x 26 metres).
Spectator Capacity: 2,500.
Senior Team: Devils (Elite League).
Communications to: Anne Hall at the rink.
Tel: 02920-396669. **Fax**: 02920-396668
e-mail: info@wnir.co.uk
Colours: *home*: White, Red & Black; *away*: Red, Black & White.
website: www.thecardiffdevils.com

CHELMSFORD

Rink Address: Riverside Ice & Leisure Centre, Victoria Road, Chelmsford, Essex CM1 1FG.
Tel: 01245-615050. **Fax**: 01245-354919.
Ice Size: 184 x 85 feet (56 x 26 metres).
Spectator Capacity: 1,200.
Senior Team: Chieftains (Eng Premier Lge).
Club Secretary: Sue Green, 72 Stirrup Close, Springfield, Chelmsford, Essex CM1 6ST.
Tel/fax: 01245-461708.
e-mail: sue@braves.freeserve.co.uk
Colours: *home*: White, Blue & Red; *away*: Blue, White & Red.
website: www.chelmsfordchieftains.co.uk

COVENTRY

Rink Address: Planet Ice at Skydome Arena, Skydome Coventry, Croft Road, Coventry CV1 3AZ. **Tel**: 02476-630693. **Fax**: 02476-630674
Ice Size: 184 x 92 feet (56 x 28 metres)
Spectator Capacity (for ice hockey): 2,616.
Senior Team: Blaze (Elite League).
Communications to: Coventry Blaze IHC, The Hockey Locker, Co-op Extra Superstore, Queen Victoria Road, Coventry CV1 3LE.
Tel/fax: 02476-631352
e-mail: mikecowley@coventryblaze.co.uk
Colours: *Home:* White & Navy Blue; *away:* Navy Blue & White.
website: www.coventryblaze.co.uk

DEESIDE (QUEENSFERRY)

Rink Address: Deeside Ice Rink, Leisure Centre, Chester Road West, Queensferry, Clwyd CH5 5HA.
Tel: 01244-814725. **Fax**: 01244-836287.
Ice Size: 197 x 98 feet (60 x 30 metres).
Spectator Capacity: 1,200.
Senior Team: Flintshire Freeze (English National League North).
Club Secretary: Mark Stokes c/o the rink.
e-mail: mark.stokes@cls.glasgow.gov.uk
Colours: *home*: White, Purple & Green; *away*: Green, Purple & White.
website: www.flintshirefreeze.btinternet.co.uk

CLUB DIRECTORY

DUMFRIES

Rink Address: The Ice Bowl, King Street, Dumfries DG2 9AN.
Tel: 01387-251300, **Fax**: 01387-251686.
Ice Size: 184 x 95 feet (56 x 29 metres).
Spectator Capacity: 1,000.
Senior Team: Solway Sharks (Scot. Nat. Lge).
Communications to: Sandra Edgar, 5 St Anne's Road, Dumfries DG2 9HZ. **Tel**: 01387-264010.
e-mail: sedgar5701@aol.com
Colours: Blue, White & Green.
website: www.solwaysharks.co.uk

DUNDEE

Rink Address: Camperdown Leisure Park, Kingsway West, Dundee.
Tel: 01382-608060. **Fax**: 01382-608070
Ice Size: 197 x 98 feet (60 x 30 metres).
Spectator Capacity: 2,400.
Senior Teams: Dundee Stars (British National League) and Camperdown Stars (Scottish National League).
Club Secretary: Steve/Marie Ward, Chamber of Commerce Buildings, Panmure Street, Dundee DD1 1ED
Tel/fax: 01382-204700.
e-mail: dundeestars@btconnect.com
Colours: home: White, Red & Blue; away: Blue, Red & White.
website: www.dundeestars.com

EDINBURGH

Rink Address: Murrayfield Ice Rink, Riversdale Crescent, Murrayfield, Edinburgh EH12 5XN.
Tel: 0131-337-6933, **Fax**: 0131-346-2951.
Ice Size: 200 x 97 feet (61 x 29.5 metres).
Spectator Capacity: 3,800.
Senior Team: Capitals (British National League and Scottish National League).
Communications to: Scott Neil at the rink.
Tel/fax: 0131-313-2977.
e-mail: edcapitals@aol.com
Colours: Home: White, Red & Blue; away: Red, White & Blue.
website: www.edinburgh-capitals.com

ELGIN

Rink Address: Moray Leisure Centre, Borough Briggs Road, Elgin, Moray IV30 1AP.
Tel: 01343-550033. **Fax**: 01343-551769
Ice Size: 147.5 x 82 feet (45 x 25 metres)
Spectator capacity: 200
Senior Team: Moray Tornadoes (Scot Nat Lge)
Communications to: Mike Munro (chairman), Blaven, Dallas, Forres, Moray IV36 2SA.
Tel: 01343-890374
e-mail: mike@munro.fsworld.co.uk

FIFE

Rink Address: Fife Ice Arena, Rosslyn Street, Kirkcaldy, Fife KY1 3HS.
Tel: 01592-595100. **Fax**: 01592-595200.
Ice Size: 193.5 x 98 feet (59 x 30 metres).
Spectator Capacity: 3,280.
Senior Teams: Flyers (British National League) and Kirkcaldy Kestrels (Scottish Nat. League).
Communications to: Tom Muir c/o the arena.
Tel: 01592-651076. **Fax**: 01592-651138.
e-mail: tom@britnatleague.co.uk
Colours: Flyers - Home: White, Gold & Blue; away: Blue, White & Gold.
Website: www.fifeflyers.co.uk

GILLINGHAM

Rink Address: The Ice Bowl, Ambley Road, Gillingham Business Park, Gillingham, Kent ME8 0PP.
Tel: 01634-377244. **Fax**: 01634-374065.
Ice Size: 184 x 85 feet (56 x 26 metres).
Spectator Capacity: 1,500.
Senior Teams: Invicta Dynamos (English National League South)
Club Secretary: Jackie Mason, 17 Beckenham Drive, Maidstone, Kent ME16 0TG.
Tel: 01622-671065. **Fax**: 01622-754360.
e-mail: jackie@community-centre.demon.co.uk
Colours: Home: White, Red, Blue & Black; Away: Blue, White, Black & Red.
website: www.invictadynamos.co.uk

GOSPORT

Rink Address: Forest Way, Fareham Road, Gosport, Hants. PO13 0ZX.
Tel: 02392-511217. **Fax**: 02392-510445.
Ice Size: 145 x 73 feet (44 x 22 metres).
Spectator Capacity: 400.
Club Secretary: Peter Marshall, 15 Islands Close, Hayling Island, Hants PO11 0NA.
Tel: 02392-466809.
e-mail: peter.marshall@havant.gov.uk
website: www.solenticehockey.co.uk
Juniors and recreational teams only 2004-05

GRIMSBY

Rink Address: The Leisure Centre, Cromwell Road, Grimsby, South Humberside DN31 2BH.
Tel: 01472-323100. **Fax:** 01472-323102.
Ice Size: 120 x 60 feet (36.5 x 18 metres).
Spectator Capacity: 1,300.
Club Secretary: Allan Woodhead, Weelsby Park Riding School, Weelsby Road, Grimsby, South Humberside DN32 8PL.
Tel/Fax: 01472-346127.
Colours: *Home:* Red & White, *away:* Black, White & Red.
Juniors and recreational teams only 2004-05

GUILDFORD

Rink Address: Spectrum Ice Rink, Parkway, Guildford GU1 1UP.
Tel: 01483-444777. **Fax:** 01483-443311.
Ice Size: 197 x 98 feet (60 x 30 metres).
Spectator Capacity: 2,200.
Senior Team: Flames (British National League).
Communications to: Kirk Humphries at the rink.
Tel: 01483-452244, **Fax:** 01483-443373.
e-mail: kirk@guildfordflames.com
Colours: *Home:* Gold, Red & Black;
away: Black, Red & Gold.
website: www.guildfordflames.com

HARINGEY (LONDON)

Rink Address: The Ice Rink, Alexandra Palace, Wood Green, London N22 4AY.
Tel: 0208-365-2121. **Fax:** 0208-444-3439.
Ice Size: 184 x 85 feet (56 x 26 metres).
Spectator Capacity: 1,750.
Senior Team: Greyhounds (English Lge South).
Club Secretary: Jan Bestic, 71 Osier Crescent, Muswell Hill, London N10 1QT.
Tel/fax: 0208-444-1843.
e-mail: jan.bestic@btconnect.com
Colours: Blue, Gold, White & Silver.
website: www.haringeygreyhounds.co.uk

HULL

Rink Address: The Hull Arena, Kingston Park, Hull HU1 2DZ.
Tel: 01482-325252. **Fax:** 01482-216066.
Ice Size: 197 x 98 feet (60 x 30 metres).
Spectator Capacity: 2,000.
Senior Teams: Stingrays (British National Lge) and Kingston Jets (English Nat Lge North).
Stingrays' communications to: Mike/Sue Pack.
Tel/fax: 01908-317029 .
e-mail: info@hullstingrays.co.uk
Stingrays' colours: *Home:* White, Purple & Black, *away:* Purple, Black & Silver.
Website: www.hullstingrays.co.uk

IRVINE

Rink Address: Magnum Leisure Centre, Harbour Street, Irvine, Strathclyde KA12 8PD.
Tel: 01294-278381. **Fax:** 01294-311228.
Ice Size: 150 x 95 feet (45.5 x 29 metres).
Spectator Capacity: 750.
Senior Team: North Ayr Bruins (Scot Nat Lge)
Club Secretary: Bobby Peters, 2 Somerville Park, Lawthorn, Irvine KA11 2EL.
Tel/Fax: 01294-213755.

ISLE OF WIGHT (RYDE)

Rink Address: Planet Ice Ryde Arena, Quay Road, Esplanade, Ryde, I of Wight PO33 2HH.
Tel: 01983-615155. **Fax:** 01983-567460.
Ice Size: 165 x 80 feet (50 x 24 metres)
Spectator Capacity: 1,000.
Senior Team: *Wightlink* Raiders (English Premier League).
Club Secretary: Mavis Siddons, 6 Port Helens, Embankment Road, St Helens, Isle of Wight PO33 1XG. **Tel:** 01983-873094.
e-mail: hockey@twin2.plus.com
Colours: *Home:* White, Red & Black;
away: Red, Black & White.
website: www.wightlinkraiders.com

KILMARNOCK

Rink Address: Galleon Leisure Centre, 99 Titchfield Street, Kilmarnock, Ayr KA1 1QY.
Tel: 01563-524014. **Fax:** 01563-572395.
Ice Size: 146 x 75 feet (44.6 x 23 metres)
Spectator Capacity: 200
Club Secretary: Anne Davidson.
Address: 23 Rawson Crescent, Mauchline KA5 5AT. **Tel/fax:** 0141-577-6946.
Junior and recreational teams only 2004-05.

LEE VALLEY (LONDON)

Rink Address: Lee Valley Ice Centre, Lea Bridge Road, Leyton, London E10 7QL.
Tel: 0208-533-3156. **Fax No**: 0208-446-8068.
Ice Size: 184 x 85 feet (56 x 26 metres).
Spectator Capacity: 1,000.
Senior Team: London Racers (Elite League)
Communications to: Roger Black, 13 New North Street, London WC1N 3PJ.
Tel:0207-420-5955.
e-mail: roger@racershockey.com
Colours: *Home*: Gold & Blue;
away: Blue & Gold.
website: www.londonracers.co.uk

MILTON KEYNES

Rink Address: Planet Ice Milton Keynes Arena, The Leisure Plaza, 1 South Row, (off Childs Way H6), Central Milton Keynes, Bucks MK9 1BL.
Tel: 01908-696696. **Fax**: 01908-690890.
Ice Size: 197 x 98 feet (60 x 30 metres)
Spectator Capacity: 2,200.
Senior Teams: Lightning (English Premier Lge) and Thunder (Eng Nat Lge South).
Communications to: Harry Howton, Oldbrook House, Boycott Avenue, Oldbrook, Milton Keynes.
Tel: 01908-696993. **Fax**: 01908-696995.
e-mail: howtons.ltd@btinternet.com
Lightning's Colours: *Home*: White, Gold & Black; *away*: Black, White & Gold.
website: ww.mk-lightning.com

NEWCASTLE

Arena Address: *Metro Radio* Arena, Arena Way, Newcastle-on-Tyne NE4 7NA.
Tel: 0191-260-5000. **Fax**: 0191-260-2200.
Ice Size: 197 x 98 feet (60 x 30 metres).
Spectator Capacity (for ice hockey): 5,500
Senior Team: Vipers (British National Lge).
Communications to: Clyde Tuyl at the Arena.
Tel: 0191-242-2420. **Fax**: 0191-260-2328
e-mail: kbsvipers@wwmail.co.uk
Colours: *Home*: White, Gold & Black; *away*: Black, Gold & White.
website: www.newcastlevipers.com

Senior Team: Sunderland Chiefs (English Nat League North).
Communications to: Mike Hendry, 4 Floral Dene, South Hylton, Sunderland SR4 0NW.
Tel: 0191-534-7219. **Fax**: 0191-564-2695.
e-mail: tynetube@lineone.net
Colours: *Home*: White, Red & Blue; *away*: Blue, Red & White.

NOTTINGHAM

Rink Address: National Ice Centre, Lower Parliament Street, Nottingham NG1 1LA.
Tel: 0115-853-3000. **Fax**: 0115-853-3034.
Ice Size: 197 x 98 feet (60 x 30 metres).
Spectator Capacity (for ice hockey): 6,500.
Senior Teams: Panthers (Elite League) and Lions (English Nat League North).
Panthers' office: Gary Moran, 2 Broadway, The Lace Market, Nottingham NG1 1PS.
Tel: 0115-941-3103. **Fax**: 0115-941-8754. .
e-mail: info@panthers.co.uk
Panthers' colours: *Home*: White, Gold & Red; *away*: Black, Gold & Red.
Website: www.panthers.co.uk

OXFORD

Rink Address: The Ice Rink, Oxpens Road, Oxford OX1 1RX.
Tel: 01865-467002. **Fax**: 01865-467001.
Ice Size: 184 x 85 feet (56 x 26 metres).
Spectator Capacity: 1,025.
Senior Team: City Stars (Eng Nat Lge South)
Club Secretary: Gary Dent, 42 Westfield Way, Wantage, Oxon OX12 7EW.
Tel/fax: 01235-763264.
e-mail: garyndent@aol.com
Colours: *Home*: Red & White, *away*: amarillo.
website: www.oxfordstars.com

OXFORD UNIVERSITY

Home Ice: The Ice Rink, Oxpens Road, Oxford OX1 1RX (details above).
Communications to: Lal Aggarwal, New College, Oxford OX1 3BN.
Tel: 07939-502703.
e-mail: lalit.aggarwal@new.ox.ac.uk
Colours: Dark Blue and White.
website: www.ouihc.org/home.asp
Recreational.

PAISLEY

Rink Address: Lagoon Leisure Complex, Mill Street, Paisley PA1 1LZ.
Tel: 0141-889-4000. **Fax**: 0141-848-0078.
Ice Size: 184 x 85 feet (56 x 26 metres).
Spectator Capacity: 1,000.
Senior Team: Pirates (Scottish Nat League).
Communications to: Gil MacDonald at the rink.
e-mail: macdonal@fish.co.uk
Colours: Black & White
website: www.paisleypirates.net

CLUB DIRECTORY

PETERBOROUGH

Rink Address: Planet Ice Peterborough Arena, 1 Mallard Road, Bretton, Peterborough, Cambs PE3 8YN.
Tel: 01733-260222.   **Fax:** 01733-261021.
Ice Size: 184 x 85 feet (56 x 26 metres).
Spectator Capacity: 1,500.
Senior Teams: Phantoms (English Premier League) and Islanders (Eng Nat Lge South).
Communications to: Phil Wing, Manor Farm, Great North Road, Stibbington, Peterborough.
Tel/fax: 01780-783963
e-mail: phil.wing@peterborough-phantoms.com
Phantoms' colours: *Home:* White, Black, Silver & Red; *away:* Black, Silver, White & Red.
website: www.peterborough-phantoms.com

ROMFORD

Rink Address: Rom Valley Way, Romford, Essex RM7 0AE.
Tel: 01708-724731.   **Fax:** 01708-733609.
Ice Size: 184 x 85 feet (56 x 26 metres).
Spectator Capacity: 1,500.
Senior Team: Raiders (English Premier Lge).
Communications to: Ollie Oliver, Quattro Sports Ltd, 3 Hallsford Bridge Ind Est, Stondon Road, Ongar, Essex CM5 9RB.
Tel/Fax: 01277-822688.
e-mail: ollie@candol.co.uk
Colours: *Home:* White, Gold & Blue;
   away: Blue, Gold & White.
website: www.romfordraiders.co.uk

SHEFFIELD

Hallam FM ARENA
Address: Broughton Lane, Sheffield S9 2DF.
Tel: 0114-256-5656.   **Fax:** 0114-256-5520.
Ice Size: 197 x 98 feet (60 x 30 metres).
Spectator Capacity (for ice hockey): 10,000.
Senior Team: Steelers (Elite League).
Communications to: Betty Waring at Arena.
Tel: 0114-242-3535.   **Fax:** 0114-242-3344.
e-mail: sheffsteel@freeuk.com
Colours: *Home:* White, Blue, Orange & Teal; *away:* Black, Blue, Orange & Teal.
website: www.steelersihc.co.uk.

iceSHEFFIELD
Address: Coleridge Road, Sheffield S9 5DA.
Tel: 0114-223-3900.   **Fax:** 0114-223-3901.
e-mail: info@icesheffield.com
Spectator Capacity: 1,500 (main rink).
Senior Team: Sheffield Scimitars (English Nat Lge North)
Club Secretary: Lynn Millard, 10 Metcalfe Avenue, Killamarsh, Sheffield S21 1HW.
Tel: 0114-248-1891.
e-mail: lynnmillard40@hotmail.com
Colours: *Home:* White, Black & Blue; *away:* Black, White & Blue.
website: under construction at press-time

SLOUGH

Rink Address: The Ice Arena, Montem Lane, Slough, Berks SL1 2QG.
Tel: 01753-821555.   **Fax:** 01753-824977.
Ice Size: 184 x 85 feet (56 x 26 metres).
Spectator Capacity: 1,500.
Senior Team: Jets (English Premier League).
Club Secretary: Pauline Rost, 37 Monks Avenue, East Molesey, Surrey KT8 0HD.
e-mail: pauline.rost@ntlworld.com or woz@sloughjets.co.uk
Colours: *Home:* White, Blue & Red;
   away: Blue, White & Red.
website: www.sloughjets.co.uk

SOLIHULL

Rink Address: Hobs Moat Road, Solihull, West Midlands B92 8JN.
Tel: 0121-742-5561.   **Fax:** 0121-742-4315.
Ice Size: 185 x 90 feet (56 x 27 metres).
Spectator Capacity: 1,500.
Senior Team: Kings (English Premier Lge).
Club Secretary: Mark Dyson, 9 Coopers Mews, Neath Hill, Milton Keynes MP14 6HD.
Tel: 01908-672789.   **Fax:** 01908-548579.
e-mail: dyson808@hotmail.com
Colours: *Home:* White & Red; *away:* Black & Red.
website: www.solihullkings.co.uk

STREATHAM (LONDON)

Rink Address: 386 Streatham High Road, London SW16 6HT.
Tel: 0208-769-7771. **Fax**: 0208-769-9979.
Ice Size: 197 x 85 feet (60 x 26 metres).
Club Secretary: Judith Korol, 78 Tankerville Road, Streatham, London SW16 5LP.
Tel: 0208-480-8641
e-mail: streathamicehockey@hotmail.com
Senior Team: Redskins (English Nat Lge South).
Colours: *Home:* White & Red;
away: Black & Red.
website: www.streathamicehockey.com

SUNDERLAND

Crowtree Leisure Centre closed in June 2000 and it is uncertain if it will re-open. The Chiefs are playing at the Telewest Arena in Newcastle-on-Tyne. See entry under Newcastle.
Rink Address: Crowtree Leisure Centre, Crowtree Road, Sunderland, Tyne & Wear SR1 3EL.
Ice Size: 184 x 85 feet (56 x 26 metres).
Spectator Capacity: 1,200.

SWINDON

Rink Address: Link Centre, White Hill Way, Westlea, Swindon, Wilts SN5 7DL.
Tel: 01793-445566. **Fax**: 01793-445569.
Ice Size: 184 x 85 feet (56 x 26 metres).
Spectator Capacity: 1,650.
Senior Team: Wildcats (English Premier Lge).
Communications to: Mark Thompson, 21 Senlac Road, Romsey, Hants SO51 5RE.
Tel: 07906-024042 (mobile).
e-mail: mark.thompson@swindonwildcats.com
Colours: *Home:* White, Blue, Silver & Gold;
away: Blue, White, Silver & Gold.

TELFORD

Rink Address: The Ice Rink, St Quentins Gate, Town Centre, Telford, Salop TF3 4JQ.
Tel: 01952-291511. **Fax**: 01952-291543.
Ice Size: 184 x 85 metres (56 x 26 metres).
Spectator Capacity: 2,250.
Senior Team: Wild Foxes (Eng Premier Lge).
Club Secretary: Mrs Jen Roden, 12 Dee Close, Wellington, Telford TF1 3HJ.
Tel/fax: 01952-405506.
e-mail: jenrod@tiscali.co.uk
Colours: *Home:* White, Orange & Black; *away:* Orange, Black & White.
website: www.telfordwildfoxes.co.uk

WHITLEY BAY

Rink Address: The Ice Rink, Hillheads Road, Whitley Bay, Tyne & Wear NE25 8HP.
Tel: 0191-291-1000. **Fax**: 0191-291-1001.
Ice Size: 186 x 81 feet (56.5 x 24.5 metres).
Spectator Capacity: 3,200.
Senior Team: Warriors (Eng Nat Lge North).
Club Secretary: Stuart Graham, 12 Wark Street, Chester-le-Street, Co Durham DH3 3JP
Tel/Fax: 0191-388-0940.
e-mail: stu_warriors@hotmail.com
Colours: *Home:* White, Gold & Maroon; *away:* Maroon, White & Gold.
website: www.warriors-online.com

LEGEND

The abbreviations used in the *Annual* are -

LEAGUES

EIHL/EL	Elite Ice Hockey League
FBNL/BNL	Findus British National League
EPL	English Premier League

SCORERS

GP	-	Games Played
G	-	Goals
A	-	Assists
Pts	-	total Points
Pim(s)	-	Penalties in minutes
N	-	Netminder
Ave		Points per Games Played

NETMINDERS

GPI	-	Games Played In
Mins	-	Minutes played
SoG	-	Shots on Goal
GA		Goals Against
SO	-	Shutouts
Sv%	-	*Save percentage

TEAMS

S	-	Seasons
W	-	Win
RW		Win in regulation time (60 Mins)
OW	-	Win in overtime
RL		Loss in regulation time
OL		Loss in overtime
D	-	Draw
GF	-	Goals For
GA	-	Goals Against
Pct	-	Points gained as a percentage of total games played.

PLAYERS

(I)	'Limited' ITC holder
(N)	Netminder

TIE BREAKERS

The method using for deciding the places of teams tied on points is as follows -

Elite League
- total number of wins
- results between tied teams

British National League
English Premier League
as per IIHF Rule Book

---

*SAVE PERCENTAGE - CALCULATION METHOD
Shots on goal less goals against, divided by shots on goal, multiplied by 100.
Example: 100 shots less 10 goals scored, equals 90, divided by 100, equals 90 per cent.